What Brings a Marriage into Existence?
A Historical Re-examination
of the Canon Law
of the Latin Church

What Brings a Marriage into Existence?
A Historical Re-examination
of the Canon Law
of the Latin Church

By
Brendan Killeen

University of Scranton Press
Scranton and London

Library of Congress Cataloging-in-Publication Data

Killeen, Brendan.
  What brings a marriage into existence? : a historical re-
examination of the canon law of the Latin Church / by Brendan
Killeen.
      p. cm.
Includes bibliographical references and index.
ISBN 978-1-58966-190-5 (pbk.)
1. Marriage (Canon law)--History. I. Title.
KBR3109.K55 2009

262.9--dc22

                                                          2009019451

Distribution:
UNIVERSITY OF SCRANTON PRESS
Chicago Distribution Center
11030 S. Langley
Chicago, IL 60628

PRINTED IN THE UNITED STATES OF AMERICA

To my Parents,
Sheila and Tim Killeen

Nihil Obstat   The Rev. Dr. James Cassidy,
                                CRIC, JCL, STL

Imprimatur   The Rev. Mgr. Provost Séan Healy,
                                VG, STL, MPhil

                                Northampton, 22 April 2009

CONTENTS

ACKNOWLEDGMENTS

I wish to thank Rev. Dr. Theodore Davey C.P., formerly of Heythrop College, University of London. His guidance and support have been invaluable. I also wish to thank Rev. Dr. Dominic Byrne and Rev. Prof. Roch Pagé for their helpful advice.

I made much use of the library at Saint Mary's College, Oscott in the early stages of my research. I thank Rev. David Evans and Mr. Michael Hadcroft for assisting me in my use of that library.

In my book I refer to a work written by Rev. Prof. James Coriden. I thank him for very kindly sending me a copy of it—details of which are given in my bibliography.

I am also most grateful to Mrs. Julia Gibson for checking my text and providing me with helpful comments.

Finally, I wish to thank my friends Rev. Seamus Keenan and Sr. Celine Donnelly for their continued interest and encouragement.

Brendan Killeen
January 2010

GENERAL INTRODUCTION

What is it that actually brings a marriage into existence? That is, at one moment there are a man and woman intending to marry; at another moment they are married. What is it that brings about this change? Moreover, does this influence what is central to the marriage that has just come into existence? Also, does it indicate how the marriage may cease to exist?

The marriage laws of the Catholic Church answer these questions. These answers have evolved from written texts issued over many centuries. These sources are often quoted by canon lawyers, ecclesiastical judges, and official ecclesiastical documents. The question— What brings a marriage into existence?—has provided me with a focus with which to re-examine these sources.

It is essential that I explain the framework within which I am working. I am a practicing canon lawyer and an ecclesiastical judge within the Catholic Church who is often involved with matrimonial cases. Thus, my analysis of marriage is not based primarily on psychology or sociology. Instead, it is performed within the discipline of canon law. This is why I consider, foremost, those ecclesiastical documents which are either of a legal nature or have legal consequences. While these documents cover a number of centuries, my aim is not to produce an entire historical survey but a fresh examination of those documents which are usually quoted within the tradition of canon law as being relevant sources to the present discipline.

I hope that my analysis will enable me to contribute three things to this area of law:

1. A re-examination of those primary sources which are often quoted in regard to matrimonial law, as well as a re-examination of the historical development of this law. This re-examination is important because there is always a temptation among canon lawyers to quote the previous generation of canon lawyers—rather than quoting the primary sources.

2. An objective evaluation of the present law of marriage, in particular that found in the 1983 Code of Canon Law.[1] This Code has now been in use for some time, so an objective assessment of it would be timely.

3. Specific suggestions—made in light of this research and offered humbly in that light—for further development of the law of marriage.

The book is in two parts. The first part considers the relevant history up to the eve of the Second Vatican Council. The second part considers the Second Vatican Council and the present law of marriage. As the majority of the current law of marriage in the Latin Church is found in the 1983 Code of Canon Law, my consideration of the present law will follow the layout of the 1983 Code. Some chapters of the Code are less relevant to this book and so will be dealt with briefly. Also, elements of the Church's matrimonial law are

---

1. *1983 Code* (bibliog. I).

found outside the 1983 Code. Thus, where necessary, my examination goes beyond the Code. The structure of the second part of this book is explained more fully in the Introduction to Part Two.

Finally, I hope that my book will provide a good introduction to those who are new to the canon law of marriage, and foster lively debate among those who are already working in this field.

PART ONE

Up to the Eve
of The Second Vatican Council

—1—

The Roman Empire
Consent Makes Marriage

THAT A MARRIAGE IS BROUGHT into existence by the mutual consent of the couple is a concept common within ancient Roman culture. By the time of the Empire, marriages came about in two steps: the betrothal and the marriage proper. The betrothal carried with it no obligations.[1] As for the marriage proper, this required two elements: *consensus* and *domumductio*. *Consensus* was the mutual consent of both parties. *Domumductio* was the leading of the wife to the husband's home. Although ancient traditional ceremonies were sometimes enacted, there was no legal form for the marriage. There were no prescribed words or actions, and no public official had to be present.[2] As long as they were not slaves, it was sufficient that mutual consent was given within the context of the wife being led to the home of her new husband.[3] Thus, the mutual desire to be man and wife was an essential factor for marriage.

---

1. Carcopino, *Daily Life in Ancient Rome* (bibliog. III), 86.
2. Treggiari, "Divorce Roman Style" (bibliog. III).
3. Schillebeeckx, *Marriage: Human Reality and Saving Mystery* (bibliog. III), 241. Also, Gauthier, *Roman Law and its Contribution to the Development of Canon Law* (bibliog. III), 34–35. Ibid., 31–34, explains how slaves could not take on certain commitments and contracts themselves. To have done so could have compromised their masters' wishes.

In AD 527, Justinian became emperor. He immediately introduced a legal reform. Within a few years, under his authority, *The Digest of Justinian* was published.[4] This was a collection of legal opinions from famous experts on law. About a third of the *Digest* comprises the opinions of the great jurist Ulpian, who was murdered in AD 228. He is referred to more than any other jurist.[5] He is quoted as saying that "marriage is constituted by marital affection, not by cohabitation."[6] Not only does this reference stress the importance of marital consent, but it places the *consensus* over the *domumductio*. Indeed, Roman law acknowledged that a man and woman could live together in concubinage and not be married. The marriage only began once they started to regard themselves as man and wife.[7]

Ulpian is also quoted as saying, "For it is consent, not sleeping together, which makes marriage."[8] The jurist Scaevola agrees that marriage is brought about by consent.[9] Albert Gauthier, a Canadian professor of canon law who specialized in Roman law and who died in 1997, comments, "Neither the absence of common life, nor the absence of *deductio in domum* constitute proofs of the non existence of marriage."[10] Indeed, in the first book of his *Institutes*, the jurist Gaius states that con-

4. Krueger et al., *Corpus Iuris Civilis* (bibliog. III).

5. Smith, *A Classical Dictionary of Biography, Mythology, and Geography* (bibliog. III), 798.

6. ". . . non enim coitus matrimonium facit, sed maritalis affectio." *Digest* (bibliog. III), 24, 1, 32, 13.

7. *Digest* (bibliog. III), 39, 5, 31pr.

8. "Nuptias enim non concubitus, sed consensus facit." *Digest* (bibliog. III), 35, 1, 15. Also, *Digest* (bibliog. III), 50, 17, 30.

9. *Digest* (bibliog. III), 24, 1, 66.

10. Gauthier, *Roman Law* (bibliog. III), 38. The term *deductio in domum* is the same as *domumductio*.

sent makes a marriage legally complete even if the customary marriage ceremonies are omitted.[11]

Therefore, within Roman law there evolved the understanding that consent was both necessary and sufficient to bring about a marriage. But there was a complication. Within Roman society each family was ruled over by its oldest male ascendant—called the *paterfamilias*.[12] In order for a couple to marry, not only did they need to give consent themselves but so did the *paterfamilias* of each—both the man's and the woman's.[13] Even if the man or the woman had been previously married with the consent of the appropriate *paterfamilias* and subsequently divorced, he or she could not remarry without the new consent of the *paterfamilias*.[14]

With regard to the bride, the consent of her *paterfamilias* could be presumed, but this presumption could be overturned if he did in fact disapprove of the marriage. Unfortunately, such a presumption was not made with regard to the bridegroom's *paterfamilias*.[15] This brought about some complex legislation in order to cover certain possible situations. For example, what would happen if his *paterfamilias* was mad and so unable to give consent? If the bridegroom was still under the control of his grandfather, who was insane, then his father's consent was sufficient.[16] Similarly, if he was under the control of his insane father, then his grandfa-

---

11. Joyce, *Christian Marriage: An Historical and Doctrinal Study* (bibliog. III), 32.

12. Treggiari, "Divorce Roman Style" (bibliog. III), 31–46.

13. *Digest* (bibliog. III), 23, 2, 2.

14. *Digest* (bibliog. III), 23, 2, 18.

15. Treggiari, "Divorce Roman Style" (bibliog. III), 32.

16. *Digest* (bibliog. III), 23, 2, 9pr.

ther's consent was sufficient. What would happen if the father could not give the required consent because he had been captured in battle by the enemy? After three years, his son was allowed to marry.[17] Similarly, if the father of either a man or a woman had been captured and it was not even certain that he was still alive, then either could marry after three years.[18] Moreover, they could marry before the three years provided it was certain that the missing father would not, if he knew, object.[19]

The fact that consent was required from the couple themselves as well as each *paterfamilias* meant that conflicts were possible. What happened if a person wished to marry but his or her *paterfamilias* was against it? The jurist Marcianus says that it is the duty of the *paterfamilias* to prevent such a marriage. The same reference to Marcianus, however, says that the *paterfamilias* is not, in an illicit manner, to prevent his child from marrying. It refers to the thirty-fifth section of the *Lex Iulia*, a law of the first Roman emperor Augustus, which made it a duty for those Roman citizens who were members of the old patrician families to marry and so continue their family lines. Thus, in such families, the *paterfamilias* was obliged to allow his child to marry eventually. This rule was also decreed by the emperors Severus and Antonius, who are referred to in the text from Marcianus.[20] Augustus

17. Ibid., 23, 2, 9, 1.
18. Ibid., 23, 2, 10.
19. Ibid., 23, 2, 11.
20. "Capite trigesimo quinto legis iuliae qui liberos quos habent in potestate iniuria prohibuerint ducere uxores vel nubere, vel qui dotem dare non volunt ex constitutione divorum severi et antonini, per proconsules praesidesque

reigned from 63 BC to AD 14, Severus from 193 to 211, and Antonius from 211 to 217.[21]

What happened if a son did not wish to marry but his *paterfamilias* wanted him to? Could he be forced to marry against his will? The *Digest* says that it was the opinion of Terentius Clemens that such a son could not be forced to marry.[22] However, it is surprising that the next article of the *Digest* refers to Celsus who says that if the son was indeed compelled to go through with the marriage, then it would be legally binding. In a somewhat naive fashion, this latter article explains that although the son would not have married the woman if his father had not made him, the fact that he went through with the marriage shows that he did ultimately consent.[23]

It was theoretically possible to avoid these complications. Professor Susan Treggiari (a modern expert on Roman life) and Albert Gauthier both explain that sons and daughters could be emancipated from the control of their respective *paterfamilias*.[24] The methods of emancipation varied and were often complex, but they usually involved the exchange of money. Modestinus says that a son who had been emancipated could marry without the consent of his father.[25] A description of marriage is attributed to this jurist who was a student

---

provinciarum coguntur in matrimonium collocare et dotare. Prohibere autem videtur et qui condicionem non quaerit." Digest (bibliog. III), 23, 2, 19.

21. Smith, *A Classical Dictionary* (bibliog. III),108–10, 146, 702.

22. *Digest* (bibliog. III), 23, 2, 21.

23. Ibid., 23, 2, 22.

24. Treggiari, "Divorce Roman Style" (bibliog. III), 32, and Gauthier, *Roman Law* (bibliog. III), 31–32.

25. *Digest* (bibliog. III), 23, 2, 25.

of Ulpian.[26] He describes it as a union between a man and a woman which is a sharing of the whole of life.[27] Later, it will be seen how this description became influential in official Church documents in the twentieth century.

The nature of the matrimonial consent is elaborated further by the Roman legislation concerning divorce. Once the couple had established the marriage by their mutual consent, with the consent of each *paterfamilias*, they kept the marriage in existence by honoring the marriage (*honor matrimonii*).[28] That is, they continually consented to remain as man and wife. As Treggiari explains, their will had to continue in order for the marriage to continue.[29] If they withdrew their intention to be married then the marriage ended. From the legal point of view, divorce was informal. There was no set formula of words and no prescribed actions. Treggiari says that often it was the contracting of a second marriage which proved that the first had ended.[30] By the time of Cicero, who lived from 106 to 43 BC, both husbands and wives could divorce each other unilaterally. They could also divorce by mutual agreement.[31] Initially, divorce came about for a serious reason such as adultery. Eventually, however, no serious reason was needed and so divorce became a frequent occurrence.[32]

---

26. Smith, *A Classical Dictionary* (bibliog. III), 454.
27. "Nuptiae sunt coniunctio maris et feminae et consortium omnis vitae, divini et humani iuris communicatio." *Digest* (bibliog. III), 23, 2, 1.
28. Ibid., 24, 1, 32, 13 and 39, 5, 31pr.
29. Treggiari, "Divorce Roman Style" (bibliog. III), 33–34.
30. Ibid., 35–36.
31. Ibid., 37, and Smith, *A Classical Dictionary* (bibliog. III),170–73. Also, *Carcopino, Daily Life* (bibliog. III), 100–101.
32. Treggiari, "Divorce Roman Style" (bibliog. III), 38–46.

Indeed, Jerome Carcopino, a modern expert on Roman society, says that it eventually became epidemic.[33] This high frequency of divorce is connected with the ease with which it could be accomplished—namely, by the simple withdrawal of matrimonial consent by either party.

It has been seen that the consent of the couple, as well as that of their respective *paterfamilias*, was required to bring about the marriage. Either spouse could withdraw his or her consent and so end the marriage. Could a *paterfamilias* also end the marriage by withdrawing his consent? Treggiari suggests that up to the first century BC, a *paterfamilias* might have been able to impose a divorce,[34] but by the time of the *Digest*, a *paterfamilias* could not do so if the consent of the couple remained. Instead, if he really disapproved of the marriage, he could withdraw the protection and support he was able to give as the *paterfamilias*.[35]

---

33. Carcopino, *Daily Life* (bibliog. III), 100–101.
34. Treggiari, "Divorce Roman Style" (bibliog. III), 34.
35. *Digest* (bibliog. III), 24, 1, 32, 19, and following. Also, Ibid., 43, 30, 1, 5.

—2—

The Church's Use of the Roman Understanding that Consent Makes Marriage

BY THE TIME OF JESUS, the Roman Empire had spread and was a most formidable force. Unfortunately for the early Christians, the might of Rome was sometimes turned against them.[1] Nevertheless, the Edict of Milan, issued by Emperor Constantine in 313, gave the Church the opportunity to spread throughout the Roman Empire.[2] As it did so, it absorbed certain features of Roman culture—in particular, the principle that consent brings a marriage into existence. Gauthier proposes that this was a major influence of Roman civil law. He believes that although many of the Church Fathers promoted the notion that consent makes marriage, they were basing their arguments on civil law.[3]

James Brundage, who is among the twentieth century's leading experts on medieval canon law, agrees. He says, "Patristic writers assumed, as Roman law did,

---

1. Grant, *Augustus to Constantine* (bibliog. III), 255–64. Also, Frend, *The Rise of Christianity* (bibliog. III), 452–63.

2. Walsh, *Roots of Christianity* (bibliog. III), 246–48. Also, Frend, *The Rise of Christianity* (bibliog. III), 503, 554.

3. Gauthier, *Roman Law* (bibliog. III), 39–40.

that consent made marriage. They rejected the notion that consummation was an essential part of marriage. It made no difference whether a couple ever went to bed together; so long as they consented to marry one another, that was what counted."⁴ For example, there is Ambrose who wrote in the fourth century. In his *Book Concerning the Institution of a Virgin*⁵ he states, "When a marriage is initiated, it is then that the name of marriage is applied. It is not the loss of virginity which makes the marriage, but the matrimonial agreement. Therefore, there is a marriage when [the woman is] united with the man; not when [she is] intimately joined to the man."⁶

Saint John Chrysostom wrote in the last half of the fourth century. There is a collection of homilies, attributed to him, on parts of Matthew's Gospel. It is very doubtful whether he is the author of this work. It will be seen later, however, that its content has been very influential in the Latin tradition of the Church—this despite Chrysostom being categorized as one of the Greek Fathers. The thirty-second homily of this *Incomplete Work on Matthew*⁷ states, "It is not intercourse which makes marriage, but consent."⁸

4. Brundage, *Law, Sex, and Christian Society* (bibliog. III), 92.

5. Ambrose, *Liber de Institutione Virginis* (bibliog. III), Latin text in Migne (ed), *Patrologiae Latina* (bibliog. III), vol. 16, cols. 319–48, in particular, ch. 6 of St. Ambrose's work, found in cols. 330–32.

6. "Cum initiatur coniugium, coniugii nomen ascsiscitur. Non defloratio virginitatis facit coniugium, sed pactio coniugalis. Denique cum iungiter viro, coniugium est, non cum viri admixtione cognoscitur." Migne (ed), *Patrologiae Latina* (bibliog. III), vol. 16, cols. 330–31.

7. Chrysostom (attrib.), *Opus Imperfectum in Matthaeum, Homilia xxxii* (bibliog. III).

8. "Matrimonium non facit coitus, sed voluntas." Migne (ed), *Patrologiae Graeca* (bibliog. III), vol. 56, col. 802.

Brundage explains that, during the time of Augustine, Christian wedding ceremonies began to form. He describes how, by the sixth century, two types of ceremony had developed: "One type, commonest in Gaul, featured a nuptial blessing imparted by a priest while the newly wedded couple lay in the marriage bed. Nuptial ceremonies in Italy, by contrast, centered on a blessing bestowed upon the couple either in the church building or, more commonly, at the door of the church, at the time when they exchanged consent. Thus the symbolism of the Italian rites centered upon consent and the Church's role in marriage, while the French wedding symbolism stressed consummation and treated the nuptial ceremony as primarily a domestic affair."[9] The Italian rites, as described by Brundage, certainly manifested the Roman emphasis on consent.

What about the rite in Gaul? I would suggest that there are two important factors underlying it. The first is that the bishops of the Church in Gaul were very different from the other bishops in the Church. The historian Peter Brown explains that in the fifth century the landed aristocracy of Gaul took over the running of the Church. Brown describes it as the "aristocratization" of the Church. Thus, as Brown says, this part of the Church developed differently because its bishops had not risen "through the ranks of the clergy."[10]

The second factor is the Germanic invasion of Gaul. Despite Julius Caesar's earlier conquest, the Frankish king Clovis finally removed all Roman rule from the

---

9. Brundage, *Law, Sex, and Christian Society* (bibliog. III), 88.
10. Brown, *The Rise of Western Christendom* (bibliog. III), 64–65.

Loire Valley in 486. He then converted to Catholicism in 500.[11] Clovis and his followers were thus no friends of the Romans and were only too keen to remove the last vestiges of Roman culture. Indeed, Frend says of them, "For two centuries they had fought the Romans on the Rhine frontier. Their kings had been thrown to the beasts in the amphitheatre of Cologne by Constantine. Only exceptionally had Franks allowed themselves to become Romanized."[12] Thus it can safely be said that the type of rite Brundage describes in Gaul was not typical of the rites present at the time in the Roman Empire—most of which emphasized the role of consent in bringing a marriage into existence.

At the beginning of the seventh century, Saint Isidore of Seville wrote his *Books of Etymologies*.[13] In the seventh chapter of the ninth book he says, "Married couples are truly called as such from the first moment of the fulfillment of the betrothal, although up to that point there has been no matrimonial intercourse between them—just as Mary is called the spouse of Joseph, between whom there had not been, nor was there going to be, the slightest joining of the flesh."[14] Like Augustine, Isidore wished to uphold the fact that the marriage between Mary and Joseph was a true marriage, despite there being no sexual union between them. As

---

11. Frend, *The Rise of Christianity* (bibliog. III), 800–805.

12. Ibid., 803.

13. Isidore, *Libri Etymologiarum* (bibliog. III).

14. "Coniuges verius appellantur a prima desponsationis fide, quamvis adhuc inter eos ignoretur coniugalis concubitus, sicut Maria Joseph coniux vocatur, inter quos nec fuerat, nec futura erat carnis nulla commistio." Migne (ed), *Patrologiae Latina* (bibliog. III), vol. 82, col. 365.

the centuries passed, the tradition in the Church which maintained that it is a couple's consent that brings their marriage into existence was accepted more and more.

Eventually, in November 866, it received official backing from Pope Nicholas I. He had received questions on various issues from Bulgarian Christians. His *Replies to the Questions of the Bulgarians*[15] covers 106 points. His third point concerns marriage. The Bulgarians were concerned because they had been told by Greek priests that a marriage had to receive the blessing of a priest for it to be a true marriage. Without such a blessing, there could be no marriage.[16]

It has just been seen that Brundage refers to two types of ceremony which had evolved by the sixth century, both of which involved the blessing of a priest. In these cases, however, the blessing itself was not considered to bring the marriage into existence. It merely highlighted an aspect of marriage which was regarded as important—*consent* in the rites in Italy; *consummation* in the rite in Gaul. But this was not the opinion of the Greek priests who lived near the Bulgarians. These priests thought *the blessing* actually brought the marriage into existence.

The Pope replied, "Let the consent alone of those whose wedding is in question be sufficient according to the laws. If it happens that this consent alone is missing from marriages then all other celebrations are in vain, even when there has been intercourse—as the great

---

15. Nicholas I (bibliog. I), *Responsa ad Consulta Bulgarorum*, 13 November 866.
16. Joyce, *Christian Marriage* (bibliog. III), 44–45.

doctor John Chrysostom bears witness, who says, 'It is not intercourse which makes marriage, but consent.'"[17]

Two observations need to be made about Nicholas's response. The first is that his argument does not depend upon the quotation from the *IncompleteWork on Matthew*. Thus, the fact that the reference most probably comes from another author and not from Saint John Chrysostom does not undermine Nicholas's reasoning too much. Pope Nicholas, like so many others, wished to show that his thinking was supported by the Church's tradition. Therefore, if he could find an eminent Father of the Church who agreed with him, then his position would seem stronger. If Nicholas's argument had been, "Saint John Chrysostom said consent makes marriage and so that is the position I take," then his line of reasoning would have been completely invalidated by the fact that Chrysostom most probably said nothing of the kind. Nicholas's argument is more subtle, however. It can be paraphrased this way: Consent makes marriage and John Chrysostom agrees. This is evident from the fact that Nicholas's explanation ends with the reference to Chrysostom; it does not start with it. Therefore, the revelation that Chrysostom probably did not make the statement means that Nicholas's argument merely lacks such expert corroboration. His belief that consent makes marriage comes from another source.

---

17. ". . . ac per hoc sufficiat secundum leges solus eorum consensus, de quorum coniunctionibus agitur. Qui consensus si solus in nuptiis forte defuerit, cetera omnia etiam cum ipso coitu celebrata frustrantur, Joanne Chrysostomo magno doctore testante, qui ait: Matrimonium non facit coitus sed voluntas." Migne (ed), *Patrologiae Latina* (bibliog. III), vol. 119, col. 980.

The second observation concerns this very source. Nicholas states that consent alone is sufficient "according to the laws" (*secundum leges*). From the context, it does seem that he is referring to Roman civil law. This is certainly Gauthier's interpretation of the passage.[18] Moreover, George Hayward Joyce, a Jesuit who wrote an authoritative history of Christian marriage in 1933, actually translates the word *leges* of this passage as "civil law."[19] Thus, Nicholas bases his argument on the long-standing civil view that consent makes marriage. If consent is given, then there is a marriage, and no priest's blessing is needed. If, however, there is no consent, then nothing can bring about a marriage—neither a blessing nor consummation.[20]

18. Gauthier, *Roman Law* (bibliog. III), 40.

19. Joyce, *Christian Marriage* (bibliog. III), 45.

20. Vogel, "The Role of the Liturgical Celebrant" (bibliog. III), in particular, 74–75.

—3—

Saint Augustine
The Centrality of Love

THE RELATIONSHIP BETWEEN consent and sexual intercourse within marriage was further analyzed by Saint Augustine. In the early 390s, he involved himself in a controversy known as the ascetic debates between Jerome and Jovinian. Jerome held very strong ascetic views. Consequently, he placed the life of virginity above that of marriage. Jovinian, on the other hand, believed that marriage was a state in the Church which ranked equally with virginity. As far as he was concerned, married couples could also lead holy and virtuous lives.

Augustine had been a member of a heretical sect called the Manicheans for about nine years during the early part of his life.[1] They regarded the body to be the product of an evil deity; to them, the body was evil. As a consequence, for a married couple to have children meant that they were continuing this evil with their offspring. In short, the Manicheans were against sexual reproduction. It is thus not surprising that Jovinian

---

1. Clark (ed), *St. Augustine on Marriage and Sexuality* (bibliog. III), 32.

accused Jerome of being tainted with this heresy. It is within this context that Augustine addresses the issue. He takes the middle path. That is, he upholds the superiority of the life of virginity while maintaining the genuine and inherent goodness of marriage. He does this in two works:[2] *On Holy Virginity*[3] and *On the Good of Marriage*.[4]

In *On the Good of Marriage*, written in 401, Augustine starts with the account in Genesis 2:21–24 of the creation of the woman from the man's rib. He explains that God did not create man and woman separately with the later intention of joining them together in marriage. No, God created one from the other with the very purpose of them complementing each other. The creation of the woman from the man's side shows the inherent intimacy between the two.[5] Augustine thus uses the principle that origin determines nature. Marriage is in accordance with the divine plan. It brings together man and woman, who are created to be intimate with each other. Augustine thus acknowledges that marriage must be good because of its divine origin. He then considers the ways in which marriage is good.

Augustine states that marriage "does not seem to me to be a good solely because of the procreation of children, but also because of the natural companionship between the two sexes. Otherwise, we could not speak of marriage in the case of old people, especially if they had

2. Ibid., 42–43.

3. Augustine, *De Sancta Virginitate* (bibliog. III).

4. Augustine, *De Bono Coniugali* (bibliog. III).

5. Augustine, *De Bono Coniugali* (bibliog. III), 1.1; Migne (ed), *Patrologiae Latina* (bibliog. III), vol. 40, col. 373; Wilcox (tr), *The Fathers* (bibliog. III), vol. 27, 9.

either lost their children or had begotten none at all. But, in a good marriage, although one of many years, even if the ardor of youth has cooled between man and woman, the order of charity still flourishes between husband and wife."[6] Thus, for Augustine, the two sexes complement each other. Within marriage this complementarity gives rise to a special bond of friendship and intimacy. Love and charity are experienced within this bond, and it is for this reason that marriage can be said to be good.

This friendship is inherent to marriage. As such, it is not dependent upon having children. So even if the couple has no offspring, this great bond of friendship remains. It does not break if their children die. Moreover, it continues to exist when they are too old to have any children. It is this tie of love and friendship that was planned by God when he created woman from man. Willemien Otten, a modern theologian and historian of Christianity, says it is for this reason that Augustine regards marriages between elderly or sterile persons to be just as valid as those between younger couples and those able to have children.[7]

What about children? Augustine describes them as "the only worthy fruit, not of the joining of male and female, but of sexual intercourse."[8] Otten carefully

---

6. "Quod mihi non videtur propter solam filiorum procreationem, sed propter ipsam etiam naturalem in diverso sexu societatem. Alioquin non iam diceretur coniugium in senibus, paesertim si vel amisissent filios, vel minime genuissent. Nunc vero in bono licet annoso coniugio, etsi emarcuit ardor aetatis inter masculum et feminam, viget tamen ordo charitatis inter maritum et uxorem." *Augustine, De Bono Coniugali* (bibliog. III), 3.3; Migne (ed), *Patrologiae Latina* (bibliog. III), vol. 40, col. 375; Wilcox (tr), *The Fathers* (bibliog. III), vol. 27, 12.

7 . Otten, "Augustine on Marriage" (bibliog. III).

8. "Consequens est connexio societatis in filiis, qui unus honestus fructus

notes the distinction that Augustine makes.[9] He regards children to be "the only worthy fruit" of sexual intercourse. He is not saying that they are the only worthy fruit of marriage. It is for this reason that Augustine explains that the Church does not allow a man to divorce his barren wife. He might do so outside the Church, but his initial marriage remains because "that bond of fellowship between married couples is so strong."[10] Augustine treats cases of adultery in the same way. For example, although a man might divorce his wife outside the Church because she has committed adultery, the Church does not recognize such a divorce because the marriage remains by virtue of the bond of fellowship. Thus, if the man attempts to marry a new wife, he would be guilty of an adulterous act.[11]

Therefore, for Augustine, the first and most fundamental way in which marriage is good is the love and friendship that exists between the husband and wife. Timothy Buckley, a present-day writer on family life, acknowledges that Augustine emphasizes the place of love within marriage.[12] Moreover, Buckley states that this fact is often forgotten and that consequently,

est, non coniunctionis maris et feminae, sed concubitus." Augustine, *De Bono Coniugali* (bibliog. III), 1.1; Migne (ed), *Patrologiae Latina* (bibliog. III), vol. 40, col. 373; Wilcox (tr), *The Fathers* (bibliog. III), vol. 27, 9.

9. Otten, "Augustine on Marriage" (bibliog. III), 398–99.

10. ". . . tantum valet illud sociale vinculum coniugum." Augustine, *De Bono Coniugali* (bibliog. III), 7.7; Migne (ed), *Patrologiae Latina* (bibliog. III), vol. 40, cols. 378–79; Wilcox (tr), *The Fathers* (bibliog. III), vol. 27, 18.

11. Augustine, *De Bono Coniugali* (bibliog. III), 15.17; Migne (ed), *Patrologiae Latina* (bibliog. III), vol. 40, col. 385; Wilcox (tr), *The Fathers* (bibliog. III), vol. 27, 31.

12. Buckley, *What Binds Marriage? Roman Catholic Theology in Practice* (bibliog. III), 43–47.

"Augustine does not receive a good press today when it comes to sexual ethics."[13]

Augustine gives another reason why marriage is good: "Marriage has also this good, that carnal or youthful incontinence, even if it is bad, is turned to the honorable task of begetting children, so that marital intercourse makes something good out of the evil of lust."[14] Thus, marriage provides the legitimate context in which the sexual faculties may be used.

Later, in *On the Good of Marriage*, Augustine gives three other reasons why marriage is good.[15] The first two pertain to the marriages of all people. The third refers only to the marriages of Christians. The first is that marriage provides an occasion for having children. The second is that the marriage partners are called to remain faithful to each other. It is this mutual fidelity which helps the husband and wife to avoid unlawful intercourse.[16] The third, which relates to Christian marriages, is that the couple enjoys the sanctity of the sacrament of marriage. Each of these three dimensions of marriage is good. Consequently, marriage as a whole is good.

---

13. Ibid., 43.

14. "Habent etiam id bonum coniuga, quod carnalis vel iuvenilis incontinentia, etiamsi vitiosa est, ad propagandae prolis redigitur honestatem, ut ex malo libidinis aliquid boni faciat copulatio coniugalis." Augustine, *De Bono Coniugali* (bibliog. III), 3.3; Migne (ed), *Patrologiae Latina* (bibliog. III), vol. 40, col. 375; Wilcox (tr), *The Fathers* (bibliog. III), vol. 27, 13.

15. Augustine, *De Bono Coniugali* (bibliog. III), 24.32; Migne (ed), *Patrologiae Latina* (bibliog. III), vol. 40, cols. 394–95; Wilcox (tr), *The Fathers* (bibliog. III), vol. 27, 47–48.

16 . Augustine, *De Bono Coniugali* (bibliog. III), 6.6; Migne (ed), *Patrologiae Latina* (bibliog. III), vol. 40, cols. 377–78; Wilcox (tr), *The Fathers* (bibliog. III), vol. 27, 16–17.

Not everybody agreed with Augustine's solution to the ascetic debate. A certain Julian of Eclanum wrote a paper to someone called Turbantius. Although "To Turbantius" has since been lost, it is known that Julian regarded Augustine's view of marriage to be Manichean. He believed that Augustine was teaching that marriage and reproduction are evil. Augustine responded with his work *Against Julian*,[17] which he wrote in about 421 to 422.[18]

In *Against Julian*, Augustine is more positive toward the role of sexual intercourse within marriage, but he still regards it as only one of the many elements of marriage. In fact, he does not think that it is a necessary element. He elaborates on this when he explains why the marriage between Mary and Joseph was a true marriage despite there being no intercourse. He gives two reasons. First, a marriage does not cease when the couple ceases to have intercourse.[19] For example, marriages of the elderly remain in existence.[20] The second reason is that in the marriage of Mary and Joseph the three goods of children, fidelity, and the sanctity of the sacrament were present. He explains that the good of children was manifested in Jesus Christ. Fidelity was evident in that there was no adultery. Finally, the ho-

---

17. Augustine, *Contra Julianum* (bibliog. III); Migne (ed), *Patrologiae Latina* (bibliog. III), vol. 44, cols. 641–874; Schumacher (tr), *The Fathers* (bibliog. III), vol. 35.

18. Clark (ed), *St. Augustine on Marriage and Sexuality* (bibliog. III), 86–87.

19. Augustine, *Contra Julianum* (bibliog. III), 5, 12, 46; Migne (ed), *Patrologiae Latina* (bibliog. III), vol. 44, col. 810; Schumacher (tr), *The Fathers* (bibliog. III), vol. 35, 287–88.

20. Here Augustine repeats what he said two decades earlier in *De Bono Coniugali* (bibliog. III), 3.3; Migne (ed), *Patrologiae Latina* (bibliog. III), vol. 40, col. 375; Wilcox (tr), *Fathers* (bibliog. III), vol. 27, 12.

liness of the sacramental bond was apparent because there was no divorce. As these three goods existed, it is a sign that Mary and Joseph were truly married.

In conclusion, Augustine acknowledges that God has created men and women so that they can be intimate. Marriage is a part of the divine plan. For this reason marriage is good. Marriage is particularly good because of the intimate friendship that exists between husband and wife. Within this special bond they share love and charity. This goodness exists from the moment they marry and it remains. Therefore, according to Augustine, there is a true marriage from the moment of its initiation. That is, it is not dependent upon sexual intercourse or procreation. This is particularly evident in the marriage of Mary and Joseph.

—4—

The Indissolubility of Marriage in the Christian Roman Empire

ALTHOUGH THE CHURCH within the Roman Empire adopted the notion from civil law that a marriage is brought into being by the consent of the couple, there developed one major difference concerning the indissolubility of marriage. It has been seen that under Roman civil law marital consent had to be given continuously. Once it ceased to be given the marriage ended. This is why divorce within the Empire became very easy and very common. Brundage observes that this was the situation that Constantine inherited,[1] but divorce did become harder under this new emperor. The grounds on which a divorce could be allowed were stipulated. A man could divorce his wife for adultery, poisoning, or prostitution. A woman could divorce her husband for murder, poisoning, or grave-robbing. Brundage also notes that Constantine explicitly gave three grounds which were not sufficient for a wife to

---

1. Brundage, *Law, Sex, and Christian Society* (bibliog. III), 94.

obtain a divorce—that the husband was a drunkard, a gambler, or an adulterer.[2]

After Constantine's death, divorce became easier again under various emperors. At the beginning of the fifth century, Honorius removed the necessary grounds for divorce. Thus, it became theoretically possible to divorce for any reason. One limiting factor, however, was that a person who obtained a divorce for insufficient reasons incurred a heavy penalty such as deportation or loss of property. Moreover, the individual might not have been allowed to remarry.[3] Later, Emperor Theodosius II allowed divorces and remarriages without any penalties being imposed. The consequence was that divorces occurred simply by spouses withdrawing consent—as they had done before Constantine's reform. But another change by the same Theodosius meant that divorces became harder again for he insisted that there had to be provable grounds.[4]

It can thus be seen that the civil law concerning divorce went through various changes in the Christian Roman Empire. Similarly, the Church's discipline within the Empire varied. Gradually, however, the Church's understanding of the indissolubility of marriage emerged. Thus, unlike civil law, the Church eventually believed that once marital consent was given, it could not be withdrawn. For example, it has been seen how Augustine believed that the bond of fellowship in a marriage is so strong that it cannot be broken. Although the state

---

2. Ibid. Also, Noonan, "Novel 22" (bibliog. III), in particular, 42.

3. Noonan, "Novel 22" (bibliog. III), 45–46.

4. Brundage, *Law, Sex, and Christian Society* (bibliog. III), 95–96, and Noonan, "Novel 22" (bibliog. III), 49–52.

may allow a civil divorce, the marriage does in fact still exist. Moreover, if the individual attempts to marry another person, then he or she commits adultery.[5]

In 405, Pope Innocent I wrote to Exsuperius, the Bishop of Toulouse.[6] Exsuperius had asked for advice on certain issues, including how to deal with divorced and remarried members of the Church.[7] In the sixth chapter of his response, the Pope states that both parties of a second attempted marriage are guilty of adultery[8] and that they are to be excommunicated.[9] Two years later, one of the synods of North Africa, called the Eleventh Council of Carthage, stated, "We decree that according to the evangelic and apostolic discipline neither a husband dismissed by his wife, nor a wife dismissed by her husband may marry another; but that they are to remain as they are or to be reconciled to one another. If they despise [this law] they ought to be subjected to penance. And on this subject an imperial law ought to be promulgated."[10]

Theodore Mackin, a modern writer who has written eminent accounts of the historical development of the Catholic Church's understanding of marriage,

---

5. Augustine, *De Bono Coniugali* (bibliog. III), 7:7 and 15:17; Migne (ed), *Patrologiae Latina* (bibliog. III), vol. 40, cols. 378–79 and 385.

6. Innocent I (bibliog. I), *Ad Exsuperium*, 20 February 405.

7. Joyce, *Christian Marriage* (bibliog. III), 319–20.

8. Innocent I, *Ad Exsuperium,* 20 February 405, col. 500.

9. Ibid., col. 501.

10. "Placuit ut, secundum evangelicam et apostolicam disciplinam, neque dimissus ab uxore, neque dimissa a marito, alteri coniungatur, sed ita maneant, aut sibimet reconcilientur: quod si contempserint, ad poenitentiam redigantur, in qua causa legem imperialem petendam promulgari." Eleventh Council of Carthage (bibliog. I), canon 102 (sometimes numbered as canon 8), circa 407. English translation in Mackin, *Divorce and Remarriage* (bibliog. III), 228.

makes some observations on this canon.[11] First, it rests
its authority on the teachings of the synoptic Gospels
(evangelic) and of Saint Paul (apostolic).[12] Second, the
Council met after the restrictions on divorce by Emper-
or Constantine had been weakened and before divorces
became harder again under Theodosius II. That is, at a
time when the civil law was liberal—hence, the call for
a new corrective imperial law.

Mackin's third observation is that the canon's teaching on indissolubility appears to be absolute. That is, it
does not allow for any exception. This is important because there was, and still is, a debate over Matthew
19:9 which has Jesus saying, "Now I say this to you:
anyone who divorces his wife—I am not speaking of
an illicit marriage—and marries another, is guilty of
adultery."[13] The expression *illicit marriage* is a translation of the Greek word πορνεια. It is also possible to
translate this word as "adultery." Thus, the text from
Matthew could mean that anyone who divorces his wife
and marries another is guilty of adultery *except* in the
case of him divorcing his wife because she has committed adultery. But the Greek term, πορνεια, can have
at least three other meanings:[14] a relationship that is not
really a marriage because of some legal impediment; a
betrothal; an incestuous union which is not a true marriage.[15] In all these cases the man *would* be able to divorce his wife and marry another without being guilty

---

11. Mackin, *Divorce and Remarriage* (bibliog. III), 228–29.
12. ". . . ut secundum evangelicam et apostolicam disciplinam."
13. Wansbrough (ed), *The New Jerusalem Bible,* Standard Edition.
14. Mackin, *Divorce and Remarriage* (bibliog. III), 60–64.
15. Meier, *Matthew* (bibliog. III), 51.

of adultery for the simple reason that his first marriage was not a real marriage. However we translate the word πορνεια, though, the canon from the Eleventh Council of Carthage does not refer to any exception to the rule that a divorced person may not remarry.

In the middle of the fifth century, Attila the Hun invaded northern Italy and captured many men. Their wives did not know whether they were dead or still alive. Consequently, as time passed, some of the wives remarried, and problems arose when the first husband returned from captivity. This presented a pastoral problem for one local bishop, Nicetas of Aquileia, who wrote to the Pope for guidance.[16] Leo I replied, explaining that in such a case the first marriage would still be in existence.[17] Thus, the second attempted marriage had to end. Leo acknowledged that a second union would have resulted from an honest mistake. For this reason, he stated that no penalty should be imposed by the Church, but if the wife refused to end the second union, then she would be guilty of adultery and so must be excommunicated.

Just over three centuries later, in the 790s, the Council of Friuli was convened in northeast Italy.[18] This time the key person from Aquileia was Paulinus who presided over the Council. The tenth canon of the Council explicitly teaches that the bond of marriage is indissoluble.[19] Moreover, it also states that there is no ex-

---

16. Joyce, *Christian Marriage* (bibliog. III), 321, and Mackin, *Divorce and Remarriage* (bibliog. III), 231.
17. Leo I (bibliog. I), *Epistula clix*, 21 March 458, especially cols. 1136–37.
18. Council of Friuli (bibliog. I), circa 796–97.
19. Ibid., canon 10.

ception to this rule—not even in the case of adultery. With regard to Matthew's Gospel, the canon states that a study of Saint Jerome shows that the Gospel teaches that a man whose wife has committed adultery is free to dismiss her, but he must not remarry because his first marriage still exists.[20] Thus, the Council clearly teaches that Matthew's Gospel contains no exception at all to the indissolubility of marriage.

In summary, it can be said that the Roman Empire became an excellent vehicle for the spread of Christianity. Just as the Empire contained different traditions, then so did the Church. From within the Church of the Empire, however, there emerged, slowly but surely, two principles about marriage and consent. The first is based upon Roman civil law—namely, that consent makes marriage. Thus, marriage does not begin with consummation or the reception of a priest's blessing. The second principle—namely, that once marital consent has been given it cannot be withdrawn—generally disagrees with Roman civil law. This second principle reaffirms the understanding that marriage is indissoluble. Eventually, Church authorities made it clear that this indissolubility does not allow for exceptions, such as cases involving adultery.

---

20. It has already been seen that St. Augustine says that such a man must not remarry. Augustine, *De Bono Coniugali* (bibliog. III), 15.17; Migne (ed), *Patrologiae Latina* (bibliog. III), vol. 40, col. 385; Wilcox (tr), *The Fathers* (bibliog. III), vol. 27, 31.

—5—

The Ancient Germanic Tradition
Consent Makes Marriage but Needs Proof

THE TERM *GERMANIC* IS GENERIC. Although the Roman Empire grew in size so that it covered many lands, there remained a number of regions outside its boundaries. In these regions lived many tribes. To the sophisticated Graeco-Roman world these peoples were barbarians. Generally, their languages fell within the Germanic family. Thus, the term *Germanic* is often applied to them.

The Church historian and theologian Henry Chadwick illustrates the diversity of these tribes.[1] Within the Germanic tradition he lists Goths, Vandals, Alans, Suevi, Visigoths, Burgundians, Heruls, Ostrogoths, and Franks. It is not surprising that the Roman Empire, despite all its might, had difficulty in standing up against such a large array of tribes. By the fourth century, the Germanic tribes had made incursions into areas of the Roman Empire. With them they brought their own customs, including those related to marriage and the family.

---

1. Chadwick, *The Early Church* (bibliog. III), 247–57.

33

James Brundage suggests that the tribal law of the
Germanic peoples was founded upon two principles.
The first involved an essential link between the tribe
as a whole and an individual member with regard to
rights and obligations. Thus, if an individual took on
certain obligations, then it was the tribe's responsibility
to ensure that these obligations were met. Similarly, if
an individual had the right to something, then the tribe
had the responsibility of protecting him so that he received it.

One example of the latter, given by Brundage, is
peace and security. The tribe would protect the individual from foreign enemies. The second principle was
that of *reciprocal revenge*. That is, if an individual suffered unjust injury at the hands of another, then the
tribe would balance the situation by inflicting injury on
the guilty party or, if that was not possible, on his family. Gradually, Germanic kings, as opposed to the whole
tribe, took on the role of protecting rights and obligations and providing justice in the case of injury. Later,
toward the end of the fifth century, these kings had the
norms they used in such cases written down in collections of laws, known as codes. Examples of these codes
are the *Leges Alamannorum, Leges Visigothorum*, and
the *Leges Burgundionum*.[2]

It is within the context of the ancient tribal customs
that the primitive Germanic understanding of marriage
can be seen. It was essentially a contract, not between
the bride and bridegroom, but between their tribes. Under this contract, the bride was transferred from the

---

2. Brundage, *Law, Sex, and Christian Society* (bibliog. III), 125–26.

protection of her father or guardian to that of her husband. He now had the rights to her, as well as the obligation to protect her.[3] Within this convention, there developed three forms of marriage.

The first form of marriage was by purchase (*Kaufe-he*). This form had two parts—the betrothal and the marriage proper. In different Germanic regions and at different times, the distinction made between these two parts varied as far as ritual was concerned. For example, the Anglo-Saxon word for the betrothal was *Beweddung*, which eventually included the marriage ceremony itself—hence the modern English word *wedding*. Joyce explains that the betrothal was very important, being regarded as "at least the initial portion of the contract itself."[4] Before the marriage, however, a betrothed person could refuse to go through with the marriage and even marry another person. In those areas where the betrothal and marriage proper were regarded virtually as one act, the prospective bridegroom or his father paid an agreed amount to the woman's father or guardian. The bride was thus purchased by her husband. The marriage contract was based upon this purchase. It was necessary for a certain amount to be handed over to the bride's family. Joyce says that even the equivalent of a token farthing could be used if the bridegroom was from a poor family.[5]

Where the betrothal and the marriage proper were considered to be clearly distinct acts, the betrothal was

---

3. Schillebeeckx, *Marriage: Human Reality and Saving Mystery* (bibliog. III), 256.
4. Joyce, *Christian Marriage* (bibliog. III), 48.
5. Ibid., 51.

an agreement (*Muntvertrag*) between the prospective husband, or his father, and the woman's father or guardian. These negotiations involved the fixing of the amount to be paid by the bridegroom's side to the bride's family. The marriage itself began with the bride being publicly handed over to the head of the bridegroom's family. This transfer (*Anvertrauung*) was then followed by the wedding ceremony (*Trauung*). In this the members of the bride's family encircled her to witness the transfer and to make public their agreement to the marital contract.[6]

The transfer of the bride was symbolic of a deeper reality. She no longer belonged to the family in which she grew up. Instead, she was now a member of her husband's family. Moreover, he now had legal power (*Munt*) over her.[7] Joyce says that this transfer of guardianship became an essential part of marriage throughout the Germanic race.[8] Indeed, the theologian Edward Schillebeeckx states, "The handing over of the bride by her father or guardian (*Vormund*) was the most important condition in Germanic law of the validity of the marriage."[9]

Later, in some areas, what was emphasized was not so much the actual handing over of the bride but the fact that she had been handed over. Thus, the existence of conjugal life was essential proof of the existence of a marriage.[10] The transfer of the bride ensured that she

6. Brundage, *Law, Sex, and Christian Society* (bibliog. III), 128.
7. Ibid., 128–29.
8. Joyce, *Christian Marriage* (bibliog. III), 49.
9. Schillebeeckx, *Marriage: Human Reality and Saving Mystery* (bibliog. III), 257.
10. Joyce, *Christian Marriage* (bibliog. III), 52.

always belonged to a family. Thus, there would be somebody to protect her. It is for this reason that marriage by purchase (*Kaufehe*) was seen to protect the woman and to preserve the structure of society. The necessary public contract, with the exchange of money, gave a certainty as to who actually had guardianship over her. Also, the inheritance rights of her children would be known. If she was under the guardianship of her husband, then their children would be his genuine heirs. Consequently, it is not surprising that Brundage suggests that this was the preferred type of marriage.[11]

In today's world, marriage by purchase is seen as extremely demeaning to women. This system of marriage regarded them as property which could be bought and sold. Unfortunately, the second form of marriage was even worse. This was marriage by abduction (*Raubehe*). The woman would be captured and taken by force, without her consent or that of her family. Brundage explains that this is why this method is sometimes described as "marriage by rape." When the codes of law were written, they discouraged this type of marriage and even imposed fines on men who committed such acts.[12]

The third form of marriage was by the mutual consent (*Friedelehe*) of the man and the woman. If marriage by abduction can be termed "marriage by rape," then marriage by mutual consent can be described as "marriage by elopement." The man took the woman from her fam-

---

11. Brundage, *Law, Sex, and Christian Society* (bibliog. III), 129.
12. Ibid.

ily with *her* consent but without *her family's* consent.[13] In one respect this method of marrying was somewhere between the other two methods. Marriage by purchase involved the consent of the bride and her family; whereas marriage by abduction involved neither. Marriage by mutual consent was a middle way, however, involving the consent of the woman but not her family.

Although marriage by mutual consent avoided the legal penalties incurred by abduction, it lacked the contractual element found in marriage by purchase because neither the husband nor his father paid any money over to the bride's family. Consequently, the husband could not claim to have guardianship (*Munt*) over her. She might live with him, but she was still a member of the family in which she grew up. It was this family that had guardianship over her. Despite the fact that the husband lacked this legal power, this method of marrying had its advantages. First, the husband or his father did not have to part with any money. Second, the marriage did not depend upon the consent of her family.[14]

These three forms of marriage existed in early Germanic law, but marriage by abduction became much less acceptable as time went on. Changes in society and law increasingly discouraged it. With regard to marriage by purchase, women gradually gained more independence. This emancipation meant that they were no longer regarded as property. Thus, the notion that the guardianship (*Munt*) of a woman could be purchased from her family by her husband became less relevant. Consequently, of the three forms, marriage by mutual

---

13. Ibid.
14. Ibid.

consent eventually became the most significant. More-over, the mutual exchange of consent came to be seen as the central part of the proceedings.[15]

Schillebeeckx gives the example of marriage in Up-per Bavaria by the time of the eleventh century. The importance of the consent of the couple was such that the form of marriage could now be split into three phas-es: the betrothal, the mutual consent to marry, and the wedding feast. The last of these involved the leading of the bride to the husband's home. This was followed by the festive meal and her solemn entry into the bridal chamber. Although the mutual consent of the couple brought about the marriage, Schillebeeckx explains, "The third phase, however—the *domumductio* [the leading home] of the bride and the consummation of the marriage—gradually came to be regarded as con-clusive evidence of the legal validity of the marriage contract."[16] It is because consummation provided such important legal proof of the existence of the marriage that Brundage states, "Sexual intercourse was essential to Germanic marriage, however, and no marital union was binding without it."[17]

When one considers the Germanic tradition, I would suggest that one must distinguish between the required marital consent and the legal proof of its existence. Consent in itself is an internal disposition of some-one's will and so cannot be seen. Within the Germanic tradition, the consent of both the man and the woman

15. Schillebeeckx, *Marriage: Human Reality and Saving Mystery* (bibliog. III), 258, and Joyce, *Christian Marriage* (bibliog. III), 50.
16. Schillebeeckx, *Marriage: Human Reality and Saving Mystery* (bibliog. III), 258.
17. Brundage, *Law, Sex, and Christian Society* (bibliog. III), 131.

eventually became necessary. For example, without the woman's consent, the marriage would have been by abduction (*Raubehe*). For legal reasons, however, it was necessary to verify that consent had been given. Thus, external proofs became important. Depending upon local custom and law, the mutual consent of the couple would be expressed externally in a particular way. For example, somebody may have been authorized to ask them publicly if they both wished to marry (although Joyce raises doubt as to whether it was indeed a strict legal requirement for the bride's internal consent to be manifested externally in such a way).[18]

The importance of the mutual consent of the bride and bridegroom can be illustrated another way. Brundage considers what the difference was, in Germanic thought, between marriage and concubinage. He states, "Marriage in Germanic law consisted simply of sexual intercourse accompanied by an intention to live together permanently and to have children. The intention to form a permanent union was what distinguished marriage from concubinage."[19]

Did Germanic law regard marriage to be indissoluble? The simple answer is in the negative. As might be expected of such cultures, it was fairly easy for a husband to divorce his wife but not so easy for her to divorce him. For example, Brundage states,

> The Burgundian woman who attempted to divorce her husband was to be smothered in mire, but the Burgundian man who wished to divorce his wife could do

18. Joyce, *Christian Marriage* (bibliog. III), 52.
19. Brundage, *Law, Sex, and Christian Society* (bibliog. III), 130.
20. Ibid., 131.

so on any of the three grounds: adultery, sorcery, or tomb-violation. If he chose, however, he could also divorce his wife without citing reasons, but in this case he was required to pay her a sum equal to her marriage price and was also subject to a fine. Visigothic women, by contrast, could repudiate their husbands for sodomy or for having forced the wife to have sexual relations with another man.[20]

Brundage also explains that the first year of a marriage was generally regarded by Germanic law as a trial period. If the woman became pregnant during that time then the marriage was regarded as permanent—although, as has just been seen, a divorce could be obtained if the necessary conditions were met. If the woman did not conceive a child during the first year, then it was much easier to dissolve the union.[21]

In conclusion, it is difficult to give a single, straightforward account of marriage as found within the ancient Germanic tradition. Even the term *tradition* is debatable. It might be more accurate to speak of the Germanic traditions (in the plural) because of the various tribes. While the great variations in place and time provide a diverse picture of marriage, the following summary can be made.

There were three ancient ways of contracting marriage—by purchase, by abduction, and by mutual consent. As the role of women in society developed, the third form of marriage became the most prevalent. Within this form, the mutual exchange of consent was central. Indeed, it was this intention to remain together

---

21. Ibid.

as man and wife that made the union a marriage—as opposed to mere concubinage. With regard to inheritance and other legal consequences, however, it was necessary to have proof that a marriage did exist. The mutual consent was insufficient proof because it was internal and so could not be seen. Consummation was external proof that there was a marriage. Other proofs would include the woman's pregnancy, offspring, and marital cohabitation.

I would say that there is an unfortunate tendency to make a black and white distinction between the ancient Roman view of marriage and marriage in the Germanic traditions. It is often said that in Roman law it was consent that brought a marriage into existence, whereas in Germanic law it was cohabitation or consummation. Yes, within Roman law the role of consent was essential in bringing a marriage into existence, whereas consummation and cohabitation were not important legally. Within Germanic law, however, one also finds that consent became essential in the creation of a marriage—although for legal purposes it had to be verified externally.

—6—

Archbishop Hincmar of Rheims
His Unsupported Emphasis
on Consummation

WHEN POPE NICHOLAS I wrote his reply to the Bulgarian Church he had a very important contemporary—Archbishop Hincmar of Rheims, who held office from 845 until his death in 882. While Pope Nicholas was upholding the centrality of *consent alone* with regard to the validity of marriage, Hincmar was teaching that marital consent must be followed by sexual intercourse. In the 1970s, the Catholic writer on marriage and sexuality, André Guindon, recognized Hincmar's influence on the Church's understanding of marriage.[1] Indeed, Guindon says, "The importance of his stand on carnal copulation as an essential factor in the constitution of the marriage cannot be stressed enough."[2] In short, Hincmar teaches that marriage begins with the consent of the couple but that it is not complete until it has been consummated sexually.[3]

Hincmar was involved in an actual marriage case

---

1. Guindon, "Case for a 'Consummated' Sexual Bond before a 'Ratified' Marriage" (bibliog. III).
2. Ibid., 144.
3. Joyce, *Christian Marriage* (bibliog. III), 54.

and was asked to give a theological judgment. The case involved an Aquitanian nobleman named Stephen. He married the daughter of Regimund, another aristocrat. After the wedding ceremony, Stephen said that he could not consummate the marriage. He explained that, prior to the wedding, he had had an affair with a close relation of his intended wife. He thus argued that the marriage was invalid because of the impediment of affinity. Furthermore, his conscience forbade him to consummate the marriage.

The case had two important elements. First, there was the alleged impediment of affinity which, if proved, would have resulted in the marriage being declared null and void. The second was the fact of non-consummation. With regard to the first element, Stephen refused to name the relative of his wife with whom he had had the affair. As a result, the existence of the impediment of affinity could not be proved. Therefore, if Stephen wanted to be declared free from the obligations of the marriage, his only hope was the fact that the marriage had not been consummated. Accordingly, in 860 he referred the matter to the bishops assembled at the Synod of Touzy.[4] They in turn asked Hincmar for his opinion. In response to their request, Hincmar wrote "Concerning the Marriage of Stephen and the Daughter of Count Regimund."[5] In it he gives reasons why he believes that, although a marriage begins with the wedding ceremony, it is not complete until it has been consummated sexually.

Hincmar upholds the importance of the wedding

---

4. Ibid.
5. Hincmar of Rheims, *De Nuptiis Stephani* (bibliog. III).

ceremony. For example, he makes reference to the apocryphal story of the wedding of Saint John the Evangelist. It was told how Jesus called Saint John to follow him at his wedding. It was on this occasion that Jesus turned the water into wine. Hincmar observes that Saint John was called "not only before the joining of the flesh, but also before the pronouncement of the marriage."[6] That is, John was called from the wedding ceremony and not after it.[7] Thus, they were not married. Consequently, they were free to marry in the future and so "either of them was not bound to remain in a state of continence."[8] Hincmar contrasts this with the case of Saint Peter who was married and whose wife adhered to strict continence.[9]

Hincmar also stresses the importance of the marriage ceremony in the case of Mary and Joseph. He examines the passage in Matthew's Gospel where it says that it was discovered that Mary was pregnant before she and Joseph came together.[10] Hincmar draws attention to the fact that this means the discovery was made before the wedding.[11] He explains that when Matthew speaks of the period before Mary and Joseph "came together," this coming together does not refer to them living together as man and wife but to them coming

---

6. ". . . non solum ante carnis unionem, verum et ante nuptiarum percelebrationem." Migne (ed), *Patrologiae Latina* (bibliog. III), vol. 126, col. 148.

7. ". . . non post celebratas nuptias, sed de nuptiis." Ibid.

8. ". . . non legitur utrum in continentia manserit." Ibid.

9. ". . . sicut de beati Petri uxore, quae continentissime perseveravit." Ibid.

10. Matthew 1:18.

11. "Et haec sibimet ita concinere sacra demonstrat auctoritas, dicens de Maria et Joseph: 'Antequam,' inquit, 'convenirent' (Matth. I), id est, antequam nuptiarum solemnia rite celebrarent." Migne (ed), *Patrologiae Latina* (bibliog. III), vol. 126, col. 148.

together at a wedding ceremony, which would precede them living together.[12] Thus, Mary's pregnancy was discovered before she was married to Joseph. Indeed, it was at the wedding that she "began to be a wife" with respect to Joseph.[13]

Although Hincmar sees the importance of the wedding ceremony, he does not regard a marriage to be complete until it has been consummated. This is because, according to Hincmar, sexual intercourse between spouses makes their marriage share in the bond that exists between Christ and the Church. He bases his argument on Saint Augustine: "Not all weddings make the conjugal bond, such as those which are not followed by the union of the sexes—just as a man is not always the son and heir of him whose heir he is known to be. Marriages do not have in themselves the symbolism of Christ and the Church, as the blessed Augustine says, if they [the spouses] do not avail themselves of each other maritally—that is, if the union of the sexes has not followed up the marriages."[14]

Augustine is drawing a distinction between external appearances and the deeper realities. For example, everyone might believe that a man is the son and heir of another man, but this might not actually be so. Similarly, a marriage might appear to have the conjugal

---

12. "Verbo enim conveniendi, non ipsum concubitum, sed nuptias, quae praecedere solent concumbendi tempus, insinuat . . . ." Ibid.

13. ". . . esse coniux incepit." Ibid.

14. ". . . non omnes nuptiae coniugalem copulam faciunt, quas non sequitur commistio sexuum: sicut nec semper illius est filius omnis et haeres, cuius esse noscitur haeres. Nec habent nuptiae in se Christi et Ecclesiae sacramentum, sicut beatus Augustinus dicit, si se nuptialiter non utunter, id est, si eas non subsequitur commistio sexuum." Migne (ed), *Patrologiae Latina* (bibliog. III), vol. 126, col. 137.

bond when, in fact, it does not. Despite the externals, the deeper reality might be that the symbolism of the union between Christ and his Church is absent. This absence is caused by the lack of any sexual consummation. Hincmar's use of Augustine does seem powerful, but I would suggest that it is worth applying the same principle to it—that is, distinguishing between what is on the surface from the deeper reality. Superficially, Hincmar's argument is based upon the authority of Augustine, the great father of the Church. When examined more closely, however, the reference cannot be found in any of Augustine's works. This point is also made by George Joyce and the modern writer on theology, Philip Reynolds.[15]

Hincmar appeals to another father of the Church to support his position—Pope Saint Leo I. Again, Hincmar makes reference to a text which appears to maintain that intercourse in marriage is necessary for the bond between Christ and the Church to be made present. From Leo, Hincmar quotes, "The fellowship of marriage was, from the beginning, instituted so that in addition to the union of the sexes it would have in itself the symbolism of Christ and the Church."[16] Again it is worth examining the reference more closely.

Pope Leo had received a marriage case from Bishop Rusticus of Narbonne. A certain man was living with a freed woman as if they were man and wife, but they had not fulfilled the requirements of civil law concern-

---

15. Joyce, *Christian Marriage* (bibliog. III), 56. Also, Reynolds, "Marriage, Sacramental and Indissoluble" (bibliog. III), especially 129–30.

16. ". . . societas nuptiarum ita ab initio constituta sit, ut praeter sexuum coniunctionem haberet in se Christi et Ecclesiae sacramentum." Migne (ed), *Patrologiae Latina* (bibliog. III), vol. 126, col. 137.

ing marriage.[17] Bishop Rusticus asked the Pope for his advice, and Leo replied with an epistle.[18] In it, he said that there was not a true marriage between the couple. He argued that for there to be a genuine marriage the couple would have to be of equal standing. Thus, there could be no marriage between a person who was free and one who was from a lower, servile, background. It is only when the two have equal standing and equal freedom that they can share in the symbolism of the relationship between Christ and the Church.[19] In short, one could say that the Church is the Bride of Christ and not his slave. It is this equality which Leo believed was necessary between spouses. Therefore, when Leo spoke of the "union of sexes" and "the symbolism of Christ and the Church,"[20] he was referring to the equal standing of the spouses. He was not referring to sexual intercourse. Hincmar's use of Leo's words involves taking them out of context and giving them a whole new meaning.

Hincmar gives another reason why a marriage is not complete until there is intercourse. He says, "We have taught that just because there was a betrothal with endowment and a wedding ceremony, there is not a marriage if it lacked the union of the sexes, and thus the hope of offspring and the symbolism of faith."[21] It has been seen how Augustine gave three dimensions

---

17. Joyce, *Christian Marriage* (bibliog. III), 56–57.

18. Leo I (bibliog. I), *Epistula clxvii*, circa 458–59.

19. Migne (ed), *Patrologiae Latina* (bibliog. III), vol. 54, col. 1204.

20. "sexuum coniunctionem" and "Christi et Ecclesiae sacramentum." Migne (ed), *Patrologiae Latina* (bibliog. III), vol. 126, col. 137.

21. ". . . docuimus propter talem desponsationem, dotationem, atque pro talibus nuptiis, sicut istae fuerunt, non esse coniugium, quibus defuit coniunctio sexuum, ac cum prolis spe fidei sacramentum." Migne (ed), *Patrologiae Latina* (bibliog. III), vol. 126, col. 145.

of marriage which are in themselves good and which therefore make marriage as a whole good.[22] These are the goods of children, fidelity, and the sanctity of the sacrament. It has been noted how Hincmar makes reference to Augustine, albeit erroneously. It might be that Hincmar was conscious of these three goods when he wrote the passage in question. Certainly, Hincmar refers to offspring. He argues that if sexual intercourse does not occur, then there is no hope of the couple having children. According to Hincmar, this results in the couple's relationship not being a true marriage. It is noteworthy that he does not say that it is the absence of offspring which means there is no marriage but the absence of the "hope of offspring."[23] Thus, a married couple could have intercourse and produce no children. What is important for Hincmar is that intercourse takes place. He does not take into consideration, however, that in certain marriages intercourse can occur but still without any hope of children—for example, in cases of sterility and when the spouses are elderly.

Hincmar also says that the absence of intercourse results in the absence of the "symbolism of faith."[24] Whether or not he was thinking of Augustine's three goods of marriage, this most probably refers to fidelity. Therefore, it is probably better translated as the "symbolism of fidelity" or "symbolism of faithfulness." If this is so, then Hincmar is repeating his argument that

---

22. Augustine, *De Bono Coniugali* (bibliog. III), 24, 32; Migne (ed), *Patrologiae Latina* (bibliog. III), vol. 40, cols. 394–95.

23. "prolis spe"; Migne (ed), *Patrologiae Latina* (bibliog. III), vol. 126, col. 145.

24. "fidei sacramentum"; ibid.

sexual intercourse makes present between the couple the relationship between Christ and the Church. If there is no intercourse, then this symbolism is not present and the marriage does not share in the totally faithful bond that Christ has forged with his Church.

In summary, Hincmar taught that marriage begins with the wedding ceremony but that it is not complete until there has been sexual intercourse.[25] For him, intercourse makes present the special bond between Christ and the Church. He bases his argument on Saint Augustine and Saint Leo. Unfortunately, no such reference in Augustine's works can be found. As for Leo, he is quoted out of context. The other argument given by Hincmar is that sexual intercourse is necessary for a true marriage because without it there would be no hope of a couple having children, but this does not take into account sterile or elderly spouses.

It is not clear why Hincmar attributed such an argument to Augustine and Leo. It might be that he was genuinely mistaken or that he thought that such an argument was something they *would* have used. In any case, it will be seen later that his reference to Augustine and Leo has had a major influence on the Church's teaching on marriage.

It is often stated that Hincmar's emphasis on sexual intercourse was based upon Germanic law. I do not think that this is the case, however. In my section on Germanic law I showed that the role of consent in marriage eventually became central. The problem was that consent is internal and so cannot be seen. Thus, some

---

25. Brundage, *Law, Sex, and Christian Society* (bibliog. III), 136.

form of external evidence was necessary to prove that a marriage had occurred. One such proof was sexual intercourse. In this respect, it would have been tempting for ecclesiastical authorities to make use of Hincmar's teaching. Brundage agrees, "Hincmar's coital theory of marriage possessed some juristic virtues: it enumerated a set of conditions for marriage that were, in large part, susceptible of verification by witnesses or by inference from circumstantial evidence. These features made it possible to resolve questionable cases by reference to actions, rather than impressions about intentions."[26]

This does not mean that within Germanic law intercourse was necessary for a marriage to be fully recognized. Other types of proof—such as cohabitation— could be used instead. Indeed, Reynolds goes so far as to say this: "It is true that in the *Grágás,* a vernacular Icelandic code compiled in the twelfth and thirteenth centuries, a marriage was formally concluded when the groom was led with lights to his wife's bed. Unless husband and wife were observed to go to bed together by at least six witnesses, the marriage was not valid. But I have found no evidence in the *leges* (that is, in the early medieval Germanic codes composed in continental Europe) that consummation was required for the perfection of marriage or even that it had any legal significance."[27]

It can be seen that Hincmar's view on the bringing of a completed marriage into existence differed from the general view that had developed in the Church. There

26. Ibid., 137.
27. Reynolds, "Marriage, Sacramental and Indissoluble" (bibliog. III), 131. (Italics and brackets in the original.)

was one point of agreement, however. This concerned the indissolubility of a completed marriage. King Lothar II of the Franks wanted to divorce his wife Theutberga because they had not produced an heir. Instead, he wished to marry his mistress Waldrada, by whom he had a potential heir. The case was presented to Hincmar. By late 860 he gave his judgment in "Concerning the Divorce of Lothar and Theutberga."[28] In it he asks certain relevant questions, which he then answers at some length. Mackin suggests that there are twenty-three questions. This is certainly the numbering given in the edition of Migne.[29] However, the medieval historian Valerie Flint suggests that there are in fact thirty. She suggests that Migne based his edition on a text from 1645. She claims that the manuscript to which she has had access dates from 860 itself, although it is not Hincmar's original.[30] In either case, Hincmar answers the questions in such a way that Lothar never obtained a divorce.

In his answer to the second question (*Responsio 2*),[31] Hincmar says, "A man cannot dismiss his wife for any reason other than adultery, and no other reason, and if he has dismissed her then while she is living he cannot marry another, nor can she marry another while her husband is alive, because it is written: What God has joined man must not separate (Matthew 10:9)."[32] Hincmar's reference to Matthew's Gospel is important.

28. Hincmar of Rheims, *De Divortio Lotharii et Tetbergae* (bibliog. III); Migne (ed), *Patrologiae Latina* (bibliog. III), vol. 125, cols. 619–772.
29. Ibid. Also, *Mackin, Divorce and Remarriage* (bibliog. III), 254.
30. Flint, *"Hinkmar von Reims"* (bibliog. III).
31. Migne (ed), *Patrologiae Latina* (bibliog. III), vol. 125, cols. 641–45.
32. "Et vir non potest uxorem suam dimittere quancunque de causa, et nulla alia nisi sola fornicationis causa, et si dimiserit eam, vivente illa non potest aliam

It is this Gospel which could be interpreted to allow divorce and remarriage in the exceptional case of adultery. But just as the Council of Friuli had done about seventy years before, Hincmar states explicitly that although adultery is grounds for dismissal, neither spouse may remarry while the other is still alive. His reference to "What God has joined" indicates that Hincmar believes that the bond of marriage remains, even in the case of adultery and any subsequent dismissal.

To conclude, it can be said that Hincmar believes that although marriage begins with the wedding ceremony, it is not complete until there has been consummation, but once the marriage is complete it cannot be completely dissolved for any reason.

---

ducere, nec illa viro suo vivente alteri nubere, quia scriptum est: Quod Deus coniunxit homo non separet (Matth. x. 9)." Migne (ed), *Patrologiae Latina* (bibliog. III), vol. 125, col. 642.

—7—

Twelfth-Century France
Marriage is Centered on Love and Created by Consent

Three Thinkers Who
Promoted the Role of Consent

DESPITE ARCHBISHOP HINCMAR'S emphasis on the role
of sexual intercourse within marriage, most of the
Church's tradition acknowledged that it is the consent
of the couple that brings a marriage into existence. This
understanding had been present in the Roman Empire
before Christ and was adopted by the Church throughout the Empire. Even in the Germanic regions, consent
came to be understood as the factor necessary to bring a
marriage into existence—although external proof was
required. This appreciation of the role of mutual consent reached a climax in twelfth-century France. Three
great thinkers wrote about the necessity and the sufficiency of marital consent. They are Ivo of Chartres,[1]
Hugh of Saint Victor, and Peter Lombard. Each provides a theological basis for saying that consent alone
brings a marriage into existence.

---
1. Sometimes written Yves of Chartres.

Ivo of Chartres
Restricting Divorce and Remarriage
While Supporting Love and Consent

Ivo was Bishop of Chartres from 1091 until his death in
1116. He is remembered for three works. The first is the
short *Collectio Tripartita*. This was incorporated into
his second work, the *Decretum*, which was completed in 1095.[2] As Theodore Mackin observes, Ivo was
a strong believer in papal authority while remaining
faithful to Frankish practice.[3] Thus, the *Decretum* is a
large collection of laws and legal principles from both
the Roman and the Frankish traditions. Ivo draws upon
an earlier collection by Burchard of Worms,[4] papal decrees, Justinian's writings on Roman law, Church Fathers, and other writers. Ivo's *Decretum* is an impressive legal collection, but its size makes it difficult to
use. Consequently, shortly after producing his *Decretum*, Ivo published his third major work, the *Panormia*.[5] It is based upon the *Decretum* but it is arranged
systematically to make it easier for the reader to refer
to particular themes.[6]

The *Panormia* is an important tool for understanding Ivo's view of marriage. The content is not original
because it is a collection of other writers' works. Ivo
stamps his identity on the work by deciding not only
what to include and what to omit, but also by determin-

---

2. Migne (ed), *Patrologiae Latina* (bibliog. III), vol. 161, cols. 47–1036.
3. Mackin, *Divorce and Remarriage* (bibliog. III), 261.
4. Burchard of Worms, *Decretorum Libri Viginti* (bibliog. III); Migne (ed),
Patrologiae Latina (bibliog. III), vol. 140, cols. 537–1058. (Written from about
1008 to 1012.)
5. Migne (ed), *Patrologiae Latina* (bibliog. III), vol. 161, cols. 1045–1344.
6. Mackin, *Divorce and Remarriage* (bibliog. III), 261.

ing how the subject matter is arranged. As with many other compilers of legal texts, Ivo's own opinions are present in his collection like a watermark. On the surface, the words belong to others and seem objective, but when held up to the light and examined more closely, Ivo's own thoughts can be seen underneath them.

For example, Mackin explains that Ivo wished to restrict divorce and remarriage and so he excluded the more liberal Frankish, Celtic, and Anglo-Saxon legislation: "Because Yves's *Panormia* is so clearly a careful selection from and rearrangement of the material in his *Decretum*, we may take for granted that the *Panormia* comes closest to an expression of his own mind on dissolution and remarriage."[7] It has been seen how, in the Roman Empire, Theodosius II and Justinian freely permitted divorce and remarriage. Mackin explains that Ivo took legal texts completely out of context: "This enables him, for one thing, to quote restrictive decrees from Theodosius II and Justinian, who in general proposed a most permissive divorce legislation."[8]

Ivo's own tendency was to restrict divorce and remarriage. Schillebeeckx observes that around the twelfth century there was an evolution in the concept of indissolubility. Roughly speaking, until then the Church Fathers had addressed the question of the permissibility of divorce and remarriage. This was to be developed by the scholastics, who examined the actual possibility of such actions.[9] Mackin suggests that Ivo

---

7. Ibid.

8. Ibid., 262.

9. Schillebeeckx, *Marriage: Human Reality and Saving Mystery* (bibliog. III), 284.

was still addressing the earlier issue of permissibility and impermissibility.[10]

It is within this context that Ivo refers to authorities, such as Pope Gregory II, who had permitted divorce and remarriage when one of the spouses is impotent.[11] Mackin observes that Ivo uses these authorities to argue that impotence is a ground for dissolving a marriage. It does not appear that Ivo considers impotence to be an impediment to marriage which would make any attempted marriage null and void from the beginning. Instead, he accepts that such a marriage can exist but that it can be dissolved in order to allow remarriage.[12]

Mackin argues that Ivo expands the question of impotence to the lack of sexual intercourse generally. Ivo cites canon 27 of the Frankish Council of Verberies which was held around 756. This canon allows a wife to leave her husband if she swears on the cross that she has never had intercourse with him.[13] As Mackin notes, the central issue is no longer impotence but intercourse. There are two important points about this canon. First, this "Council" was a civil gathering and not an ecclesiastical one. Joyce states, "In this assembly laity took part as well as churchmen, so that it had not the character of an ecclesiastical synod properly so called. Its decisions had force as royal capitularies, not as

10. Mackin, *Divorce and Remarriage* (bibliog. III), 264.

11. Ivo of Chartres, *Panormia* (bibliog. III), book 7, chapters 112–13; Migne (ed), *Patrologiae Latina* (bibliog. III), vol. 161, cols. 1273–76.

12. Mackin, *Divorce and Remarriage* (bibliog. III), 264–65.

13. "Si qua mulier proclamaverit quod vir suus nunquam coisset cum ea, exeant inde ad crucem; et si verum fuerit separentur. Et ita fiat quod vult." Ivo of Chartres, *Panormia* (bibliog. III), book 7, ch.118; Migne (ed), *Patrologiae Latina* (bibliog. III), vol. 161, col. 1276.

synodical decrees, though they seem to have been practically treated as such and found their way into many collections of canons."[14] Thus, canon 27 does not have the force of ecclesiastical authority behind it.

The second point to be made is that Mackin does not say whether the woman concerned could remarry. So, was Ivo using Canon 27 to allow a wife simply to leave her husband if they had not had intercourse? Or, was he saying that the marriage could actually be dissolved? Ivo does not include any reference to the woman being able to remarry. Considering how strict Ivo was with regard to divorce and remarriage, it certainly cannot be presumed that he would have allowed the woman to remarry. Indeed, the canon is also quoted by Burchard of Worms.[15] Again, although reference is made to the possibility of separating (*separentur*), no mention is made of remarriage. Remarriage would be an indication that the first marriage is actually dissolved. Thus, I would not agree with Mackin that Ivo expands the case of impotence to cover the absence of sexual intercourse generally. On the contrary, Ivo regards impotence to be grounds for dissolution and thus remarriage; whereas the lack of sexual intercourse is grounds only for separation.

This raises the issue of how Ivo viewed the role of intercourse within marriage. In his *Panormia* he quotes from Ambrose's *Book Concerning the Institution of a*

---

14. Joyce, *Christian Marriage* (bibliog. III), 342.

15. "Si qua mulier proclamaverit, quod vir suus nunquam cum ea coisset, exeant inde ad crucem: et si verum fuerit, separentur, et illa faciat quod vult." Burchard of Worms, *Decretorum Libri Viginti* (bibliog. III), book 9, ch. 41; Migne (ed), *Patrologiae Latina* (bibliog. III), vol. 140, col. 821. Migne numbers this canon as 17.

Virgin.[16] It has been seen that Ambrose regarded the name of marriage to be applied properly once the spouses had given consent. He did not think it necessary to have to wait until after they had consummated their union sexually. Ivo gives strength to the consensual argument by also referring to the letter of Pope Leo I to Bishop Rusticus.[17] This was the very letter which Hincmar had quoted out of context in order to prove that intercourse was necessary for marriage. Ivo uses the letter to show that when Leo referred to marriage involving "the sacrament of Christ and the Church,"[18] he made no reference to sexual intercourse at all. Thus, as Brundage notes, Ivo's use of Leo's letter is to show that the symbolism of the relationship between Christ and his Church is present in a marriage irrespective of whether or not it has been consummated.[19]

In order to obtain a clear and balanced view of Ivo's thinking, it is necessary to go beyond the *Panormia* and look at his letters. In letter 134, addressed to Daimbert the Archbishop of Sens,[20] he refers to the homily attributed to Saint John Chrysostom[21] and to the re-

16. Ivo of Chartres, *Panormia* (bibliog. III), book 6, ch. 14; Migne (ed), *Patrologiae Latina* (bibliog. III), vol. 161, cols. 1246–47. Ambrose, *Liber de Institutione Virginis* (bibliog. III), ch. 6; Migne (ed), *Patrologiae Latina* (bibliog. III), vol. 16, cols. 330–31.

17. Leo I (bibliog. I), *Epistula clxvii*, circa 458–59.Relevant passage in Migne (ed), *Patrologiae Latina* (bibliog. III), vol. 54, cols. 1204–05. Ivo's use is in Ivo of Chartres, *Panormia* (bibliog. III), book 6, ch. 23; Migne (ed), *Patrologiae Latina* (bibliog. III), vol. 161, cols. 599–600. Also in Ivo of Chartres, *Panormia* (bibliog. III), book 6, ch. 35; Migne (ed), *Patrologiae Latina* (bibliog. III), vol. 161, col. 615.

18. "Christi et Ecclesiae sacramentum." Migne (ed), *Patrologiae Latina* (bibliog. III), vol. 54, col. 1204.

19. Brundage, *Law, Sex, and Christian Society* (bibliog. III), 188.

20. Ivo of Chartres, *Epistula cxxxiv* (bibliog. III)..

21. Migne (ed), *Patrologiae Latina* (bibliog. III), vol. 162, col. 144.

sponse of Pope Nicholas to the Bulgarian Church.[22] It has been seen that both of these state that consent alone brings a marriage into existence. Professor Schoovaerts, an expert on Ivo, observes that he argues that just as sexual intercourse unites two bodies, consent must also unite two people.[23] Ivo says, "Nature has ordered, and ecclesiastical human law has just as much confirmed, because of those whose bodies have only to be one by conjugal copulation, then of those same persons the consent of their minds must be similar."[24] Ivo repeats the necessity and sufficiency of consent in letters 99[25] and 148.[26] In each of these letters, he refers to Ambrose's *Book Concerning the Institution of a Virgin*, Isidore of Seville's *Book of Etymologies*, and Pope Nicholas's response to the Bulgarians. Again, Ivo wishes to show that he agrees with the Church's most authoritative writers—or, more to the point, that they agree with him.

It has been seen that in Pope Leo's reply to Bishop Rusticus of Narbonne he explains that for a genuine marriage to exist the couple must be of equal standing. If one party is free and the other is from a servile background, then a marriage cannot exist between them be-

---

22. Ibid., cols. 143–44.

23. Schoovaerts, "*L'Amour et le Mariage*" (bibliog. III), 307.

24. ". . . quod et natura disposuit, et lex tam ecclesiastica quam mundana firmavit, quia quorum per coniugalem copulam unum debet fieri corpus, eorumdem pariter animorum debet esse consensus." Migne (ed), *Patrologiae Latina* (bibliog. III), vol. 162, col. 143. Schoovaerts, "*L'Amour et le Mariage*" (bibliog. III), uses a translation which renders animorum consensus as "consent of hearts." I would suggest that "consent of minds" is another possibility. In fact, Schoovaerts (312–13) notes that some versions of letter 134 refer simply to consensus ("consent").

25. Migne (ed), *Patrologiae Latina* (bibliog. III), vol. 162, cols. 118–19.

26. Ibid., cols. 153–54.

cause they cannot share in the symbolism of the relationship between Christ and his Church.[27] It seems that Ivo takes a position similar to Leo's, with the pastoral consequence that such persons are not recognized as married. This brought criticism from the Bishop of Evreux who accused Ivo of dissolving certain marriages between free men and slaves, as well as marriages between free women and slaves.[28] Ivo replied to the Bishop with a letter.[29] In it he explains that he is not dissolving such marriages because they have never existed in the first place.

The whole of Ivo's argument is based upon the principle of love and so puts love at the center of marriage. When a man and woman marry, they should love one another. This love involves wanting the best for the other party. Now, in Ivo's time, if one of them was from a servile background, the civil law held that the free spouse was reduced to the rank of a slave so that they had to live as a couple in servitude. Ivo argues that if the party who is free is unaware at the time of marriage that the other is not free, then there can be no marriage. Ivo explains that this is because the servile party cannot truly love the free party if he or she is willing to reduce the free party to the rank of a slave.[30]

What if the free party knows of the servile rank of the other at the time of entering marriage? Ivo's letter goes on to explain that such a marriage holds because consent has been given: "But if a free man has taken

27. Leo I (bibliog. I), *Epistula clxvii, circa* 458–59.
28. Schoovaerts, *"L'Amour et le Mariage"* (bibliog. III), 320.
29. Ivo of Chartres, *Epistula ccxlii* (bibliog. III)..
30. Migne (ed), *Patrologiae Latina* (bibliog. III), vol. 162, col. 250.

a slave-girl in marriage, he does not have the freedom to dismiss her if, first knowing her condition and consenting, they have contracted marriage, because consent makes marriage, not intercourse."[31] Thus, in this letter Ivo gives two principles. The first is that mutual love is at the center of marriage. This is based upon the theological concept that marriage must reflect the love between Christ and the Church. The second is that consent makes marriage. Ivo bases this on the long tradition of the Church.

Schoovaerts wonders if Ivo manages to hold these two principles together. He refers to the two parts of the letter which have just been examined: "Finally, this letter is deceptive. Because in the first part, where the person is unaware of the other's state, the principle of love is normative for the marriage and the non-love imposes the dissolution of the couple; in the second part, where the person knows the other's rank and consents to the marriage, love is no longer in the picture."[32]

I would suggest that Ivo does not set these two principles against each other. On the contrary, they must both be followed in order for a marriage to exist. In the first part of his letter, where the free person is unaware of the servile rank of the other, Ivo is dealing with a case where the element of love is missing and

31. "Si quis autem liber ancillam in matrimonium duxerit, non habebat licentiam dimittere eam, si prius scientes conditionem suam et consentientes matrimonium contraxerunt, quia coniugium consensus facit, non coitus." Ibid.

32. "Finalement cette lettre est décevante. Car dans la première partie où la personne ignore l'état de l'autre, le précepte de l'amour est normatif pour le mariage et le non-amour impose la dissolution du couple; dans la deuxième partie où la personne connaît le rang de l'autre et consent au mariage, l'amour n'est plus dans le tableau." Schoovaerts, *"L'Amour et le Mariage"* (bibliog. III), 322.

thus there is no marriage. In the second part of the letter, where the servile rank is known, Ivo's emphasis on consent is *not* to the detriment of marital love. Just because he does not make explicit reference to love does not mean that it is missing. Indeed, in such a case love must be present. That is, a man knows that a woman is a slave and that if he marries her, he too will become a slave. Aware of this, he consents to marry her. If I encountered this situation in real life I would, quite naturally, say that the man must love the woman deeply in order to give up his freedom for her.

In summary, Ivo believes that love is at the very center of marriage. By giving consent, a couple enters into this shared life of love which symbolizes the bond between Christ and his Church. This symbolism is present irrespective of whether the marriage has been consummated. Finally, with regard to divorce and remarriage, Ivo is restrictive in his understanding.

Hugh of Saint Victor
Consent and Consummation are Important, but Only Consent is Necessary

The death of Hugh of Saint Victor in the early 1140s meant the loss of a great scholar who had taught just outside Paris on Mont Sainte-Geneviève. Dominique Poirel, who is an authority on medieval writers such as Hugh, explains how a bishop sent Hugh a copy of a theologian's work which argued that because Mary was truly the wife of Joseph, then she could not have remained a virgin. Hugh's task was to uphold both Mary's virginity as well as the fullness of her marriage.[33] The result was Hugh's *On the Virginity of the Blessed Virgin Mary*.[34] In this work, he asks a rhetorical question. In doing so he gives a definition of marriage: "For what is marriage unless it is the lawful fellowship between a man and a woman in which it is clear that each owes himself to the other by mutual consent?"[35]

In this definition, Hugh is primarily describing marriage as a fellowship (*societas*). This is reminiscent of Augustine's emphasis on marriage providing companionship. Augustine believed that it is within the companionship of marriage that love and friendship are exchanged. Hugh's definition states that this fellowship is brought about by the mutual consent of the couple. Through this consent, each owes (*debet*) himself or herself to the other. This definition is followed by an explanation of this *owing*, which provides an insight into what Hugh believes both are consenting to when they enter marriage: "This owing is to be considered in two ways, that one certainly reserves oneself for the other and that one does not refuse oneself to the other. One reserves oneself, that is, after giving consent one does not switch to another fellowship. One does not refuse, that is, one does not separate oneself from the common fellowship of one with the other."[36] Thus, through con-

---

33. Poirel, *"Love of God, Human Love"* (bibliog. III), especially, 100–101.

34. Hugh of St. Victor, *De Beatae Mariae Virginitate* (bibliog. III).

35. "Quid enim est coniugium nisi legitima societas inter virum et feminam, in qua videlicet societate ex pari consensu uterque semetipsum debet alteri?" Migne (ed), *Patrologiae Latina* (bibliog. III), vol. 176, col. 859.

36. "Debitum autem hoc duobus modis consideratur, ut scilicet et se illi conservet, et se illi non neget. Conservet videlicet ne post talem consensum ad alienam societatem transeat. Non neget ut ab ea quae ad invicem est communi societate se non disiungat." Ibid.

sent, each spouse gives himself or herself to the other in a faithful and permanent way. Hugh emphasizes this permanence: "Therefore free consent lawfully given between a man and a woman, which obliges each to the other, is that which makes marriage. And the marriage is the fellowship itself, held together by such consent, where neither is released from the debt whilst the other is alive."[37]

What about the marriage between Mary and Joseph? Hugh explains that, as well as consent to marriage, there is consent to intercourse. He acknowledges that this second form of consent has characteristics similar to the first. For example, it also brings about a union between the man and the woman.[38] Moreover, this consent also gives rise to a mutual indebtedness in which both parties reserve themselves for each other and do not refuse themselves to each other. [39]

There is, however, one major difference between these two types of consent. Whereas consent to marriage brings about the marriage, consent to intercourse is "a consequence, not a producer, of marriage."[40] Therefore, Hugh understands the relationship between marriage, intercourse, and the two types of consent in

---

37. "Spontaneus ergo consensus inter virum ac feminam legitime factus, quod uterque alteri debitorem sui se spondet; iste est qui coniugium facit. Et coniugium est ipsa societas tali consensu foederata quae altero vivente alterum a debito non absolvit." Ibid.

38. "Est adhuc alius consensus, scilicet carnalis commercii ad invicem exigendi atque reddendi, similem inter virum et mulierem pactionem constituens." Ibid.

39. "Quod debitum in hoc quoque consensu dupliciter (sicut in priori commemoravi) exhibendum est, ut videlicet uterque se alteri conservet, et neuter alteri se neget." Ibid.

40. ". . . comes et non effector coniugii." Ibid.

terms of cause and effect. Initially there is consent to
marriage. This in turn produces marriage. This applies
to all married couples—including Mary and Joseph.
What then might follow is that the husband and wife
consent to intercourse. They do not have to, but if they
do, then intercourse follows. This did not happen in the
case of Mary and Joseph.

Hugh was thus able to uphold the validity of the
marriage of Mary and Joseph while maintaining the
virginity of Mary. Intercourse is dependent upon marriage, not the other way around. Indeed, compared to
other marriages, Hugh regards Mary's "to be a more
genuine and holy a marriage, because it was held together by the bond of charity—and not by concupiscence of the flesh or by the flame of lust."[41] This marital
bond of charity is recognized by Hugh to be essential.
It has been seen that in his definition Hugh describes
marriage as a fellowship. It is within this very fellowship that charity is at work.

Hugh understands charity and love to be central to
marriage. He refers to Saint Paul's Letter to the Ephesians: "'The two become one in the flesh. This great
sacrament is in Christ and the Church' (Ephesians
5). The two become one in heart. This greater sacrament is in God and the soul."[42] Hugh acknowledges
that intercourse within marriage is a sacrament of the

---

41. ". . . potius tanto verius et sanctius coniugium esse, quod in solo charitatis
vinculo, et non in concupiscentia carnis et libidinis ardore foederatum est." Migne (ed), *Patrologiae Latina* (bibliog. III), vol. 176, col. 860.

42. "'Erunt duo in carne una, sacramentum hoc magnum est in Christo et
Ecclesia' (Ephes. v). Erunt duo in corde uno: sacramentum hoc maius est in Deo
et anima." Ibid.

relationship between Christ and his Church—that is, it signifies it and shares in it. But he believes that the sacrament is greater in the realm of love. The joining of hearts shares in the union of God and the soul. With regard to this, Poirel highlights a most pertinent passage from Hugh's work.[43] I give my own translation of it:

> It is rightly said that a man leaves his father and his mother and cleaves to his wife and they become two in one flesh. Therefore, in his cleaving to his wife is the sacrament of the invisible fellowship which must be established between God and the soul. In the two being in one flesh is the sacrament of the invisible sharing which has been established in the flesh between Christ and the Church. Therefore, that they are two in one flesh is a great sacrament of Christ and the Church; but the greater sacrament, that they are two in one heart, in one love, is of God and the soul.[44]

In this passage, Hugh emphasizes the role of love within marriage. Moreover, this love does not have to be sexual. Before any sexual union takes place the two people are joined in marriage by love. Indeed, as soon as the married couple leave their parents and live together, they form a fellowship of love. This fellowship is a sacrament of the bond between God and the soul—that is, it signifies the bond and shares in it. It is within this fellowship that sexual union might take place. When it does, it is a sacrament of the bond

---

43. Poirel, "Love of God, Human Love" (bibliog. III), 104.

44. "Recte ergo dicitur: Relinquet homo patrem suum et matrem suam, et adhaerebit uxori suae, et erunt duo in carne una, ut in eo quod adhaeret uxori suae sacramentum sit invisibilis societatis, quae in spiritu facienda est inter Deum et animam; in eo autem quod duo sint in carne una, sacramentum sit invisibilis participationis quae in carne facto est inter Christum et Ecclesiam. Magnum igitur sacramentum, Erunt duo in carne una, in Christo et Ecclesia; sed maius sacramentum, Erunt duo in corde uno, in dilectione una, in Deo et anima." Migne (ed), *Patrologiae Latina* (bibliog. III), vol. 176, col. 864.

between Christ and the Church. This second sacrament is important, but the first is more so. Thus, according to Hugh, marriage is far more than a lawful occasion for sex; it is a loving union between a man and a woman. It is a loving community in which each spouse sacrifices himself or herself for the other. This sacrifice involves the whole person—body, heart, spirit, and soul. In this way they can live together in tranquility and joy.[45] This is why Schillebeeckx says, "Interpersonal relationship, including the material cares of daily life, was for Hugh the primary and essential task of marriage."[46]

After he wrote On the Virginity of the Blessed Virgin Mary, Hugh produced a much larger work, On the Sacraments of the Christian Faith.[47] The eleventh part of the second book of this treatise is entitled On the Sacrament of Marriage.[48] This provides one with another opportunity to discover Hugh's thoughts on marriage. There he gives a definition of marriage which seems to be based upon the one he used in On the Virginity of the Blessed Virgin Mary: "Marriage is that fellowship, which is consecrated by the covenant of mutual espousal, when each by free promise obliges himself or herself to the other so that from then on neither may switch to the fellowship of another while the other [spouse] is alive, nor may he or she separate from that fellowship which is mutually fixed."[49] Again, Hugh

45. Ibid., col. 860–61.
46. Schillebeeckx, *Marriage: Human Reality and Saving Mystery* (bibliog. III), 321.
47. Hugh of St. Victor, *De Sacramentis Fidei Christianae* (bibliog. III).
48. Hugh of St. Victor, *De Sacramento Coniugii* (bibliog. III); Migne (ed), *Patrologiae Latina* (bibliog. III), vol. 176, cols. 479–520.
49. "Haec ergo societatis coniugium est, quae foedere sponsionis mutuae

defines marriage as a fellowship which is brought about by the mutual consent of the couple. Cyrille Vogel, an expert in the canon law and liturgy of the medieval period, notes that for Hugh consent is so central to marriage that it does not have to be given publicly in a religious ceremony.[50] The consent alone is both necessary and sufficient.[51]

Toward the beginning of *On the Sacrament of Marriage*, Hugh states that at the very beginning of creation God established marriage "in a covenant of love" (*in foedere dilectionis*).[52] For this reason, it is a sacrament of the spiritual bond that exists between God and the individual soul. This is true of all marriages, including those of non-Christians. Moreover, this sacramentality does not depend upon marriages being consummated sexually; it exists from the moment of consent. With regard to the sexual dimension of marriage, before humanity sinned, marriage had the purpose of producing children for the continuation of the human race. This purpose changed once humanity sinned. Marriage then provided a remedy for sin—that is, a lawful context in which sexual activity could occur. Hugh says, "The institution of marriage is two-fold: one before sin as a duty; the second after sin as a remedy. The first so that nature could be multiplied; the second so that nature could be rescued and

consecratur, quando uterque voluntaria promissione debitorem se facit alteri, ut deinceps neque ad alienam altero vivente societatem transeat, neque se ab illa quae ad invicem constat societate disiungat." Migne (ed), *Patrologiae Latina* (bibliog. III), vol. 176, col. 485. A similar translation can be found in Mackin, *What is Marriage?* (bibliog. III), 158.

50. Vogel, *"The Role of the Liturgical Celebrant"* (bibliog. III), 82.
51. Migne (ed), *Patrologiae Latina* (bibliog. III), vol. 176, cols. 488–94.
52. Ibid., col. 481.

vice restrained."[53] However, this change in purpose did not change the fact that marriage is a covenant of love.[54]

Hugh emphasizes the dimension of love within marriage by referring to Saint Augustine's *On the Good of Marriage*.[55] He repeats Augustine's view that marriage is not good solely because of the procreation of children. It is good because of the fellowship, or companionship, that exists between the spouses. Otherwise, elderly couples and those without children could not be said to be married, despite sharing a life of charity.[56] Hugh continues, "In marriage, the holiness of the sacrament is of more value than the fruitfulness of the womb."[57] To prove his point further, he quotes Jesus's words from John's Gospel, "'The flesh' he said, 'offers nothing; it is the spirit that gives life' (John 6). If therefore what is in the flesh is great then, of the two, what is in the spirit is greater."[58]

It has been seen that Hugh regards the fellowship of the couple, with its spiritual bond of love, to be a sacrament of the bond between God and the soul. It has also been seen that he regards the sexual side to be the sacrament of the union between Christ and the Church. Schillebeeckx argues that Hugh placed such weight on the

---

53. "Institutio coniugii duplex est: una ante peccatum ad officium; altera post peccatum ad remedium. Prima ut natura multiplicaretur; secunda ut natura exciperetur, et vitium cohiberetur." Ibid.

54. Ibid.

55. Augustine, *De Bono Coniugali* (bibliog. III), 1.1; Migne (ed), *Patrologiae Latina* (bibliog. III), vol. 40, col. 373.

56. Migne (ed), *Patrologiae Latina* (bibliog. III), vol. 176, col. 481.

57. "In nuptiis plus valet sanctitas sacramenti, quam fecunditas ventris." Migne (ed), *Patrologiae Latina* (bibliog. III), vol. 176, col. 481.

58. "'Caro', inquit, 'nihil prodest, spiritus est qui vivificat' (Joan. VI). Si ergo magnum est quod in carne est, maius utique est quod in spiritu est." Migne (ed), *Patrologiae Latina* (bibliog. III), vol. 176, col. 482.

life of love between the spouses that he would have preferred to have called this the sacrament of Christ and the
Church. Schillebeeckx suggests that the tradition of the
Church prevented him from doing so. As Schillebeeckx
notes, however, Hugh does state, "Just as we have said
that the sacrament of Christ and the Church is in the
joining of the flesh, so also we have shown that the sacrament of the same is in the covenant of fellowship."[59]

Hugh's clear distinction between the loving fellowship of the couple and the sexual side of their relationship is brought out further by his consideration of Augustine's three goods of marriage. Augustine had said
that one reason why marriage is good is because it involves three factors, each of which is good. These are
children, fidelity, and the sanctity of the sacrament of
marriage.[60] Hugh explains that the first two goods pertain to the sexual side of marriage; whereas the good of
the sacrament pertains to the fellowship itself. As the
sexual dimension is not essential, the first two goods
can be missing from a marriage without affecting its
validity. That is, there can be no children and no fidelity. With regard to the former, it has been seen how
Hugh regards a marriage without children to be still
a marriage. Similarly, if one spouse is unfaithful, the
marriage does not cease to exist.[61] However, the third
good (the good of the sacrament) must apply to all
marriages (including non-Christian ones) because

59. "Ut sicut in copula carnis Christi et Ecclesiae sacramentum diximus, ita
etiam in foedere societatis eiusdem sacramentum ostendamus." Migne (ed), *Patrologiae Latina* (bibliog. III), vol. 176, col. 495. Also, Schillebeeckx, *Marriage:
Human Reality and Saving Mystery* (bibliog. III), 323.

60. Augustine, *De Bono Coniugali* (bibliog. III), 24.32; Migne (ed), *Patrologiae Latina* (bibliog. III), vol. 40, cols. 394–95.

61. Migne (ed), *Patrologiae Latina* (bibliog. III), vol. 176, cols. 494–96.

every marriage is essentially a fellowship which is a sacrament of the bond between God and the soul. Indeed, if this good should be absent, then it must be because there is no marriage.[62]

From the definition of marriage used by Hugh in this treatise, it must be noted that the couple's mutual consent binds them together for life. That is, their consent gives rise to the indissolubility of their marriage: "Marriage is that fellowship, which is consecrated by the covenant of mutual espousal, when each by free promise obliges himself or herself to the other so that from then on neither may switch to the fellowship of another while the other [spouse] is alive, nor may he or she separate from that fellowship which is mutually fixed." [63]

Mackin makes a valuable comment on this. Hugh is arguing that the consent of a man and woman creates a marriage that is indissoluble. This permanent fellowship is therefore a sacrament of the permanent bond between God and the soul. Thus, Hugh is arguing that the marriage is a sacrament because it is indissoluble—not that it is indissoluble because it is a sacrament. In other words, the indissolubility of marriage comes from the consent of the couple—not from its sacramental nature.[64]

The dependence of marriage's indissolubility upon the couple's consent has a surprising consequence within Hugh's work. He seems to allow for the

---

62. "Sacramentum autem ita inseparabile esse videtur, ut sine illo omnino coniugium esse non possit." Ibid., col. 495.

63. "Haec ergo societatis coniugium est, quae foedere sponsionis mutuae consecratur, quando uterque voluntaria promissione debitorem se facit alteri, ut deinceps neque ad alienam altero vivente societatem transeat, neque se ab illa quae ad invicem constat societate disiungat." Ibid., col. 485.

64. Mackin, *Divorce and Remarriage* (bibliog. III), 331–32.

possibility of a marriage being dissolved. He compares marriage to baptism and receiving the Eucharist: "Although baptism is to confer the remission of sins, and it is rightly said that baptism confers the remission of all sins; and although the value of the sacrament of the body of Christ is to confer fellowship and sharing with Christ, and it is rightly said that partaking of the body of Christ confers spiritual sharing with Christ; yet, one who pretends to accept baptism does not experience the forgiveness of sins, and one who eats the body of Christ unworthily in no way through it merits any spiritual sharing with Christ."[65] The point here is that an individual can be prevented from receiving the spiritual rewards of baptism and the Eucharist. Similarly, someone might not receive the spiritual effect of marriage—namely, indissolubility. Although Hugh regards all marriages to be sacramental, only the consent of Christians can produce an indissoluble marriage.[66] As Philip Reynolds observes, "Hugh's position is that indissolubility is an essential norm or characteristic of marriage which, like the efficacy of baptism, is only realized when marriage is where it should be: among the faithful."[67] Thus, only Christians receive the full spiritual reward of marriage—that is, indissolubility.

---

65. "Sieut baptismi est remissionem peccatorum conferre, et vere dicitur cum dicitur quod baptismus remissionem omnium peccatorum confert; et sicut sacramenti corporis Christi virtus et societatem et participationem Christi conferre, et vere dicitur cum dicitur quod susceptio corporis Christi confer spiritualem participationem Christi; et tamen qui fictus baptismi sacramentum accipit, remissionem peccatorum non percipit, et qui indigne manducat corpus Christi, nequaquam per id meretur spiritualem participationem Christi." Migne (ed), *Patrologiae Latina* (bibliog. III), vol. 176, col. 498.

66. Migne (ed), *Patrologiae Latina* (bibliog. III), vol. 176,, cols. 504–10.

67. Reynolds, "Marriage, Sacramental and Indissoluble" (bibliog. III), 136.

To summarize Hugh, it can be said that he regards marriage to be a fellowship of love brought about by the mutual consent of the spouses. In their consent, they sacrifice themselves to one another—as indeed they are called to do throughout their married life. This life of love is a sacrament of the bond between God and the individual soul. This applies to all marriages irrespective of whether or not they have been consummated. Sexual intercourse is a sacrament of the bond between Christ and the Church. Initially, intercourse was meant for procreation; now it provides a remedy for sin. Although both types of sacramentality apply to marriage, the former is the more important. Finally, the consent of the couple gives rise to indissolubility, which is present in the marriages of the baptized.

Peter Lombard
The Pinnacle of the Consensual View of Marriage

The third important writer of twelfth-century France is Peter Lombard. In the 1150s, while at the University of Paris, he compiled his four *Books of the Sentences*.[68] These are a collection of the teachings and opinions of ecclesiastical authorities and learned scholars. Like Ivo in his *Panormia*, Peter arranged his collection under various headings, and like Ivo—by deciding what to include and what to exclude, as well as how it was to be arranged—he was able to favor his own opinions.[69]

---

68. Patres Collegii S. Bonaventurae (eds), Petri Lombardi, *Libri IV Sententiarum* (bibliog. III).
69. Mackin, *What is Marriage?* (bibliog. III), 164–65.

His treatment of marriage is covered in Book 4, from distinction 26 to distinction 42.[70] Like Ivo and Hugh, Peter believes that consent is both necessary and sufficient for marriage. He considers at which point a marriage begins. After referring to Ambrose's *Book Concerning the Institution of a Virgin*, Isidore of Seville's *Book of Etymologies*, and Augustine, he concludes, "From this evidence it is shown that from the time which follows the free consent and wedding (which alone makes marriage) the betrothed man and woman are truly a married couple."[71]

But there is a problem. If marriage is compared to engagement, then it can be argued that consent, in itself, is insufficient for marriage. A man and a woman wish to marry each other and so they get engaged. The fact that they wish to marry means they are consenting to marry. They are not married, however. They are only engaged. Thus, their consent is insufficient. Both Joyce and Schillebeeckx highlight a distinction which Peter makes.[72] He speaks of "consent about the future" and "consent about the present."[73] When a man and woman become engaged, they consent to marriage—

---

70. Peter Lombard, *Sententiarum* (bibliog. III). Latin text in Migne (ed), *Patrologiae Latina* (bibliog. III), vol. 192, cols. 839–962. Distinctiones xxvi– xlii are found in columns 908–43.

71. "Ex his evidenter insinuatur quod ex tempore quo intercedit consensus voluntarius ac maritalis (qui solus Coniugium facit) veri coniuges sunt sponsus et sponsa." Peter Lombard, *Sententiarum* (bibliog. III), 27: 5; Migne (ed), *Patrologiae Latina* (bibliog. III), vol. 192, col. 911.

72. Joyce, *Christian Marriage* (bibliog. III), 62, and Schillebeeckx, *Marriage: Human Reality and Saving Mystery* (bibliog. III), 290.

73. "consensus de futuro" and "consensus de praesenti." Peter Lombard, *Sententiarum* (bibliog. III),28: 1–3; Migne (ed), *Patrologiae Latina* (bibliog. III), vol. 192, cols. 914–16. Also Peter Lombard, *Sententiarum* (bibliog. III), 27: 3; Migne (ed), *Patrologiae Latina* (bibliog. III), vol. 192, cols. 910–11.

but marriage in the future. On the other hand, when they get married, they consent to marry at that moment in time (in the present). Thus, with regard to marriage, it is brought into existence by consent about the present: "For the efficient cause of marriage is consent, not without qualification, but through words expressed, not about the future, but about the present. For if they consent about the future saying: 'I will take you later as my husband' and 'I [too] with you as my wife' this consent is not efficacious of marriage."[74]

The requirement that marital consent is based in the present is clear, but to what are they consenting? Peter says that they cannot be consenting to live together, or else a brother and sister could marry. Moreover, they cannot be consenting to sexual intercourse, or else Mary and Joseph would not have been married. Instead, they must be consenting to marital fellowship.[75] This is the same as Hugh's position.

It is important to note that there are other major similarities between Peter and Hugh. Peter also speaks of the institution of marriage being two-fold: before humanity sinned and after.[76] The first institution commanded the use of the sexual faculty for the generation of children and thus for the increase of the human race.

---

74. "Efficiens autem causa Matrimonii est consensus, non quilibet, sed per verba expressus, nec de futuro, sed de praesenti. Si enim consentiunt in futurum, dicentes: Accipiam te in virum, et: Ego te in uxorem, non est iste consensus efficax Matrimonii." Peter Lombard, *Sententiarum* (bibliog. III), 27: 3; Migne (ed), *Patrologiae Latina* (bibliog. III), vol. 192, col. 910.

75. Peter Lombard, *Sententiarum* (bibliog. III),28: 3; Migne (ed), *Patrologiae Latina* (bibliog. III), vol. 192, cols. 915–16. Also, Mackin, *What is Marriage?* (bibliog. III), 166.

76. Peter Lombard, *Sententiarum* (bibliog. III), 26: 2; Migne (ed), *Patrologiae Latina* (bibliog. III), vol. 192, cols. 908–09.

Because of sin, however, the second institution allows sexual activity between couples as a remedy for concupiscence.[77] Another similarity concerns Peter's treatment of Augustine's three goods of marriage. He, too, argues that the good of children and the good of fidelity can be separated from marriage,[78] but that the good of the sacrament cannot.[79]

It is with regard to the sacramental nature of marriage that Peter differs from Hugh. It has been seen how Hugh wished to emphasize the role of love within marriage. He thus spoke of the fellowship of marriage and how it is a sacrament of the spiritual love between God and the soul. At the same time, he spoke of sexual intercourse being the sacrament of the union of Christ and his Church. Against Hugh, it could be argued that marriage is *one* reality, so sexual intercourse should not be separated from the rest of marriage. Furthermore, it could be said that intercourse should not be afforded a sacramentality all of its own. These accusations cannot be made against Peter, who tends to take marriage as a whole (including intercourse) and speaks of just one symbol or sacrament—namely, the union of Christ and the Church.[80] As Reynolds notes, "Peter Lombard managed to make marriage into one sacrament again by making the two signified unions aspects of the same

---

77. Peter Lombard, *Sententiarum* (bibliog. III), 26: 2–4; Migne (ed), *Patrologiae Latina* (bibliog. III), vol. 192, cols. 908–09.

78. Peter Lombard, *Sententiarum* (bibliog. III), 31: 3; Migne (ed), *Patrologiae Latina* (bibliog. III), vol. 192, col. 919.

79. Peter Lombard, *Sententiarum* (bibliog. III), 31: 2; Migne (ed), *Patrologiae Latina* (bibliog. III), vol. 192, cols. 918–19.

80. Peter Lombard, *Sententiarum* (bibliog. III), 26: 6; Migne (ed), *Patrologiae Latina* (bibliog. III), vol. 192, cols. 909–10. Also, Schillebeeckx, *Marriage: Human Reality and Saving Mystery* (bibliog. III), 324.

union between Christ and the Church: that is, the spiritual union of charity and the physical union through conformity of nature."[81]

If marriage is a sacrament of Christ's bond with the Church, then where in marriage is this sacramentality primarily found? Peter states, "The consent of the spouses signifies the spiritual bond of Christ and the Church, which comes through charity. The union of sexes [also] signifies that, which comes through the expression of nature."[82] As Reynolds and Schillebeeckx observe, in the first half of this statement Peter is saying that it is the actual consent of the couple which is the sacrament of the relationship between Christ and the Church.[83] That is, it signifies the bond and participates in it. This is a major development of Hugh's position, which regarded sacramentality to be based in the fellowship of the couple and also in intercourse.

With Peter Lombard, the consensual view of marriage reached a pinnacle. Consent alone brings a marriage into existence and this very consent is the sacrament of Christ's bond with his Church. Thus, for instance, the consent of Mary and Joseph made their marriage complete. What about sexual intercourse? In the second half of his statement, Peter says that intercourse enables the body to express physically the consent of the spouses.

---

81. Reynolds, "Marriage, Sacramental and Indissoluble" (bibliog. III), 139.
82. "Consensus enim coniugum copulam spiritualem Christi et Ecclesiae, quae fit per charitatem, significat. Commixtio vero sexuum illam significat, quae fit per naturae conformitatem." Peter Lombard, *Sententiarum* (bibliog. III), 26: 6; Migne (ed), *Patrologiae Latina* (bibliog. III), vol. 192, col. 910.
83. Reynolds, "Marriage, Sacramental and Indissoluble" (bibliog. III), 145, and Schillebeeckx, *Marriage: Human Reality and Saving Mystery* (bibliog. III), 293.

That is, consent is internal to the mind and so is unseen; whereas intercourse enables it to be expressed.

The Combined Challenge
to the Legacy of Hincmar of Rheims

Ivo of Chartres, Hugh of Saint Victor, and Peter Lombard all regard consent alone to bring a marriage into existence. Also, each sees the importance of love within marriage. Indeed, they equate marriage with the fellowship of love. Ivo interprets this fellowship to symbolize the bond between Christ and the Church. Hugh interprets it to be a sacrament of the bond between God and the soul. For him, sexual intercourse is a sacrament of the bond between Christ and the Church. Peter Lombard takes marriage as a whole and speaks only of it being a sacrament of the bond between Christ and the Church. For him, this sacramentality exists within the marital consent itself. It expresses itself within all aspects of the fellowship of love, including sexual intercourse. Thus, intercourse expresses what is already there; it adds nothing new to the marriage. As Schillebeeckx notes, Peter's work was accepted by the Frankish church as authoritative.[84] Only a few centuries earlier, in the same church, Archbishop Hincmar of Rheims had taught the importance of sexual intercourse within marriage. Now, under the influence of Peter Lombard, only consent matters. For example, ecclesiastical courts would now regard non-consummated marriages to be just as indissoluble as consummated ones.

---

84. Schillebeeckx, *Marriage: Human Reality and Saving Mystery* (bibliog. III), 294.

—8—

Gratian

Gratian and His Decretum

THE TWELFTH CENTURY saw the consensual understanding of marriage reach its climax with Peter Lombard of Paris. At that time, however, Paris was not the
only place where the question of marriage was being
considered. In Italy, at Bologna, another great scholar
was at work. He was Gratian, and his writings have
been most influential on the Catholic Church's understanding of marriage and the corresponding canon
law—even up to the present day.

Many aspects of Gratian's life remain a mystery,
but it is generally believed that he was a monk.[1] Like
many others who were concerned with the Church's legal practices, Gratian would have been overwhelmed
by the amount of material available. There existed large
collections of opinions from Popes, bishops, Church
Fathers, saints, and theologians. Although it was possible to classify the various opinions according to subject
matter, there remained a major problem. On any one issue, there could be a whole variety of opinions—some

---

1. Noonan, "Gratian Slept Here" (bibliog. III).

contrary to others. As a consequence, one person could follow the advice of one Church authority who advocated one thing, while another could follow the advice of an equally outstanding authority who taught something totally different.

It was within this context that Gratian compiled his *Concordia Discordantium Canonum (Concordance of Discordant Canons)*.[2] As the name suggests, Gratian wished to harmonize the various teachings of Church authorities so that, on any given matter, there would be one clear position. In order to achieve such an impressive goal, Gratian systematically took parts of the Church's discipline and examined them one by one. For each part, he collected various opinions. Then, by analyzing each opinion and commenting on it, he attempted to synthesize the various views and draw out a single conclusion. We know that this mammoth work was completed sometime after 1139, because it contains canons from the Second Lateran Council which met that year. We also know that it was finished before 1155, because Peter Lombard was using it in Paris at that time.[3] And in the sixteenth century, after the close of the Council of Trent, a special commission of cardinals and experts was established. Its function was to correct any mistakes found in Gratian's *Concordia Discordantium Canonum*. They completed their work in 1582.[4]

The *Decretum*—the short name for the *Concordia Discordantium Canonum*—is divided into three parts.[5]

---

2. Gratian, *Concordia* (bibliog. III).
3. Noonan, "Gratian Slept Here" (bibliog. III), 159.
4. Cicognani, *Canon Law* (bibliog. III), 285–86.
5. Cunningham, "When Gratian Worked for the Tribunal" (bibliog. III), 638. Also, Brundage, *Law, Sex, and Christian Society* (bibliog. III), 230–32.

The first part examines the foundations and sources of the Church's law. It deals with such practical matters as the rights and obligations of clergy and the administration of Church property. It is divided into 101 distinctions, each of which considers a particular point of law. Each distinction is subdivided into short chapters, each of which contains an opinion of a Church authority on the matter being covered in that particular distinction. These are interwoven with Gratian's own comments and conclusions (each one of these is called a *dictum*).

The second part of the *Decretum* consists of thirty-six cases (*causae*). Each case begins with a problem of a practical nature, usually in the form of a brief story. Gratian breaks the problem down into questions so that, by answering all the questions, the solution to the problem can be found. Gratian answers each question in turn. As he does so, he subdivides each one into brief chapters. As with the first part, each chapter contains the opinion of an ecclesiastical authority, and again, Gratian adds his own *dicta*. This second part considers marriage, monks, and the administration of property. Although the layout is very systematic, it is interrupted in question three of case thirty-three by a treatise on penance, which is divided into seven distinctions.

Finally, the third part of the *Decretum* is similar in structure to the first part, but it consists of only five distinctions. These deal with liturgical matters, such as the consecration of a church and the sacraments. It does not contain Gratian's *dicta*.

Gratian Introduces Consummation into the Consensual View of Marriage

I have just alluded to the fact that Gratian examines marriage in the second part of the *Decretum*. To be exact, cases twenty-seven to thirty-six are related to marriage. Case twenty-seven would have been most relevant in his day because it was not unusual for there to be a lengthy interval between the agreement to marry and the actual handing over of the bride to the man. Gratian quotes from Augustine to suggest that the delay encourages the man to value his wife more highly.[6]

The case thus begins with a brief account of a man who is betrothed to a certain woman. She renounces this betrothal and gives herself to another man and marries him. The first man demands to have her back. Gratian asks two questions: Is there marriage between the betrothed? And is the betrothed woman allowed to break from the first man and marry another?[7] It is the second question which is most pertinent to this book. This is because, in it, Gratian examines what it is that actually brings a marriage into existence.

The question consists of about fifty chapters—some of which have been added by later commentators. In chapter two, Gratian pinpoints the difficulty. If cohabitation brings about a marriage, then a brother and sister

---

6. Gratian, *Concordia* (bibliog. III), P. 2, C. 27, Q. 2, ch. 39. Gratian's reference is not exact. It should be to Augustine's Confessions, book 8, ch. 3.

7. "Quidam votum castitatis habens desponsavit sibi uxorem; illa priori condicioni renuncians, transtulit se ad alium, et nupsit illi; ille, cui prius desponsata fuerat, repetit eam. (Qu. I) Hic primum queritur, an coniugium possit esse inter voventes? (Qu. II) Secundo, an liceat, sponsae a sponso recedere, et alii nubere?" Gratian, *Concordia* (bibliog. III), Part 2, Case 27, Introduction.

can marry. But if intercourse is necessary for marriage, then Mary and Joseph were not married.[8] Moreover, not only did Mary not have intercourse with Joseph, but she never intended to.[9] Gratian sets about finding a solution to the problem. He cites authorities who had taught that consent makes marriage. Similarly, he cites those who argued that intercourse brings a marriage into existence. He harmonizes these two positions and provides a compromise.

The list of authorities—used by Gratian—who held that consent makes marriage is impressive. He quotes from the work attributed to Saint John Chrysostom which says that consent, not intercourse, makes marriage;[10] the reply of Pope Nicholas I to the Bulgarians;[11] Saint Ambrose, who said that it is the matrimonial agreement and not the loss of virginity which makes marriage;[12] Saint Isidore of Seville, who said that a couple is truly described as married from the moment the betrothal is fulfilled despite matrimonial intercourse not having taken place;[13] and a similar argument from Saint Augustine, who also referred to Mary and Joseph being truly married.[14] Gratian also uses Augustine's argument that Mary and Joseph were really married because they fulfilled his three goods of marriage. That is, the good of children was accomplished in the person of Jesus; the good of fidelity was fulfilled by the

---

8. Gratian, *Concordia* (bibliog. III), Part 2, Case 27, Question 2, ch. 2.
9. Ibid., ch. 3.
10. Ibid., ch. 1.
11. Ibid., ch. 2.
12. Ibid., ch. 5 and 35.
13. Ibid., ch. 6.
14. Ibid., ch. 9.

absence of infidelity; the good of the sacramental bond was achieved by the absence of divorce.[15]

Against these authorities, Gratian places those who believed that sexual intercourse was necessary for a true marriage to exist. At first sight, this list seems very impressive. It contains Saints Augustine, Pope Leo I, Ambrose, and Jerome. A closer inspection reveals a different picture, however. In chapter sixteen, Gratian quotes from Augustine, "There is no marriage between those who have not joined together by the union of the sexes."[16] But even after a careful reading of Augustine, one cannot find this quotation. Theodore Mackin agrees.[17] Indeed, the sixteenth-century commission established to correct the *Decretum* stated that this quotation cannot be found in the works of Augustine.[18]

Some chapters later, Gratian gives a similar quotation which he also says is from Augustine: "There is no doubt that a woman does not belong to a marriage when it is known that there has been no union of the sexes."[19] Again, this cannot be found in Augustine's works. This fact was noted by Friedberg in his edition of the *Decretum*.[20] Both of Gratian's references to Au-

---

15. Ibid., ch. 10. Other similar arguments involving Mary and Joseph are found in chapters 40–45.

16. "Non est inter eos matrimonium, quos non copulat conmixtio sexuum." Gratian, *Concordia* (bibliog. III), Part 2, Case 27, Question 2, ch. 16.

17. Mackin, *Divorce and Remarriage* (bibliog. III), 283.

18. *Notationes Correctorum to Gratian, Concordia* (bibliog. III), Part 2, Case 27, Question 2, ch. 16.

19. "Non dubium est, illam mulierem non pertinere ad matrimonium, cum qua docetur non fuisse conmixtio sexus." Gratian, *Concordia* (bibliog. III), Part 2, Case 27, Question 2, dictum after ch. 39.

20. This edition is the one that I am using in this book. Friedberg (ed), *Quinque Compilationes Antiquae* (bibliog. III) notes that the same is to be said of this second "quotation" from Augustine as is said of the first. Footnote 379 to Gratian, *Concordia* (bibliog. III), Part 2, Case 27, Question 2, dictum after ch. 39.

gustine are very similar to the one used by Archbishop Hincmar of Rheims: "Not all weddings make the conjugal bond, such as those which are not followed by the union of the sexes."[21] Moreover, like the one given by Hincmar, these cannot be found in any of Augustine's works.

Hincmar's false quotation from Augustine had continued, "Marriages do not have in themselves the symbolism of Christ and the Church, as the blessed Augustine says, if they [the spouses] do not avail themselves of each other—that is, if the union of the sexes has not followed up the marriages."[22] Similarly, Gratian's second "quotation" from Augustine is followed by an explanation that a completed marriage must contain the symbolism of Christ and the Church.[23]

Gratian also seems to rely on Hincmar with regard to Pope Leo I. It has been seen that Leo thought it necessary for a man and a woman to be of equal standing if they are to marry. Thus, he did not think that there could be a genuine marriage between a person who was free and a slave. His reasoning is based upon the symbolism of the relationship between Christ and his Church. That is, the Church is the Bride of Christ and not his slave. Therefore, Leo regarded marriage to involve not only sexual intercourse but also a relationship based upon

---

21. ". . . non omnes nuptiae coniugalem copulam faciunt, quas non sequitur commistio sexuum." Hincmar of Rheims, *De Nuptiis Stephani* (bibliog. III); Migne (ed), *Patrologiae Latina* (bibliog. III), vol. 126, col. 137.

22. "Nec habent nuptiae in se Christi et Ecclesiae sacramentum, sicut beatus Augustinus dicit, si se nuptialiter non utunter, id est, si eas non subsequitur commistio sexuum." Hincmar of Rheims, *De Nuptiis Stephani* (bibliog. III); Migne (ed), *Patrologiae Latina* (bibliog. III), vol. 126, col. 137.

23. "Ad matrimonium perfectum subintelligendum est, tale videlicet, quod habeat in se Christi et ecclesiae sacramentum." Gratian, *Concordia* (bibliog. III), Part 2, Case 27, Question 2, dictum after ch. 39.

equality. Thus, Leo says, "the fellowship of marriage was, from the beginning, instituted so that *in addition to* (*ut praeter*) the union of the sexes it would have in itself the symbolism of Christ and the Church."[24] Hincmar took Leo's words out of context and used them erroneously to imply that sexual intercourse makes present the symbolism of Christ and the Church.[25]

Just a few decades before Gratian, Leo's phrase had reached Ivo of Chartres, who used it when considering marriage in his *Panormia*. But the word *not* (*non*) had been inserted into the text so that it now stated that *without* sexual intercourse the symbolism of Christ and his Church would be absent: "The fellowship of marriage was, from the beginning, instituted so that apart from the union of the sexes the marital union does not have in itself the symbolism of Christ and the Church."[26] It has already been seen that, despite this, Ivo concluded that a marriage shares in the symbolism of Christ and the Church irrespective of whether it has been consummated.[27] However, Gratian also uses a corrupted version of Leo's teaching, which is virtually the same as the one used by Ivo, in order to illustrate the necessity of intercourse with regard to the symbolism:

24. ". . . societas nuptiarum ita ab initio constituta sit, ut praeter sexuum coniunctionem haberet in se Christi et Ecclesiae sacramentum." (Emphasis is mine.) Leo I (bibliog. I), *Epistula clxvii*, circa 458–59.

25. Hincmar of Rheims, *De Nuptiis Stephani* (bibliog. III); Migne (ed), *Patrologiae Latina* (bibliog. III), vol. 126, col. 137.

26. ". . . societas nuptiarum ita ab initio constituta sit ut praeter sexus coniunctionem non habeant in se nuptiae coniunctionis Christi et Ecclesiae sacramentum." Ivo of Chartres, *Panormia* (bibliog. III), book 6, ch. 23; Migne (ed), *Patrologiae Latina* (bibliog. III), vol. 161, col. 1248. Ivo cites Pope Leo II and not Leo I.

27. Migne (ed), *Patrologiae Latina* (bibliog. III), vol. 161, cols. 599–600 and 615.

"The fellowship of marriage was, from the beginning, instituted so that apart from the union of the sexes marriage does not have in itself the symbolism of Christ and the Church."[28] Thus, not only does Gratian use Leo I out of context, but he also uses a corrupted version of his words.

Gratian also quotes from Ambrose: "In every marriage the union is understood to be spiritual, which the bodily joining of those united confirms and completes."[29] Using this as a basis for his argument, Gratian is able to declare, "Behold, marriage which is initiated by the pledge is not completed."[30] A thorough reading of Ambrose's works, however, does not reveal the whereabouts of this quotation. In fact, the sixteenth-century correctors said that this text cannot be found in the writings of Ambrose.[31]

Two chapters later, Gratian quotes Ambrose again: "It is called a marriage when the pledged woman is handed over and enjoyed by him [the husband]."[32] Earlier, it was seen how Gratian quoted from Ambrose when giving the consensual argument. Ambrose had stated that it is the marital pledge and not the loss of virginity

---

28. ". . . societas nuptiarum ita a principio sit instituta, ut preter conmixtionem sexuum non habeant in se nuptiae Christi et ecclesiae sacramentum." Gratian, *Concordia* (bibliog. III), Part 2, Case 27, Question 2, ch. 17.

29. "In omni matrimonio coniunctio intelligitur spiritualis, quam confirmat et perficit coniunctorum conmixtio corporalis." Gratian, *Concordia* (bibliog. III), Part 2, Case 27, Question 2, ch. 36.

30 . "Ecce, quod in desponsatione coniugium initiatur, non perficitur." Gratian, *Concordia* (bibliog. III), Part 2, Case 27, Question 2, dictum after ch. 35.

31. *Notationes Correctorum* to Gratian, *Concordia* (bibliog. III), Part 2, Case 27, Question 2, ch. 36.

32. "Ambrosius ad Paternum . . . Si quis desponsata sibi et tradita utatur coniugium vocatur." Gratian, *Concordia* (bibliog. III), Part 2, Case 27, Question 2, ch. 38.

which begins a marriage. Despite this, Gratian is quoting Ambrose again so as to portray him opposing the consensual position. This new quotation from Ambrose has to be considered carefully, as well as in the light of his other statements. In practice, a betrothed woman marries and is handed over to her new husband, after which sexual intercourse may occur. Thus, at the time she has intercourse with him, she is his wife because they have married, but this is not the same as saying that the marriage only exists from the moment she has intercourse. Gratian uses Ambrose's text in such a way that he ignores the interpretation which says the woman is already married when she has intercourse.

Gratian also cites Jerome, stating that marriages "are begun by the contract of the betrothed and are completed by the joining of their bodies."[33] Again, no such reference can be found in the works of Jerome. It has just been seen that the sixteenth-century correctors state that a quotation from Ambrose cannot be found. At the same time, they also state that this text attributed to Jerome cannot be seen in his writings.[34]

Gratian thus lists the ecclesiastical authorities who maintained that a marriage begins with the consent of the couple, as well as those who argued that a marriage is not complete until there has been sexual intercourse. From these two schools of thought he creates a synthesis. To do this, he distinguishes between "an initiated marriage" (*coniugium initiatum*)[35] and "a confirmed marriage"

---

33. ". . . sponsali conventione initiantur, et conmixtione corporum perficiuntur." Gratian, *Concordia* (bibliog. III), Part 2, Case 27, Question 2, ch. 37.

34. *Notationes Correctorum* to Gratian, *Concordia* (bibliog. III), Part 2, Case 27, Question 2, ch. 36.

35. Gratian, *Concordia* (bibliog. III), Part 2, Case 27, Question 2, dictum after ch. 34.

(*coniugium ratum*). A marriage begins with the consent of the marriage partners; this is an initiated marriage. But the marriage is *completed* by sexual intercourse; this is a confirmed marriage. Such a synthesis
was intended to be faithful to both schools of thought.
It acknowledges that marriage begins with consent. At
the same time, it recognizes the importance of sexual
intercourse which perfects and completes a marriage.
Gratian concludes, "It is known that a marriage is begun by a pledge and perfected by uniting. Between a
pledged man and a pledged woman there is, from that
time, a marriage—but initiated. Between those en-
joined there is a confirmed marriage."[36]

As Mackin observes,[37] Gratian does not make use
of Peter Lombard's distinction between *consent about
the future* (*consensus de futuro*) and *consent about
the present* (*consensus de praesenti*). Thus, Gratian's
terminology is ambiguous. For example, *desponsatio*
could mean an intention to marry in the future—that
is, an intention to be engaged. On the other hand, it
could mean an intention to marry in the present. Hence,
desponsatio could refer to either engagement promises
or wedding vows. It is for this reason that, where there
is a doubt, I have translated it as "pledge." The word
pledge is sufficiently neutral so as not to impose a false
meaning on the text. Whichever interpretation is used,
however, a marriage without sexual intercourse is not
complete as far as Gratian is concerned.

---

36. "Sed sciendum est, quod coniugium desponsatione initiatur, conmixtione
perficitur. Unde inter sponsum et sponsam coniugium est, sed initiatum; inter
copulatos est coniugium ratum." Gratian, *Concordia* (bibliog. III), Part 2, Case
27, Question 2, dictum after ch. 34.

37. Mackin, *What is Marriage?* (bibliog. III), 160.

Brundage provides a good summary of Gratian's synthesis of the consensual and the coital theories: "As Gratian explained matters, these two theories were not contradictory; rather, they complemented one another. Each described one facet and one stage in the process of creating a marital union, and neither was sufficient without the other."[38] This is evident in chapter thirty-four, where Gratian quotes from an assembly of bishops at Toledo: "It is established by sacred council that if a man abducts a woman betrothed to another man he is to be punished with public penance and remain without any hope of marrying. And if that woman had not consented to the crime, she is not to be denied permission to marry another."[39] Thus, although the man may have raped the woman, the fact that she did not consent to the abduction means that she did not give marital consent and so cannot be regarded as married to him. Therefore, she is not to be denied the opportunity to marry another man. This example makes it clear that Gratian believes that just as consent requires intercourse to complete a marriage, so intercourse requires marital consent.

Mackin comments, "For creating a marriage the consent and the subsequent intercourse act as necessary co-causes, each insufficient without the other, but in co-operative tandem producing their effect."[40] It is noteworthy that Gratian does not seem too concerned about in which order these two co-causes occur. For

---

38. *Brundage, Law, Sex, and Christian Society* (bibliog. III), 236.

39. "Statutum est a sacro conventu, ut si quis sponsam alterius rapuerit, publica penitencia mulctetur, et sine spe coniugii maneat. Et si ipsa eidem crimini consentiens non fuerit, licentia nubendi alii non negetur." Part 2, Case 27, Question 2, ch. 34.

40. Mackin, *Divorce and Remarriage* (bibliog. III), 282.

example, he refers to Jacob who had consented to marry Rachel but was tricked into having intercourse with Leah. Gratian argues that if Jacob had intercourse with Rachel, to whom he had consented to marry, then he was married to her. Both co-causes would be present—consent followed by intercourse. Gratian also argues, however, that if Jacob consented to marry Leah, having had intercourse with her, then he was married to her. In this latter scenario both co-causes exist but with the marital consent coming after intercourse.[41]

There is a lot written about Gratian and he deservedly receives much praise for his *Decretum*. Moreover, his marital synthesis does appear to be an excellent compromise between the consensual and coital theories. But I disagree.

Although he was a most brilliant scholar, his synthesis lacks validity. The consensual theory had worthy adherents, referred to by Gratian. The advocates of the coital theory, however, were virtually non-existent. The best Gratian could do, like Hincmar before him, was to quote some ecclesiastical authorities out of context and to attribute false quotations to others. He may have been acting with the best intentions, having inherited erroneous references from earlier collections, but the fact remains that he attempted to synthesize the consensual theory, which had a long tradition, with the coital theory, which had very few credible proponents.

---

41. Gratian, *Concordia* (bibliog. III), Part 2, Case 29, Question 1.

Consequences of Gratian's Theory
Pertaining to Spouses Entering Religious Life,
Clandestine Marriages, and Impotence

Gratian's synthesis has dramatic consequences. It has been seen that the tradition, up to the time of his work, emphasized the role of consent. Moreover, this consent brought about a marriage which was primarily a fellowship of love. Gratian changed this by putting more emphasis on the sexual dimension of marriage. Indeed, according to him, the sacrament of the bond between Christ and the Church is made present through sexual intercourse.[42]

In chapters nineteen to twenty-eight of the question I have been examining, Gratian looks at the Church's practice of allowing one or both spouses to enter religious life with a vow of continence. Gratian's emphasis on sexual intercourse results in his making much use of a concept which Brundage calls *marital debt*.[43] Gratian bases his argument on Saint Paul: "The wife does not have authority over her own body, but the husband does; and in the same way, the husband does not have authority over his own body, but the wife does."[44] Gratian regards this quotation from Saint Paul to have a sexual meaning. Therefore, he alludes to the previous verse of Saint Paul, "The husband must give to his wife what she has a right to expect, and so too the wife to her husband."[45] Gratian thus argues that a husband

---

42. Ibid., Case 27, Question 2, ch. 17, and dictum after ch. 39.

43. Brundage, *Law, Sex, and Christian Society* (bibliog. III), 241.

44. "Mulier sui potestatem corporis non habet, sed vir; similiter et vir potestatem sui corporis non habet, sed mulier." Gratian, *Concordia* (bibliog. III), Part 2, Case 27, Question 2, ch. 19. The Biblical reference is 1 Corinthians 7:4.

45. 1 Corinthians 7:3. Referred to in Gratian, *Concordia* (bibliog. III), Part 2,

has the right to have sex with his wife when he so demands. Similarly, the wife has this right with regard to her husband.[46] I agree with Brundage who states that, for Gratian, consent to marry does not create a duty to consummate.[47] However, the duty to have sexual intercourse originates with the first act of intercourse. Thus, a married couple need not have intercourse, but if they do, then either spouse can rightfully demand it on any subsequent occasion. This teaching of Gratian is most evident in his treatment of a spouse's entry into religious life, which I shall now briefly examine.

If a husband wishes to enter religious life with a vow of continence after his marriage has been consummated, then he must obtain permission from his wife. This is because the consummation of their marriage has produced the "marital debt." Thus, his wife, before anyone else, has a right to his body. But if the marriage has not been consummated, then the woman has no such claims over the man and so he can enter religious life, with a vow of continence, without her permission. The same would apply to a woman who wishes to enter religious life.[48]

The fact that the wife has the same right as her husband with regard to demanding intercourse is surprising, given the cultural and social setting of

Case 27, Question 2, dictum after ch. 18: "Item Apostolus precipit, ut uxor reddat debitum viro, et vir uxori." ("As the Apostle taught, so a wife must give what is owing to her husband, and the husband to his wife.")

46. Gratian, *Concordia* (bibliog. III), Part 2, Case 27, Question 2, dictum after ch. 18, ch. 19, dictum after ch. 26, and dictum after ch. 28. Also, Case 30, Question 1, ch. 2; Case 32, Question 2, dictum after ch. 2; and Case 33, Question 5, ch. 5, and dictum after ch. 11.

47. Brundage, *Law, Sex, and Christian Society* (bibliog. III), 241.

48. Gratian, *Concordia* (bibliog. III), Part 2, Case 27, Question 2, dictum after ch. 26, and dictum after ch. 28. Also, Case 33, Question 5, dictum after ch. 11, and dictum after ch. 20.

Gratian. Brundage says, "This parity in respect to the conjugal debt was Gratian's most emphatic venture in the direction of a doctrine of equality between the sexes."[49] Gratian is not consistent in his thoughts on equality, however. Indeed, elsewhere he says, "The woman has no authority, but remains under her husband's rule in everything."[50]

Despite Gratian's emphasis on intercourse, he does not ignore the importance of consent, especially if it is manifested at a Church ceremony. Indeed, it is consent which brings about an initiated marriage. Moreover, a spouse cannot just walk out of a marriage, even an unconsummated one, which has been publicly celebrated by the Church—let alone form another marriage with a third person. Indeed, such an action would violate the blessing bestowed by the Church's priest.[51]

Concerning such a blessing, Gratian does not regard it as essential. Although he is against clandestine marriages, he says that once they have been entered into they are to be as binding as public marriages.[52] Raymond Decker, who specializes in the relationship between religion and law, suggests that Gratian was opposed to clandestine marriages because they lacked proof and so could easily be denied. This undermined the stability of society and the Church. If

49. Brundage, *Law, Sex, and Christian Society* (bibliog. III), 242.

50. "Nulla est mulieris potestas, sed in omnibus viri dominio subsit." Gratian, *Concordia* (bibliog. III), Part 2, Case 33, Question 5, ch. 17. Also, Brundage, *Law, Sex, and Christian Society* (bibliog. III), 255.

51. Gratian, *Concordia* (bibliog. III), Part 2, Case 27, Question 2, dictum after ch. 50.

52. Ibid., C. 30, Q. 5, especially chapters 8 to 11.

Gratian denied that they were true marriages, however, he himself would be undermining many such marriages and thus society and the Church.[53]

What if there cannot be sexual intercourse because of impotence? In order to examine Gratian's answer to this question it is necessary to note his interpretation of the possible exceptive clause in Matthew's Gospel.[54] He refers to a quotation attributed to Clement[55] and concludes, "From this authority it is most obviously shown that whoever leaves his wife because of fornication is not able to marry another while she is alive, and if he does then it would be a matter of adultery."[56] Thus, although Gratian regards adultery as a permissible ground to leave one's spouse, he does not believe that it dissolves the marriage. That is, Matthew does not provide an exception to the indissolubility of marriage.

With this in mind, Gratian answers the question about impotence. There are two possible scenarios. First, the marriage is consummated and impotence develops afterwards. It has already been seen that such a marriage would be regarded by Gratian to have been completed by the act of intercourse which occurred prior to the onset of impotence. Thus, such a marriage would be sacramental and indissoluble. Moreover, the spouses would have sexual rights over each other.

---

53. Decker, "Institutional Authority versus Personal Responsibility" (bibliog. III), in particular, 56–57.

54. Matthew 19:9.

55. Gratian, *Concordia* (bibliog. III), Part 2, Case 32, Question 7, ch. 16.

56. "His auctoritatibus evidentissime monstratur, quod quicumque causa fornicationis uxorem suam dimiserit, illa vivente aliam ducere non poterit, et, si duxerit, reus adulterii erit.", Ibid., dictum after ch. 16.

Therefore, in such a case, the impotence could not dissolve the marriage.[57]

The second scenario is when the impotence exists before any consummation so that the marriage has to remain unconsummated. In this case, the marriage could never be completed. It could not participate in the unbreakable bond that exists between Christ and his Church. Therefore, if the husband was impotent, his wife could leave him and marry another.[58] One other question needs to be asked about this case. Is the unconsummated marriage actually dissolved? Gratian does use language which suggests that it is: "Behold, the inability to pay the debt dissolves the bond of marriage."[59] However, Gratian also observes that the impotence is based upon something more fundamental: "But also, this is brought about by a natural inability."[60] One interpretation of Gratian's thinking is that the marriage is not dissolved, for the simple reason that it never existed in the first place.[61] That is, it is prevented from existing by natural reasons.

This view is supported by two factors. One, Gratian is willing to let a woman marry a second man only if the first man's impotence is *natural*. He expresses

---

57. "Ecce, inpossibilitas coeundi, si post carnalem copulam inventa fuerit in aliquo, non solvit coniugium." Ibid., Case 27, Question 2, dictum after ch. 29.

58. "Si vero ante carnalem copulam deprehensa fuerit, liberum facit mulieri alium virum accipere." Ibid.

59. "Ecce, quod impossibilitas reddendi debitum vinculum solvit coniugii." Ibid., Case 33, Question 1, dictum after ch. 3. There is an inconsistency in Gratian's thinking here. It has been seen that he believed the marital debt came about from the first act of intercourse; not from consent. Thus, if there has been no sexual intercourse because of impotence, then Gratian should not be arguing that the marital debt cannot be satisfied—because no such debt exists.

60. "Sed hoc de naturali impossibilitate statutum est." Ibid.

61. Mackin, *Divorce and Remarriage* (bibliog. III), 284, 290–91.

doubt as to whether the Church could allow her to do so if she brought about the impotence herself by sorcery.[62] Two, Gratian seems to allude to the actual practice of certain Church authorities who would allow a woman to leave her impotent husband and marry another man. Gratian argues logically as follows: No married person can separate from his or her spouse and marry another. Instead, he or she must either remain single or return to the original spouse. There is no exception to this rule (not even if the original spouse has committed adultery). Thus, the fact that such a woman may marry another man can only mean that there was never a marriage in the first place.[63] If such an interpretation is correct, then sexual intercourse within marriage is so important to Gratian that its natural impossibility means there can be no marriage at all—not even an initiated one.

Gratian and Marriages between Unbaptized Spouses (the Pauline Privilege)

The twenty-eighth case in Gratian's marriage section begins with an outline.[64] Two unbaptized persons marry. The man converts and receives baptism. His wife refuses to live with him because he is a Christian. She leaves him and he marries a Christian

---

62. Gratian, *Concordia* (bibliog. III), Part 2, Case 33, Question 1, dictum after ch. 3.

63. "Unde apparet, illos non fuisse coniuges; alioquin non liceret eis ab invicem discedere, excepta causa fornicationis; et sic discedentes oportet manere innuptos, aut sibi invicem reconciliari." Gratian, *Concordia* (bibliog. III), Part 2, Case 27, Question 2, dictum after ch. 29.

64. Gratian, *Concordia* (bibliog. III), Part 2, Case 28. I shall also be using Mackin, *Divorce and Remarriage* (bibliog. III), 285–88.

woman. Eventually, this second woman dies and the man is ordained. Finally, he becomes a bishop. Gratian asks three questions: (1) Can true marriage exist between those who are not baptized? (2) Was the man able to take a second wife while the first one was still alive? (3) Has the man actually been married twice?

To answer the first question, Gratian uses the concept of *a legitimate marriage (legitimum coniugium)*.[65] This is a marriage which is celebrated in such a way that it satisfies local laws and customs. Gratian says that non-Christians are able to have legitimate marriages. He goes on to say, however, that there is an essential difference between the marriages of non-Christians and those of Christians. Christians, through intercourse, can make present the indestructible bond that exists between Christ and his Church. When this occurs, Christian couples cannot dissolve their marriages. On the other hand, the marriages of non-Christians can never make present Christ's bond with his Church. Therefore, they can be dissolved by the couples themselves through such means as divorce.

Gratian explains that Christian marriages can be either legitimate or not. If they are legitimate, then by definition they have been celebrated in accordance with local laws and customs.[66] It has been seen that Gratian recognized clandestine Christian marriages, although he objected to them. These marriages would have no public ceremonies, as determined by local rules and customs, and so would not be legitimate.

---

65. Gratian, *Concordia* (bibliog. III), Part 2, Case 28, Question 1, dictum after ch. 17.

66. Ibid.

With regard to the second question, Gratian says that the man was allowed to take a second wife.[67] He bases his reasoning on Saint Paul: "But if the unbeliever chooses to leave, then let the separation take place: in these circumstances, the brother or sister [that is, the Christian spouse] is no longer tied. But God has called you to live in peace."[68] Gratian notes that Saint Paul says that the Christian party is not bound by the marriage when the non-Christian spouse *departs* of his or her own choice. He explains that the conditions given by Saint Paul would not be satisfied if the non-Christian spouse was forcibly *dismissed* by the Christian.

The expression, *no longer tied*, is a translation of the Greek word δεδούλωται which has the same root as δοῦλος, which means "a slave."[69] Thus, the Christian spouse is no longer enslaved. This can be interpreted in two very different ways: in one interpretation, the marriage still exists, but the Christian party is no longer bound by its obligations, such as living with his or her spouse; in the other, the marriage itself no longer exists. The fact that Gratian says the man is permitted to remarry means that he takes the second interpretation of Paul's text.

There is nothing in the text, however, to indicate that Paul did indeed mean the second interpretation. As the Scripture scholar Gordon Fee observes, "This statement is the source of the notorious 'Pauline Privilege,' in which the text is understood to mean that

---

67. Ibid., Case 28, Question 2, especially dictum after ch. 2.
68. 1 Corinthians 7:15.
69. Liddell and Scott, *An Intermediate Greek-English Lexicon* (bibliog. III), 210.

the believer is free to remarry. But despite a long tradition that has so interpreted it, several converging data indicate that Paul is essentially repeating his first sentence: that the believer is not bound to maintain the marriage if the pagan partner opts out."[70] Fee goes on to outline the "converging data."[71] The entire context in which 1 Corinthians 7:15 is found has nothing to do with remarriage. Indeed, elsewhere Paul explicitly rules out remarriage.[72] Moreover, there is nothing to connect the verb *tied* with the bond of marriage. Thus, is the Christian free to remarry? Fee concludes that Paul just does not consider the question: "All of this is not to say that Paul *disallows* remarriage in such cases; he simply does not speak to it at all."[73]

The third question, as to how many times the man married, is important because he went on to become a bishop. Gratian has in mind another of Saint Paul's instructions—this time, that a presiding elder "must have an impeccable character [and be] husband of one wife."[74] Gratian acknowledges the opinion attributed to Saint Jerome that baptism gives a new start and so the wife before the man's baptism does not count.[75] However, it is retorted that baptism dissolves sin and not marriage,[76] in which case the man would have been married twice—once before his baptism and once after.

---

70. Fee, *The First Epistle to the Corinthians* (bibliog. III), 302.
71. Ibid., 303.
72. 1 Corinthians 7: 11.
73. Fee, *The First Epistle to the Corinthians* (bibliog. III), 303. (Emphasis in the original.)
74. 1 Timothy 3:2.
75. Gratian, *Concordia* (bibliog. III), Part 2, Case 28, Question 3, ch. 1.
76. Ibid., ch. 2.

The Revolution Caused by Gratian

It must be said that Gratian's *Decretum* has made an invaluable contribution to the Church. It is a treasury of texts from many ecclesiastical authorities. Moreover, Gratian's attempt to harmonize conflicting opinions was a most noble project. But in the area of marriage, his contribution has been unfortunate. It is the common view that he provided a masterly synthesis of two equally valid traditions—the consensual school and the coital school. I would disagree.

From the previous sections it has been seen that, until Gratian, the consensual tradition had been constant and strong. The main proponent of the coital theory was Archbishop Hincmar of Rheims whose crucial sources were either false or taken out of context. In the same way, Gratian uses erroneous texts in order to support the coital tradition. It is for this reason that I would say that he has diluted and polluted the consensual tradition of the Church.

As a consequence, Gratian shifts the emphasis away from love to sexual intercourse. It is intercourse which completes marriage, making it an indissoluble sacrament. Moreover, the notion of marriage being a fellowship of love is overshadowed by the concept of marital debt. Marriage is reduced to the spouses having sexual rights over each other. As a result, impotence becomes a serious obstacle to entering marriage.

Finally, Gratian gives a strict interpretation to Matthew's Gospel, allowing no exception to the rule against divorce and remarriage. Despite this, however, he interprets Paul broadly, permitting a convert to Christianity—who was legitimately married—to divorce and re-marry should the unbaptized spouse refuse to remain.

Like Gratian himself, the *Concordia Discordan-tium Canonum* is somewhat shrouded in mystery. I have already noted in passing that some of its chapters were added by later scholars. There are in existence various manuscripts which give rise to two versions of the *Decretum*—a shorter one and a longer one. It had been thought that the longer version was the original and that the shorter one was a summary of it. But it is now believed that the shorter version is the original.[77] Irrespective of which chapters were added later, it will be seen that the *Decretum* as a whole, as handed down from generation to generation, has had a dramatic ef-fect on the Church's understanding of marriage.

The eminent professor of canon law, Gaetano Cicog-nani, who later became a Cardinal in 1953, explains that it was a private work—that is, it was never an of-ficial legal text of the Church.[78] Thus, its conclusions are not by themselves legally binding; they are merely opinions. In practice, however, this great work has in-fluenced various Popes and, consequently, the canon law of marriage. It thus marks a turning point in the development of the Church's official understanding of what it is that brings a marriage into existence. After the *Decretum*, consent alone would no longer be con-sidered to be sufficient for a full marriage to exist.

---

77. Larrainzar, *"El Decreto de Graciano del Códice Fd"* (bibliog. III). Also, Viejo-Ximénez, *"'Concordia' y 'Decretum' del Maestro Graciano"* (bibliog. III). Also, Winroth, The Making of Gratian's Decretum (bibliog. III).

78. Cicognani, *Canon Law* (bibliog. III), 287–88.

—9—

Gratian Influences the Universities and the Church

Collections of Law after Gratian

IN THIS SECTION I shall show how Gratian's *Decretum* influenced two Popes—Alexander III and Innocent III. Through these two Popes, the *Decretum* shaped the marriage law of the Catholic Church. Moreover, its effect is still felt today.

When the *Decretum* was completed, it proved to be an essential treasury of ecclesiastical texts. Nevertheless, bishops from all over the world continued to write to the Pope and ask his judgment on various matters. Each reply, called a *decretal*, became an additional source of law. Thus, very soon, Gratian's work needed to be updated. This process began toward the end of the twelfth century. In about 1191, Bernard of Pavia produced a supplementary collection of decretals—his *Breviarium Extravagantium*. This work was later to be called the *Compilatio Prima* (*The First Collection*). It was systematically arranged into five books, the fourth of which considered marriage.

Later, in 1210, Pope Innocent III (of whom more shall be said) commissioned Pietro Beneventano to put together his decretals. This collection left a gap. The decretals issued after 1191 and before Innocent III had not been compiled. This omission was soon rectified by John of Wales. His collection became known as the *Compilatio Secunda* (*The Second Collection*) and the one of Innocent III's decretals was known as the *Compilatio Tertia* (*The Third Collection*). Shortly afterwards, Johannes Teutonicus produced the *Compilatio Quarta*. This fourth collection of decretals contained the last ones of Innocent III as well as the constitutions of the Fourth Lateran Council. Finally, in 1226, Pope Honorius III commissioned Tancred to publish a fifth collection—the *Compilatio Quinta*—which contained his decretals. Together, these works are often referred to as the five collections or compilations of antiquity.[1] Unlike Gratian's *Decretum*, these collections officially had the force of law.[2]

Although these five collections were arranged systematically, anyone who used them had to be prepared to go from one to another. This made it difficult to trace the decretals written on any particular point of law. To remedy this, Pope Gregory IX commissioned Raymond of Peñafort to prepare a new collection which would replace all five. In 1234, the work was promulgated. It is known as the *Liber Extra* or the *Decretals of Gregory IX*.[3] As Brundage points out, this collection clarified the Church's legal position on various matters

---

1. Friedberg (ed), *Quinque Compilationes Antiquae* (bibliog. III). .
2. Brundage, *Law, Sex, and Christian Society* (bibliog. III), 326–27. Also, Wernz, *Ius Decretalium* (bibliog. III), 357–60.
3. Gregory IX, *Decretales* (bibliog. III).

in two ways. First, it gathered together decretals from the five collections and included relevant ones which had been omitted. Second, and more radically, Pope Gregory delegated Raymond to write new decretals on matters where previous decretals were either contradictory or silent. Following the layout of the *Compilatio Prima* and the other collections, the *Liber Extra* is divided into five books, with marriage being examined in the fourth. This masterly work had the force of law for nearly seven hundred years. It was replaced by a code of law in 1917.[4]

The five collections and the *Liber Extra* provide an invaluable insight into the minds of two Popes, Alexander III and Innocent III, who have had a considerable influence on marital law.[5]

Gratian's Influence on the Church through Pope Alexander III

Pope Alexander III started life as Roland Bandinelli. He was a follower of Gratian at Bologna and was himself a professor there in theology and ecclesiastical law. Sometime before 1148, an abridgment to the second part of Gratian's *Decretum* was published under the title *Summa* (or *Stroma*) by a Master Roland.[6] Within a few years, this author produced a theological

---

4. Brundage, *Law, Sex, and Christian Society* (bibliog. III), 327.

5. Coriden, *The Indissolubility Added to Christian Marriage by Consummation* (bibliog. III). I am indebted to James Coriden, professor of canon law, for sending me a copy of this paper. Although he wrote it before the Second Vatican Council and the 1983 Code of Canon Law, it provides an excellent account of the contribution of Alexander III and Innocent III to the development of the canon law of marriage.

6. Thaner (ed), *Summa Magistri Rolandi* (bibliog. III).

treatise called the *Sententiae*,[7] and both of these works are important in themselves.

The thinking in the *Summa* is very similar to Gratian's. For example, it distinguishes between an initiated marriage and a confirmed marriage. Moreover, it recognizes consent and sexual intercourse as necessary co-causes of a confirmed marriage. Consequently, it allows an engagement and even an unconsummated marriage to be dissolved for a pressing reason—such as the desire (by at least one party) to enter religious life, or the discovery of impotence. Furthermore, the necessity of intercourse means that one party can leave an unconsummated marriage and enter a new marriage with another—the consummation of which supersedes the first. The reason given is that a consummated marriage contains the sacrament of Christ and his Church.[8]

As Coriden observes, the *Sententiae* shows a shift in Roland's thinking.[9] The *Summa* emphasized Gratian's distinction between an initiated marriage and a confirmed marriage. The *Sententiae* focuses more on the distinction made by Peter Lombard concerning consent about the future (becoming engaged) and consent about the present (entering marriage). This shift means that the type of consent given must be examined. Hence, emphasis is slightly taken away from intercourse and placed on consent.

In 1159, Roland Bandinelli became Pope Alexander III. Coriden, like many, presumes that this was the

---

7. Gietl (ed), *Sentenzen Rolands* (bibliog. III).
8. Coriden, *The Indissolubility Added to Christian Marriage by Consummation* (bibliog. III), 7–11.
9. Ibid.

same Roland who wrote the *Summa* and the *Sententiae*, but more recent scholarship has called this presumption into question.[10] It is because of this that Brundage suggests that any analysis of Alexander III's thinking must concentrate on his decretals, as opposed to the *Summa* or the *Sententiae*.[11] I would agree for an additional reason. That is, whatever Alexander III may have written prior to becoming Pope did not influence the Church; this was achieved through his papal decrees.

Indeed, his influence on the Church's discipline of marriage can be seen from the *Liber Extra*. Brundage provides pertinent statistics.[12] As mentioned, the fourth book of the *Liber Extra* is concerned with marriage. This book is divided into twenty-one titles, and eighteen of these contain decretals from Alexander. Moreover, of the total 156 decretals, sixty are by him.

As Coriden explains, an examination of Alexander's decretals is difficult for three reasons. First, few are dated, so it is hard to put them into chronological order to see if there is any development in his thinking. Second, when they give responses to actual cases, they only give brief outlines of the facts. And third, since they were written over a period of time, there is no consistency in the terms and expressions used.[13] Despite these problems, however, it is possible to piece together Alexander's understanding of marriage.

Alexander received a case from the Archbishop of

---

10. Weigand, "*Magister Rolandus und Papst Alexander III*" (bibliog. III). Also, *Brundage, Sex, Law, and Marriage* (bibliog. III), 59–83.

11. Brundage, *Sex, Law, and Marriage* (bibliog. III), 59–61.

12. Ibid., 65–66.

13. Coriden, *The Indissolubility Added to Christian Marriage by Consummation* (bibliog. III), 12.

Salerno. A girl consents to marry a certain man but marries another. The Archbishop wished to know to whom the girl was married. In his reply, Alexander uses the distinction between consent about the future and consent about the present. He explains that if present consent had been exchanged with the first man, then she was married to him. In such an instance, even if she had intercourse with the second man and not the first, she would still be married to the first and so must return to him.[14] If Alexander had used Gratian's distinction between an initiated marriage and a confirmed marriage then he might have come to a different conclusion. If the first union had not been consummated but the second had, then the second would be a completed marriage. It would thus have taken precedence over the first. By applying the distinction used by Peter Lombard, however, it is only necessary to determine which type of consent has been exchanged. For this reason, Alexander acknowledges that his decision is not in keeping with previous papal decisions.[15] It will be seen that it was most unusual for Alexander and other Popes to break from the matrimonial decisions of their predecessors.

His thinking on the matter is also illustrated in the decretal *Tua fraternitas*.[16] Here he explains that consent about the present makes a marriage irrespective of whether or not it is consummated. Thus, couples who have exchanged present consent are not free to marry

14. Decretals are traditionally named after their opening words. This decretal is Alexander III (bibliog. I), decretals, 1159–81: *Licet praeter.*

15. Coriden, *The Indissolubility Added to Christian Marriage by Consummation* (bibliog. III),12–13.

16. Alexander III (bibliog. I), decretals, 1159–81: *Tua fraternitas.*

others. Consent about the future, on the other hand, is only an engagement and so does not prevent either party from marrying another.[17]

Alexander's decretals show a consistency in his thought. In particular, there are two consequences of his emphasis on present consent. First, present consent alone is sufficient and so no public or ecclesiastical ceremony is required. In other words, he recognizes clandestine marriages. He is against them in principle because they undermine society. A man could marry a woman secretly and then deny it. But if the man exchanges present consent, then Alexander feels obliged to uphold the marriage.[18] Indeed, he accepts that under certain circumstances, it might be necessary to marry secretly.[19]

The second consequence of Alexander's emphasis on present consent means that it has to be genuine. If everything relies upon this consent, then any problem with it threatens the very existence of the marriage. Thus, for example, if parents make their children marry through the use of force or threats, then the children are not really giving true consent. In such cases, the marriages would not exist.[20]

Was consummation irrelevant to Alexander's understanding of marriage? The answer is no. It has been seen that there is a theory that, before becoming Pope, he wrote an abridgment to Gratian's *Decretum*. If this

---

17. Coriden, *The Indissolubility Added to Christian Marriage by Consummation* (bibliog. III), 15.

18. Alexander III (bibliog. I), decretals, 1159–81: *Solet frequenter.*

19. Alexander III (bibliog. I), decretals, 1159–81: *Quod nobis.* Also, *Brundage, Law, Sex, and Christian Society* (bibliog. III), 335–36.

20. Alexander III (bibliog. I), decretals, 1159–81: *Quum locum.* Also, *Brundage, Law, Sex, and Christian Society* (bibliog. III), 335.

is so, then it might explain why he incorporates sexual intercourse into his understanding of the creation of marriage. Even if the theory is incorrect, the decretals of Alexander show that he felt that he was unable to ignore the role of intercourse within marriage. That is, even if he had not had the direct link with Gratian, he was aware that Gratian had influenced many bishops and universities with his emphasis on consummation. It is for this reason that Alexander gives a second way in which a marriage can come into existence.

In one decretal *Ex parte C.*, Alexander has to judge a case involving consent about the future. A man and a woman exchange future consent and so are engaged. They live together and have children. Eventually, the man leaves the union and claims that he has entered marriage with another woman.[21] Now, if the man had exchanged present consent with the first woman then, as just seen, he would be married to her. But in this case, the consent was about the future—it was only an engagement. Alexander rules that future consent followed by intercourse creates a binding marriage. As the man had children by the first woman, it can be concluded that he had intercourse with her. Consequently, they are bound to each other in marriage. Alexander orders the man to return to the first wife. Coriden notes other decretals in which Alexander says that consent about the future followed by intercourse creates a marriage.[22]

Therefore, Alexander gives two ways in which a

21. Alexander III (bibliog. I), decretals, 1159–81: *Ex parte C.* Also, Brundage, *Sex, Law, and Marriage* (bibliog. III), 72.

22. Coriden, *The Indissolubility Added to Christian Marriage by Consummation* (bibliog. III), 17. These are Alexander III (bibliog. I), decretals, 1159–81: *De*

marriage can come about: through the exchange of present consent, and by an engaged couple having sexual intercourse. How is the second of these methods related to the first? There are two possibilities. First, when an engaged couple has sexual intercourse, it is to be regarded as *equivalent* to them exchanging present consent. That is, it brings about a marriage. Second, that couple's sexual intercourse is an *indication* that they have in fact exchanged present consent, and it is this present consent which creates the marriage. Coriden states that there is no evidence of the second explanation in Alexander's writings. Thus, the first possibility seems the more plausible.[23]

It has been seen that, before Gratian, there had been a long and authoritative tradition within the Church which taught that consent brings a marriage into existence. On the other hand, the theory that sexual intercourse creates marriage had few advocates. Gratian's *Decretum* with its so-called synthesis changed this. After Gratian, both consent and intercourse came to be regarded as important in the creation of a marriage, and consequently, Alexander had to satisfy both the consensual aspect of marriage and the coital aspect. He did this, not by attempting to unite the two aspects, but by keeping them separate and describing *two* ways in which a marriage can be created. One way satisfies the consensual emphasis—namely, that present

illis, in Gregory IX, *Decretales* (bibliog. III), 4, 5, 3; *Veniens ad nos; Significavit nobis; De illis autem; Literae quas tua; Veniens ad apostolicam; Ex literis*, in Gregory IX, *Decretales* (bibliog. III), 4, 14, 1; and *Ex transmissa*.

23. Coriden, *The Indissolubility Added to Christian Marriage by Consummation* (bibliog. III), 16–17.

consent makes a marriage. The other way acknowledges the coital emphasis and says that engaged couples are married if they have intercourse.

It has been seen how the author of the *Summa* said that a consummated marriage contains the sacrament of Christ and his Church. Coriden makes this important observation about Alexander: "But in his decretals he failed to refer to this symbolism."[24] Although Coriden did not consider such a possibility, this omission could be taken as evidence that Alexander did not in fact write the *Summa*. Either way, Alexander does link intercourse with indissolubility in his decretals.[25] Indeed, he argues that a marriage is not absolutely indissoluble until it has been consummated. In the decretal *Ex publico*, he says that when Jesus condemned those who divorced and remarried, he was only referring to those who attempted to leave consummated marriages. Thus, unconsummated marriages do not fall under Jesus's prohibition.[26]

The fact that a marriage is not totally indissoluble until it has been consummated has consequences for the two ways in which a marriage can be created. If it comes about through the exchange of present consent, then it is not absolutely indissoluble until there is intercourse. If, however, the marriage is formed by an engaged couple having intercourse, then it is immediately totally indissoluble.

This teaching of Alexander runs throughout many

24. Ibid., 30.

25. O'Callaghan, "Studies in Moral Questions" (bibliog. III), in particular, 167–68.

26. Alexander III (bibliog. I), decretals, 1159–81: *Ex publico*. Also, Joyce, *Christian Marriage* (bibliog. III), 431–32.

of his decretals. Like Gratian, he has a concept of marital debt. Thus, once a marriage is consummated, a spouse has the right to demand of the other sexual activity when he or she so wishes. Alexander rules that not even leprosy can terminate this right.[27] Elsewhere, he says that an unconsummated marriage can be dissolved by one of the spouses entering religious life— even if the other is opposed. But the marriage cannot be dissolved once it has been consummated, although the couple could agree to live in continence.[28] Alexander's decretal *Verum post consensum* says that in the case of an unconsummated marriage, the spouse left behind when the other enters religious life is free to remarry.[29] This is proof that Alexander regards the unconsummated marriage to be actually dissolved.

Coriden quotes from a reply of Alexander to the Archbishop of Mayence which was not included in the *Liber Extra*.[30] The case involves a couple exchanging present consent. Before they consummate the marriage, the man enters a second union and consummates it. It has already been seen that Alexander would uphold the first marriage because present consent has been exchanged. But what is interesting in his reply to the Archbishop is that he says the man "could not

---

27. Alexander III (bibliog. I), decretals, 1159–81: *Pervenit ad nos:* and *Quoniam ex multis.* Also, Brundage, *Law, Sex, and Christian Society* (bibliog. III),335.

28. Alexander III (bibliog. I), decretals, 1159–81: *Commissum.* Also, Coriden, *The Indissolubility Added to Christian Marriage by Consummation* (bibliog. III), 18.

29. Alexander III (bibliog. I), decretals, 1159–81: *Verum post consensum,.* Also, Coriden, *The Indissolubility Added to Christian Marriage by Consummation* (bibliog. III), 19.

30. Coriden, *The Indissolubility Added to Christian Marriage by Consummation* (bibliog. III), 13.

be separated from the first [woman] without the judgment of the Church."[31] Alexander does not say whether the man could be separated *with* the judgment of the Church. If Alexander is allowing for such a possibility, then he believes that the Church has the authority to dissolve an unconsummated marriage simply on the grounds that it has not been consummated. The dissolution would not require specific conditions external to the marriage, such as the desire to enter religious life. Nevertheless, Coriden rightly cautions against reading too much into these words of Alexander.[32]

What is certain, though, is that Alexander regards intercourse within marriage to be so important that impotence allows the Church to declare a marriage null. This is evident in his decretals *Ex literis* and *De illis*.[33] In his decretal *Consuluit*, he states that if a couple cannot consummate their marriage, then they should live together as brother and sister.[34] Brundage wonders if there is an inconsistency between the first two decretals and *Consuluit* that made Raymond of Peñafort omit the latter from the *Liber Extra*.[35] I personally see no discrepancy. Alexander regards intercourse to be so important that a couple experiencing impotence cannot be man and wife. This is his position in the first two decretals. Although the man and woman concerned are not

31. ". . . cum a primo sine iudicio Ecclesiae separari non debuit." Coriden, *The Indissolubility Added to Christian Marriage by Consummation* (bibliog. III), 13.

32. Ibid., 14.

33. Alexander III (bibliog. I), decretals, 1159–81: *Ex literis*, in Gregory IX, *Decretales* (bibliog. III), 4, 15, 3; and *De illis*, in Gregory IX, *Decretales* (bibliog. III), 4, 2, 9.

34. Alexander III (bibliog. I), decretals, 1159–81: *Consuluit*.

35. Brundage, *Sex, Law, and Marriage* (bibliog. III), 70–71.

married, hopefully they will still live together and support each other in exactly the same way that a brother and sister can live together despite not being married. This is indeed Alexander's opinion in *Consuluit.*

There are two other decretals which stress the strong link which Alexander makes between intercourse and indissolubility. The first concerns conditional consent. It has been seen how Alexander understands the role of consent in creating a marriage. Alexander acknowledges the practice of attaching a condition to the consent. That is, the consent might take the form: "I marry you provided that X is the case." Consequently, if X is the case then they are married. If, however, it is not the case, then they are not married and each party is free to marry another person. Such a practice would be acceptable to Alexander because consent has to be completely free.

In another decretal *De illis*, he believes that intercourse removes any condition attached to the consent.[36] Therefore, in the paradigm just considered, if X was not the case, the couple would still be married if they had consummated their union. Alexander's reasoning is not clear. It might be that he believes that a couple who has married conditionally must have removed the condition if they have had intercourse. But there is no direct evidence for this interpretation. On the other hand, it might be that such a marriage is simply *equivalent* to one created without any condition. Either way, *De illis* is consistent with Alexander's other decretals.

36. Alexander III (bibliog. I), decretals, 1159–81: *De illis*, in Gregory IX, *Decretales* (bibliog. III), 4, 5, 3. Also, Brundage, *Sex, Law, and Marriage* (bibliog. III), 74–75.

That is, once a marriage is consummated it cannot be dissolved—not even if, attached to the consent, there is a condition which has not been fulfilled.

The second decretal concerns a man who exchanges consent with a woman whom he believes to be free. Later, he discovers that she is in fact a slave. In this decretal *Proposuit nobis M.*, Alexander rules that the man is not bound by the marriage unless it has been consummated.[37] There are similarities with the decision given in *De illis*. First, it acknowledges the role of consent in creating the marriage. Thus, if the consent is based upon an erroneous belief (namely, that the woman is free), then it must itself be faulty, so there can be no genuine marriage. Second, it links absolute indissolubility with consummation. Thus, even if the marriage was entered into by error, it cannot be dissolved once it has been consummated. Whatever was wrong at the start is rectified through consummation.

In summary, Alexander III taught the traditional view that consent brings a marriage into existence. By using the distinction of Peter Lombard, concerning consent about the future and consent about the present, he was able to be more precise in his description of the consent needed to create a marriage. Although Alexander was Pope, Gratian was regarded as a genius and his *Decretum* was being studied by the universities. Thus, Alexander could not ignore the role of consummation. Through his decretals, he taught that a marriage can come about by an engaged couple having sexual intercourse. This method is in addition to the traditionally

---

37. Alexander III (bibliog. I), decretals, 1159–81: *Proposuit nobis* M. Also, Brundage, *Sex, Law, and Marriage* (bibliog. III), 75.

held one whereby present consent creates a marriage. Similarly, although he teaches that a marriage is generally indissoluble, he follows Gratian's position that a marriage is not *absolutely* indissoluble until it has been consummated.

Huguccio
An Authoritative Gratian Scholar

Before I examine the contributions of Pope Innocent III, it is necessary to consider a major canonist who was influential toward the end of the twelfth century and the beginning of the thirteenth. He was Hugh of Pisa, known as Huguccio. Again, I shall make use of Coriden who gives a good summary of Huguccio's teaching on marriage.[38]

Huguccio's background is uncertain. He was both a student and a teacher at Bologna.[39] In about 1188, he wrote his *Summa,* which was an authoritative commentary on Gratian's *Decretum.*[40] For a long time it has been accepted that Huguccio taught canon law to a certain student called Lothario of Segni, who later became Pope Innocent III. It is noteworthy that a study of Innocent III has the same problems as a study of Alexander III. It has been seen that it is debated whether or not Alexander was the author of the *Summa,* which was an important abridgment to the second part of Gratian's *Decretum.* Similarly, there is a debate concerning the extent of Huguccio's link with Innocent. This debate

---

38. Coriden, *The Indissolubility Added to Christian Marriage by Consummation* (bibliog. III), 34–44.

39. Muller, *Huguccio* (bibliog. III), 21–108.

40. Roman (ed), *"Summa d'Huguccio"* (bibliog. III).

is relevant because it could explain how Gratian influenced Innocent through Huguccio.

Coriden takes the accepted view that Innocent had been a student of Huguccio and that, like him, he was a canon lawyer. Since Coriden, however, experts on medieval canon law have seriously questioned this. For example, Kenneth Pennington suggests that Innocent III was more a theologian than a canonist and that if he had been taught by Huguccio then it was only for a brief period.[41] Either way, Huguccio was an important scholar in his own right and his understanding of marriage requires a closer examination.

Huguccio, like Alexander III, does not use Gratian's distinction between an initiated and a confirmed marriage. Instead, he uses the distinction which Lombard made between future consent and present consent.[42] Again, like Alexander, Huguccio argues that present consent alone is sufficient to bring a marriage into existence. The sufficiency of present consent means that as long as a couple's consent is manifested in some fashion externally, no public ceremony is required. Thus, clandestine marriages are to be recognized as genuine.[43]

The fact that a true marriage is brought about by present consent alone means that it is, to a degree,

---

41. Pennington, *Popes, Canonists and Texts 1150–1550* (bibliog. III), essay 1: "The Legal Education of Pope Innocent III" (page numbering starts fresh with each essay), and essay 2: "Further Thoughts on Pope Innocent III's Knowledge of Law."

42. Roman (ed), *"Summa d'Huguccio"* (bibliog. III), 746. Also, Coriden, *The Indissolubility Added to Christian Marriage by Consummation* (bibliog. III), 35–36.

43. Roman (ed), *"Summa d'Huguccio"* (bibliog. III), 749–55, 761–63, 804–05. Also, Coriden, *The Indissolubility Added to Christian Marriage by Consummation* (bibliog. III),36–38.

indissoluble from the start. Huguccio says that present consent signifies the union between God and the
individual soul, but this bond is not absolutely indissoluble because the soul can be separated from God
by sin. Thus, a marriage brought about by present consent alone is not absolutely indissoluble. It can be dissolved by the entry of one of the spouses into religious
life.[44] This gave Huguccio the theological basis for the
practice of dissolving marriages through entry into religion. He could therefore give support to Pope Alexander III who allowed it. Moreover, he could defend the
discipline which had developed in the Church whereby a spouse, after exchanging present consent, had two
months in which he or she could either consummate the
marriage or enter religious life. If he or she did not consummate the marriage and, instead, chose the greater
good (*maius bonum*)[45] within the two months, then the
marriage was dissolved and the other spouse was free
to remarry.[46]

Huguccio uses a second symbolism. He regards sexual intercourse as signifying the union between Christ
and the Church. Now, unlike the bond between God
and the individual soul, this union cannot be broken.
Therefore, a marriage which has been consummated
shares in this unbreakable bond and so is absolutely
indissoluble. Only the death of one of the spouses can

---

44. Roman (ed), "*Summa d'Huguccio*" (bibliog. III), 795. Also, Coriden, *The Indissolubility Added to Christian Marriage by Consummation* (bibliog. III), 41–42.

45. Roman (ed), "*Summa d'Huguccio*" (bibliog. III), 779.

46. Ibid., 756, 779–80. Also, Coriden, *The Indissolubility Added to Christian Marriage by Consummation* (bibliog. III), 38–39.

dissolve it.[47] Like the first symbolism, the second gives
Huguccio the theological basis for defending the practice of the Church.

For Huguccio, each symbolism is so central that it
applies to every marriage—including those of the unbaptized. Indeed, he supports this by appealing directly to Saint Paul's letter to the Ephesians.[48] Huguccio
explains that when Saint Paul said that marriage symbolizes the relationship between Christ and the Church,
he made no distinction between the marriages of Christians and those of non-Christians.[49] The consequence is
that any marriage which has been consummated is absolutely indissoluble. This supersedes the earlier teaching of Hugh of Saint Victor, who said that only the marriages of the baptized are indissoluble.[50]

What about unconsummated marriages? Like Alexander, Huguccio says that when Jesus prohibited
divorce and remarriage he was referring only to consummated marriages.[51] Thus, Scripture provides no objection to the Church's practice of allowing the dissolution of an unconsummated marriage so that one spouse
may enter religious life—and the other remarry.

It is difficult to determine exactly why Huguccio's
theory of marriage is so similar to Alexander's. There
are a number of factors. First, because Pope Alexander

47. Roman (ed), "*Summa d'Huguccio*" (bibliog. III), 764. Also, Coriden, *The
Indissolubility Added to Christian Marriage by Consummation* (bibliog. III),
41–42.
48. Ephesians 5:31–32.
49. "Hoc enim probatur auctoritate Apostoli indistincte et generaliter loquen-
tis de matrimonio tam fidelium quam infidelium ubi dicitur: Hoc est magnum
sacramentum, ego autem dico in Christo et Ecclesia." Roman (ed), "*Summa
d'Huguccio*" (bibliog. III), 764.
50. Migne (ed), *Patrologiae Latina* (bibliog. III), vol. 176, 504–10.
51. Roman (ed), "*Summa d'Huguccio*" (bibliog. III), 779. Also, Coriden, *The*

had taught so authoritatively on marriage through his decretals, Huguccio would have been impelled to construct a theory which did not contradict him. Second, both Huguccio and Alexander were influenced by Gratian. Even if Alexander was not the author of the *Summa*, he found himself governing a Church which had been greatly influenced by Gratian's scholarly *Decretum*, on which Huguccio was an expert. Neither could ignore the tradition that had developed—a tradition which upheld the importance of intercourse within marriage.

It is not surprising that Huguccio's emphasis on intercourse means that he also teaches that impotence prevents a marriage from taking place. Even if they are regarded as husband and wife, the discovery that one of them was impotent at the time the marriage was entered into is sufficient for the other to be free to marry a new partner.[52]

Another consequence of this emphasis is that Huguccio teaches how a marriage can come about by a couple exchanging future consent and following it with intercourse. That is, an engaged couple having intercourse are in fact married. He acknowledges that Alexander also taught this. Unlike Alexander, however, he clearly states that sexual intercourse by an engaged couple is an indication that they have in fact exchanged present consent.[53] Thus, it is not the intercourse which

---

Indissolubility Added to Christian Marriage by Consummation (bibliog. III), 43.

52. Roman (ed), "*Summa d'Huguccio*" (bibliog. III), 782. The existing marriage would be upheld if impotence only developed during the actual course of the marriage. Also, Coriden, *The Indissolubility Added to Christian Marriage by Consummation* (bibliog. III), 44.

53. Roman (ed), "*Summa d'Huguccio*" (bibliog. III), 755, 801, 804. Also, Coriden, *The Indissolubility Added to Christian Marriage by Consummation* (bibliog. III), 44.

creates the marriage, but the present consent—the existence of which is manifested by the intercourse. This difference does not undermine Alexander's position. On the contrary, it firmly underpins his argument. Both ways of marrying (exchanging present consent, or exchanging future consent and then having intercourse) are based upon the ancient understanding that consent makes marriage.

Pope Innocent III
Uniformity of Church Practice
Based on Gratian

The Popes who followed Alexander III gave very similar judgments on marriage cases. The teachings of Lucius III, Urban III, and Celestine III were consistent with Alexander's teaching.[54] The next Pope to consider in more depth is Innocent III. He became Pope in 1198. As Brundage explains, "The new Pope [Innocent III] insisted more fiercely than Alexander had on the principle that Catholic marriage law must be uniform and that local variations on fundamental issues must be discouraged."[55] Innocent is important because it was his teaching on marriage, promoted through his decretals, that became universal.

Innocent III, like Alexander III and Huguccio, uses the distinction between future consent and present consent.[56] Present consent alone creates a marriage. This consent should be expressed externally in

---

54. Coriden, *The Indissolubility Added to Christian Marriage by Consummation* (bibliog. III),23–26.

55. Brundage, *Law, Sex, and Christian Society* (bibliog. III), 338.

56. Innocent III (bibliog. I), decretals, 1198–1216: *Tuas dudum*.

words or signs.[57] Innocent also allows a marriage created through present consent, which has not been consummated, to be dissolved by the entry of one of the
spouses into religious life.[58] Although it is difficult to
evaluate his opinion on this last point, in the decretal
Ex parte tua, he acknowledges that he is permitting the
practice because he does not feel that he can go against
the decisions of previous Popes: "However, we are unwilling to turn suddenly away from the footsteps of our
predecessors in this matter."[59]

I would say that this is very important. Just as Huguccio felt that he had to support the judgments of such
Popes as Alexander III, so did Innocent. Sexual intercourse had become an important factor in the Church's
matrimonial discipline. Innocent felt he had no authority to contradict this tradition and the Popes who had
upheld it. The consequence was that Innocent also became a part of this tradition, continuing it and strengthening it. Similarly, the Popes who followed him did not
feel that they had the authority to contradict him.

The fact that Innocent inherited a tradition which
gave much weight to consummation shows itself in four
other areas. In each of these areas his teaching is consistent with Alexander's. First, he reaffirms that a consummated marriage, unlike an unconsummated one, is
absolutely indissoluble. Only the death of a spouse can
break the marital bond. Not even entry into religious life

---

57. Innocent III (bibliog. I), decretals, 1198–1216: *Quum apud sedem.*

58. Innocent III (bibliog. I), decretals, 1198–1216: *Fraternitatis tuae.*

59. ". . . nos tamen nolentes a praedecessorum nostrorum vestigiis in hoc ar-
ticulo subito declinare." Innocent III (bibliog. I), decretals, 1198–1216: *Ex parte
tua*. Also, Coriden, *The Indissolubility Added to Christian Marriage by Consummation* (bibliog. III), 48–49.

can dissolve it.[60] Second, he says that the exchange of future consent followed by sexual intercourse results in a marriage. He takes Huguccio's position and says that the act of intercourse is a sign that present consent has in fact been exchanged.[61] Innocent uses this principle in his decretal *Tuas dudum*. In this decretal he deals with a concrete example. An engaged person meets a new partner and marries him. This marriage is consummated. To whom is the person married? Like Alexander, Innocent says that if present consent had been exchanged with the first partner, then the individual in question would be married to him. Otherwise, the consummation of the union with the second suggests that present consent had been exchanged with him—in which case, the second union would be the true marriage.[62]

The third area which emphasizes the role of intercourse is impotence. In the decretal *Fraternitatis tuae*, he deals with an actual case in which a couple was unable to consummate marriage because of a severe discrepancy in the sizes of their sexual organs. Innocent rules that both are free to remarry.[63] With regard to impotence, Brundage explains, "Innocent III's successor, Honorius III, decided that inability to consummate a marriage after three years of vain efforts constituted sufficient proof that the condition was real."[64] The fourth area concerns those who have married conditionally. In

---

60. Innocent III (bibliog. I), decretals, 1198–1216: *Constitutus in praesentia*.

61. Innocent III (bibliog. I), decretals, 1198–1216: *Tua nos duxit*. Also, Coriden, *The Indissolubility Added to Christian Marriage by Consummation* (bibliog. III), 49–50.

62. Innocent III (bibliog. I), decretals, 1198–1216: *Tuas dudum*.

63. Innocent III (bibliog. I), decretals, 1198–1216: *Fraternitatis tuae*. Also, *Brundage, Law, Sex, and Christian Society* (bibliog. III), 339.

64. Brundage, *Law, Sex, and Christian Society* (bibliog. III), 339. Honorius III's decretal is Honorius III (bibliog. I), decretal, 1216–27: *Literae vestrae*.

these cases, as Alexander had said, sexual intercourse makes any condition of the consent irrelevant.[65]

Innocent appears to have doubts when it comes to the marriages of the unbaptized.[66] In his decretal *De infidelibus*, he argues that the marriages of non-Christians are as indissoluble as those of Christians. His reasoning is very similar to Huguccio's. He says the principle that a marriage is created by freely given consent and is made absolutely indissoluble by sexual intercourse pertains to all marriages.[67] This would suggest that he was against dissolving non-Christian marriages except on grounds used to dissolve Christian ones.

This is consistent with another decretal. In *Gaudemus in Domino*, he considers a problem which was to become more common a few centuries later with the spread of missionary work. He is faced with the issue of an unbaptized man who has more than one wife and who becomes a Christian. He rules that he must remain with his first wife and dismiss the others.[68] Innocent's decision shows that he regards the man's first non-Christian marriage to be as indissoluble as if it were a Christian marriage. This is confirmed by a second example in the same decretal. Innocent states that a non-Christian who marries, divorces, and then becomes a Christian must dismiss any present partners and return to his first wife. If she has remarried, then he is still bound to her and so cannot remarry until she dies.

There is, however, a problem. The Church had been

---

65. Innocent III (bibliog. I), decretals, 1198–1216: *Per tuas*. Also, Coriden, *The Indissolubility Added to Christian Marriage by Consummation* (bibliog. III), 50.

66. Brundage, *Law, Sex, and Christian Society* (bibliog. III), 340.

67. Innocent III (bibliog. I), decretals, 1198–1216: *De infidelibus*.

68. Innocent III (bibliog. I), decretals, 1198–1216: *Gaudemus in Domino*.

allowing the dissolution of non-Christian marriages on the basis of the first letter written by Saint Paul to the Corinthians.[69] It has been seen how Gratian defended this practice.[70] It is impossible to look into Innocent's mind to see if there was indeed any conflict between following a line of reasoning similar to Huguccio's and having to defend the practice of the Church. Either way, he did issue another decretal in which he defends the Church's discipline. In *Quanto te*,[71] he examines the case of two married non-Christians. One converts to Christianity and receives baptism. The non-Christian spouse refuses to live with him or makes it most difficult for him to live out his Christian duties. Innocent declares the Christian free to remarry.

Gratian's Legacy

It is not certain whether the Master Roland who wrote an abridgment to the second part of Gratian's *Decretum* was Roland Bandinelli who became Pope Alexander III. It is also not clear whether Huguccio, who wrote an authoritative commentary on the *Decretum*, personally taught the future Innocent III at any length. But what is absolutely certain is that Gratian's *Decretum* had so influenced the Church that such scholars as Master Roland and Huguccio were focusing on it. Therefore, both Alexander III and Innocent III took on the leadership of the Church at a time when its scholars, universities, and clergy were concentrating on the *Decretum*.

---

69. 1 Corinthians 7:15.

70. Gratian, *Concordia* (bibliog. III), Part 2, Case 28, Question 2, especially dictum after ch. 2.

71. Innocent III (bibliog. I), decretals, 1198–1216: *Quanto te*.

It has been seen how, up until Gratian, the consensual understanding of marriage had been constant and strong. Through his *Decretum*, like Hincmar of Rheims previously, Gratian shifted more importance onto consummation. By this, attention was drawn away from marital love and was focused more on sexual intercourse. Consequently, although Alexander III makes it clear that present consent creates a marriage, he cannot ignore the new emphasis on the role of intercourse in the creation of marriage and its indissolubility. For example, a marriage is created when an engaged couple has intercourse. Moreover, intercourse is regarded as so important that impotence is a bar to marriage. It has been seen that Alexander's teaching on marriage is then given a theological basis by Huguccio. Consequently, Alexander's decisions—such as those concerning the dissolution of unconsummated marriages by entry into religious life—appear to be very well-founded.

Innocent III wishes to uphold the traditional teaching that consent makes marriage. Thus, like Alexander and Huguccio, he uses Lombard's distinction between future consent and present consent. He stresses that present consent makes marriage, but he cannot ignore the decisions of his predecessors. Thus, he acknowledges Alexander's teaching that engagement followed by intercourse creates a marriage. At the same time, as Huguccio had done, he upholds the primacy of present consent in the creation of all marriages. Therefore, intercourse between the engaged is an indication that present consent has been exchanged.

Although he is hesitant about permitting the dissolution of unconsummated marriages by entry into religious life, he does so because he feels that he cannot go
against his predecessors. Consequently, he maintains
the distinction between an unconsummated marriage,
which is *relatively* indissoluble, and a consummated one
which is *absolutely* indissoluble. Similarly, although his
understanding of marriage applies equally to both the
marriages of Christians and non-Christians, he bows to
the tradition which had developed that allows the dissolution of a marriage between two non-Christians where
one converts and the other refuses to remain.

Gratian was regarded as a genius, and his *Decretum* as a scholarly masterpiece. Consequently, Alexander III felt obliged to give decisions which incorporated
Gratian's conclusions. Huguccio was also strongly influenced by the great Gratian. Furthermore, Huguccio
felt religiously obliged to give theological support to
decisions given by Alexander. Finally, Innocent III felt
reluctant to go against the decisions of his predecessor
Alexander. Thus, Innocent had to support him, and a
new tradition was started in the Church.

The marriage section of the *Liber Extra* contains
many of Alexander's decretals. This authoritative collection was the official law of the Church for seven centuries. Moreover, the decretals of Innocent halted any
contrary practices. Although Gratian's *Decretum* in itself was never an official source of ecclesiastical law, it
influenced the Church universally and powerfully for
many centuries.

—10—

The Sixteenth Century
A Time of New Challenges
for the Church

The Council of Trent and Marriage

DURING THE SIXTEENTH CENTURY, the Catholic Church felt that it was being confronted by a number of errors and criticisms. The Protestant Reformation was seen to give rise to the necessity of affirming that marriage is one of the sacraments instituted by Christ.[1] Also, the Church's teaching on monogamy was being questioned. King Henry VIII of England was in dispute with Rome because he wished to remarry. Philip Melanchthon argued that since holy men in the Old Testament, such as Abraham and David, had more than one wife, polygamy could not be said to be against divine law. Melanchthon thus suggested that, instead of Henry questioning the validity of his existing marriage, he could simply take another wife.[2] Indeed, it was argued by some that although Christ had forbidden divorce and remarriage he never referred to simultaneous polygamy.[3]

---

1. Schillebeeckx, *Marriage: Human Reality and Saving Mystery* (bibliog. III), 359.
2. Hillman, "Polygamy and the Council of Trent" (bibliog. III), in particular, 363–64.
3. Ibid., 365.

131

Luther also criticized the Church's practice of dissolving marriages. First, he said that marriages can be dissolved not only by reason of impotence but also for adultery and the refusal to have sexual intercourse. He taught that the Church is wrong to say that adultery does not dissolve marriage. Second, he taught that the Church has no authority to dissolve marriages for any other reason.[4] Luther also said that the Church was negligent in allowing clandestine marriages. Such marriages gave rise to abuses. For example, married men would pretend that they were single in order to "remarry." To halt such crimes, Luther wanted marriages to be put under stricter control. Indeed, he wanted the consent of both sets of parents to be a necessary condition for a valid marriage. Without such consent, he would regard the marriage to be invalid—even if there had been sexual intercourse and children produced.[5]

As Schillebeeckx observes, the whole matter of the Church's jurisdiction over marriage was also questioned.[6] In the early years of the Church, it was the state which determined the regulations concerning the celebration of marriage. Was the Church now going beyond its authority with its rules on marriage? This was a dangerous question, because if the control of marriage shifted too far away from the Church, then marriage might be seen only in secular terms and would, as a consequence, not be understood sacramentally.

---

4. Lehman (ed), *The Christian in Society* (bibliog. III), in particular, Luther, "Sermon on the Estate of Marriage" in vol. 45, 17–49. For example, Luther would not accept the Church's practice of dissolving unconsummated marriages by religious profession.

5. Luther, "On Marriage Matters," ibid., vol. 46, 259–320.

6. Schillebeeckx, *Marriage: Human Reality and Saving Mystery* (bibliog. III), 361.

It was decided to convene a council so that the Church could address the issues raised by the Protestant Reformation—including those concerning marriage. It took some time to draw together so many bishops as well as experts in theology and law. Eventually, the Council of Trent opened on the thirteenth day of December in 1545.[7] As the eminent twentieth-century Catholic historian Hubert Jedin notes, "It was a difficult and laborious start. It took a long time to get the technical machinery of the Council functioning."[8] Indeed, matters relating to marriage were not discussed until 1563.

At the twenty-fourth session, under Pope Pius IV, the Council promulgated its "Doctrine Concerning the Sacrament of Marriage."[9] In it, the Council teaches that marriage was from the very beginning perpetual and indissoluble. To support this, it quotes from Genesis: "This one at last is bone of my bones and flesh of my flesh! This is why a man leaves his father and mother and becomes attached to his wife, and they become one flesh."[10] The Council notes that Christ himself confirmed this teaching: "They are no longer two, therefore, but one flesh," and "So then, what God has united, human beings must not divide."[11] Trent's text goes on to state that marriage is a sacrament instituted by Christ. Thus, the natural love which exists in marriage is

---

7. Jedin, *A History of the Council of Trent* (bibliog. III), 13.
8. Ibid., 14.
9. Council of Trent (bibliog. I), Session 24, *Doctrina de Sacramento Matrimonii,* 11 November 1563. English translation in Schroeder (tr), *The Canons and Decrees of the Council of Trent* (bibliog. III), 180–82.
10. From Genesis 2:23.
11. Matthew 19:6 and Mark 10:9.

perfected by the grace of the sacrament. Moreover, this grace confirms the indissoluble bond and sanctifies the spouses. Therefore, Christian marriage confirms the indissolubility which is present naturally in marriage.

Trent uses the letter written by Saint Paul to the Ephesians in order to support its teaching that marriage is a sacrament: "Husbands should love their wives, just as Christ loved the Church and sacrificed himself for her," and "This mystery (*sacramentum*) has great significance, but I am applying it to Christ and the Church."[12] Nevertheless, as Schillebeeckx observes, the Council's final draft only states that Saint Paul "suggests" (*innuit*) that marriage is a sacrament.[13] Thus, Trent avoids basing its teaching about the sacramentality of marriage solely on Saint Paul. In doing so, any attack by the Protestant Reformers on this interpretation of Paul would not gravely undermine the Catholic Church's argument.

The Council concludes its "Doctrine Concerning the Sacrament of Marriage" with twelve canons.[14] Each canon condemns a particular statement about marriage which was regarded as erroneous by Trent. In this way, each canon either defends or promotes a certain teaching of the Council about marriage.

The very first canon condemns those who deny that marriage is a sacrament instituted by Christ. In doing

---

12. Ephesians 5:25 and 5:32. The whole of Trent's quotation of 5:32 reads, "Sacramentum hoc magnum est; ego autem dico, in Christo et in Ecclesia." Denzinger, *Enchiridion Symbolorum* (bibliog. III), 415.

13. Schillebeeckx, Marriage: Human Reality and Saving Mystery (bibliog. III), 359, and Denzinger, *Enchiridion Symbolorum* (bibliog. III), 415.

14. Denzinger, *Enchiridion Symbolorum* (bibliog. III), 416–17, and Schroeder (tr), *The Canons and Decrees of the Council of Trent* (bibliog. III), 181–82.

so, the Council is reaffirming that marriage is a spiritual matter and so falls within its competency. This authority of the Church is defended by six other canons which I shall now outline. Canon three refers to Leviticus which lists those family members who cannot have intercourse together (for example, brother and sister).[15] The canon states that these very people cannot marry. Moreover, it asserts that the Church has the authority to dispense from some of these prohibitions, where the relationship is not too close, as well as introduce other ones.

Similarly, the next canon states that the Church can establish impediments which prevent marriage. Two such impediments are given in canon nine: neither a cleric in sacred orders nor a religious with a solemn vow of chastity can marry validly. Canon eight defends the Church's authority to allow married couples to live apart.[16] The eleventh canon upholds the Church's power to prohibit the celebration of marriage at certain times of the year. Then, canon twelve reaffirms that ecclesiastical judges are competent to hear marriage cases. It is important to note that none of these canons denies the jurisdiction of civil authorities over marriage, but the canons make it clear that marriage is primarily a spiritual matter and so the Church also has real jurisdiction.

Philip Melanchthon's suggestion that polygamy could be permissible is condemned by canon two. Canon seven states that adultery does not dissolve marriage. Even the innocent party cannot remarry while the other party is still alive, and to do so would itself

---

15. Leviticus 18:6–18.

16. Such couples would still be married to each other, however, and so could not enter into marriage with others.

be adultery. It is important to note that the canon does not actually condemn those who teach that remarriage is permissible in the case of adultery. Its condemnation is for those who teach that the Church is wrong to say that such remarriages are not allowed. The distinction is small but very important. The Greek Church allowed remarriage in the case of adultery, but it did not teach that the Latin Church was wrong to forbid it. On the other hand, Luther not only said that such remarriages were permissible, but that the Church was wrong to prohibit them.[17] Thus, the Council's seventh canon manages to condemn Luther while not damaging relations with the Greek Church.[18]

The indissolubility of marriage is also upheld by canon five, which confirms that a marriage cannot be dissolved by heresy, troublesome cohabitation,[19] or by the voluntary absence of one spouse from the other. But the next canon, against Luther, defends the Church's practice of dissolving unconsummated marriages by religious profession.

Therefore, Trent's "Doctrine Concerning the Sacrament of Marriage" upholds the sacramentality of marriage, the Church's authority over marriage, and its practices. Moreover, it condemns those who call these into question.[20]

17. Lehman (ed), *The Christian in Society* (bibliog. III), vol. 45, 30–35.

18. Denzinger, *Enchiridion Symbolorum* (bibliog. III), 416, footnote to canon 7. Also, Schillebeeckx, *Marriage: Human Reality and Saving Mystery* (bibliog. III), 359–60.

19. "Troublesome cohabitation" was not regarded by the Catholic Church as a reason to dissolve a Christian marriage. As will be seen in this section, however, it could give rise to the dissolution of a non-Christian one by the granting of the Pauline Privilege if the non-Christian spouse was the cause of the trouble.

20. For the sake of completeness, the only canon I have not referred to is number ten. This condemns those who teach that the married state is higher than

The Council of Trent
and How Consent is to be Exchanged

It has been seen that one of Luther's complaints against the Church was that it tolerated clandestine marriages. The Council of Trent discussed the matter. There was a problem. Luther was correct in saying that clandestine marriages would sometimes give rise to abuses—such as a husband denying that he was married and so committing bigamy. But what could be the alternative? The Church had been teaching authoritatively that present consent exchanged by a couple is sufficient to create a marriage. To say that a clandestine marriage is invalid, where such mutual consent has been given, would be to contradict this teaching. Consequently, the bishops and their experts in theology and law debated the issue thoroughly. One side thought that as consent was sufficient it was not possible to declare clandestine marriage invalid; the other side of the debate was in favor of such a declaration to halt abuses. The debate was fought on a number of fronts.

With regard to Scripture, it was noted that there is no biblical text which supports the prevention of clandestine marriages.[21] One proponent of invalidating clandestine marriages said, however, that in Adam's marriage, God himself acted as his father who consented, that he was the priest who gave the blessing, that he was the bridesman who performed and that,

the state of virginity or celibacy, as well as those who teach that it is not better to remain in virginity or celibacy than to marry.

21. Societas Goerresiana (ed), *Concilium Tridentinum* (bibliog. III), vol. 9, 642. An excellent article on the debate is Di Mattia, "*La Dottrina*" (bibliog. III), in particular, 477–88.

together with the angels, he witnessed the marriage. Thus, every marriage since the first one has been celebrated openly and publicly. Hence, no marriage ought to be celebrated secretly. If it is, then it is from Satan. Therefore, clandestine marriages must be prevented.[22]

Those wishing to prohibit clandestine marriages not only won the scriptural argument, they also used logical arguments *a fortiori*. They said that if parents can prevent clandestine marriages, then so can the Church.[23] Moreover, if secular princes and even pagan princes can prohibit them, then the Church must also have the same authority.[24]

During the previous year, at the twenty-first session of the Council, communion under both kinds was discussed, as well as the reception of communion by small children. It had been stated then, in the final draft, that the Church has the authority to determine or change the way in which sacraments are received while preserving the very substance of them. The Council declared that it has this authority with regard to the Eucharist. It can thus determine whether or not communion should be received under one or both kinds as well as the minimum age for reception.[25] The final text quotes from the first letter written by Saint Paul to the Corinthians:

---

22. Societas Goerresiana (ed), *Concilium Tridentinum* (bibliog. III), 9, 387. Also, Di Mattia, "*La Dottrina*" (bibliog. III), 480.

23. Societas Goerresiana (ed), *Concilium Tridentinum* (bibliog. III), 9, 380. Also, Di Mattia, "*La Dottrina*" (bibliog. III), 480.

24. Societas Goerresiana (ed), *Concilium Tridentinum* (bibliog. III), 9, 650. Also, Di Mattia, "*La Dottrina*" (bibliog. III), 482–83.

25. Council of Trent (bibliog. I), Session 21, *Doctrina de Communione sub utraque Specie et Parvulorum*, 16 July 1562. English translation in Schroeder (tr), *The Canons and Decrees of the Council of Trent* (bibliog. III), 133.

"People should think of us as Christ's servants, stewards entrusted with the mysteries of God."[26]

In order for the Church to be "entrusted with the mysteries of God," it is necessary for it to be given sufficient power to determine their use. Chapter eleven of the same letter of Saint Paul is also used: "So then, my brothers, when you meet for the Meal, wait for each other; anyone who is hungry should eat at home. Then your meeting will not bring you condemnation. The other matters I shall arrange when I come."[27] The Council quotes the final sentence to show that Saint Paul himself had the authority to regulate the way in which the Eucharist was celebrated.[28] Trent teaches that the bishops, as successors to Saint Paul and the Apostles, must also have this authority.

Now, it was thought by a number at Trent that they had the same authority with regard to marriage. That is, they could determine the way in which marriages are to be celebrated—so that secret ones could be declared invalid. But those opposed to invalidating clandestine marriages pointed out that, although the Church has the authority to regulate the sacraments, it is not able to change what is essential to them. Thus, the Patriarch of Venice argued that the Church has no authority to state that consent is insufficient for a valid marriage—because consent is essential to marriage.[29]

---

26. 1 Corinthians 4:1. Denzinger, *Enchiridion Symbolorum* (bibliog. III), 406.

27. 1 Corinthians 11:33–34.

28. Denzinger, *Enchiridion Symbolorum* (bibliog. III), 406.

29. Societas Goerresiana (ed), *Concilium Tridentinum* (bibliog. III), 9, 407 and 643. Also, Di Mattia, "*La Dottrina*" (bibliog. III), 481, 484.

He distinguished between what is essential to marriage and what is accidental. Consent is essential, but the external ceremonies are only accidental. Thus, a clandestine marriage has all that is essential and necessary.

This distinction seemed to be winning the debate, but those wishing to ban clandestine marriages came up with their own distinction. They distinguished between the sacrament of marriage and the contract.[30] When a Christian marriage exists, it is a sacrament, but it is brought about by a form of contract between the couple—that is, they agree to marry each other. Thus, even if the Church does not have the authority to regulate matters pertaining to the essentials of the sacrament of marriage, it does have the authority to determine how the contract is to be made. Hence, if the required form of contract is not followed, then the contract is invalid. No contract means that there is no marriage and thus no sacrament.[31]

Those in favor of such a distinction used another *a fortiori* argument. They pointed out that the Church's tribunals have the authority to declare a person's consent to be invalid—for example, in the case of a man marrying out of fear. He does not really wish to marry, but is too frightened not to. Now, if the Church can declare consent (which is essential to marriage) to be invalid, then how much easier it is for the Church to declare the marital contract invalid because it does not follow the prescribed form.[32]

This argument persuaded more members of the

30. Societas Goerresiana (ed), *Concilium Tridentinum* (bibliog. III), 9, 404.
31. Ibid., 650.
32. Ibid. Also, Di Mattia, "*La Dottrina*" (bibliog. III), 483.

Council to support the prevention of clandestine marriages. It raised a fundamental question, however. Why should those marriages which fail to follow the prescribed formula be invalid? The Patriarch of Aquila provided the reason: Those persons attempting to enter such marriages would in fact be "unable" (*inhabiles*) to marry.[33] This answer satisfied many, but those opposed to banning clandestine marriages put up one last obstacle. "Inability" had traditionally been linked with a cause inherent to the person—inseparably joined to him. For example, a man who is already married is unable to marry another woman. Wherever he goes, he cannot remove this obstacle. But the inability associated with not following the prescribed form of marriage is not inherent to the person. The answer to this problem now seems obvious, but it was a breakthrough at the Council. The inability comes about through the act not the person.[34] Therefore, if the Church were to lay down a public form of marriage, then anyone not following it would, by the very act itself, be unable to marry. Hence, his or her marriage would be invalid—despite the giving of consent. The majority of those at Trent voted in favor of this, although fifty remained opposed to it.[35]

It was thus agreed that clandestine marriages were to be prohibited. The way in which this was to be done was by demanding that there be sufficient witnesses to

---

33. Societas Goerresiana (ed), *Concilium Tridentinum* (bibliog. III), 9, 643. Also, Di Mattia, "*La Dottrina*" (bibliog. III), 483.

34. Societas Goerresiana (ed), *Concilium Tridentinum* (bibliog. III), 9, 644. Also, Di Mattia, "*La Dottrina*" (bibliog. III), 485.

35. Societas Goerresiana (ed), *Concilium Tridentinum* (bibliog. III), 9, 977. Also, Di Mattia, "*La Dottrina*" (bibliog. III), 487.

a marriage. Initially three witnesses were proposed. It was suggested that one of these be a public notary. Instead, it was decided that it would be more convenient to have the parish priest, or another authorized priest, whose presence might be needed in any case in order to dispense from certain impediments.[36]

Schillebeeckx's interpretation of the Council's decision seems to me to be both correct and pertinent. The necessity of the presence of a priest was not meant to detract from the state's authority over marriage. It was simply meant to provide a convenient way of proving that the marriage had occurred. The necessity of a priest did have the side-effect of transferring more marriages away from the civil authorities to the Church, but there is no proof that this was either deliberately or principally intended.[37] It has already been seen that although Trent made it clear that the Church has authority over marriage, it did not deny that the state also has jurisdiction.

The Council's "Decree Concerning the Reform of Matrimony" was promulgated on 11 November 1563. It is commonly known by the first word of its text—*Tametsi*.[38] It begins with an acknowledgment that consent, freely given, creates a marriage. For this reason, children can genuinely marry without the consent of their parents. This counters Luther who taught that

---

36. Societas Goerresiana (ed), *Concilium Tridentinum* (bibliog. III), 9, 656, and 760–71, and 888–90.
37. Schillebeeckx, *Marriage: Human Reality and Saving Mystery* (bibliog. III), 366.
38. Council of Trent (bibliog. I), Session 24, *Canones super Reformatione circa Matrimonium*: Decretum Tametsi, 11 November 1563. English translation in Schroeder (tr), *The Canons and Decrees of the Council of Trent* (bibliog. III), 183–85.

such permission was necessary for validity.[39] *Tametsi* goes on to say that, for good reasons, the Church has forbidden children to marry without their parents' permission. That is, although such marriages are valid, they are unlawful. Despite its rejection of Luther's position regarding the marriage of children, *Tametsi* does accept that clandestine marriages can give rise to serious abuses. Therefore, as agreed by the debate, it proposes that in future all marriages be public.

Tametsi requires the parish priest of the parties to announce publicly during Mass, on three successive feast days, the names of those intending to marry. In this way, anyone who knows why a marriage should not take place (for example, if the man is already married) has an opportunity to inform the priest and so prevent the wedding. To avoid delay, however, the rule about announcing names may be relaxed. What is necessary, though, is that the marriage takes place in the presence of the couple's parish priest and two or three other witnesses. Without this, the marriage is invalid.

Moreover, severe ecclesiastical penalties are to be applied to priests or lay people who ignore this new precept. Once the priest has heard the couple's mutual consent, he is to declare them married in accordance with local rites and customs. This priest, or another with permission, is to bestow the Church's blessing. *Tametsi* exhorts couples not to live together until they have received such a blessing. As a further tool for preventing abuse, the decree instructs priests to keep

39. Lehman (ed), *The Christian in Society* (bibliog. III), vol. 46, 259–320.

marriage registers that will provide proof of marriages. Finally, it addresses the spiritual good of the couple. It exhorts them to go to Confession and to attend Mass before marrying. Failing that, it encourages them to receive these sacraments at least three days before consummating their marriage.

What were the consequences of *Tametsi*? In short, they can be put into two categories: foreseen and unforeseen. With regard to the foreseen consequences, *Tametsi* was not intended to be retroactive. That is, clandestine marriages which had already been celebrated remained valid. Indeed, for the instruction to come into force in a particular parish it had to be promulgated (read out) in that parish. It would then come into force thirty days later. Only then would clandestine marriages in that parish be invalid. Moreover, it was agreed that the decree should not be promulgated in Protestant areas and regions with few priests. Otherwise, the majority of marriages in these areas would be invalid because very few would be celebrated in front of a Catholic priest.[40]

There were also unforeseen consequences. In many parishes, priests never read out the decree and so it was not promulgated. Thus, clandestine marriages remained valid in those parishes. Also, it eventually became very difficult to remember in which parishes the decree was actually in force. Another problem was that the priest required for the wedding was the parish priest of the couple. This gave rise to many complications: What if the man and the woman were from different parish-

---

40. Barry, "The Tridentine Form of Marriage" (bibliog. III), in particular, 163.

es? Who was their parish priest? What if the wedding was to take place outside the parish of their own parish priest? What if the man lived in a parish where *Tametsi* had been promulgated and his bride lived in one where it had not? Later, questions arose about the validity of non-Catholic and mixed marriages celebrated in areas where the decree was in force.[41]

Another unfortunate consequence arose from the fact that the priest was only required to *hear* the exchange of consent. It was not necessary for him to say or do anything. He was only involved passively. In short, his presence alone would be sufficient as long as he could hear. This meant that it was possible for young members of the Church to marry against their parents' wishes: "But *Tametsi* scored no decisive victory over young Catholics in their campaign to marry partners of their choice. Many took to the practice of 'the surprise marriage.' By careful plotting they could arrange, with two or three sympathetic friends, to break into the pastor's residence in the small hours of the morning, shake the pastor awake and quickly pronounce their wedding vows in his hearing. They thus fulfilled the requirement of *Tametsi*: they had declared their consent *in facie Ecclesiae*, and the pastor would afterward have to admit that he had heard their vows."[42]

It was a number of centuries before the problems with *Tametsi* were rectified. In 1741, Pope Benedict XIV excluded non-Catholics from the requirements of *Tametsi* when they either married amongst themselves

41. Ibid., 163–64. Also, Dunderdale, "The Canonical Form of Marriage" (bibliog. III), in particular, 45.
42. Mackin, *What is Marriage?* (bibliog. III), 222, footnote 5.

or married Catholics.[43] Although this exemption from Benedict was initially intended only for the Low Countries, it was gradually extended to other countries.[44] Then, in 1907, the Sacred Congregation of the Council, under Pope Pius X, issued its decree, *Ne temere*, which simplified the norms of *Tametsi*.[45]

Ne temere acquired the force of law on 19 April 1908 and immediately clarified matters in three ways. First, it was universal. Hence, it did not need to be promulgated separately in each parish. There was thus no question as to whether or not it had been promulgated for a particular parish. Second, the priest who was required to be present was the parish priest of the place in which the wedding was being celebrated (or another priest with the necessary faculties). Hence, complicated questions relating to where the couple lived and who was their parish priest were no longer so important. Third, the priest had to take an active role in the wedding. It was no longer sufficient that he be merely present. He had to *ask* in a deliberate manner for the consent of each party as well as hear it. Thus, "the surprise marriage" became a thing of the past.[46]

Unlike *Tametsi*, *Ne temere* provides a solution to another difficult pastoral problem. What would happen if a Catholic couple wishes to marry when there is no authorized priest available? Would marriage be impossible? What about any natural right to marry that the

---

43. Benedict XIV (bibliog. I), Declaration, *Matrimonia quae in locis,*, 4 November 1741.
44. Barry, "The Tridentine Form of Marriage" (bibliog. III), 163.
45. Sacred Congregation of the Council (bibliog. I), Decree *Ne temere*.
46. Bouscaren and Ellis, Canon Law: *A Text and Commentary*, 573–74.

couple might have? Would any children have to be illegitimate? *Ne temere* introduces the "extraordinary" form of marriage for when no priest is available for a period of a month. It allows the exchange of consent in front of two witnesses alone.

In summary, despite the practical problems with *Tametsi*, the Council of Trent manages to clarify the Church's teaching on marriage. It makes it clear that the Church has jurisdiction over marriage because it is a spiritual matter. Indeed, marriage is one of the sacraments instituted by Christ. This jurisdiction means that the Church can define impediments which prevent marriage as well as dispense from them. One example of the Church's authority over marriage is the introduction of the necessity of marrying in front of a priest and witnesses in order to prevent clandestine marriages. Trent upholds the ancient teaching that mutual consent makes marriage, but it teaches that the Church has the authority to determine how this consent is to be exchanged.

Sixteenth-Century Extensions to Gratian's Pauline Privilege

Trent taught how a marriage comes into existence. But what sort of marriage is it? Once a marriage has been created, how indissoluble is it? On this subject it has been seen that Saint Paul's First Letter to the Corinthians contains a passage which can be interpreted in two ways.[47] One of the interpretations suggests that a marriage can be dissolved, albeit under a strict set of circumstances. Saint Paul considers the case of a non-

---

47. 1 Corinthians 7:12–16, especially verse 15.

Christian married couple—one of whom converts to Christianity. The unbaptized spouse refuses to live with the Christian party and leaves. Saint Paul says that the separation can take place and that the Christian spouse "is no longer tied." The ambiguity arises with this phrase. Is Paul saying quite simply that the Christian party, although still bound by the marriage, does not have to live with his or her spouse? On the other hand, is Paul being more radical? Is he saying that the Christian is no longer bound by the marriage itself—and so is free to remarry?

There is very little evidence to suggest that the early Church allowed such remarriages. While the Church developed her understanding of certain aspects of marriage, such as indissolubility, it is quite possible that regional variations under certain ecclesiastical authorities might have allowed remarriages. The authorities examined so far, however, certainly have very little to say on the matter.

It has been noted how the twelfth-century scholar Hugh of Saint Victor taught that only the marriages of Christians are indissoluble. He explains that one does not automatically receive the spiritual benefits of the sacraments. That is, if one does not receive baptism sincerely, then one does not experience the forgiveness of sins which baptism can bring. Similarly, if one partakes of the Eucharist unworthily, then one does not merit any spiritual sharing with Christ. In the same way, if one is not baptized, then one cannot enjoy the spiritual fruits of marriage—such as indissolubility.[48]

---

48. Hugh of St. Victor, *De Sacramento Coniugii* (bibliog. III).

It has also been seen that the influential writer Gratian examined the subject. In his *Decretum*, he concludes that the Christian spouse can remarry.[49] Moreover, Gratian bases his argument explicitly on the passage of Saint Paul.

It is not until Pope Innocent III that one finds an authoritative statement permitting remarriage in the case in question. In two decretals, *De infidelibus* and *Gaudemus in Domino*, he states that the marriages of non-Christians are as indissoluble as those of Christians.[50] The Church—influenced by Gratian—had been allowing converts to Christianity to remarry, however, if their unbaptized spouses refused to live with them or made it very difficult for them to carry out their Christian duties. Thus, in another decretal, *Quanto te*, Innocent III allows such a remarriage.[51] In doing so, Innocent draws his authority more from the existing practice of the Church than from Saint Paul's text.

Therefore, since the twelfth and thirteenth centuries, the Church, both officially and universally, has allowed a convert to remarry when the unbaptized spouse refuses to cohabit peacefully. This has become known as the Pauline Privilege. From that time until the present, two conditions have been necessary: the first marriage is between two non-Christians, and it is the unbaptized spouse, not the convert to Christianity, who is responsible for the failure of the marriage.

Although the Pauline Privilege provided a solution

49. Gratian, *Concordia* (bibliog. III), Part 2, Case 28, Question 2.

50. Innocent III (bibliog. I), decretals, 1198–1216: *De infidelibus* and *Gaudemus in Domino*.

51. Innocent III (bibliog. I), decretals, 1198–1216: *Quanto te*.

to a particular type of pastoral problem, another problem had arisen by the sixteenth century. The Spanish
and Portuguese had colonies in South America and the
Indies. In these areas, the Catholic Church began to
grow in number with many new converts.[52] It was not
uncommon for an unbaptized man to have more than
one wife. If such a man wished to be baptized and enter the Catholic Church, it was necessary for him to
keep his first wife and dismiss the others. But what if
he could not remember which was his first wife? In
1537, Pope Paul III issued his apostolic constitution *Altitudo* which gave a solution.[53] Pope Paul confirmed the
teaching that such a man should keep his first wife. In
cases where he could not remember which was his first
wife, however, he was free to pick any one of his wives
and dismiss the rest. After he was baptized he was to
marry this woman.

Although Pope Paul's solution seems simple, it has
a number of consequences. It acknowledges the validity of the man's first non-Christian marriage. As a result, his subsequent marriages are not recognized; this
is why he should keep his first wife. What is original
about *Altitudo* is that it permits the man to choose any
wife if he cannot remember which was his first. For
example, he could choose a woman who was in fact
his third wife. Because the Church recognizes his first
marriage, it does not recognize his third. (He cannot
validly have more than one wife.) Thus, the woman of

52. Woestman, Special Marriage Cases (bibliog. III), 47
53. Paul III (bibliog. I), Apostolic Constitution, *Altitudo,* 1 June 1537. The
relevant passage is given as Document VI in the 1917 Code of Canon Law: *1917
Code* (bibliog. I), 750–51.

his choice is not really his wife; hence the requirement to go through a form of marriage with her.

What about his first marriage? It is dissolved so that he can marry this other woman. Like the Pauline Privilege, *Altitudo* permits the dissolution of a non-Christian marriage. It is not an application of the Pauline Privilege, however, because it is not necessary that the first wife either refuse to be baptized or to live peacefully with her convert husband. Hence, Pope Paul introduced a new ground for dissolving marriages based upon the fact that a marriage between two unbaptized persons is not absolutely indissoluble.

The use of the dissolution outlined in *Altitudo* could give rise to the two following scenarios. The first is that the man could actually choose his first wife without knowing it. He would thus go through a second form of marriage with her. It can be argued that in such a case the ceremony would have no effect, for he is already married to her. The second is that the man receives baptism and is about to marry a woman who was not his first wife, when his first wife is also baptized without him knowing it. In this case, his first marriage is a Christian one, for both he and his first wife are baptized. Would *Altitudo* allow dissolution of that marriage? Mackin explains that it would because the marriage was not consummated *after* it became a Christian marriage. That is, in this particular case, the dissolution is not based upon the marriage being a non-Christian one but on it being unconsummated.[54]

Finally, the reason for the dispensation given in

---

54. Mackin, *Divorce and Remarriage* (bibliog. III), 395–97.

Altitudo was that a number of unbaptized men who wished to be baptized could not remember who their first wives were. As Mackin notes, "The availability of this dispensation is also reported to have been the cause of suspicious failures of memory on the part of men who not unexpectedly preferred a younger wife."[55] Moreover, situations would arise when one of the wives would, like her husband, wish to be baptized, but she would not be the wife chosen by her husband. That is, the husband preferred to remain with an unbaptized wife and dismiss the one wishing to embrace Christianity with him.

In 1571, in order to address these problems, Pope Pius V promulgated his apostolic constitution *Romani Pontificis*.[56] An unbaptized man (with more than one wife), who wished to be baptized, could remain with the wife who wished to be baptized with him. Moreover, this favor was not dependent upon the state of the man's memory. That is, he could keep such a woman as his wife even if she was not his first wife and he knew who his first wife was. His first marriage would be dissolved. Like *Altitudo*, this apostolic constitution allowed the dissolution of the first marriage on the basis that it was not a Christian marriage.

By the end of the sixteenth century, another pastoral difficulty had arisen. The problem was in Africa and was caused by the slave trade. A typical case would be this: Two non-Christians would meet and marry. Later, one of them would be captured and taken into slavery.

---

55. Ibid., 396.

56. Pius V (bibliog. I), Apostolic Constitution, *Romani Pontificis,* 2 August 1571. The relevant passage is given as Document VII in *1917 Code* (bibliog. I), 751–52.

Consequently, a great distance would separate them. Then, one of them would wish to be baptized and re-marry a Christian. What could be done? The Pauline Privilege would require the first spouse to refuse to live in peace with the new convert to Christianity, but it was impossible to reach this spouse in order to ascertain this. In 1585, Pope Gregory XIII issued his apostolic constitution *Populis*.[57] In it, he allowed such non-Christian marriages to be dissolved so that a spouse could be baptized and remarry another baptized person. Again, the reason for the dissolution was that the first marriage was not a Christian one. William Woestman, professor of canon law, notes that this favor applied to monogamous marriages as well as polygamous ones.[58]

Would the convert who remarried have to leave his second spouse if it was later discovered that the first spouse had also been baptized? *Populis* says that the second marriage would be upheld. That is, the dissolution of the first marriage would still be recognized. As in the case of *Altitudo*, even if both parties of the first marriage receive baptism they have not consummated their marriage as Christians. Any sexual intercourse between them occurred before the marriage was a Christian one. Thus, as a Christian marriage, it is un-consummated and so can be dissolved on this basis.

These three apostolic constitutions of the sixteenth century supplemented the Catholic Church's use of the Pauline Privilege. They allowed a marriage to be

---

57. Gregory XIII (bibliog. I), Apostolic Constitution, *Populis*, 25 January 1585. The relevant passage is given as Document VIII in *1917 Code* (bibliog. I), 752–54.
58. Woestman, *Special Marriage* Cases (bibliog. III), 47–48.

dissolved on the basis that it was not a Christian marriage. Moreover, such a non-Christian marriage could be dissolved even if there had been sexual intercourse. By the end of that century, the Church's matrimonial discipline recognized only one type of marriage which possessed absolute indissolubility—namely, a marriage between two baptized persons which had been consummated sexually *after* both spouses had been baptized. Such a marriage could only be dissolved by the death of a spouse. No other type of marriage had this absolute indissolubility. Consequently, under the appropriate conditions, a marriage might be open to dissolution— for example, if it was not Christian, if there had been no sexual intercourse, or if there was intercourse in the marriage only prior to both spouses receiving baptism.

The great contributor to the Church's thinking, Saint Thomas Aquinas, wrote after Gratian, Alexander III, and Innocent III. Consequently, by his time, the question as to what brings a marriage into existence had been formally settled. Indeed, this is the reason why I refer so little to Aquinas. But he contributed to the debate about whether Christians should marry non-Christians. For a very long time within the Church, there had been some hesitation about allowing such marriages. In the Supplement to the *Summa Theologica*, compiled from his notes after his death in 1274, one finds the opinion that there cannot be a fitting marriage between a Christian and a non-Christian. The chief reason given is that marriage involves bringing up children to worship God. This religious and spiritual education is the duty of both parents. If they are of different faiths, then there will be a conflict. Thus, the conclusion given is that the difference in faith is an impediment to any marriage.[59]

Over the centuries, Church discipline varied considerably from region to region. Some areas allowed Christians to marry non-Christians; in other areas it was considered unlawful. Moreover, some ecclesiastical authorities regarded the difference in faith to be such that it was an actual impediment to marriage— making any attempted marriage invalid. Thus, in order to marry, it was not just a matter of needing permission but also a dispensation from the impediment. This impediment became known as "disparity of worship." In 1749, Pope Benedict XIV made the requirement for a dispensation universal.[60]

Indeed, as Woestman observes, until the 1917 Code of Canon Law, this rule applied to all the baptized—including Christians outside the Catholic Church.[61] That is, the Catholic Church would not recognize the validity of a marriage, for example, between a member of the Church of England and an unbaptized person unless such a dispensation had been obtained. It must be noted that, even with a dispensation, a marriage between a baptized person and an unbaptized spouse would not be recognized as absolutely indissoluble. It has just been seen that for the marriage to be absolutely indissoluble the unbaptized spouse would have to receive baptism and the marriage would then have to be consummated.

---

59. Aquinas, *Summa Theologica* (bibliog. III), Quest. 59, Art. 1, 318–19.

60. Benedict XIV (bibliog. I), Brief, *Singulari nobis,* 9 February 1749. Also, Noldin and Schmitt, *Summa Theologiae Moralis* (bibliog. III), 582.

61. Woestman, *Special Marriage Cases* (bibliog. III), 53.

The End of the Sixteenth Century

The sixteenth century was an important century for the development of the Church's understanding of marriage. The question of what brings a marriage into existence came under fresh examination. The role of consent had been officially accepted since Alexander III and Innocent III. By the end of this century, however, the Catholic Church taught that it could determine the manner in which marital consent is to be exchanged.

The so-called synthesis of Gratian, four centuries earlier, meant that consummation was also considered to be important, especially with regard to indissolubility. Also, Gratian had interpreted the passage from Saint Paul's First Letter to the Corinthians to mean that a convert to Christianity is free to enter a new marriage if his or her unbaptized spouse refuses to cohabit peacefully. This interpretation influenced Pope Innocent III who gave papal authority to the Pauline Privilege, as it became known. During the sixteenth century, this privilege was extended to other cases. Thus, by the end of the century, not only was it possible to find authoritative Church teaching on the creation of marriage but also on its dissolution. All these are ultimately based upon the principle enunciated by Gratian that only a consummated marriage between baptized spouses can participate in the indissoluble bond that exists between Christ and his Church. Thus, any other type of marriage is incomplete and is therefore open to dissolution. The effects of Trent and the three apostolic constitutions on the Church's matrimonial discipline can still be seen today.

The 1917 Code of Canon Law
The Need for
One Comprehensive Book of Laws

The 1917 Code's Purpose and Layout

THE *LIBER EXTRA* (or the *Decretals of Gregory IX*) of 1234 provided the Church with an authoritative source of law for many centuries. To this were added other official texts, such as papal decrees—for example, the three sixteenth-century apostolic constitutions on marriage: *Altitudo, Romani Pontificis,* and *Populis.* All these laws had to be known by any canon lawyer. As the years went by, in every area of the Church's life, new laws were promulgated. Thus, the work of the canonist became more and more complicated. By the end of the nineteenth century, it became clear that the Church's law needed to be revised.[1]

At the beginning of the twentieth century, Pope Pius X began the process of drafting a new book which would systematically contain the laws governing the

---

1. Van de Wiel, *History of Canon Law* (bibliog. III), 165.

Church. A special commission of cardinals was established, with Pius X as chairman and Cardinal Pietro Gasparri as secretary. Various drafts of each law were drawn up for consideration, and every bishop was invited to participate in the process. In 1914, two events occurred which could have seriously hindered the process—war broke out in Europe, and Pius X died. But in 1917, his successor, Pope Benedict XV, promulgated the Code of Canon Law which assumed the force of law the following year. A commission of cardinals, called *Pontificia Commissio ad Codicis Canones Authentice Interpretandos*, was established to provide authentic interpretations of the Code if doubts arose about the meaning of its text.[2] Also, Cardinal Gasparri gradually issued the sources for all the canons, showing on what they are based.[3]

When the Code was promulgated, who was bound by it? Canon 12 of the Code states that purely ecclesiastical laws[4] apply to those people who have been baptized, have the use of reason, and have completed their seventh year.[5] Thus, the Code was meant for all the baptized, including non-Catholics, as long as they

---

2. Ibid., 165–67. Also, Bouscaren and Ellis, *Canon Law: A Text and Commentary* (bibliog. III), 4–5.

3. Gasparri (ed), *Codex Iuris Canonici Pii X* (bibliog. III). Also, Gasparri (ed), *Codex Iuris Canonici Fontes* (bibliog. III). Van de Wiel, *History of Canon Law* (bibliog. III), 167 notes that the last three volumes of the latter work were completed under Iustinianus Serédi.

4. "Purely ecclesiastical laws" (Legibus mere ecclesiasticis) are laws established solely by the Church. There are also divine laws (established by God) and natural laws (established by nature). Divine and natural laws apply to everyone.

5. *1917 Code* (bibliog. I), canon 12: "Legibus mere ecclesiasticis non tenentur qui baptismum non receperunt, nec baptizati qui sufficienti rationis usu non gaudent, nec qui, licet rationis usum assecuti, septimum aetatis annum nondum expleverunt, nisi aliud iure expresse caveatur."

had the use of reason and were old enough. This was an ambitious goal, but the Code provides for some exceptions. For example, canon 1 says that the Code generally does not apply to members of the Oriental (or Eastern) churches. Also, as will be seen later in this section, non-Catholics (whether baptized or not) are exempt from the canonical form of marriage when they marry amongst themselves.[6] Again, as will be seen, baptized non-Catholics are exempt from the impediment of disparity of worship when they marry unbaptized persons.[7]

The final draft of the Code follows the structure used by such ancient Roman jurists as Gaius and Justinian. They classified laws into three categories: persons, things, and actions. Cardinal Gasparri, as secretary of the commission which drafted the Code, followed this format, but he needed a section to cover ecclesiastical crimes and penalties, so he added a fourth section. He also provided a section on general norms, which preceded—and was intended to help interpret the laws given in—these four sections.[8] This makes a total of five sections. In the final draft, each section is referred to as a book—thus, the Code consists of five books. Within each of these books are individual laws, called canons. These are numbered consecutively throughout the entire Code, starting with canon 1 at the beginning of Book One and ending with canon 2414 at the end of Book Five.

---

6. *1917 Code* (bibliog. I), canon 1099 §2.
7. *1917 Code* (bibliog. I), canon 1070 §1.
8. Van de Wiel, *History of Canon Law* (bibliog. III), 168.

The canons on marriage are found in Book Three, which considers *things*. The first part of the book considers the sacraments. It is here that canons 1012 to 1143 give the Church's laws on marriage. The canons are systematically arranged into a group of introductory canons followed by twelve chapters. As the canons on marriage are already arranged logically, I shall go through them in order. It is not my intention to provide a commentary on each of them. Instead, I shall focus on those canons which are relevant to the question: What brings a marriage into existence?

The Nature of Marriage According to the 1917 Code

The introductory canons on marriage go from canons 1012 to 1018. Canon 1012 refers to marriage as a contract (*contractum matrimonialem*).[9] Moreover, it states that a marriage between baptized persons must always be a sacrament.[10] Cardinal Gasparri cites the Council of Trent as one of the sources of this canon.[11] That is, canon 1 of *Canons Concerning the Sacraments in General* (*Canones de Sacramentis in Genere*) from the *Decree Concerning the Sacraments* (*Decretum de Sacramentis*) of Session 7, and also canon 1 of *Canons Concerning the Sacrament of Marriage* (*Canones de Sacramento Matrimonii*) from *Doctrine Concerning*

---

9. *1917 Code* (bibliog. I), canon 1012 §1: "Christus Dominus ad sacramenti dignitatem evexit ipsum contractum matrimonialem inter baptizatos."

10. *1917 Code* (bibliog. I), canon 1012 §2: "Quare inter baptizatos nequit matrimonialis contractus validus consistere, quin sit eo ipso sacramentum."

11. Gasparri (ed), *Codex Iuris Canonici Pii X* (bibliog. III), 290. Also, Gasparri (ed), *Codex Iuris Canonici Fontes* (bibliog. III), vol. 9, cols. 121, 130.

the Sacrament of Marriage (*Doctrina de Sacramento Matrimonii*) of Session 24.[12] It has been seen that although Trent uses the letter written by Saint Paul to the Ephesians (5:25 and 5:32) to support its teaching on the sacramentality of marriage, it does not base its authority solely on this letter. That is, Trent simply states that Paul "suggests" (*innuit*) that marriage is a sacrament.

Canon 1013 §1 says that the primary end of marriage is the procreation and education of children. It goes on to say that the secondary end is mutual help and the remedy for concupiscence.[13] Thus, marriage has the primary purpose of generating and educating children. Its secondary purpose is that it enables spouses to help each other, as well as providing them with a legitimate context in which they can engage in sexual activity.

The lack of authoritative sources used by Gasparri is noteworthy.[14] The weightiest he cites is an encyclical, *Arcanum*, written by Pope Leo XIII only a few decades earlier in 1880,[15] but even the use of this work is dubious. In the encyclical, Leo extols the two properties of unity and indissolubility, which he says have belonged to marriage from the very beginning. He then states that the introduction of Christian marriage has brought about the additional gift of being a sacrament.[16] Leo

---

12. Denzinger, *Enchiridion Symbolorum* (bibliog. III), 382, 416.

13. *1917 Code* (bibliog. I), canon 1013 §1: "Matrimonii finis primarius est procreatio atque educatio prolis; secundarius mutuum adiutorium et remedium concupiscentiae."

14. Gasparri (ed), *Codex Iuris Canonici Pii X* (bibliog. III), 290.

15. Ibid. Also, Gasparri (ed), *Codex Iuris Canonici Fontes* (bibliog. III), vol. 9, col. 163. Also, Leo XIII (bibliog. I), Encyclical, *Arcanum*, 10 February 1880. English text in Carlen (ed), *The Papal Encyclicals 1873–1903* (bibliog. III), 29–40.

16. Carlen (ed), *The Papal Encyclicals 1873–1903* (bibliog. III), 30–31.

says, however, that the perfection of Christian marriage is not found only in its unity, indissolubility, and sacramentality. He gives two further benefits of the introduction of Christian marriage. First, it now has a higher purpose than before. It is no longer just for the continuation of the human race, but of the Church. Second, Christian marriage has defined the rights and duties of spouses—to love each other, to be faithful to their marriage vows, and to provide mutual help.[17]

It is necessary to look at the first benefit more closely. Leo says, "For, first, there has been vouchsafed to the marriage union a higher and nobler purpose than was ever previously given to it. By the command of Christ, it not only looks to the propagation of the human race, but to the bringing forth of children for the Church."[18] It is important to note that Leo is not saying that the generation of children for the Church is the highest and noblest purpose of Christian marriage. Instead, he says that it is a higher and nobler purpose than generating children for the human race (which was all that marriage could achieve before Christ). Leo is making a comparative statement and not a superlative one. Thus, from this encyclical, one cannot conclude that the generation and education of children is the primary purpose of marriage.

Canon 1013 §1 is in stark contrast with Saint Augustine's understanding that marriage is for the intimate friendship between a man and a woman—a friendship in which love and charity are shared, a friendship

---

17. Ibid., 31–32.
18. Ibid., 31. "Nam primo quidem nuptiali societati excelsius quiddam et nobilius propositum est, quam antea fuisset; ea enim spectare iussa est non modo ad propagandum genus humanum, sed ad ingenerandam Ecclesiae sobolem." *Acta Sanctae Sedis* 12 (1879), 389.

which exists from the moment they marry and is not dependent upon their having children. Furthermore, the canon does not allow for the French tradition of the twelfth century and its emphasis on love within marriage as taught by Ivo Chartres, Hugh of Saint Victor, and Peter Lombard.

Paragraph 2 of the same canon explains that the essential properties of marriage are unity (*unitas*) and indissolubility (*indissolubilitas*). It also notes that in Christian marriages these properties acquire a particular firmness because such marriages are sacraments.[19] Gasparri cites the second canon of the Council of Trent's *Canones de Sacramento Matrimonii*, which was produced by its twenty-fourth session, as one of the authoritative sources.[20] This Tridentine canon condemns anyone who teaches that Christians may have more than one wife simultaneously. When canon 1013 §2 says that a marriage enjoys unity, it means that the spouses' relationship is exclusive and does not allow a third party to share in its intimacy. Moreover, this exclusivity is perpetual by virtue of the marriage being indissoluble. That is, apart from the death of a spouse, a marriage cannot be dissolved to enable the spouses to enter new marriages. (It will be seen, however, that the 1917 Code gives exceptions to this general rule.)

Paragraphs 1 and 3 of canon 1015 give useful definitions. Paragraph 3 calls a valid marriage between

---

19. *1917 Code* (bibliog. I), canon 1013 §2: "Essentiales matrimonii proprietates sunt unitas ac indissolubilitas, quae in matrimonio christiano peculiarem obtinent firmitatem ratione sacramenti."

20. Gasparri (ed), *Codex Iuris Canonici Fontes* (bibliog. III), vol. 9, col. 130. Also, Gasparri (ed), *Codex Iuris Canonici Pii X* (bibliog. III), 290. Also, Denzinger, *Enchiridion Symbolorum* (bibliog. III), 416.

unbaptized persons "legitimate" (*legitimum*).[21] Behind this definition is the important acknowledgment that the marriage of two unbaptized persons can be valid. Paragraph 1 gives two definitions which provide a fundamental distinction.[22] It calls a valid marriage between two baptized persons "ratified" (*ratum*) if it has "not yet been completed by consummation" (*nondum consummatione completum est*). Once consummated, however, the marriage is said to be "ratified and consummated" (*ratum et consummatum*). The way in which this distinction is worded suggests that an unconsummated Christian marriage is incomplete. This is supported by the rest of paragraph 1 which describes sexual intercourse as "the conjugal act to which the matrimonial contract is ordered by nature and by which spouses become one flesh."

It is noteworthy that Gasparri gives only two sources for this paragraph: Gratian and Pope Innocent III.[23] The reference to Gratian is his quotation from Saint Ambrose.[24] Gratian boldly quotes, "In every marriage the union is understood to be spiritual, which the bodily joining of those united confirms and completes."[25] But, as noted previously, this cannot be found in any

---

21. *1917 Code* (bibliog. I), canon 1015 §3: "Matrimonium inter non baptizatos valide celebratum, dicitur legitimum."

22. *1917 Code* (bibliog. I), canon 1015 §1: "Matrimonium baptizatorum validum dicitur ratum, si nondum consummatione completum est; ratum et consummatum, si inter coniuges locum habuerit coniugalis actus, ad quem natura sua ordinatur contractus matrimonialis et quo coniuges fiunt una caro."

23. Gasparri (ed), *Codex Iuris Canonici Fontes* (bibliog. III), vol. 9, cols. 45 and 90. Also, *Gasparri (ed), Codex Iuris Canonici Pii X* (bibliog. III), 291.

24. Gratian, *Concordia* (bibliog. III), Part 2, Case 27, Question 2, ch. 36.

25. "In omni matrimonio coniunctio intelligitur spiritualis, quam confirmat et perficit coniunctorum conmixtio corporalis."

of Ambrose's works. The reference to Innocent III is to his decretal *Quanto te*.[26] As seen earlier, however, this decretal is more concerned with authorizing the existing practice known as the Pauline Privilege than with considering the role of intercourse within marriage.

Canon 1016 upholds the Church's authority over matrimonial matters. It states that the marriages of baptized persons are governed by canon law as well as divine law. The canon acknowledges the competency of civil authorities, though, with regard to the civil effects of marriage.[27] For example, the 1917 Code asks that civil law be respected with regard to the adoption of children and the minimum age for marriage.[28] It is surprising that Gasparri does not cite the Council of Trent as a basis for this canon, especially considering how Trent wished to maintain the Church's jurisdiction over marriage—albeit not to the exclusion of civil authorities in respect of the civil aspects of marriage.[29]

Canon 1017 considers engagements. Paragraph 3 makes the important statement that an engaged person cannot be compelled to marry—even if the engagement is valid and there is no just reason excusing its fulfillment. Later, it will be seen how canon 1081 §1 teaches that it is the consent of the couple which brings about the marriage. Canon 1017 §3 is in conformity with this

---

26. Innocent III (bibliog. I), decretals, 1198–1216: *Quanto te.*

27. *1917 Code* (bibliog. I), canon 1016: "Baptizatorum matrimonium regitur iure non solum divino, sed etiam canonico, salva competentia civilis potestatis circa mere civiles eiusdem matrimonii effectus."

28. *1917 Code* (bibliog. I), canons 1059, 1080, and 1067 §2.

29. Gasparri (ed), *Codex Iuris Canonici Pii X* (bibliog. III), 291–92. Also, Gasparri (ed), *Codex Iuris Canonici Fontes* (bibliog. III), vol. 9, cols. 120–35.

principle—that is, even an engaged person cannot be compelled to marry because such a marriage would lack true marital consent and so would be invalid.

The introductory canons on marriage cover diverse matters, but they provide a picture of how marriage is understood in the 1917 Code. It is a contract between a man and a woman with the primary purpose of having children and educating them. Indeed, marriage is ordered to the conjugal act. It is through this sexual act that the spouses become one flesh. Consummation completes the marriage. Marriage also provides an opportunity for the spouses to help one another and offers a remedy for concupiscence. It is both indissoluble and exclusive of third parties. These properties are even more pronounced in the marriages of Christians because their marriages are sacraments.

Marriage Preparation and Impediments, Especially Impotence

The first chapter goes from canon 1019 to canon 1034 and considers the necessary preparations for the celebration of marriage. The Council of Trent is referred to extensively, in particular its *Decree Concerning the Reform of Matrimony*.[30] Trent's attempt to halt abuses is codified in this chapter.[31] Canons 1019 to 1021 require the priest to ensure that each party is free to marry, that there is no impediment, and that they are properly instructed. In order to prevent someone being forced to

---

30. Council of Trent (bibliog. I), Session 24, *Canones super Reformatione circa Matrimonium: Decretum Tametsi*, 11 November 1563.

31. Gasparri (ed), *Codex Iuris Canonici Pii X* (bibliog. III), 293. Also, Gasparri (ed), *Codex Iuris Canonici Fontes* (bibliog. III), vol. 9, col. 131.

marry against his or her will, canon 1020 §2 says that the priest must ensure that both parties freely consent to the marriage—especially the woman. The principle behind this canon is that only genuine consent creates a marriage.

Trent called for the names of those intending to marry to be announced publicly beforehand at Mass. Thus, if someone knew of a reason why a person should not be allowed to go through a wedding ceremony (for example, if he or she was already married), then the priest could be informed and the wedding prevented. This publication of the banns of marriage was regarded as an effective way to bring any impediments to the attention of the Church's authorities.[32] Canons 1022 to 1031 lay down norms for the publication of banns.[33]

Canon 1033 says that the priest is to instruct the parties wishing to marry about the sanctity of the sacrament of marriage and the obligations of marriage, including their duties toward their children. The same canon repeats Trent's exhortation that the parties go to Confession and receive Holy Communion before they marry.[34]

It has been seen how Luther taught that children who attempted to marry without the permission of their parents did so invalidly—and how Trent replied by stating that, although such marriages were discouraged by the

---

32. Council of Trent (bibliog. I), Session 24, *Canones super Reformatione circa Matrimonium: Decretum Tametsi*, ch. 1.

33. Gasparri (ed), *Codex Iuris Canonici Pii X* (bibliog. III), 293–95. Also, Gasparri (ed), *Codex Iuris Canonici Fontes* (bibliog. III), vol. 9, col. 130.

34. Gasparri (ed), *Codex Iuris Canonici Pii X* (bibliog. III), 296. Also, Gasparri (ed), *Codex Iuris Canonici Fontes* (bibliog. III), vol. 9, col. 130. Also, Council of Trent (bibliog. I), Session 24, *Canones super Reformatione circa Matrimonium: Decretum Tametsi*, ch. 1.

Church, they were still valid.[35] This position is taken up by canon 1034, which instructs priests to dissuade minors[36] from marrying without their parents' knowledge or against their reasonable wishes.

The second chapter of the Code's marriage section runs from canon 1035 to 1057. It gives general principles regarding impediments to marriage. Canon 1036 gives two definitions and in doing so makes a fundamental distinction. Paragraph one defines an *impedient impediment* (*impedimentum impediens*) to be a grave prohibition against marrying. But if the marriage goes ahead without a dispensation, it is still valid—albeit unlawful.[37] Paragraph two defines a more serious type of impediment, the *diriment impediment* (*impedimentum dirimens*). Such an impediment not only gravely prohibits the marriage but makes it invalid if it should proceed without the diriment impediment being dispensed.[38]

Canon 1038 declares the Church's authority over impediments to marriage. Based on Trent, paragraph one states that only the Church has the authority to interpret when divine law forbids or invalidates marriage.[39] Similarly, paragraph two says that the Church

---

35. Council of Trent (bibliog. I), Session 24, *Canones super Reformatione circa Matrimonium: Decretum Tametsi*, ch. 1.

36. That is, those not yet twenty-one years old, per *1917 Code* (bibliog. I), canon 88 §1.

37. *1917 Code* (bibliog. I), canon 1036 §1: "Impedimentum impediens continet gravem prohibitionem contrahendi matrimonium; quod tamen irritum non redditur si, non obstante impedimento, contrahatur."

38. *1917 Code* (bibliog. I), canon 1036 §2: "Impedimentum dirimens et graviter prohibet matrimonium contrahendum, et impedit quominus valide contrahatur."

39. Gasparri (ed), *Codex Iuris Canonici Pii X* (bibliog. III), 297. Also, Gasparri (ed), *Codex Iuris Canonici Fontes* (bibliog. III), vol. 9, col. 130. Also, Council of Trent (bibliog. I), Session 24, *Canones de Sacramento Matrimonii*, 11 November 1563, canon 3.

has the exclusive right to establish both impedient and diriment impediments for those who are baptized.[40] This paragraph also uses Pope Benedict XIV as an authority.[41] As already seen, Benedict had declared that all Christians needed to be dispensed from the impediment of disparity of worship in order to marry an unbaptized person validly.[42]

Chapter three is covered by canons 1058 to 1066 and lists the various impedient impediments to marriage. Canon 1058 prohibits someone marrying who has made a simple vow to remain a virgin, to remain perfectly chaste, to stay unmarried, to receive sacred orders, or to enter religious life. The next canon respects civil law with regard to adoption. That is, if the civil authorities prohibit a marriage because of a relationship arising from adoption, then so does the Church. Canon 1060 prohibits marriage between Catholics and baptized non-Catholics. Finally, canons 1065 and 1066 describe other marriages which should be avoided unless a grave reason suggests otherwise. Canon 1065 deters Catholics from marrying lapsed Catholics and canon 1066 discourages the celebration of the marriages of unrepentant public sinners.

Chapter four runs from canon 1067 to canon 1080

---

40. Gasparri (ed), *Codex Iuris Canonici Pii X* (bibliog. III), 297. Also, Gasparri (ed), *Codex Iuris Canonici Fontes* (bibliog. III), vol. 9, cols. 130–31. Also, Council of Trent (bibliog. I), Session 24, *Canones de Sacramento Matrimonii*, canons 3, 4, and 9. Also, Council of Trent (bibliog. I), Session 24, *Canones super Reformatione circa Matrimonium: Decretum Tametsi*, chapters 1 and 6.

41. Gasparri (ed), *Codex Iuris Canonici Fontes* (bibliog. III), vol. 9, col. 155, and vol. 2, cols. 193–99. Also, *Benedict XIV* (bibliog. I), Brief, *Singulari nobis*, 9 February 1749.

42. Canon 1070 §1 of the 1917 Code restricts this impediment to Catholics who marry unbaptized persons; *1917 Code* (bibliog. I).

and lists the diriment impediments to marriage. These impediments are more serious than those in the preceding chapter because, without a dispensation, they invalidate any attempted marriage. Of these various diriment impediments, only canon 1068 concerning impotence is central to my book and so I shall concentrate on it.

Gasparri cites Gratian as one of the main sources for canon 1068.[43] It has been seen how Gratian taught that if a man enters marriage and proves to be impotent, his wife can leave him and marry another. It is not clear whether Gratian regarded the first marriage to be dissolved or simply not to exist in the first place. In favor of dissolution he says, "Behold, the inability to pay the debt dissolves the bond of marriage."[44] But he also suggests that the marriage never truly existed. He bases his argument on the practice of the Church in allowing remarriage in cases of impotence. He notes that spouses cannot separate and marry others—not even in the case of adultery.[45] Thus, when the Church allows spouses to remarry because of impotence, they could not have been truly married in the first place.[46] Whichever explanation is used, Gratian describes impotence to be the result of a "natural inability" (*naturali impossibilitate*).[47] Hence, impotence is a natural inability to

---

43. Gasparri (ed), *Codex Iuris Canonici Pii X* (bibliog. III), 304. Also, Gasparri (ed), *Codex Iuris Canonici Fontes* (bibliog. III), vol. 9, cols. 45–47.

44. "Ecce, quod impossibilitas reddendi debitum vinculum solvit coniugii." Gratian, *Concordia* (bibliog. III), Part 2, Case 33, Question 1, dictum after ch. 3.

45. Gratian, *Concordia* (bibliog. III), Part 2, Case 32, Question 7, dictum after ch. 16.

46. Gratian, *Concordia* (bibliog. III), Part 2, Case 27, Question 2, dictum after ch. 29.

47. Gratian, *Concordia* (bibliog. III), Part 2, Case 33, Question 1, dictum after ch. 3.

consummate a marriage—that is, it makes it impossible to complete the marriage.

Gratian's opinion is codified in canon 1068 §1.[48] This paragraph states that a person cannot marry validly if he or she is suffering from impotence. As there are different types of impotence, the canon gives two criteria which both have to be met in order for the impotence to be a diriment impediment. First, the impotence has to be antecedent (*antecedens*)—that is, actually existing at the time the marriage is contracted. Thus, for example, if a man becomes impotent during the course of his marriage through an accident it would not affect the validity of his existing marriage. Second, the condition must be perpetual (*perpetua*). Thus, if the condition can be cured, then the impotence is not perpetual and, consequently, does not prevent a valid marriage from taking place. One commentary says that the impotence is deemed to be perpetual if it can be cured but *only* by means which are illicit or dangerous.[49]

The canon explains that if the impotence fulfills both of these criteria, then the marriage cannot be celebrated—irrespective of whether it is the man or the woman who suffers the impotence, irrespective of whether the other party knows about the condition, and irrespective of whether the condition is absolute (*absoluta*) or relative (*relativa*). This last distinction needs an explanation. Impotence is absolute if the sufferer would

---

48. *1917 Code* (bibliog. I), canon 1068 §1: "Impotentia antecedens et perpetua, sive ex parte viri, sive ex parte mulieris, sive alteri cognita sive non, sive asboluta sive relativa, matrimonium ipso naturae iure dirimit."

49. Bouscaren and Ellis, *Canon Law: A Text and Commentary* (bibliog. III), 525.

manifest impotence with any other sexual partner. It is relative if the sufferer only manifests the condition with a particular individual or class of individuals—for example, when there is a very serious difference in the size of sexual organs.

Paragraph 3 of the canon states that sterility does not affect the validity or the legality of marriage.[50] There is thus a distinction made between impotence and sterility. A good explanation of the difference is found in the classic commentary on the 1917 Code by the two Jesuit scholars Timothy Lincoln Bouscaren and Adam Ellis: "In general *impotence* may be defined as *incapacity for the marital act, sterility*, as *incapacity for generation*. Even though persons be perfectly capable of normal copula, generation may be impossible because of some condition adverse to it in one or both parties. In such a case one or both are *sterile*; but sterility neither invalidates the marriage nor renders it illicit. On the other hand, if they are incapable of the marital act itself, they are *impotent*."[51]

Matrimonial Consent

The fifth chapter goes from canon 1081 to canon 1093 and considers matrimonial consent. Canon 1081 §1 states that it is the consent of the couple that creates the marriage. Moreover, as this consent has to be genuine, it can only come from the two individuals themselves. Thus, the same paragraph states that no human power

50. *1917 Code* (bibliog. I), canon 1068 §3: "Sterilitas matrimonium nec dirimit nec impedit."

51. Bouscaren and Ellis, *Canon Law: A Text and Commentary* (bibliog. III), 523. (Emphasis in the original.)

can supply the required consent.[52] That is, any consent given by a third party, or parties, would be artificial and so would not have the effect of producing a marriage. Among the references given by Gasparri which support the consensual position are a number to Gratian.[53] In particular, one finds Gratian's use of the reply of Pope Nicholas I to the Bulgarians, the writings of Saint Ambrose, Saint Isidore of Seville, and (the work attributed to) Saint John Chrysostom.[54] It can be concluded that paragraph one of this canon is faithful to the Church's traditional teaching that consent makes marriage.

What does this consent actually consist of? The second paragraph of the canon explains. It states, "Matrimonial consent is an act of the will by which each party gives and accepts a perpetual and exclusive right over the body, ordered toward acts which are of themselves apt for the generation of children."[55] One would expect this second paragraph to be as well supported by tradition as the first, but Gasparri gives very few references.[56] As in the first paragraph, he does cite Gratian however. In fact he gives three references.

The first reference is to the beginning of Gratian's examination of whether consent or sexual intercourse

52. *1917 Code* (bibliog. I), canon 1081 §1: "Matrimonium facit partium consensus inter personas iure habiles legitime manifestatus; qui nulla humana potestate suppleri valet." The wording of the canon leaves open the possibility of consent being supplied by divine power.

53. Gasparri (ed), *Codex Iuris Canonici Pii X* (bibliog. III), 308. Also, Gasparri (ed), *Codex Iuris Canonici Fontes* (bibliog. III), vol. 9, cols. 44–45.

54. Gratian, *Concordia* (bibliog. III), Part 2, Case 27, Question 2, chapters 1, 2, 5, and 6.

55. *1917 Code* (bibliog. I), canon 1081 §2: "Consensus matrimonialis est actus voluntatis quo utraque pars tradit et acceptat ius in corpus, perpetuum et exclusivum, in ordine ad actus per se aptos ad prolis generationem."

56. Gasparri (ed), *Codex Iuris Canonici Pii X* (bibliog. III), 309.

makes marriage.[57] In this chapter, however, Gratian does not come to any major conclusion. He merely outlines the problem of the relationship between consent and intercourse in order to begin his examination of the matter in the following chapters. Moreover, it is within this very chapter that he acknowledges that Mary, although truly married to Joseph, not only did not have intercourse with him, but never intended to. That is, there was never any question of Joseph performing generative acts with Mary.

The second reference to Gratian actually refers to an addition to the *Decretum* by a later commentator, probably a master at the law school at Bologna called Paucapalea. Indeed, this chapter is missing from various versions of the *Decretum*.[58] Moreover, it does not address the issue of what consent is. Instead it considers why a man cannot have two wives.

The third reference is to a sizeable passage of the *Decretum*.[59] It is primarily concerned with errors about a spouse which someone can make when entering marriage—for example, marrying the wrong person or believing that he or she has a certain quality which is in fact missing.[60]

From these three references, one certainly cannot arrive at the bold statement of what consent is, as found

57. Gratian, *Concordia* (bibliog. III), Part 2, Case 27, Question 2, ch. 3.

58. Gratian, *Concordia* (bibliog. III), Part 2, Case 27, Question 2, ch. 51. Also, Cicognani, *Canon Law* (bibliog. III), 277–78.

59. Gratian, *Concordia* (bibliog. III), Part 2, Case 29, Question 1.

60. Indeed, this passage from Gratian is cited by Gasparri as the source for canon 1083 §1, which considers the consequence of making an error about the other person when marrying. Gasparri (ed), *Codex Iuris Canonici Pii X* (bibliog. III), 309. Also, Gasparri (ed), *Codex Iuris Canonici Fontes* (bibliog. III), vol. 9, col. 45.

in canon 1081 §2. Undoubtedly, matrimonial consent is an act of the will. This canon is not greatly supported by tradition, however, when it states in such a narrow way how this consent gives mutual rights over the spouses' bodies for procreative acts. In short, there is little to support its reduction of marital consent to a consideration of just the sexual and generative aspects of marriage.

If an individual is to give marital consent, what does he or she require? The 1917 Code gives two answers: sufficient knowledge so that the individual knows to what he or she is consenting, and sufficient freedom to give genuine consent. Canons 1082 and 1083 consider the knowledge required. Canon 1082 §1 says that contracting parties must know that marriage is a permanent society between a man and a woman for the procreation of children.[61] Two things are noteworthy about this canon. First, there is no reference to marital love and support. Instead, emphasis is placed on the procreative dimension of marriage. Second, Gasparri cites just one reference and this is to a matrimonial decision, given only three decades earlier, concerning a young woman who claimed to have been forced into marriage by her mother.[62] Surprisingly, the decision does not provide a detailed examination of the knowledge required for marriage.

The other canon on knowledge, canon 1083, says that the couple must have sufficient knowledge of each other. It states that a marriage is invalid if someone should marry the wrong person or make an error regarding a

---

61. *1917 Code* (bibliog. I), canon 1082 §1: "Ut matrimonialis consensus haberi possit, necesse est ut contrahentes saltem non ignorent matrimonium esse societatem permanentem inter virum et mulierem ad filios procreandos."

62. Gasparri (ed), *Codex Iuris Canonici Pii X* (bibliog. III), 309. Also, Sacred Congregation of the Council (bibliog. I), Response, *Ventimilien*, 19 May 1888.

quality of the other person so that it amounts to marrying the wrong person. One part of the canon gives a definite example.[63] It says that if a free person marries someone in the belief that he or she is free, when in fact he or she is in slavery, then the marriage is invalid.[64]

Canon 1087 considers the freedom required to give genuine marital consent. It states that an individual who is compelled to marry through force or grave fear does so invalidly. This canon is based upon the principle that it is the consent of the couple themselves that creates the marriage. If true consent is not given by one of the parties, then the marriage cannot come about. As canon 1081 §1 says, no other human power can supply this consent.

Canon 1086 §2 considers cases where, despite the externals, an individual does not give genuine marital consent. It examines the situation where either party, or both, at a wedding ceremony makes his or her marital promises but does not mean them. In other words, true consent is not given and so the marriage is invalid. To be precise, the canon's second paragraph states that if either or both parties exclude, by a positive act of the will, either marriage itself, all rights to the conjugal act, or an essential property of marriage, then the marriage is invalid.[65]

To exclude marriage itself means that the party concerned does not really intend to be married. He or she is going through the wedding ceremony for another

---

63. *1917 Code* (bibliog. I), canon 1083 §2 2°.
64. It has been seen that this was the opinion of Ivo of Chartres.
65. *1917 Code* (bibliog. I), canon 1086 §2: "At si alterutra vel utraque pars positivo voluntatis actu excludat matrimonium ipsum, aut omne ius ad coniugalem actum, vel essentialem aliquam matrimonii proprietatem, invalide contrahit."

reason—for example, to obtain citizenship of the other party's country. To exclude all rights to the conjugal act means to deny rights to that act which is open to the generation of children. To exclude an essential property of marriage, according to canon 1013 §2, means to exclude unity or indissolubility. The exclusion of the former would involve the party not intending to keep the marital relationship exclusive. For example, he or she might keep in mind the possibility of being unfaithful if the opportunity should arise. The exclusion of the latter means that the party concerned does not intend the marriage to be a lifelong commitment. For example, he or she might reserve the right to seek a divorce if the relationship does not succeed.

Finally, canon 1092 allows conditions to be added to a person's matrimonial consent. This does seem strange. It is based upon the fact that marriage is a contract which is brought about by the consent of the parties. If this consent is to be given freely, then the parties concerned should be at liberty to add conditions to it. The canon covers various possibilities which could arise. If someone adds a condition about a future event which is either necessary or impossible, then the condition is considered to have not been made.[66] For example, "I marry you if the sun rises tomorrow" (necessary) or "I marry you if the sun does not rise tomorrow" (impossible).[67] The same is true—that is, the condition is considered not to have been made—if the condition is

66. *1917 Code* (bibliog. I), canon 1092 1°: "Si sit de futuro necessaria vel impossibilis vel turpis, sed non contra matrimonii substantiam, pro non adiecta habeatur."

67. Examples from Bouscaren and Ellis, *Canon Law: A Text and Commentary* (bibliog. III), 567.

about a future event which, although not contrary to the substance of marriage, is immoral. For example, "'I marry you if I am successful in tomorrow's bank-robbery.'" But if the condition is about a future event which is contrary to the substance of marriage, then the marriage is invalid.[68] This is because the condition attached to the matrimonial consent is such that it nullifies it. For example, "I marry you if we have no children."

If the condition concerns the past or present, then the marriage is valid depending on whether or not the condition is met.[69] For example, "I marry you if you have not been to prison" (past) or "I marry you if you are a virgin" (present). Thus, in the first example, if the individual has not been to prison then the marriage is valid; if he has, then it is invalid. Similarly, in the second example, if the woman is a virgin then the marriage is valid; if she is not, then it is invalid.[70]

The third part of the canon is probably the hardest to comprehend. It concerns a condition about the future which does not fall into any of the categories already seen: necessary, impossible, immoral, or contrary to the substance of marriage. For example, "I marry you here and now on the condition that my parents agree tomorrow."[71] According to the canon and its commentators, the validity of the marriage is suspended until the condition is fulfilled.[72] That is, if the

---

68. *1917 Code* (bibliog. I), canon 1092 2°: "Si de futuro contra matrimonii substantiam, illud reddit invalidum."

69. *1917 Code* (bibliog. I), canon 1092 4°: "Si de praeterito vel de praesenti matrimonium erit validum vel non, prout id quod conditioni subest, exsistit vel non."

70. Bouscaren and Ellis, *Canon Law: A Text and Commentary* (bibliog. III), 570.

71. Ibid., 569.

72. 1917 Code (bibliog. I), canon 1092 3°: "Si de futuro licita, valorem matri-

parents give their approval, then the marriage is valid; otherwise it is invalid. Four things need to be noted. First, the matrimonial consent can be withdrawn before the future condition is fulfilled—for example, before the parents give their approval. If this happens, either party is free to marry someone else. Second, before the condition is determined, it can be revoked so that there is no condition attached to the matrimonial consent. For example, the condition is removed before the parents agree or disagree to the marriage. Hence, the couple is married irrespective of what the parents say. It has been seen that Pope Alexander III taught that sexual intercourse between them makes any condition attached to the matrimonial consent irrelevant.[73] This decree is cited by Gasparri as a source.[74] Certainly, under the 1917 Code, an ecclesiastical judge would have to consider whether intercourse, in a particular case, was indeed an indication that the condition had been revoked.

The third point to be noted is that consent is actually given in the present, although it involves a future event. Thus, the individual is consenting to marry here and now. This is different from the person consenting to marry in the future, which is merely an engagement— which can be broken off (canon 1017 §3). Fourth, during the period between the parties consenting to marry in the present and the condition being fulfilled in the future, the validity of the marriage is suspended. Thus, in the example just given, its validity is suspended until

---

monii suspendit." Also, Bouscaren and Ellis, *Canon Law: A Text and Commentary* (bibliog. III), 569–70.

73. Alexander III (bibliog. I), decretals, 1159–81: *De Illis*, in Gregory IX, *Decretales* (bibliog. III), 4, 5, 3.

74. Gasparri (ed), *Codex Iuris Canonici Pii X* (bibliog. III), 311.

the parents agree to the marriage. This part of the canon, from a legal point of view, allows couples to exist in a state of matrimonial limbo—matrimonial consent has been exchanged but the validity of the marriage is suspended.

The Prescribed Form of Marriage

Chapter six runs from canon 1094 to canon 1103 and considers the form that the celebration of marriage must take. It is based upon the Council of Trent's call for marriages to be celebrated publicly, as well as the later decree from the Sacred Congregation of the Council, *Ne temere*, which simplified the norms laid down by Trent.[75] Canon 1094 states that marriages are to be celebrated before the parish priest or Ordinary[76] of the place, or before a delegated priest. Moreover, there are to be at least two witnesses present. Canons 1095 to 1097 give rules regarding the delegation of priests.

Canon 1098 codifies the extraordinary form of marriage which was introduced by *Ne temere*. If no priest is available (or none can be reached) and this situation will probably last a month, then the couple may marry in front of two witnesses alone. The canon also allows marriages in the presence of just witnesses when there is danger of death.

The Council of Trent wished to halt abuses such as bigamy. It thus required marriage registers to be kept.

---

75. Ibid., 312. Also, Gasparri (ed), *Codex Iuris Canonici Fontes* (bibliog. III), vol. 9, cols. 130 and 257, and vol. 6, cols. 867–70. Also, Council of Trent (bibliog. I), Session 24, *Canones super Reformatione circa Matrimonium: Decretum Tametsi*, especially ch. 1. Also, Sacred Congregation of the Council (bibliog. I), Decree, *Ne temere*, 2 August 1907.

76. For example, the Bishop or his Vicar General—*1917 Code* (bibliog. I), canon 198.

Similarly, the Sacred Congregation of the Council's decree *Ne temere* called for the baptismal registers of Catholics to be amended to record any marriages. These two requirements are repeated by canon 1103.[77]

Chapter seven goes from canon 1104 to 1107 and gives norms for the secret celebration of marriage. For example, in a parish a man and woman, although unmarried, are regarded as husband and wife because they have cohabited for a long time. They wish to marry, but do not want other parishioners to know that they are not really married. This chapter allows the marriage to be celebrated secretly and without any banns being published. The marriage is still to be recorded in a special book, however.[78] Chapter eight is very short and consists of only two canons, 1108 and 1109, which consider the time and place of the wedding ceremony.

The Effects of Marriage

The ninth chapter examines the effects of a valid marriage and runs from canon 1110 to canon 1117. It is pertinent to highlight three effects. The first two are given by canon 1110 and are based upon the teaching of Trent:[79] A bond—which is, by nature, perpetual and exclusive—is created between the man and the woman; and, because marriage between the baptized is a

77. Gasparri (ed), *Codex Iuris Canonici Pii X* (bibliog. III), 315.

78. *1917 Code* (bibliog. I), canon 1107.

79. *1917 Code* (bibliog. I), canon 1110: "Ex valido matrimonio enascitur inter coniuges vinculum natura sua perpetuum et exclusivum; matrimonium praeterea christianum coniugibus non ponentibus obicem gratiam confert." Also, Gasparri (ed), *Codex Iuris Canonici Pii X* (bibliog. III), 317–18. Also, Gasparri (ed), *Codex Iuris Canonici Fontes* (bibliog. III), vol. 9, col. 130. Also, Council of Trent (bibliog. I), Session 24, *Canones de Sacramento Matrimonii*, canons 1 and 5.

sacrament, it confers grace upon the spouses, as long as they do not refuse it.

The third effect of a valid marriage is explained by canon 1111. It states that "from the very beginning of the marriage" (*ab ipso matrimonii initio*) both spouses have the same right and duty with regard to those acts proper to conjugal life.[80] Gasparri cites Gratian as a source for this canon.[81] Although the canon agrees with Gratian on one fundamental point, it disagrees on another. It has been seen that Gratian regarded the husband and the wife to have equal rights to sexual intercourse. This is indeed the position of canon 1111, but Gratian taught that the right to sexual intercourse originates from the first act of intercourse. That is, it comes about via consummation and not the exchange of consent. Thus, spouses are not bound to have intercourse, but once they do, either spouse can demand it on any subsequent occasion.[82] This is different from the canon, which states that the right to intercourse exists "from the very beginning of the marriage."

This difference has practical consequences. For Gratian, because the right to intercourse only comes about via consummation, then either spouse is free to leave an unconsummated marriage and enter religious

---

80. *1917 Code* (bibliog. I), canon 1111: "Utrique coniugi ab ipso matrimonii initio aequum ius et officium est quod attinet ad actus proprios coniugalis vitae."

81. Gasparri (ed), *Codex Iuris Canonici Pii X* (bibliog. III), 318. Also, Gasparri (ed), *Codex Iuris Canonici Fontes* (bibliog. III), vol. 9, cols. 44–47. Also, Gratian, *Concordia* (bibliog. III), Part 2, Case 27, Question 2, ch. 24; Case 32, Question 2, ch. 3; Case 33, Question 5, chapters 1–3, 5, 6, and 11.

82. Gratian, *Concordia* (bibliog. III), Part 2, Case 32, Question 2, ch. 3; and Case 33, Question 5, chapters 5 and 11.

life—even if the other party should object.[83] It has been seen that the discipline developed within the Church whereby spouses, after marrying, had two months in which they could either consummate their marriage or enter religious life. If one chose the religious life, then the other was free to remarry. But as canon 1111 says, the right to intercourse exists from the very beginning of marriage, so it prevents a married person from simply leaving an unconsummated marriage in order to enter religious life. The two-month rule is removed.

Indeed, canon 542 1° states that any married person enters a novitiate invalidly. Moreover, an invalid novitiate makes any religious profession invalid (canon 572 §1 3°). Under the 1917 Code, could a married person enter religious life? They could, theoretically, receive a dispensation from the Holy See to enter a novitiate. Moreover, if unconsummated, that person's marriage could be dissolved. This type of dissolution will be seen shortly when canon 1119 is examined. The rights of the spouses regarding intercourse in such cases will then be considered.

The Dissolution of Marriage

The tenth chapter of the 1917 Code's section on marriage goes from canon 1118 to canon 1132. It is divided into two articles. The first considers the actual dissolution of the bond of marriage. The second gives rules for separation from bed, table, and cohabitation while the

---

83. Gratian, *Concordia* (bibliog. III), Part 2, Case 27, Question 2, dictum after ch. 26, and dictum after ch. 28. Also, Case 33, Question 5, dictum after ch. 11, and dictum after ch. 20.

marriage bond remains intact. The first article is relevant to this book's topic.

It has been seen that, by the end of the sixteenth century the Catholic Church clearly taught that for a marriage to be absolutely indissoluble two conditions have to be met. If they are met, then only the death of a spouse can break the marital bond and free the other party to remarry. The first condition is that it must be a Christian marriage—that is, a marriage between a baptized man and a baptized woman. It is only when both spouses are baptized that the marriage is a sacrament. The second condition is that the marriage must be consummated sexually at a time when both spouses are baptized. These two conditions are enshrined in canon 1118, which states that a marriage which is ratified (*ratum*) and consummated (*consummatum*) cannot be dissolved by any human power, or by any cause except death.[84] Canon 1015 §1 defines a ratified and consummated marriage to be a valid marriage between baptized persons which has been consummated sexually. Initially, it is surprising that there are not many sources cited by Gasparri for canon 1118.[85] One must remember, however, that the principles on which this canon is based do not have a long tradition within the Church. They came about through the influence of such writers as Hincmar of Rheims and Gratian and were not finalized until the three papal decrees of the sixteenth century which I examined earlier.

---

84. *1917 Code* (bibliog. I), canon 1118: "Matrimonium validum ratum et consummatum nulla humana potestate nullaque causa, praeterquam morte, dissolvi potest."

85. Gasparri (ed), *Codex Iuris Canonici Pii X* (bibliog. III), 319.

The consequence of canon 1118 is that if a marriage lacks just one of the two conditions, then it is not absolutely indissoluble. That is, if it is not between two baptized persons, or if it is unconsummated, then it is open to dissolution. This is the basis for the canons which follow.

Canon 1119 states that an unconsummated marriage between baptized spouses or between a baptized spouse and an unbaptized one can be dissolved.[86] It says that the dissolution can take place by solemn religious profession or, if there is a just cause, by a dispensation from the Apostolic See.[87] Whichever method of dissolution is used, the Apostolic See has to be involved because a dispensation has to be obtained in order for a married person to enter the novitiate of a religious order. Among the authorities given by Gasparri for this canon is the Council of Trent, which stated definitively that solemn religious profession can dissolve an unconsummated marriage.[88] With regard to dissolution by means other than religious profession, Gasparri cites the decretal of Alexander III, *Ex publico*, which argued

---

86. Although the canon does not state it, an unconsummated marriage between two unbaptized persons can be dissolved a fortiori. In practice, however, such a marriage would only come to the attention of the Church's authorities if one of the spouses wished to marry a Catholic. In such a case, it is possible that the marriage would be dissolved for a different reason—namely, that it is not a sacrament.

87. *1917 Code* (bibliog. I), canon 1119: "Matrimonium non consummatum inter baptizatos vel inter partem baptizatam et partem non baptizatam, dissolvitur tum ipso iure per sollemnem professionem religiosam, tum per dispensationem a Sede Apostolica ex iusta causa concessam, utraque parte rogante vel alterutra, etsi altera sit invita."

88. Gasparri (ed), *Codex Iuris Canonici Pii X* (bibliog. III), 319–20. Also, Gasparri (ed), *Codex Iuris Canonici Fontes* (bibliog. III), vol. 9, col. 130. Also, Council of Trent (bibliog. I), Session 24, *Canones de Sacramento Matrimonii*, canon 6.

that when Jesus condemned those who divorced and remarried, he was referring only to those who attempted
to leave consummated marriages. That is, unconsummated marriages do not fall under Jesus's prohibition
and so can be dissolved.[89]

Canon 1119 states that the dissolution can take place
at the request of both parties or just one party—even if
the other is unwilling. Consider, however, that canon 1111
says the right to intercourse exists from the moment the
marriage is contracted. Does canon 1119 contradict canon 1111 by allowing an unconsummated marriage to be
dissolved against the wishes of one of the spouses? Not
completely. As the right to intercourse exists from the
very beginning of the marriage, neither party can simply
end the marriage himself or herself by entering religious
life—as had been the practice. Only the competent authority (the Apostolic See) can allow the dissolution, and
then only for a greater good. The dissolution will only
be granted if one party wishes to enter religious life or
if there is a just cause. If the other spouse is unwilling to
have the marriage dissolved, then the just cause must be
such that it outweighs his or her wishes—for example,
the irretrievable breakdown of the marriage.

The Pauline Privilege is covered by canons 1120 to
1124 and also canon 1126. The first paragraph of canon 1120 reaffirms the Church's practice of using the
Privilege to dissolve marriages contracted between unbaptized persons (even if consummated).[90] It has been

89. Gasparri (ed), *Codex Iuris Canonici Pii X* (bibliog. III), 319–20. Also, Alexander III (bibliog. I), decretals, 1159–81: *Ex publico*.

90. *1917 Code* (bibliog. I), canon 1120 §1: "Legitimum inter non baptizatos mat-rimonium, licet consummatum, solvitur in favorem fidei ex privilegio Paulino."

seen that Gratian was in favor of this.[91] Consequently, Gasparri cites him as one of the sources for this canon.[92] Canons 1121 to 1124 determine the procedure that is to be followed when the Pauline Privilege is used. This procedure ensures that the conditions necessary for granting the Privilege are satisfied: that the unbaptized spouse is unwilling to cohabit peacefully with the spouse who has converted, that the unbaptized spouse is unwilling to receive baptism, and that the baptized spouse is not responsible for the breakdown of the marriage. Canon 1126 answers an important question: When is the marriage which was contracted between the unbaptized spouses actually dissolved? The canon states that dissolution occurs when the baptized party contracts a new marriage. Therefore, it is at this point that the unbaptized spouse is free to enter another marriage.[93] This was the opinion of Pope Benedict XIV, who is the main source of this canon.[94]

One of the requirements for the Pauline Privilege is that the marriage to be dissolved was contracted by two unbaptized persons. It is for this reason that canon 1120 §2 states that the Privilege cannot be applied to a marriage contracted between a baptized person and an unbaptized person.[95] Nevertheless, such a marriage, even

---

91. Gratian, *Concordia* (bibliog. III), Part 2, Case 28.

92. Gasparri (ed), *Codex Iuris Canonici Pii X* (bibliog. III), 320. Also, Gasparri (ed), *Codex Iuris Canonici Fontes* (bibliog. III), vol. 9, col. 45.

93. *1917 Code* (bibliog. I), canon 1126: "Vinculum prioris coniugii, in infidelitate contracti, tunc tantum solvitur, cum pars fidelis reapse novas nuptias valide iniverit."

94. Gasparri (ed), *Codex Iuris Canonici Pii X* (bibliog. III), 322. Also, Gasparri (ed), *Codex Iuris Canonici Fontes* (bibliog. III), vol. 9, col. 154. Also, Benedict XIV (bibliog. I), Epistle, *Postremo mense*, 28 February 1747. Also, Benedict XIV (bibliog. I), Apostolic Constitution, *Apostolici ministerit*, 16 September 1747.

95. *1917 Code* (bibliog. I), canon 1120 §2: "Hoc privilegium non obtinet in

if consummated, is not a Christian one; the non-bap-
tism of one of the spouses means the marriage is not a
sacrament. It is thus still open to dissolution. Although
the 1917 Code does not address the dissolution of such
a marriage, I shall show later how the Catholic Church
did start dissolving this type of marriage shortly after
the promulgation of this Code.

Finally, canon 1125 extends the three apostolic constitutions of the sixteenth century, *Altitudo*, *Romani
Pontificis*, and *Populis*, which were written for particular circumstances in specific places, to other regions with the same conditions.[96] Thus, the 1917 Code
makes the dissolution of non-Christian marriages more
available.

Convalidations and Second Marriages

The eleventh chapter on marriage runs from canon
1133 to 1141 and gives norms for convalidation—that
is, ways in which invalid marriages can be made valid.
For example, if a marriage is invalid because of an impediment, it is necessary that the impediment ceases
to exist or is dispensed and that marital consent is re-
newed.[97] If a marriage is invalid because one of the parties has not given genuine consent, then it is necessary
that this consent is given.[98] As canon 1081 §1 makes
clear, nobody else can supply this consent. If, however,

matrimonio inter partem baptizatam et partem non baptizatam inito cum dispen-
satione ab impedimento disparitatis cultus."

96. Paul III (bibliog. I), Apostolic Constitution, *Altitudo,* 1 June 1537. Also,
Pius V (bibliog. I), Apostolic Constitution, *Romani Pontificis,* 2 August 1571.
Also, Gregory XIII (bibliog. I), Apostolic Constitution, *Populis,* 25 January
1585.

97. *1917 Code* (bibliog. I), canon 1133.

98. Ibid., canon 1136.

a marriage is invalid because the wedding was not celebrated correctly (that is, in accordance with canonical form), then it can be made valid by the couple contracting anew using the correct form.[99]

Finally, the twelfth chapter consists of just two canons, 1142 and 1143, which are concerned with second marriages. Canon 1143 states that a woman who has received the nuptial blessing may not receive it again at another wedding ceremony.[100] Thus, for example, a woman who receives the nuptial blessing and whose husband subsequently dies may not receive another blessing if she marries a second time. If one keeps in mind that both spouses receive the nuptial blessing, it might seem unusual that this canon only prevents women from receiving the blessing more than once. The reason is that the nuptial blessing is understood to sanctify the husband and wife who participate in the bond that exists between Christ and the virgin Church. Moreover, the wife symbolizes the Church—the virgin bride of Christ. A woman celebrating her second marriage is presumed to be no longer a virgin and so is unable to symbolize the virginity of the bride of Christ.

Consequences of the 1917 Code— Greater Emphasis on the Sexual Dimension at the Expense of Love

Many parts of the 1917 Code merely reiterate the Church's teaching and discipline that were already in existence. For example, in accordance with Trent, the

---

99. Ibid., canon 1137.
100. *1917 Code* (bibliog. I), canon 1143: "Mulier cui semel benedictio sollemnis data sit, nequit in subsequentibus nuptiis eam iterum accipere."

Code makes it clear that the Church has authority over marriage. This can be seen by its insistence on Catholics following canonical form, as determined by Trent and the later decree *Ne temere*. Moreover, Trent's teaching that the Church can define impediments to marriage is emphasized by those listed in the Code.

Canon 1081 §1 repeats the traditional teaching that consent makes marriage. Indeed, Gasparri cites Gratian who in turn refers to Pope Nicholas I, Ambrose, Isidore of Seville, and the work attributed to John Chrysostom. Consequently, any major defect in an individual's matrimonial consent makes the marriage invalid. For example, if he or she is compelled to marry through force or grave fear. Furthermore, as the consent has to be freely given then the spouses can add conditions to it.

The 1917 Code inherits a situation which emphasizes the sexual dimension of marriage. As Gratian was influential in this respect, it is not surprising that one finds many references to him in the sources. For example, Gratian's teaching that impotence prevents a true marriage from taking place is codified. That is, according to canon 1068 §1, a marriage is invalid if impotence exists at the time the couple enters marriage and the condition is perpetual.

The Code repeats the Church's position that the marriage bond is both perpetual and exclusive. Hence, neither spouse is free to leave the other and enter a new marriage with a third person. In accordance with Trent, however, a marriage is only absolutely indissoluble if it is a sacrament and has been consummated as one. That is, it must be between two baptized persons who, subsequent to both baptisms, have had sexual intercourse during the course of their marriage. If these conditions are not met, then the marriage can be dissolved. Thus, as taught by Trent and the three apostolic constitutions of the sixteenth century, a marriage can be dissolved by the Church if it is not between two baptized persons (for example, by way of the Pauline Privilege) or if it has not been consummated. The dissolution can only come from the Church—not from the couple themselves.

It would be a mistake to think that the 1917 Code does not make any innovations with regard to the Church's matrimonial law. These developments to the Church's practice give rise to changes in the official understanding of marriage. Canon 1081 is a good example. Although its first paragraph repeats the traditional principle that consent makes marriage, its second paragraph attempts to describe this consent. It states, "Matrimonial consent is an act of the will by which each party gives and accepts a perpetual and exclusive right over the body, ordered toward acts which are of themselves apt for the generation of children."[101] Although Gasparri lists many authoritative sources who actually support the first paragraph, he does not for the second. It is this second paragraph which restricts matrimonial consent to matters of a sexual nature—the right to each other's body for the conjugal act.

Canon 1111 introduces into the Church's universal discipline the principle that this right over the body ex-

---

101. *1917 Code* (bibliog. I), canon 1081 §2: "Consensus matrimonialis est actus voluntatis quo utraque pars tradit et acceptat ius in corpus, perpetuum et exclusivum, in ordine ad actus per se aptos ad prolis generationem."

ists from the very beginning of the marriage. One consequence of this is the suppression of the practice which allowed a married person, who had not yet consummated the marriage, to enter religious life—by his or her own choice—within two months from the time of giving consent. That person's spouse now has a right to intercourse during those two months. Only the Church can override the spouse's right—and then only if it is to bring about a greater good.

The Code's emphasis on the sexual dimension of marriage is highlighted by its understanding of the marriage contract. Canon 1012 speaks of marriage as a contract (*contractum matrimonialem*). It is canon 1015 §1 which attempts to describe this contract. It states that it is, by nature, ordered toward the conjugal act. Moreover, it is through this act that the spouses become one flesh.[102] Just as canon 1081 §2 reduces matrimonial consent to the sexual, so canon 1015 §1 restricts the marriage contract to the sexual. Moreover, just as Gasparri did not cite many authoritative sources for canon 1081 §2, so he only gives two for canon 1015 §1. One is Gratian's use of Saint Ambrose—which reference, remember, cannot be found in any of Ambrose's works. The other is to a decretal by Innocent III which, as was seen, is more concerned with the effect of baptism on marriage than the effect of intercourse.

The canons also highlight unity, indissolubility, and the sexual act being directed toward procreation. For example, canon 1013 §2 states that the essential

---

102. ". . . coniugalis actus, ad quem natura sua ordinatur contractus matrimonialis et quo coniuges fiunt una caro."

properties of marriage are unity and indissolubility. Canon 1110 says that as soon as a marriage comes into existence, there is a bond between the couple which is perpetual (that is, indissoluble) and exclusive (that is, it unites the couple in an exclusive manner). Then, the following canon says that the spouses have the right to conjugal acts. These three dimensions of marriage are also emphasized by canon 1086 §2 which says that if a party should exclude, by a positive act of the will, either marriage itself or one of these three dimensions of marriage, then the marriage is invalid.

Now, these three dimensions of marriage were also highlighted by Saint Augustine.[103] He said that because each of these dimensions is in itself good, then marriage as a whole is good. But this was very much an addition to the main reason why Augustine thought marriage is good—namely, the companionship between the husband and wife. It is within this bond of friendship that love and charity are shared. Moreover, this friendship exists from the very beginning of the marriage and is not dependent upon the couple having children.[104] Despite this, the canons do not refer to this aspect of marriage. The canons do not address the example of a man who goes through a wedding ceremony intending to enter marriage, to remain faithful, to keep the marriage permanent, and to have children—but who has no

---

103. Augustine, *De Bono Coniugali* (bibliog. III), 24.32; Migne (ed), *Patrologiae Latina* (bibliog. III), vol. 40, cols. 394–95. Also, Augustine, *Contra Julianum* (bibliog. III), 5, 12, 46; Migne (ed), *Patrologiae Latina* (bibliog. III), vol. 44, col. 810.

104. Augustine, *De Bono Coniugali* (bibliog. III), 3.3; Migne (ed), *Patrologiae Latina* (bibliog. III), vol. 40, col. 375.

intention of exchanging love and charity in a life of intimate companionship.

The Italian jurist Arturo Jemolo also noticed this
omission. In 1941, he raised the following hypothetical
case. A woman belongs to a family which has committed crimes against a man and his family. Such actions
have caused great injury. The man seeks revenge. He
marries the woman with the intention of being cruel to
her and to return the injuries. As Jemolo observed, the
Code does not state that such an intention would make
the marriage invalid.[105]

The Code even gives a restricted list of those aspects of marriage which an individual must know about
in order to marry validly. Canon 1082 §1 says that he
or she must know that marriage is a permanent society between a man and a woman for the procreation of
children. Again, emphasis is on the sexual and no reference is given to the fact that marriage involves mutual
love and support. This canon certainly is not in keeping with the thinking of Saint Augustine or with those
ideas prevalent in twelfth-century France. It is, perhaps, not surprising that Gasparri cites only one negligible source for this canon.[106]

Again, the lack of sources is noteworthy when one
considers canon 1013 §1. This canon states that the primary end of marriage is the procreation and education
of children. The secondary end is mutual help and the
provision of a remedy for concupiscence. There is no

105. Wrenn, *Annulments* (bibliog. III), 144, 196–97. Also, Wrenn, "Refining the Essence of Marriage" (bibliog. III). Also Jemolo, A, *Il Matrimonio nel
Diritto Canonico* (bibliog. III), 76.
106. Gasparri (ed), *Codex Iuris Canonici Pii X* (bibliog. III), 309.

authoritative tradition in the Church on which this canon is based. Again, weight is given to the sexual. That
is, procreation is the primary purpose of marriage. To
be fair, the canon does include within the primary end
the education of any children who might result from
a marriage. But even the secondary end of marriage
emphasizes the sexual. That is, if one is tempted by
sexual urges, then marriage provides an opportunity to
express them in a way that is legitimate and not sinful.
What about love? One could argue that love falls under
the secondary end of marriage—mutual help (*mutuum
adiutorium*). The canon does not state this explicitly,
however. Moreover, even if love is included in this, it is
only a secondary end.

The 1917 Code is a most brilliant and scholarly
work. It manages to codify the laws of the Church in a
single volume. It maintains the principle that consent
makes marriage, but its canons on marriage are biased.
Gratian emphasized the sexual dimension of marriage
at the expense of love. The Code not only maintains
this bias but actively increases it, and it does so with
very little support from the tradition of the Church.

—12—

Between the 1917 Code and the Second Vatican Council
A Period of Dispute

Pope Pius XI and How Love Must Pervade Marriage

THE UNDERSTANDING OF MARRIAGE given by the 1917 Code became the basis for much controversy during the period between its promulgation and the Second Vatican Council. One major contributor to the debate was Pope Pius XI. On the last day of 1930 he issued his encyclical *Casti connubii*.[1] In his introduction, he explains that the encyclical is meant to instruct people, especially Christian spouses, about the truth of marriage, and to protect them from error.[2]

Pius regards an individual marriage to be the result of a co-operation between the couple and God. In particular, a marriage is constituted both by the will of God and the will of man. With regard to God, he has institut-

---

1. Pius XI (bibliog. I), Encyclical, *Casti connubii*, 31 December 1930. The English text is in Husslein (ed), *Social Wellsprings* (bibliog. III), vol. 2, 122–73.
2. Husslein (ed), *Social Wellsprings* (bibliog. III), vol. 2, 125.

ed marriage and has given Christian marriage the dignity of a sacrament. Therefore, its laws are divine and cannot be changed by humans. For example, its bond unites two people in a perpetual manner. What about the will of man? Pius says, "Although matrimony is of its very nature of divine institution, the human will, too, enters into it and performs a most noble part."[3]

When a couple enters marriage, the partners do so by their consent. Moreover, this consent is so necessary that no human power can supply it. Here, Pius makes explicit use of canon 1081 §1. He explains that the role of the individuals' wills is to decide whether or not to enter marriage. It does not involve deciding what sort of marriage (for example, dissoluble, indissoluble); this has already been determined by God. When a man and a woman wish to marry, they exchange consent. In doing so, their souls are united. Pius explains that their souls are united more intimately than their bodies. From the union of their souls, a sacred and inviolable bond arises.

It has been seen how Saint Augustine taught that the main reason why marriage is good is because of the fellowship of love and charity that is created between the spouses. In addition to this, marriage is good because it has three characteristics (children, fidelity, and sacramental dignity), each of which is good in itself. It has also been seen how the 1917 Code tends to ignore Augustine's primary reason for saying that marriage is

---

3. Ibid., 126. "At, quamquam matrimonium suapte natura divinitus est institutum, tamen humana quoque voluntas suas in eo partes habet easque nobilissimas." *Acta Apostolicae Sedis* (bibliog. III) 22 (1930), 541.

good. Instead it concentrates on the three characteristics, or goods, of marriage. Pius XI explicitly refers to these three goods in his encyclical and then uses them as its main headings. It will shortly be seen, however, that Pius XI puts love at the very center of marriage— as Augustine did. This fact can easily be overlooked if one just considers the main headings of his encyclical. Indeed, a cursory reading of *Casti connubii* can lead to the erroneous conclusion that the Pope was concentrating solely on Augustine's three goods of marriage at the expense of love.

Pius describes the benefits that marriage has for the family and society. He starts with those benefits related to the good of children. He says that it is within marriage alone that the procreative faculty may be used. He explains that Christian parents produce children not only for the continuation of the human race but also for the furtherance of the Church on earth. Moreover, parents must educate their children, especially in religious matters. It is for these reasons that the primary end of marriage is the procreation and education of children. Here, Pius explicitly uses canon 1013 §1. It has been seen how the teaching of this particular canon cannot, with any degree of certainty, be traced back to before the 1917 Code.

With regard to the good of fidelity, Pius says that spouses become one flesh through marriage. He bases this teaching on the twenty-fourth Session of the Council of Trent.[4] Consequently, sexual relationships with third parties are excluded. Polygamy and polyandry are

---

4. Denzinger, *Enchiridion Symbolorum* (bibliog. III), 415.

also forbidden, as is divorce and remarriage. Pius then goes on to speak of marital love:

> [Conjugal fidelity] blooms more freely, more beauti-fully and more nobly, when it is rooted in that more excellent soil, the love of husband and wife which pervades all the duties of married life and holds pride of place in Christian marriage. For matrimonial faith demands that husband and wife be joined in an especially holy and pure love, not as adulterers love each other, but as Christ loved the Church. This precept the Apostle laid down when he said, "Husbands, love your wives just as Christ loved the Church" (Ephesians 5:25, Colossians 3:19), that Church which of a truth He embraced with a boundless love not for the sake of His own advantage, but seeking only the good of his Spouse.[5]

This beautiful description of marital love is in stark contrast with the somewhat cold canons of the 1917 Code. For Pius, marital love is special. It is more than just sexual attraction, which even adulterers can experience. Instead, it is a sharing in Christ's love for the Church—a Church which Christ loves so much that he died for her. Pius does not see love as something peripheral to marriage. On the contrary, he says that it "pervades all the duties of married life and holds pride of place in Christian marriage."

---

5. Husslein (ed), *Social Wellsprings* (bibliog. III), vol. 2, 132–33. "Haec autem, quae a Sancto Augustino aptissime appellatur castitatis fides, et facilior et multo etiam iucundior ac nobilior efflorescet ex altero capite praestantissimo: ex coniugali scilicet amore, qui omnia coniugalis vitae officia pervadit et quemdam tenet in christiano coniugio principatum nobilitas. Postulat praeterea matrimonii fides ut vir et uxor singulari quodam sanctoque ac puro amore coniuncti sint; neque ut adulteri inter se ament, sed ut Christus dilexit Ecclesiam; hanc enim regulam Apostolus praescripsit, cum ait: "Viri, diligite uxores vestras sicut et Christus dilexit Ecclesiam"; quam certe immensa illa caritate, non sui commodi gratia, sed Sponsae tantum utilitatem sibi proponens, complexus est." *Acta Apostolicae Sedis* (bibliog. III) 22 (1930), 547–48.

He goes on to say that marital love "must have as its primary purpose that man and wife help each other day by day in forming and perfecting themselves in the interior life."[6] Thus, marriage is a vocation. For Christian spouses, it should help them to perfect themselves spiritually. This is the primary purpose of marital love. Does this contradict canon 1013 §1 which states that the primary purpose of marriage is the procreation and education of children? Pius seems aware of this tension and gives the following explanation: "This mutual interior molding of husband and wife, this determined effort to perfect each other, can in a very real sense . . . be said to be the chief reason and purpose of matrimony, provided matrimony be looked at not in the restricted sense, as instituted for the proper conception and education of the child, but more widely, as the blending of life as a whole and the mutual interchange and sharing thereof."[7]

Marriage can thus be looked at in two ways—in a wide sense and in a restricted sense. In the wide sense, marriage can be seen as a sharing of life. This sharing has as its chief purpose the spiritual perfection of the spouses. This is also the primary purpose of marital love, which takes "pride of place" in Christian marriage and pervades all its duties. Thus, in the wide sense, marriage can be seen as filled with love—a love which shares in Christ's love for his Church. This love helps the spouses to grow spiritually. In the more restricted

---

6. Husslein (ed), *Social Wellsprings* (bibliog. III), vol. 2, 133. ". . . immo hoc in primis intendat, ut coniuges inter se iuventur ad interiorem hominem plenius in dies conformandum perficiendumque." *Acta Apostolicae Sedis* (bibliog. III) 22 (1930), 548.

7. Husslein (ed), *Social Wellsprings* (bibliog. III), vol. 2, 133. "Haec mutua

sense, marriage can be seen as instituted by God for the continuation of the human race and the Church. Looked at in this way, the primary purpose of marriage has to be the procreation and education of children. Therefore, the teaching of canon 1013 §1 about the primacy of procreation and education is within the context of the more restricted understanding of marriage.

If Pius's intention was to defend the 1917 Code's teaching on marriage, it is debatable whether he was successful. He makes it clear that canon 1013 §1 relies upon a narrow vision of marriage. One could go further and say that this limited vision is not broad enough to take in the concept of love, which Pius says is so central to marriage.

So far, I have been examining the encyclical's explanation of the benefits of marriage. Pius has divided these according to the three goods of Saint Augustine. The remaining good is that of sacramental dignity. All marriages, to a degree, are indissoluble.[8] Between Christians (that is, those who are baptized), marriage is always a sacrament. Pius bases this on canon 1012.[9] This sacramentality means that Christian marriage is an efficacious sign of grace. One result of this grace is greater indissolubility.[10] Indeed, Christian marriage

---

coniugum interior conformatio, hoc assiduum sese invicem perficiendi studium, verissima quadam ratione, ut docet Catechismus Romanus, etiam primaria matrimonii causa et ratio dici potest, si tamen matrimonium non pressius ut institutum ad prolem rite procreandam educandamque, sed latius ut totius vitae communio, consuetudo, societas accipiatur." *Acta Apostolicae Sedis* (bibliog. III) 22 (1930), 548–49.

8. Husslein (ed), *Social Wellsprings* (bibliog. III), vol. 2, 135–36.

9. Ibid., 138–39.

10. Ibid., 135.

shares in the bond that exists between Christ and the Church. And this bond is fully manifested in those Christian marriages which have been consummated. As a consequence, such marriages are absolutely in- dissoluble. In keeping with the existing teaching of the Church and the 1917 Code, the encyclical gives two types of marriage which do not have absolute indissol- ubility: certain natural marriages between non-Chris- tians and unconsummated marriages. Pius says that these two exceptions are based on divine law.[11]

The encyclical then goes on to list those acts and opinions which are contrary to the Church's teaching on marriage. Again, Pius divides them according to Augustine's three goods.[12] He concludes his encyclical by giving ways in which these errors and dangers can be corrected.[13]

In order to summarize *Casti connubii*, it can be said that Pius XI provides two ways of looking at mar- riage—in a broad sense and in a more restricted sense. This allows an appreciation of marriage that is much richer and deeper than that given in canon 1013 §1, which simply states that the primary purpose of mar- riage is the procreation and education of children.

Heribert Doms and His Emphasis on Love

A number of scholars also called into question this teaching of canon 1013 §1. Among these were Dietrich von Hildebrand, Bernadin Krempel, Ernst Michel, and

11. Ibid., 136–37.
12. Ibid., 143–59.
13. Ibid., 159–73.

Heribert Doms.[14] In 1935, for example, Doms wrote a treatise on marriage in German entitled *Vom Sinn und Zweck der Ehe*.[15] It was translated into French in 1937, and, in 1939, it was translated into English by George Sayer as "The Meaning of Marriage."[16] This work, available in the main European languages, became very influential.[17]

Doms gives various reasons why the primary purpose of marriage is not the procreation and education of children. From the legal perspective, he observes that the object of the marital contract is the other person as a whole and not just his or her body.[18] The giving of oneself and the taking of the other within the marital contract does include the sexual, but it is more than that.

Doms then argues from the psychological point of view. He claims that marital love is stronger than parental love—which he says usually develops later within the marriage. Thus, the bond between parent and child is not stronger than the marriage bond which exists between the couple. Moreover, this marriage bond exists before the couple has children. Any children that are born are taken up into this love. He notes that when two people marry, they do so in order to form a "two-in-oneship"—that is, they wish to unite their lives to become one. They are not primarily concerned with forming a relationship that involves a third person—namely, a child.[19]

---

14. Heribert Doms is sometimes referred to as Herbert Doms.
15. "The Sense and Purpose of Marriage."
16. Doms, *The Meaning of Marriage* (bibliog. III).
17. Mackin, *What is Marriage?* (bibliog. III), 245.
18. Doms, *The Meaning of Marriage* (bibliog. III), 3–4.
19. Ibid., 7, 15–16.

Doms then looks at the matter biologically. He argues that the fact that a couple can have intercourse while the woman is already pregnant means that intercourse must have some other purpose than just having children.[20] Moreover, pregnancy does not always result from one act of intercourse, which often has to be repeated. Doms says, "We shall certainly be making a mistake if we subordinate the act in its primary content to procreation, because in a very great number of circumstances (for instance, during pregnancy or just after the change of life) this purpose cannot in fact be fulfilled."[21]

Doms also considers the issue from the perspective of gender. He starts from the fact that human beings are divided into two genders. He argues that this must be for more than just generative purposes. Even the lowest of organisms that do not have gender, such as protozoa, are able to procreate. The existence of two genders within humanity must have a deeper purpose.

Doms observes that the Catholic Church takes the non-procreative dimension of gender seriously. For example, it does not ordain women. Thus, the Church does acknowledge that there is more to gender than the use of sexual organs to have children. Indeed, with regard to the individual, gender is a major contributory factor in the formation of personality. Between individuals, the existence of two genders assists in the formation of communities and the promotion of communal activity.[22]

---

20. Ibid., 7–8.
21. Ibid., 68.
22. Ibid., 11–14.

Although Doms rejects the notion that the procreation and education of children is primary to marriage,
he regards sexual intercourse to be very important.
This is not a contradiction because, as just seen, sexual
intercourse may not necessarily result in the generation
of children. In his treatise on marriage, Doms introduces his belief in the importance of sexual intercourse
by continuing his consideration of gender. Gender per-
meates the whole person. Thus, the sexual act can express the whole person, including the spiritual. Sexual
intercourse is more than the use of the sexual organs; it
involves the whole person. In short, intercourse is the
freely willed and total giving of one personality to another. As this total self-giving involves the whole person, including the spiritual, it not only expresses the
spiritual but realizes it.[23]

Doms regards marriage to be the only context in
which the relationship between a man and woman can
be fulfilled. It provides a stable environment for a total
sharing of their lives—a unity of life—and describes
this as a "two-in-oneship." The nurturing of this partnership takes priority over having children, but this
two-in-oneship finds its greatest expression and real-
ization in sexual intercourse. This is the primary role
of intercourse, though intercourse can also result in
children. If it does, then the dignity of the marriage is
increased; the two-in-oneship is enriched. That is, it
goes from being a husband-wife relationship to a fa-
ther-mother one. The love from this two-in-oneship
spills over from the spouses onto the children.

---

23. Ibid., 14–15.

Doms does seem to be aware that he is contradicting canon 1013 §1, with its teaching on the primary and secondary ends of marriage. He attempts to reconcile his views with this canon. He states that the "meaning" of marriage is the fulfillment of the two-in-oneship—that is, the fulfillment of the love that exists between a man and a woman within that unique partnership in which they are so united that they are as one.[24] It is for this reason that sexual intercourse has the immediate purpose of realizing the spouses' two-in-oneship. Intercourse has two ulterior purposes, however. One is biological—that is, it can produce children. The second is personal—it can provide mutual help and a remedy for concupiscence.[25] Doms goes on to explain that society gives priority to the first of the ulterior purposes because it needs children to continue. The other ulterior purpose is secondary.

Thus, Doms attempts to reconcile his understanding with the Catholic Church's teaching. In the broad sense, the meaning of marriage is the fulfillment of the two-in-oneship. Sexual intercourse is for this purpose. But intercourse can also be seen in a more restricted sense. That is, it can generate children who are to be educated—the primary end of marriage. Also, intercourse provides mutual help between the spouses and is an occasion to remedy concupiscence—the secondary ends of marriage.[26] Thus, it is possible to understand Doms's teaching on the ends of marriage in terms of the "broad" and "restricted" categories of Pius

24. Ibid., 86.
25. Ibid., 85.
26. Ibid., 87–88, 95.

XI. It could be argued that Doms was simply following the teaching put forward by this Pope only a few years before. In doing so, Doms would not appear to be contradicting canon 1013 §1. Unfortunately for Doms, the Church's authorities did not agree.

The Official Condemnation of Doms's Emphasis

On 3 October 1941, Pius XII gave his annual address to the Roman Rota.[27] He spoke of the two ends of marriage: "There are two tendencies to be avoided: first the one which, in examining the constituent elements of the act of generation, considers only the primary end of marriage, as though the secondary end did not exist, or were not the *finis operis* established by the Creator of nature himself; and secondly the one which gives the secondary end a place of equal principality, detaching it from its essential subordination to the primary end—a view which would lead by logical necessity to deplorable consequences."[28] Although Doms and his teaching is not condemned, Pius XII thought it necessary to uphold the teaching of canon 1013 §1. Mutual help and the remedy for concupiscence form the secondary end and cannot be put on the same level as the primary end. Any challenge to the primary end would be "deplorable."

Just over two years later, a marriage case came before the Rota. As is usual, three judges heard the case. One of them, Arthur Wynen, wrote the sentence that

27. Pius XII (bibliog. I), Address to the Sacred Roman Rota, 3 October 1941. English text in Woestman (ed), *Papal Allocutions* (bibliog. III), 11–16.
28. Woestman (ed), *Papal Allocutions* (bibliog. III), 13.

gave the judges' decision and their reasons for it.[29] The sentences of the Rota are not usually published in the *Acta Apostolicae Sedis*. This publication is reserved for more important official documents promulgated by the Pope or his delegates for the attention of the Church throughout the world. But the sentence of Arthur Wynen *was* published in this journal.[30] As Mackin observes, this move "suggests the importance it [the sentence] had in the minds of the Church's appointed judges."[31]

Wynen observes that it is agreed by many that some ends of marriage are primary and others secondary. Indeed, he boldly states that this is taught by various constitutions and encyclicals of Popes as well as by theologians, canonists, moral theologians, and the words of canon law.[32] Wynen then says that the primary end of marriage is the generation and education of children. He cites canon 1013 §1, the encyclical *Casti connubii* and the 1941 Papal Allocution to the Rota.[33] He continues to say that the secondary end of marriage is mutual help and the remedy for concupiscence. Here he cites Leo XIII's encyclical *Arcanum* and Cardinal Gasparri's list of sources for canon 1013 §1. It has already been shown that *Arcanum* cannot be used as a basis for this canon and that Gasparri's sources are virtually nonexistent.

---

29. The other two judges were William Heard and Albert Canestri.

30. Wynen, Rotal decision of 22 January 1944 (bibliog. II).

31. Mackin, *What is Marriage?* (bibliog. III), 219.

32. "Ex variis Summorum Pontificum Constitutionibus et Litteris Encyclicis, ex communi Theologorum, Canonistarum, Moralistarum doctrina, ex explicitis Iuris Canonici verbis constat plures esse matrimonii fines, quorum alius est primarius, alius secundarius." *Acta Apostolicae Sedis* (bibliog. III) 36 (1944), 184.

33. Ibid., 185–87.

Wynen then examines the relationship between the primary and secondary ends of marriage. He points out that mutual help can exist between two people of the opposite sex outside marriage—for example, between a brother and a sister. He thus considers what it is that distinguishes mutual help within marriage from mutual help outside it. He explains that, within marriage, mutual help is directed toward the procreation and education of children. That is, the secondary end of marriage is directed toward the primary end.

Wynen heeds the caution of Pius XII in his allocution to the Rota in 1941. He makes it clear that the secondary end of marriage is a distinct end—that it is not a part of the primary end. It is directed toward the primary end, however, and is subordinate to it.

It has been seen that canon 1086 §2 states that a marriage is null if a party excludes either marriage itself, all rights to the conjugal act, or unity or indissolubility. Wynen and his two associate judges make an important legal distinction. If a person does not intend the primary end of marriage when marrying, then his matrimonial consent is so defective that the marriage is null. If the individual does not intend the secondary end, however, then the validity of the marriage is not affected. This is because the secondary end is not as important as the primary end and is in fact directed toward it. In other words, a person could validly enter marriage with an intention to exclude the secondary end of marriage. In a way, all Wynen does is to show that Gasparri's canon 1086 §2 does not say that a marriage is null if a party excludes mutual help, which is a part of the secondary end.

Wynen's sentence was very influential on other ecclesiastical judges. Its appearance in the *Acta Apostolicae Sedis* guaranteed this. The consequences were major. If, at the time of marriage, an individual intended either not to have sexual intercourse or not to have children, then the marriage was null. If he did not intend mutual help, however, then the validity of the marriage was not affected. In short, love could be excluded from the marriage. This certainly was not the tradition of the Church. Furthermore, it did not agree with Pope Pius XI's description of the centrality of love within marriage. The primary end of marriage (the procreation and education of children) was gradually pushing out the other dimensions of marriage.

Less than three months later, another statement on marriage was published in the *Acta Apostolicae Sedis* —this time by the Holy Office.[34] This congregation had the role of upholding the Catholic Faith and correcting those who taught opinions contrary to it. The decree concludes by upholding the primary and secondary ends of marriage as understood by such persons as Wynen. Any views appearing to be different are condemned. Consequently, Doms's book was withdrawn.

Finally, on 29 October 1951, Pius XII gave an allocution to the Association of Catholic Midwives.[35] Again, he upholds the primary and secondary ends of

---

34. Holy Office (bibliog. I), Decree, *De finibus matrimonii*, 1 April 1944. English text in Mackin, *What is Marriage?* (bibliog. III), 235–36.

35. Pius XII (bibliog. I), *Allocutio Conventui Unionis Italicae inter Obstetrices*, 29 October 1951.

marriage. He explains that the secondary end of mutual help and remedy for concupiscence is subordinate to the primary end of procreation and education. He states that the family is not a mere "biological laboratory" for the production of children, however. He also acknowledges that sexual intercourse is both pleasurable and is an expression of the union of the husband and wife, but he emphasizes that these are both subordinate to the primary purpose of having children.

—13—

Conclusion to Part One

WHAT CAN BE SAID about the canon law of marriage on the eve of the Second Vatican Council? Canon 1081 §1 repeats the traditional teaching that a marriage is brought into existence by the consent of the couple. This teaching is found within the Roman Empire. It was adopted by the Church and promoted by scholars such as Saint Ambrose, Saint Isidore of Seville, and Pope Nicholas I. Furthermore, the role of consent in the creation of marriage also became important legally within the Germanic tribes.

Nevertheless, such scholars as Hincmar of Rheims and Gratian, using dubious sources, introduced the role of sexual consummation into the Church's law. Gratian's *Decretum* influenced many Popes from Alexander III and Innocent III on, and consequently the entire Church. Gratian's position is eventually reinforced by Cardinal Gasparri and the 1917 Code. Thus, the second paragraph of canon 1081 describes matrimonial consent as "an act of the will by which each party gives and accepts a perpetual and exclusive right over the body, ordered toward acts which are of themselves apt for the generation of children." Indeed, according to canon 1015 §1 of the 1917 Code, sexual intercourse is so central to marriage that the marital contract is, by nature, ordered toward it. The importance of sexual intercourse means that the 1917 Code, like Gratian, considers impotence to be a natural bar to marriage.

Gratian teaches that, although a marriage begins with the consent of the couple, it is not complete until there has been sexual intercourse. This intercourse, when it is between baptized spouses, makes present the indissoluble bond that exists between Christ and his Church. Thus, according to Gratian and the 1917 Code, a consummated Christian marriage is absolutely indissoluble. Conversely, an unconsummated marriage is not complete. Similarly, marriages involving at least one unbaptized spouse also lack absolute indissolubility. This teaching became clear by the end of the sixteenth century, which saw the issuing of three important papal constitutions: *Altitudo*, *Romani Pontificis*, and *Populis*.

Finally, canon 1013 §1 on the primary and secondary ends of marriage emphasizes the procreative dimension of marriage. This particular canon proved to be very controversial in the period leading up to the Second Vatican Council. It has been seen that there was no real tradition behind this canon and that the sources cited by Gasparri are negligible. In *Casti connubii*, Pius XI opens the door to developing this canon. If marriage is seen in the restricted sense, being for the continuation of the human race and the Church, then its primary end will be the procreation and education of children. But it is possible to look at marriage in a broader sense—as a partnership of life and love in which the spouses help to perfect each other.

Soon, however, Wynen's sentence upholds the procreation and education of children to the detriment of mutual help and love. That is, couples can marry without any intention to love and care for each other and their marriages are still regarded as valid. Finally, the Holy Office condemns any teaching likely to undermine the priority of procreation and education. This condemnation is confirmed by Pius XII in his allocution to midwives. Thus, by the early 1950s, the door opened by *Casti connubii* is firmly closed. The resulting official understanding of marriage is very different from the firm tradition within the Church which puts love at the center of marriage. This tradition has been upheld by such authorities as Saint Augustine, Ivo of Chartres, Hugh of Saint Victor, Peter Lombard, and Pope Pius XI.

PART TWO

The Second Vatican Council And Current Marriage Law

— 1 —

Introduction to Part Two

THIS SECOND PART involves an examination of the present law of marriage as found in the Latin tradition of the Catholic Church. The majority of this law is contained within the 1983 Code of Canon Law. In order to set the scene historically, it is important to mention that on 25 January 1959 Pope John XXIII announced that he was going to convene a council and revise the 1917 Code of Canon Law. This eventually resulted in the 1983 Code of Canon Law. It will be seen that this revised Code is intimately linked with the Second Vatican Council. Thus, it is necessary to consider the Council's treatment of marriage before examining the 1983 Code.

In order to help the reader understand this second part, I shall explain its layout.

Chapter 2 considers the Second Vatican Council's treatment of marriage. It will be seen that all attempts to produce a document on marriage failed. Indeed, the Council very nearly ended without any major statement on marriage. The Council did produce sixteen documents on various issues such as the liturgy, the Church, ecumenism, and the apostolate of the laity. Although none of these documents is purely about marriage, eight of them refer to it in a way that is of some significance. One of these documents is the *Pastoral Constitution on the Church in the Modern World*, which is often known by its opening words *Gaudium et spes*.[1] This document was among the last to be produced by the Council and it provides the fullest Conciliar treatment of marriage. I shall examine the first seven of these eight Conciliar documents. Then I shall consider *Gaudium et spes*—specifically, the history of its drafting and its treatment of marriage.

Chapter 3 gives a description of the 1983 Code of Canon Law. It briefly explains how the Code was drafted, for whom it is meant (that is, who is bound by it), and its structure.

I shall then examine the Code's treatment of marriage by analyzing its marriage section. This runs from canon 1055 to canon 1165. I shall focus on those canons relevant to this book. The Code's marriage section consists of eight introductory canons (1055 to 1062) followed by ten chapters of further canons. As the Code contains most of the Church marriage law, I shall generally follow the order found within the Code. Any experienced canon lawyer will already be familiar with this ordering, but anyone new to this subject could easily be confused. Thus, I shall now explain the ordering.

Chapter 4 looks at the very nature of marriage as it is depicted in the first two of the introductory canons (1055 and 1056).

---

1. Vatican II (bibliog. I), *Gaudium et spes,* 7 December 1965. Also in *Sacrosanctum* (bibliog. III).   English translation in Flannery (ed), *Vatican Council II* (bibliog. III), 903–1002.

Chapter 5 focuses on what the Code says brings a marriage into existence—namely, the consent of the couple. This chapter also examines how the Code describes this consent. In order to do this, the chapter considers canon 1057 of the Code's introductory canons on marriage.

Chapter 6 examines the nature of consummation. It will be seen that although a marriage begins with the consent of the couple, consummation remains very important legally. Thus, it is necessary to be clear about what is meant by consummation. This chapter concentrates on canon 1061 of the Code's introductory canons on marriage.

Chapter 7 picks up the theme of the previous chapter by examining the practice of dissolving non-consummated marriages. Although this chapter does not follow the order of the Code, it is convenient to consider non-consummation in the light of the previous chapter.

Chapter 8 briefly examines the first of the Code's chapters on marriage which is concerned with pastoral care and marriage preparation.

Chapter 9 examines the second and third of the Code's marriage chapters, which consider impediments to marriage. In particular, I focus on canon 1084 concerning the impediment of impotence. Thus, this chapter is linked with the earlier chapters, 6 and 7. That is, Chapter 6 describes what is meant by consummation, Chapter 7 examines the dissolution of marriages which have not been consummated, and Chapter 9 considers those instances where consummation cannot take place because of impotence. Chapter 9 is in two parts: the first examines the present law concerning impotence; the second dares to suggest some possible developments to this law.

Chapter 10 acts as an introduction to the three chapters which follow. If marriage begins with the consent of the couple, then it is necessary to explore what is required for this consent to be given properly. I classify the requirements into three categories: sufficient mental faculty, sufficient knowledge, and genuineness. This classification will enable me to consider the canons found in the fourth chapter of the 1983 Code's marriage section.

Chapter 11 focuses on the first type of requirement for consent to be given—sufficient mental faculty. It begins with an examination of canon 1095. It will be seen that some people are psychologically incapable of giving true marital consent. This has resulted in some ecclesiastical judges drawing comparisons between the law on psychological incapacity for marriage and the physical incapacity caused by impotence. I explore these comparisons. Finally, I boldly suggest a comparison of my own—namely, comparing the act of consummation to the act of giving consent. By doing so, I apply the present law on what is required mentally for giving consent to the act of consummation.

Chapter 12 focuses on the second requirement for consent to be given—sufficient knowledge.

Chapter 13 considers the third requirement for consent to be given properly— it has to be genuine. It considers three instances. The first is where somebody goes through a wedding ceremony saying the correct things but not actually meaning them. The second is concerned with the practice of adding conditions to consent. The third involves people being forced or frightened into going through a wedding ceremony.

Chapter 14 considers the wedding ceremony. It examines the form of marriage as described in the fifth chapter of the Code's marriage canons. It then looks at marriages between Catholics and other baptized Christians (called "mixed marriages"), as well as marriages celebrated secretly. Mixed marriages and marriages celebrated secretly are covered by the sixth and seventh marriage chapters of the Code respectively.

Chapter 15 briefly looks at the effects of marriage as given in the 1983 Code's eighth chapter of marriage canons. This brief examination will consist mainly of a comparison with the 1917 Code.

Chapter 16 examines the various practices of dissolving non-sacramental marriages—that is, marriages where at least one spouse is not baptized. These practices are described both within chapter nine of the 1983 Code's marriage canons and outside the Code. I look at the Pauline Privilege, which involves the dissolution of a marriage entered into by two unbaptized persons. Then I consider applications of the Pauline Privilege to particular circumstances. Finally, I look at dissolutions in Favor of the Faith, where one party was baptized at the time of entering marriage.

Chapter 17 very briefly looks at the Code's tenth and final chapter of marriage canons. This considers how marriages not recognized by the Church can be corrected. This short consideration of the subject emphasizes the teaching that it is the consent of the couple which brings a marriage into existence. This final chapter of Part Two is then followed by the General Conclusion of this book.

—2—

The Second Vatican Council and Marriage

Attempts to Draft a Document on Marriage

ON JANUARY 25, 1959, Pope John XXIII announced that he was going to convene a council and that he was going to revise the 1917 Code. About a year later, he established ten preparatory commissions, each of which was to begin considering a particular area of the Church's life and teaching. These preparatory commissions were coordinated by the Central Preparatory Commission and accompanied by two secretariats.[1] The Italian historian, Giuseppe Alberigo, explains that the preparatory commissions produced seventy schemas. He quotes the then Joseph Ratzinger, later Pope Benedict XVI: "This was more than double the quantity of texts produced by all the previous councils put together."[2]

Initially, some of the preparatory commissions received schemas from various congregations. The Sacred Congregation for the Discipline of the Sacraments drafted one on marriage. Unfortunately, instead of

1. Vorgrimler (ed), *Commentary on the Documents of Vatican II* (bibliog. III), vol. 1, 4.
2. Alberigo (ed), *History of Vatican II* (bibliog. III), vol. 2, 69.

227

allowing canon law to be based upon theology, this congregation did the opposite. It worked its way through the marriage canons of the 1917 Code of Canon Law. Moreover, it declared that there should be no changes to anything contained in canons 1012 to 1018.[3] This is important because canon 1013 §1 was the controversial one about the primary and secondary ends of marriage.

In March 1962, the same congregation drafted a more detailed schema on the sacraments.[4] In the section on marriage, the draft refers to canon 1081. Paragraph one of this canon states that consent makes marriage. This teaching has a long tradition in the Church. But the canon has a second paragraph which describes marital consent as being an act of the will whereby the partners exchange the right to those acts which are apt for the procreation of children.[5] It has been seen that there is very little tradition on which to base this paragraph. Theodore Mackin observes that the congregation's schema acknowledges that consent makes marriage, but then simply says that when marital consent is exchanged so are those rights which are proper to making a marriage.[6] This could be an indication that the congregation in question was beginning to think beyond the existing marriage canons. Whether this is true

---

3. *Acta et Documenta* (bibliog. III), Series I, vol. 3, 93–102, especially 93. Also, Mackin, *What is Marriage?* (bibliog. III), 248.

4. *Acta et Documenta* (bibliog. III), Series II, vol. 3, 499–557.

5. *1917 Code* (bibliog. I), canon 1081 §2: "Consensus matrimonialis est actus voluntatis quo utraque pars tradit et acceptat ius in corpus, perpetuum et exclusivum, in ordine ad actus per se aptos ad prolis generationem."

6. Mackin, *What is Marriage?* (bibliog. III), 249. Theodore Mackin provides an excellent account of the attempts to draft a document on marriage. This has been most helpful to my work. Also, *Acta et Documenta* (bibliog. III), Series II, vol. 3, part 1, 528.

or not, neither schema of the congregation was taken up by the appropriate preparatory commission.

The Congregation of the Holy Office also produced a schema—"Schema for the Ecumenical Council."[7] In paragraph 24 of Part 4 it gives recommendations as to what the Council should teach about marriage. It gives a long list of subjects so that the Church's teaching could be upheld and any errors corrected. The list includes the ends of marriage, birth control, consummation, impotence, abortion, and mixed marriages.[8]

The Prefect of the Holy Office was Cardinal Alfredo Ottaviani. He was also the president of the Theological Commission which had been established to help prepare for the Council. Doctrinal matters would be referred to this commission. This Theological Commission expanded paragraph 24 into an entire schema on marriage— "On Chastity, Virginity, Marriage, and the Family."[9] The Theological Commission explained that the schema contains parts of two previously proposed documents: "On Christian Chastity and Modesty"[10] (which was part of a proposed constitution called "On the Moral Order"),[11] and a constitution called "On Marriage and the Family."[12] In May 1962, the Theological Commission's schema on marriage went before the Central Preparatory Commission for its approval.

---

7. *Schema Pro Concilio Oecumenico in Acta et Documenta* (bibliog. III), Series I, vol. 3, 3–17.

8. Ibid., 13. Mackin, *What is Marriage?* (bibliog. III), 249.

9. *De Castitate, Virginitate, Matrimonio, Familia in Acta et Documenta* (bibliog. III), Series II, vol. 2,, part 3, 893–937.

10. *De Castitate et Pudicitia Christiano.*

11. *De Ordine Morali.*

12. *De Matrimonio et Familia.*

Mackin gives an excellent account of the schema and the debate over it.[13]

The schema did not treat marriage positively. It concluded its chapters with a list of errors that the Theological Commission thought should be condemned by the Second Vatican Council:

> It [the Council] condemns severely the errors and theories denying that there is an immutable divine order regarding the properties and ends of marriage. And it rejects explicitly as a supreme calumny the assertion that the indissolubility of marriage comes not from God but is something invented cruelly by the Church and cruelly held to. What is more, it condemns the theories which subvert the right order of values and makes the primary end of marriage inferior to the biological and personal values of the spouses, and proclaim that conjugal love is in the objective order itself the primary end.[14]

This example illustrates how the schema was closed to any possible changes to the Church's teaching on the ends of marriage.

Certainly, it was not permissible to regard marital love as the primary end. This is emphasized in another part of the schema: "What is more, marriage has in itself—that is, independently of the intention of the contracting parties—its own objective ends that have been established by God. Among these ends—and this we know from the plan of its divine institution, from nature itself, as well as from the Church Magisterium—

13. Mackin, *What is Marriage?* (bibliog. III), 249–57.
14. *De Castitate, Virginitate, Matrimonio, Familia,* paragraph 16, in *Acta et Documenta* (bibliog. III), Series II, vol. 2, part 3, 910. Translation in Mackin, *What is Marriage?* (bibliog. III), 250–51.

the one and only primary end is the procreation and nurture of children, even if in a particular instance a marriage is infertile."[15] These are powerful words considering how this teaching on the primary end of marriage has no authoritative tradition prior to Gasparri's 1917 Code of Canon Law.

The Theological Commission's schema then explains the secondary ends of marriage in the same way as Wynen did in his Rotal sentence. It states that the secondary ends are mutual help and the avoidance of concupiscence, but many relationships and friendships involve mutual help. What marks mutual help within a marital relationship is that as a secondary end it is directed to the primary end. Thus, even the secondary end of marriage has to be understood in terms of the primary end.[16]

When the schema went before the Central Preparatory Commission in May 1962, most of the cardinals thought it was acceptable and suggested only a few minor changes. But four cardinals had major misgivings: Julius Döpfner of München-Freising, Bernhard Jan Alfrink of Utrecht, Emile Léger of Montreal, and Leo Joseph Suenens of Malines-Bruges.[17]

Cardinal Döpfner was greatly concerned about the schema's treatment of marital love. It merely condemned those who claimed that it is the primary end. Döpfner asked a rhetorical question: "But does not

---

15. *De Castitate, Virginitate, Matrimonio, Familia,* paragraph 13 in *Acta et Documenta* (bibliog. III), Series II, vol. 2, part 3, 909. Translation in Mackin, *What is Marriage?* (bibliog. III), 251.

16. *Acta et Documenta* (bibliog. III), Series II, vol. 2, part 3, 909. Mackin, *What is Marriage?* (bibliog. III), 251–52.

17. Mackin, *What is Marriage?* (bibliog. III), 252.

marital love, in the objective order itself and according
to God's intent, somehow constitute the very form and
soul of marriage, in such a way that without true marital love the ends themselves of marriage can neither be
conceived of nor be rightly attained?"[18]

Cardinal Alfrink continued the attack.[19] He said that
Catholics use the language of psychology when talking
about marriage. They speak in terms of the human, the
theological, and the biblical. But the Church's Magisterium uses juridical language and speaks of marriage
in terms of a contract. Alfrink observed that the schema is no different. He said that it would only disap-
point Catholics, who understand marriage primarily as
a sharing of life by a man and woman who love each
other and wish to have children.

He then appealed to Scripture. He quoted Genesis 2:24—"A man leaves his father and mother and
becomes attached to his wife, and they become one
flesh." He acknowledged that this attachment has a sexual dimension, but it is also psychological, he argued.
That is, the marriage partners are also united in the
bond of marital love. Moreover, the passage from Genesis makes it clear that the man leaves his parents and
marries the woman *because* he loves her. Thus, marital love is the cause of marriage, not a consequence
of it. Cardinal Alfrink then pointed out that Scripture
uses marriage as a symbol of the relationship between
Christ and his Church. This imagery is based upon the

---

18. In *Acta et Documenta* (bibliog. III), Series II, vol. 2, part 3, 948. Translation
in Mackin, *What is Marriage?* (bibliog. III), 253.

19. *Acta et Documenta* (bibliog. III), Series II, vol. 2, part 3, 960–62. Mackin,
What is Marriage? (bibliog. III), 253–55.

centrality of love within marriage; it is not referring to its sexual dimension.

Alfrink concluded by saying that Scripture does not speak of marital love in terms of primary and secondary ends. Instead, it regards love as being constitutive of marriage. He acknowledged that one cannot say that a marriage is invalid simply because there is no love, but such a marriage would be incomplete. This marital love is expressed mutually when the partners join in the conjugal act. Alfrink noted that when spouses are engaged in such an act, their desire to express their mutual love usually comes before any intention to have a child. This is not to deny that in the objective order the primary end is the generation and subsequent education of children. Outside the juridical or objective order, however, this is not the experience of Catholics. It is for this reason that Alfrink opposed the Theological Commission's schema as it was presented and he requested that the beautiful description of marital love given by Pope Pius XI in his encyclical *Casti connubii* be included.

As Mackin notes, Cardinal Ottaviani did not take these criticisms of his schema lightly. His response was both forceful and personal: "As to the question of marital love, about which so many and endless things have been said—things that tell of the environment in which Cardinals Döpfner, Alfrink and others live—it seems to me that it must all be taken with a grain of salt."[20]

Ottaviani gave four main reasons why he thought that too great an emphasis was being put on marital

---

20. *Acta et Documenta* (bibliog. III), Series II, vol. 2, part 3, 977–78. Mackin, *What is Marriage?* (bibliog. III), 256.

love. First, it places marital love before the primary end—namely, the generation and education of children. Second, love is not essential to the nature of marriage. This is illustrated by Saint Paul's command that husbands must love their wives. That is, marital love is a duty. Third, a marriage can exist without such love. And fourth, to put love at the center of marriage easily leads to the claim that a marriage ceases to exist once a husband and wife stop loving each other.[21]

These arguments of Ottaviani did not convince the members of the Central Preparatory Commission. The majority of them began to have serious reservations about the proposed schema. Accordingly, they rejected it.[22] The legacy of Gasparri regarding the primary and secondary ends of marriage, which had lasted nearly half a century, was coming to an end.

The loss of the Theological Commission's schema meant that a new schema on marriage was needed. There was no shortage of contenders because a number of preparatory commissions were working on them. The history of these schemas is like that of a concertina. In January 1963, the Central Preparatory Commission instructed these various preparatory commissions to combine their schemas on marriage and reduce them to a single document. The task of combining them was given to the Conciliar Commission for the Discipline of the Sacraments. Consequently, six schemas were compressed into one. This new schema was called "Decree on the Sacrament of Marriage."[23] It is noteworthy that

---

21. *Acta et Documenta* (bibliog. III), Series II, vol. 2, part 3, 977–78. Mackin, *What is Marriage?* (bibliog. III), 257.

22. Mackin, *What is Marriage?* (bibliog. III), 257.

23. *Decretum de Matrimonii Sacramento,* in *Acta Synodalia* (bibliog. III), vol. 3, part 8, 1068–83.

it contains virtually nothing on the ends of marriage and so ignores the Theological Commission's rejected schema.

In July 1963, "Decree on the Sacrament of Marriage" was sent to the bishops for their comments.[24] These were passed on to the Central Preparatory Commission which concluded that the schema should be compressed even further, this time to a votum—that is, a brief suggestion or recommendation. As Alberigo says, "What had been a 'mountain' of six different schemas on marriage on the eve of Vatican II brought forth a 'mouse' of a two-page mini-document in February 1964."[25] When this further compression had been completed, the *votum* was sent to the bishops in April 1964 for their comments. It is not surprising that they thought that this treatment of marriage was far too brief. Consequently, like a concertina, it was expanded, and the new text was issued to the bishops in November of that year.[26]

It must be remembered that in January 1959 Pope John XXIII not only announced his intention to summon a Council but also to revise the Code of Canon Law. Thus, when the bishops saw the document on marriage, it was noted by many that its contents had legal implications. They agreed to refer it to the Pope so that it could be considered at some point in the future when work had started on the revision of the Code of Canon Law.[27] Consequently, it was no longer to be dealt with by the Council. This was also in accordance with Cardinal Döpfner's wishes. Like many, he was

---

24. *Acta Synodalia* (bibliog. III), vol. 3, part 8, 1145–77.
25. Alberigo (ed), *History of Vatican II* (bibliog. III), vol. 2, 482.
26. Mackin, *What is Marriage?* (bibliog. III), 258–59.
27. *Acta Synodalia* (bibliog. III), vol. 3, part 8, 552, 621–35, 652–53, 679–776.

concerned that the Council would have so many schemas and proposals to consider that it would run out of
time. He had been entrusted with the task of stream-
lining the work of the Council.[28] The concertina had
been squeezed shut permanently. The Second Vatican
Council was not going to issue a document specifically
on marriage.

Sacrosanctum Concilium

With regard to marriage, the first document to be considered is the *Constitution on the Sacred Liturgy (Sacrosanctum Concilium)* which was promulgated on 4
December 1963.[29] Since the early years of the twentieth
century, the calls for liturgical change had increased.
Pope Pius XII himself responded in 1947 by issuing
his encyclical *Mediator Dei* which reformed the Eas-
ter liturgy.[30] Then, in 1956, the Sacred Congregation
of Rites sponsored the Pastoral-Liturgical Congress in
Assisi which was attended by many bishops from several countries. The great commentator on the Council,
Heribert Vorgrimler, explains that reforms to the liturgy were being made even as the world's bishops were
preparing to go to the Council. The early 1960s saw the
introduction of new simplified rubrics; a shortened ceremony for the dedication of a church and new editions
of the Missal and Breviary.[31]

---

28. Alberigo (ed), *History of Vatican II* (bibliog. III), vol. 3, 348, 359–60.
29. Vatican II (bibliog. I), *Sacrosanctum Concilium,* 4 December 1963. Also in
Sacrosanctum (bibliog. III), 3–69. English translation in Flannery (ed), *Vatican
Council II* (bibliog. III), 1–37.
30. Pius XII (bibliog. I), Encyclical, *Mediator Dei,* 20 November 1947.
31. Vorgrimler (ed), *Commentary on the Documents of Vatican II* (bibliog.
III), vol. 1, 1–4.

This interest in liturgical renewal is illustrated well by Vorgrimler. He explains how the first preparatory commission for the proposed Council invited bishops to suggest subjects for the Council to discuss. Nearly a quarter of the replies were concerned with the liturgy.[32] Consequently, a schema on the liturgy was produced.[33] The proposed constitution was to lay down general norms and principles concerning the liturgy which would be implemented later by the appropriate departments in Rome.

This schema was so important that in October 1962 it was announced that it would be considered before any others. Progress with it was slow because it was the first one the Council had to deal with, so there were problems with procedure which had to be settled. Eventually, in November 1963, the schema as a whole was voted on by the bishops.[34] It was accepted overwhelmingly with 2,158 votes in favor and only 19 against.[35]

Articles 19 and 59 are among those which consider the sacraments generally. The former encourages pastors to foster the liturgical instruction of the members of the Church. This is so they can understand the meaning of the sacraments and appreciate the various signs and symbols used, as well as actively participate in the celebration of the sacraments. The latter article explains the purpose of the sacraments: to sanctify, to build up the Church, and to give worship to God. The

32. Ibid., 4.

33. *Schema Constitutionis de Sacra Liturgia* (Schema of the Constitution on the Sacred Liturgy).

34. Vorgrimler (ed), *Commentary on the Documents of Vatican II* (bibliog. III), vol. 1, 5–7.

35. *Acta Synodalia* (bibliog. III), vol. 2, part 5, 767.

recipients of the sacraments receive God's grace so that they may practice charity and worship God. Also, the sacraments teach by means of the signs they use. Thus, these signs must be understood by the members of the Church. The article continues by explaining the link between the sacraments and the faith of those involved in their celebration. The sacraments presuppose faith— without which their celebration would be meaningless. Moreover, they nourish and strengthen faith, as well as express it.[36]

Articles 77 and 78 apply these general principles to marriage. Article 77 calls for the rite of marriage to be revised and enriched so that the signs and symbols used may signify more clearly the grace of the sacrament. These signs should also help teach the meaning of marriage by emphasizing the duties of the spouses. In order for this to happen, bishops' conferences should be allowed to make use of local customs and ceremonies. Article 78 permits the use of the vernacular when marriage is celebrated within Mass so that the ceremony may be understood better and thus be more instructive. Moreover, marriage may also be celebrated outside Mass.[37]

It has been seen that, according to canon 1143 of the 1917 Code of Canon Law, a woman whose first husband has died cannot receive the nuptial blessing a second time if she remarries. This is because she is presumed to no longer be a virgin and so cannot symbolize the Church—the virgin bride of Christ. When article 78

36. *Sacrosanctum* (bibliog. III), 15–16, 33.
37. Ibid., 37–38.

of *Sacrosanctum Concilium* was being discussed, there were calls for it to revise the nuptial blessing. This was so that the blessing could emphasize the obligations of both the husband and the wife. This would have been in conformity with the general liturgical principles— namely, that the words of the ceremony are to be instructive. There was resistance to such a revision of the nuptial blessing, however. Some bishops did not want to weaken the imagery of the woman as the virgin bride of Christ. Thus, article 78 still emphasizes the bride. This is why it says very little about the mutual obligations of marriage. Moreover, what is said is still linked to the concept of virginal purity.[38] Hence, the only mutual marital obligation mentioned is fidelity (*mutuae fidelitatis*).[39]

In summary, *Sacrosanctum Concilium* is concerned with the capacity of the marriage ceremony to teach what marriage involves. It thus calls for richer signs and symbols to be used, including those which may have a greater meaning in a particular geographical region. It also permits the vernacular to be used. In this way, the bride and groom, as well as others present at the ceremony, may arrive more easily at an understanding of the duties of marriage.

Lumen Gentium

During the preparations for the Council, there evolved a draft document of eleven chapters concerning the

---

38. Vorgrimler (ed), *Commentary on the Documents of Vatican II* (bibliog. III), vol. 1, 54.
39. *Sacrosanctum* (bibliog. III), 38.

Church—with an appendix on the Virgin Mary. It soon became clear that this would be a most important part of the Council's work. By the end of the first session of the Council, the bishops expressed their wish that the document should be open and positive. They did not want it just to condemn errors. Similarly, they wanted more than just an apologetic. Pope John XXIII himself said that the document must have a patristic and biblical base—as opposed to a simple repetition of formulas from scholasticism.[40]

In 1963, after the first session, the Theological Commission produced a second draft. It contained four chapters and was accompanied by a list of possible improvements and suggestions. These were put before the bishops at the second session. They made their comments and eventually the Theological Commission produced a third draft with eight chapters. On 16 November 1964, Pope Paul VI issued a statement concerning the text. His involvement resulted in an explanatory note being attached to the document.[41] This note was intended to clarify the relationship between the bishops and the Pope. A few days later, the bishops voted on the whole document. It received hardly any negative votes.[42] Thus, the *Dogmatic Constitution on the Church* (*Lumen gentium*) was promulgated on 21 November 1964.[43]

---

40. Vorgrimler (ed), *Commentary on the Documents of Vatican II* (bibliog. III), vol. 1, 106–10, 126, 135–37.

41. *Nota Explicativa Praevia,* in *Acta Apostolicae Sedis* (bibliog. III) 57 (1965), 72–75. Also in *Sacrosanctum* (bibliog. III), 215–19. English translation in Flannery (ed), *Vatican Council II* (bibliog. III), 424–26.

42. *Acta Synodalia* (bibliog. III), vol. 3, part 8, 407.

43. *Vatican II* (bibliog. I), *Lumen gentium,* 21 November 1964. Also in *Sacrosanctum* (bibliog. III), 93–213. English translation in Flannery (ed), *Vatican Council II* (bibliog. III), 350–423.

References to marriage can be found at various points in *Lumen gentium*, especially in three of its chapters. In chapter five, titled "The Call to Holiness," article 41 states that everyone is called to be holy—bishops, priests, deacons, Christian spouses, widows, single people, the poor, the infirm, and the sick.[44] In chapter two, "The People of God," article 11 goes through each of the seven sacraments and explains their effects on the members of the Church. The last sacrament to be considered is marriage, but it receives the longest treatment. It begins with a reference to Ephesians 5:32 with its comparison between marriage and the love that exists between Christ and his Church. It explains that the former signifies and participates in the latter.[45]

The article's treatment of marriage must be understood within the wider theme that everyone is called to be holy. It is within this context that marriage can be seen to allow married couples and their children to attain holiness. In marriage, a man and a woman are able to assist each other spiritually. Also, the family is the place where children are born. These new citizens of human society become new members of the Church through baptism. The article describes the family as the domestic Church. It is here that parents are the first teachers of faith to their children by what they say and do. Their example will promote within their children the desire to be holy. The section concludes by urging parents to help foster the vocation that is proper to each child—taking special care if it is a calling to the religious life.

---

44. *Sacrosanctum* (bibliog. III), 167–70.
45. Ibid., 111–13.

Chapter three of *Lumen gentium* considers the hierarchical nature of the Church. It examines the role of the Pope, bishops, priests, and deacons. It is within the treatment of deacons that article 29 twice refers to marriage.[46] It explains that deacons are at a lower level of the hierarchy. They receive the imposition of bishops' hands for ministry, as opposed to priesthood. This ministry involves a three-fold service—to the liturgy, to the Gospel, and to works of charity. They are able to administer baptism within a service, distribute the Eucharist, celebrate and bless marriages in the name of the Church, give Viaticum to the dying, read the Scriptures, preach, preside over worship and the prayers of the faithful, administer sacramentals, and conduct funeral services and the burial of ashes.

The article continues by saying that the permanent diaconate should be restored in the Latin Church. It explains that, if the Pope should think it appropriate, mature married men are to be allowed to be ordained permanent deacons. It also states that suitable younger men should be admitted to the permanent diaconate— but they are to remain celibate. Consequently, article 29 not only states that deacons may celebrate marriages, but that they themselves may be married.

Orientalium Ecclesiarum and Unitatis Redintegratio

On the day *Lumen gentium* was promulgated, the Council issued another document— the *Decree on the Eastern Catholic Churches* (*Orientalium Eccle-*

46. Ibid., 149–50.

siarum).[47] The canonical form of marriage had been introduced into the Latin Church by Trent and was subsequently simplified by the decree *Ne temere*. Gradually, the canonical form was extended to the Eastern Catholic Churches. Thus, an Eastern Catholic was obliged to marry in front of a Catholic priest and witnesses for the sake of the validity of his or her marriage.

In many parts of the East, however, Orthodox Christians are in the majority with Catholics in a minority. Therefore, if an Eastern Catholic wishes to marry, then there is a good chance that the other person is Orthodox. This is problematic for two reasons. One, there is a strong tradition in the East to marry in the Church of the husband. A Catholic woman may find herself being put under pressure to marry in the Church of her Orthodox fiancé. Two, even if it were agreed to marry in front of a Catholic priest, there may be very few around in those areas that are predominantly Orthodox. Hence, many Eastern Catholics found they had to enter marriages with Orthodox Christians without following the canonical form of marriage. The Catholic Church regarded these marriages to be invalid. This did not help the spiritual development of the spouses concerned and it alienated them and their future children from the Catholic Church.[48]

In 1949, Pope Pius XII tried to reduce the problem by issuing a decree which gave patriarchs the power

---

47. *Vatican II* (bibliog. I), *Orientalium Ecclesiarum,* 21 November 1964. Also in *Sacrosanctum* (bibliog. III), 223–40. English translation in Flannery (ed), *Vatican Council II* (bibliog. III), 441–51.

48. Vorgrimler (ed), *Commentary on the Documents of Vatican II* (bibliog. III), vol. 1, 325–26.

to dispense from canonical form.[49] Thus, an Eastern Catholic could obtain a dispensation so that he or she could marry validly in an Orthodox ceremony without the need of exchanging marital consent in front of a Catholic priest. But what about those Eastern Catholics who had already attempted marriage without due canonical form? Their marriages were still invalid. In 1957, Pope Pius XII gave patriarchs the power to sanate (that is, to make valid) such marriages.[50]

Unfortunately, the bureaucracy created by the decrees of 1949 and 1957 was immense. A patriarch would have to grant a dispensation or a sanation for every Eastern Catholic who wanted to be married to an Orthodox Christian. The Holy Office and the Sacred Congregation for the Eastern Churches did extend the faculties to dispense and sanate to metropolitans and others, but the requirement to apply for dispensations for the sake of validity was still very unsatisfactory. When the Council began, the bishops from the Eastern Catholic Churches clearly expressed their frustration.[51]

In response, article 18 of *Orientalium Ecclesiarum* states that Eastern Catholics, when they marry baptized Eastern non-Catholics, are obliged to fulfill canonical form only for the sake of lawfulness—as opposed to validity. Thus, an Eastern Catholic who marries an Orthodox Christian in an Orthodox Church without any permission still enters a valid marriage, despite the law not being fully observed. Article 18 merely requires the presence of a sacred minister. As the Catholic Church

---

49. Pius XII (bibliog. I), Motu Proprio, *Crebrae allatae,* 22 February 1949.
50. Pius XII (bibliog. I), Motu Proprio, *Cleri sanctitati,* 2 June 1957.
51. *Acta Synodalia* (bibliog. III), vol. 3, part 8, 596–97.

recognizes the validity of Orthodox orders, the presence of an Orthodox priest would be sufficient.[52]

When *Orientalium Ecclesiarum* was issued, the Council also published its *Decree on Ecumenism* (*Unitatis redintegratio*).[53] These two documents are intrinsically linked, and the former recognizes the special nature of the Eastern Catholic Churches. Their rules may need to be different from those of the Latin tradition of the Church. This is not to say that their discipline is inferior. *Unitatis redintegratio* extends this principle to the non-Catholic Churches of the East. Thus, article 16 states that the discipline of these Churches has been sanctioned by Church Fathers, as well as by synods and councils.[54] These Churches have the authority to govern themselves according to their own disciplines. Indeed, they are better suited to the nature of their people. This diversity only adds to the beauty of the Church as a whole. *Unitatis redintegratio* is important legally because it means that the Second Vatican Council recognizes the autonomy of the Eastern Orthodox Churches and their discipline. Thus, for example, the Catholic Church cannot simply impose its canonical form of marriage on members of the Orthodox Churches.

Christus Dominus

On 28 October 1965, the Council issued its *Decree on the Pastoral Office of Bishops in the Church* (*Christus*

---

52. *Sacrosanctum* (bibliog. III), 233–34.
53. *Vatican II* (bibliog. I), *Unitatis Redintegratio*, 21 November 1964. Also in *Sacrosanctum* (bibliog. III), 243–74. English translation in Flannery (ed), *Vatican Council II* (bibliog. III), 452–70.
54. *Sacrosanctum* (bibliog. III), 266–67.

Dominus).[55] Its importance with regard to marriage is in the area of dispensations. The 1917 Code of Canon Law listed impediments to marriage. Some of these impediments could be dispensed by diocesan bishops. To do so, however, the bishops first had to apply to the Holy See every few years for the faculties to dispense. This gave rise to two problems. First, a large amount of paperwork was created because each diocesan bishop had to keep applying for the appropriate faculties. The second problem was ecclesiological. If a diocesan bishop is a successor of the apostles and is the shepherd of his diocese, then why can he not grant dispensations in virtue of his own office? Why does he have to rely on being granted faculties to dispense? Both these problems were in the minds of the bishops at the Second Vatican Council. Consequently, there were many demands for greater subsidiarity and for an increase in the power of diocesan bishops.[56]

These demands resulted in article 8 of *Christus Dominus*.[57] The article is in two parts. In the first, it acknowledges that bishops are successors of the apostles and that in the dioceses assigned to them they enjoy, by virtue of their office (per se), the power necessary for the exercise of their pastoral office. The first part of the article goes on to state, however, that the Pope has the authority, by virtue of his office, to reserve certain matters to himself or to others.

---

55. *Vatican II* (bibliog. I), *Christus Dominus*, 28 October 1965. Also in *Sacrosanctum* (bibliog. III), 277–330. English translation in Flannery (ed), *Vatican Council II* (bibliog. III), 564–90.

56. Vorgrimler (ed), *Commentary on the Documents of Vatican II* (bibliog. III), vol. 2, 165–97.

57. *Sacrosanctum* (bibliog. III), 283.

The second part of article 8 concerns the power to dispense and it applies the principle given in the first part. It states that diocesan bishops have the power to dispense their people provided the matter has not been reserved by the Pope. This means that there would no longer be the need for bishops to apply for faculties to dispense. *Christus Dominus* concludes with a call for the principles given in it to be adopted by the eventual revised Code of Canon Law.[58]

Gravissimum Educationis

On the day *Christus Dominus* was issued, the Council released its *Declaration on Christian Education (Gravissimum educationis)*.[59] In article 3, it states that parents have the gravest obligation (*gravissima obligatione tenentur*) to educate their children because it is primarily their responsibility.[60] Their role in education is so important that it is virtually impossible to provide a sufficient substitute. Like article 11 of *Lumen gentium*, the article stresses that the family is the most important context in which children learn the nature of love and social values. The graces received through the sacrament of marriage enable children to learn how to worship God and love others. It is within the family that the young have their first experience of society and the Church. That is, the family structure makes present both society and the Church at the domestic level.

---

58. *Vatican II* (bibliog. I), *Christus Dominus*, 28 October 1965, art. 44, in *Sacrosanctum* (bibliog. III), 320–21.

59. *Vatican II* (bibliog. I), *Gravissimum educationis*, 28 October 1965. Also in *Sacrosanctum* (bibliog. III), 387–408. English translation in Flannery (ed), *Vatican Council II* (bibliog. III), 725–37.

60. *Sacrosanctum* (bibliog. III), 392–95.

Article 8 states that society and the Church should collaborate with parents to assist them in their role as educators.[61] The responsibility of society is expanded by article 6.[62] It says that civil authorities should protect the parents' right to choose schools which they judge to be the most appropriate for their children. These civil authorities should also ensure that schools provide adequate education. Parents, in their turn, are encouraged by the article to assist schools through such means as associations of parents.

The Church's responsibility toward helping parents educate their children is given in article 3. The educational role of parents is so important that this article uses the image of a mother for the Church. It states that, like a mother, the Church has the duty to educate her children. This is because the Church has been commissioned by God to proclaim the way to salvation and to reveal Christ. The Church, by its very nature, must teach. It should do so even to those who are not members of the Church. That is, the Church must help everyone to reach perfection. This will assist society and, indeed, the whole world.

Gravissimum educationis explains that Catholic schools are very important within the Church's work of teaching. These schools must not be inward looking but should have an openness to society.[63] Article 6 requests that civil authorities allow a variety of schools—including Catholic ones. Article 8 reminds Catholic parents of

61. Ibid., 399–402.
62. Ibid., 397–98.
63. Ibid., 399–402.

the importance of supporting such schools. Where possible, they should try to send their children to them.

In summary, *Gravissimum educationis* requests that parents, society, and the Church work together for the education of children. Each part of this three-fold arrangement has rights and responsibilities with regard to the other two. Children's education, especially their Christian education, will be fostered as long as each part recognizes and performs its duties.

Apostolicam Actuositatem

The month after *Gravissimum educationis* was issued, the Council issued its *Decree on the Apostolate of the Laity (Apostolicam actuositatem)*.[64] This document is concerned with the particular contribution lay people make to the mission of the Church. It considers the role of both individuals and groups, at local, national, and international levels. In its third chapter, the document examines the special work of the parish, the family, and young people. Its treatment of the family is found in article 11.[65]

It has just been seen that *Gravissimum educationis* understands the relationship between parents and society, as well as the relationship between parents and the Church, to be important. Similarly, *Apostolicam actuositatem* regards the family to have a major contribution to make to society and the Church. In particular, the continued existence of society and the Church

64. *Vatican II* (bibliog. I), *Apostolicam actuositatem,* 18 November 1965. Also in *Sacrosanctum* (bibliog. III), 459–508. English translation in Flannery (ed), *Vatican Council II* (bibliog. III), 766–98.

65. *Sacrosanctum* (bibliog. III), 478–80.

on earth depends upon families. Family units, which are ultimately established by God, make up these two larger groupings and also provide future generations for them.

Like *Lumen gentium* and *Gravissimum educationis*, the document emphasizes the role of Christian parents in fostering their children's faith. They are the first to pass on the faith to their children. They do this by word and good example. They also assist their children to find the right vocations in life—including religious vocations. Christian spouses also help foster the faith of each other, as well as that of other relatives.

Christian couples, by their very nature, are called to assist the Church's mission in three ways. They are to give witness to the indissolubility and the holiness of the marriage bond. They are to stress the right and duty of parents and guardians to provide a Christian upbringing for their children. They are to defend the dignity and legitimate autonomy of the family. Moreover, in order to ensure that these rights are safeguarded by civil law, they are to work with members of society.

Article 11 explains that these objectives will be met as long as the family unit does three things. First, it must allow itself to be permeated by mutual love and family prayer. It must present itself as a "domestic sanctuary of the Church" *(domesticum sanctuarium Ecclesiae)*. That is, it should manifest the love and prayer found in the Church as a whole. Second, the whole family must participate in the Church's official worship. Third, it must show hospitality and practice justice and charity. The article expands upon the latter by giving various

types of work that a family could do: adopting aban-
doned children, welcoming strangers, helping schools,
giving advice and help to adolescents, helping to prepare
engaged couples for marriage, catechesis, supporting
married couples who are having problems, and helping
the elderly. In order to be more effective in these areas,
families can join together to form working groups. The
work of families gives a valuable witness to Christ, especially in parts of the world where Christianity or the
Church have only recently been introduced.

A Brief History of the
Drafting of *Gaudium et Spes*

Before I examine the treatment of marriage in *Gaudium et spes*, I shall outline the history of the document's
drafting. This will lead to a greater appreciation of its
consideration of marriage. Also, and perhaps surprisingly, it will show that this great document of the Council nearly failed to be issued because of disagreements
over the nature of marriage.

In the period of preparation for the Council, various preparatory commissions were established. Their
role was to produce schemas for eventual discussion.
Each preparatory commission corresponded to one of
the existing dicasteries (departments) of the Roman Curia. Thus, each preparatory commission was very much
grounded in the day-to-day running of the Church. This
meant that the attitude of many members of the commissions was that the proposed Council was a domestic affair of the Church.[66] Consequently, there was no

---

66. Vorgrimler (ed), *Commentary on the Documents of Vatican II* (bibliog.
III), vol. 5, 2.

willingness to dialogue with the world. It was going to be a struggle to produce a document concerning the relationship between the Church and the modern world.

Two preparatory commissions were involved with the relationship between the Church and the social order. One commission was the Commission for the Apostolate of the Laity. Its schema was intended to be more practical than theological. The schema thus lacked a firm biblical and theological basis. The other commission was the Theological Commission. Its schema provided both a biblical and a theological basis for human work, but its theology of work was negative. That is, although it describes the human person as being in the image of God with dominion over the world, it treats human labor as a punishment for the sin of Adam. Of the seventy schemas produced by the preparatory commissions, this became number seven. The Theological Commission also had a sub-commission which produced a document concerning the moral Christian order. Again, the text used the scriptural image of mankind being created in the image of God. The document was meant to counter both subjectivism and ethical relativism.[67]

At the beginning of December 1962, twenty schemas were distributed to members of the Coordinating Commission. In January 1963, the members of this commission met and outlined seventeen schemas which they suggested could be developed and eventually put before the bishops for comments. The last one

67. Ibid., 2–7.

concerned the relationship between the Church and the world. Cardinal Suenens said that this Schema 17 should make use of as many of the relevant preparatory texts as possible.[68]

In order to develop Schema 17, Suenens formed the Mixed Commission using members of the Commission for the Apostolate of the Laity and the Theological Commission. He did not want to exclude those who had already worked hard on producing a document concerning the Church's relationship with the world. Soon, Schema 17 comprised six chapters, the third of which was titled "Concerning Marriage, Chastity, and Virginity." This was changed to "Concerning Marriage, Family and Demographic Problems" and then to "Concerning Marriage and the Family." This draft of Schema 17 became known as Text Two.[69]

> The theologian Yves Congar expressed concern that the first chapter was too philosophical. He wanted the text to emphasize the concept that mankind is created in the image of God. He also wanted the moral principles given to be applied to concrete situations. Others also had reservations. In particular, many felt that the text needed a firmer theological basis. Thus, the Coordinating Commission asked Cardinal Suenens to develop the first part of the text so that it could be put before the Mixed Commission for their comments and amendments. Unfortunately, according to Alberigo, the Coordinating Commission did not consult or inform the Mixed Commission about approaching Suenens. This omission would have repercussions.[70]

At the beginning of September 1963, Suenens met

---

68. Ibid., 12.
69. Ibid., 12–17.
70. Alberigo (ed), *History of Vatican II* (bibliog. III), vol. 2, 422–27.

with theologians in the archbishop's palace at Malines. Among those invited were Yvés Congar and Karl Rahner. Congar was keen to emphasize the aspects of witness, service, and community. These had been recently highlighted by the World Council of Churches. By the middle of the month, a draft was ready. This was discussed, revised, and then sent to Rome on September 22. This text is known as Interim Text A. I shall refer to it by its more common name—the Malines Text.[71]

The Malines Text consists of three chapters. The first considers the mission of the Church—to proclaim the gospel, to promote the freedom of faith, and to evangelize the poor. This mission is based upon the fact that all humans, both rich and poor, are created in the image of God and are called by God. Furthermore, the gospel message is for everyone. The second chapter is about the need to develop the world. The third chapter brings together the ideas outlined in the first two chapters—showing how the Church's mission can benefit the world. This last chapter uses a three-fold division based upon Congar—witness, service, and community. The Church's *witness* to the world is important because the message of Christ is essential. The Church must be at the *service* of the world through acts of charity and justice. With regard to *community*, the Church is to collaborate with all men and women of good will for the benefit of humanity.[72]

The Malines Text was due to go before a meeting of the Mixed Commission on November 26. Members

71. Ibid. Also, Vorgrimler (ed), *Commentary on the Documents of Vatican II* (bibliog. III), vol. 5, 21–23.

72. Alberigo (ed), *History of Vatican II* (bibliog. III), vol. 2, 425–26.

of that commission were upset, however, that the Co-ordinating Commission had asked Cardinal Suenens to prepare a text without their knowledge. Moreover, the members of the Mixed Commission did not appreciate that the mandate given to Suenens was to prepare a theological introduction to their Text Two. He had not been asked to replace their document. This tension was particularly unfortunate because Suenens had specifically established the Mixed Commission to involve those who had worked previously on Schema 17 so that they would not be excluded from the drafting process.

The Mixed Commission did meet in November. Alberigo sets the scene: "Initially set for November 26, the first meeting was actually held on the 29th, a day when Suenens was in Florence to give a lecture scheduled long before!"[73] Indeed, the Commission was "in a state of utter confusion and refusing to consider the Malines text."[74] It is therefore not surprising that the Malines Text was rejected.[75]

A group of bishops and theologians was appointed to draft a new schema. It was decided that the document should be based upon Scripture and not purely upon theology. The members of this new commission were impressed by the recent encyclical *Pacem in Terris* which emphasized the need to read the signs of the times.[76] This encyclical stressed the importance of members of the Church being actively involved in the world. Thus, its main editor, Pietro Pavan, was

---

73. Alberigo (ed), *History of Vatican II* (bibliog. III), vol. 3, 312.
74. Ibid., vol. 2, 426.
75. Ibid., 428, and vol. 3, 312–13.
76. John XXIII (bibliog. I), Encyclical, *Pacem in Terris,* 11 April 1963.

appointed to the new commission. Bernhard Häring was appointed secretary. The commission had five sub-commissions, each with about half a dozen members. These sub-commissions considered the following five areas: the human person in society, marriage and the family, culture, the economic order and social justice, and the community of nations and peace.

During January 1964, the document was drafted and given the title *The Active Participation of the Church in the Building of the World.* Häring believed that it had managed to balance two opposing schools of thought— that it should be theological and that it should apply to concrete situations. He also felt that it was faithful to all the work that had been put into earlier texts—Text Two and the Malines Text. It also incorporated many of the suggestions that had been submitted to Rome. The text was sent to a central commission which met in Zurich at the beginning of February. In order to avoid the problems caused by the Malines Text, this commission consisted of very few people who had worked on earlier texts, thus providing a sense of impartiality and objectivity. The document is commonly known as Interim Text B. For the sake of simplicity I shall refer to it as the First Zurich Text.[77]

The First Zurich Text was written in French. Its introduction begins, "Joy and sorrow, hope and anxieties," which is the basis for the famous introduction of the eventual *Pastoral Constitution on the Church in the Modern World.* There are four chapters, the last of

77. Alberigo (ed), *History of Vatican II* (bibliog. III), vol. 3, 313–14, 407. Also, Vorgrimler (ed), *Commentary on the Documents of Vatican II* (bibliog. III), vol. 5, 26–27.

which outlines the tasks Christians must perform in the world. It is within this fourth chapter that the family and responsible parenthood are considered along with other matters such as peace and economic and social justice.[78]

The First Zurich Text was favorably received. In particular, four themes were regarded as very important: the need for the Church to enter into dialogue with the world; the Church's solidarity with humankind; the need to read the signs of the times, as indicated in *Pacem in Terris*; and the human vocation to work in the world. The First Zurich Text was quickly amended to *emphasize* these themes. This new text is usually referred to as the Second Zurich Text.[79]

This text was submitted to the Mixed Commission. Cardinal Ottaviani, the Prefect of the Holy Office, presided at the meeting. Only two years earlier, Ottaviani had seen his own document on marriage rejected. Members of the Doctrinal Commission, which was linked with the Holy Office, objected to the Second Zurich Text. In particular, they opposed its treatment of marriage, especially its failure to refer to the primary and secondary ends of marriage as described by the 1917 Code of Canon Law. These members blamed Häring personally for failing to be obedient to this position. There were sufficient people at the meeting to counter these criticisms, so the text was approved over these objections. Never-

---

78. Vorgrimler (ed), *Commentary on the Documents of Vatican II* (bibliog. III), vol. 5, 27–30.

79. Alberigo (ed), *History of Vatican II* (bibliog. III), vol. 3, 408–10. Also, Vorgrimler (ed), *Commentary on the Documents of Vatican II* (bibliog. III), vol. 5, 31–34.

theless, as Alberigo observes, "The schema passed, but Häring had to be 'sacrificed.' "[80] After 1964, Häring was not given another opportunity to be so influential.

Although the text was passed by the Mixed Commission, it was decided that its last chapter should be revised. This had a detrimental effect on its treatment of marriage. As in the First Zurich Text, this chapter considers the various tasks Christians must perform in the world. Among these, the family and parenthood are examined. It was agreed that the last chapter would be altered to provide a general theological statement concerning the role of Christians in the world. This would be a basis for examining the individual tasks to be performed; these tasks were to be examined in appendix chapters. Thus, much of the material about marriage and the family was relegated to an appendix.[81]

The required revision was made. This new text of the schema was passed to the Coordinating Commission which examined it at the end of June 1964.[82] The various schemas for consideration by the bishops were renumbered. This new schema was now called Schema 13.[83] At the beginning of July, the Pope approved it and it was sent to the bishops for their comments. They were asked to submit their observations by the beginning of October. In the meantime, a commission was formed to examine the bishops' replies. This commission soon had two sub-commissions—the first, to

---

80. Alberigo (ed), *History of Vatican II* (bibliog. III), vol. 3, 412, footnote 198.

81. Vorgrimler (ed), *Commentary on the Documents of Vatican II* (bibliog. III), vol. 5, 35.

82. Alberigo (ed), *History of Vatican II* (bibliog. III), vol. 3, 436–37.

83. *Acta Synodalia* (bibliog. III), vol. 3, part 5, 116–42.

examine issues relating to the theme (from *Pacem in Terris*) of reading the signs of the times, the second, to examine theological matters.

Bishops who had not been involved in the development of Schema 13 were invited to join these sub-commissions. For example, Archbishop Wojtyla joined the first sub-commission. He actually sent Häring a complete schema to replace Schema 13. It had already been agreed, however, that the existing Schema 13 was the one to be considered by the bishops. Also, there were concerns that because Wojtyla's schema had been written in the context of Poland it might not be fully applicable universally. Despite these problems, his schema was included in a group of documents called the Ariccia Documents. These were available to those at the Council and were influential.[84]

It has been noted that much of the material concerning marriage was moved to an appendix (appendix number two), but some aspects of marriage did remain in chapter four. This chapter is called "The Special Task to be Accomplished by Christians in the Modern World."[85] In particular, paragraph 21 is titled "The Dignity of Marriage and the Family."[86] It places love at the very center of marriage. Mackin provides the following translation: "Marriage is no mere instrument of procreation. Rather the nature itself of the indissoluble covenant between the persons, and most especially the good

---

84. Alberigo (ed), *History of Vatican II* (bibliog. III), vol. 3, 413–15. Also, Vorgrimler (ed), *Commentary on the Documents of Vatican II* (bibliog. III), vol. 5, 37.
85. *Acta Synodalia* (bibliog. III), vol. 3, part 5, 129–40.
86. Ibid., 131–33.

of the children, demand that the spouses truly love one another. And even if the marriage has no children, it is in no way deprived of its fundamental value or its indissolubility. But such is the character of marital love that marriage is of its nature oriented to the procreation and nurture of children."[87]

The text acknowledges that marriage is oriented toward the generation and education of children; it does not say, however, that this is the primary purpose of marriage. Indeed, it states that a childless marriage does not lose any of its value because the spouses are still able to love each other and enjoy an indissoluble bond. This love and indissolubility are linked to the indissoluble covenant that exists between the spouses. This covenant is based on love. Thus, marriage is far more than a legitimate context in which to have children. It is not surprising that this divergence from the 1917 Code's teaching on the ends of marriage had provoked Cardinal Ottaviani and his associates.

The second appendix to Schema 13 is titled "On Marriage and the Family."[88] Again, love is placed at the center of marriage, which is spoken of as a covenant of love: "God, seeing that it was not good for the man to be alone . . . created them male and female from the beginning. He joined them in a covenant of love [*amoris foedere*]."[89] This replaces the legal description where marriage is seen as a contract in which rights and obligations are exchanged.

---

87. Ibid., 132. Translation in Mackin, *What is Marriage?* (bibliog. III), 260. Once again, Theodore Mackin's book has been most helpful to me.

88. *Acta Synodalia* (bibliog. III), vol. 3, part 5, 158–68.

89. Ibid., 159. Translation in Mackin, *What is Marriage?* (bibliog. III), 261.

This appendix to Schema 13 acknowledges that a marriage is brought into existence by the consent of the couple. Indeed, the appendix connects marital consent with marital love. It states that love must be present in the exchange of consent, which marks the very start of the marriage. This love must then continue and, in fact, increase during the course of the marriage: "Marital consent of its essence intends the unity of this covenant, its indissolubility and the love that is devoted to the service of life. The stronger and purer the marital love, the more strongly and perseveringly will the spouses accept and realize marriage's specific traits and its essential goods. . . . No one is unaware of how seriously necessary it is that love be fully present in the act of consent, and increase throughout the entire married life. For love will fulfill and cause to be fulfilled what the consent has said and has promised."[90]

Although appendix two does not state that the procreation and education of children are the primary ends of marriage, it acknowledges that they are intrinsic to marriage and that marriage is directed toward them: "Let all acknowledge, before all else, that procreation and truly human nurture are an innate and a most specific orientation in marriage."[91] Moreover, it makes it clear that they certainly are not subordinate to any other ends of marriage: "The assertions of those who deem procreation and nurture to be something secondary which one can subordinate to its other goods, or

---

90. *Acta Synodalia* (bibliog. III), vol. 3, part 5, 161. Translation in Mackin, *What is Marriage?* (bibliog. III), 261.

91. *Acta Synodalia* (bibliog. III), vol. 3, part 5, 164. Translation in Mackin, *What is Marriage?* (bibliog. III), 261.

even radically separate from them—these contradict the very nature and orientation of marriage."[92] Mackin believes that these comments were included in order to satisfy such people as Ottaviani.[93] They failed to placate, however, because they stop short of actually saying that the primary end of marriage is the procreation and education of children. They merely state that procreation and education are not less important than the other ends.

On 20 October 1964, Schema 13 was presented to the bishops during their third session. Certain alterations were agreed upon and the schema received a positive response with 1,579 votes in favor out of 1,876. There were only 296 votes against.[94] The bishops acknowledged the importance of the material in the appendices and called for it to be placed back into the main body of the text. Thus, marriage was to be given greater prominence.[95] Sub-commissions were established to assist the revision of Schema 13. The largest sub-commission was on marriage, and it presented a draft section on marriage and the family at the beginning of February 1965.[96] This draft maintained the centrality of love within marriage. It also continued to speak of marriage as a covenant rather than as a contract. With regard to the ends of marriage, it avoided discussing them.[97] This new draft was submitted to the

---

92. *Acta Synodalia* (bibliog. III), vol. 3, part 5, 165. Translation in Mackin, *What is Marriage?* (bibliog. III), 261–62.

93. Mackin, *What is Marriage?* (bibliog. III), 261.

94. *Acta Synodalia* (bibliog. III), vol. 3, part 5, 416.

95. Vorgrimler (ed), *Commentary on the Documents of Vatican II* (bibliog. III), vol. 5, 43–44.

96. Ibid., 52–53.

97. Mackin, *What is Marriage?* (bibliog. III), 262.

bishops at their fourth session on 21 September 1965. An initial vote on the entire schema was very favorable; out of 2,157 present, there were 2,111 votes for and only 44 against.[98]

The bishops then examined the schema chapter by chapter and changes were made. The revised schema was resubmitted to the bishops on November 12.[99] Further voting took place between November 15 and 17. Out of the entire document, two issues relating to marriage caused the most debate—the ends of marriage and artificial contraception. With regard to contraception, it was noted that the schema did not contain a condemnation, as had Pius XI's *Casti connubii* and Pius XII's Allocution to the Association of Catholic Midwives. Moreover, there was uncertainty as to whether the fairly recent contraceptive pill fell under the Church's existing ban. Neither Pius XI nor Pius XII had foreseen the introduction of such a pill. Therefore, some moral theologians thought the whole matter needed to be reconsidered.

Previously, in the spring of 1963, the Pontifical Commission on Questions of the Birth Rate was established. While the matter was being discussed in Rome, other bishops gave their own interpretation. Later that year, the Dutch bishops issued a pastoral letter in which they said that it was not certain whether the contraceptive pill was definitely forbidden. In May 1964, the Bishops' Conference of England and Wales issued a statement which upheld the position found in *Casti*

---

98. *Acta Synodalia* (bibliog. III), vol. 4, part 2, 403.
99. Ibid., part 6, 421–563.

connubii. As Alberigo notes, they did not give the impression that the matter was open for debate. Meanwhile, Cardinal Suenens spoke of the need to re-examine the matter. These differences in opinion remained among the bishops present at the Council.[100]

Despite these differences, Schema 13 was once again accepted overwhelmingly.[101] As the schema was passed with a two-thirds majority, the rules of the Council stipulated that it could no longer be altered substantially—the bishops were allowed to submit written suggestions for minor alterations. They were permitted to do so until midnight of November 17. In all, there were about twenty thousand suggestions made, and for a while there was concern that the Council would run out of time.[102] A much more serious crisis was about to occur, however. This crisis centered on marriage.

One week after the deadline for minor suggestions, the Secretary of State submitted suggested alterations from Pope Paul VI himself. In particular, these concerned contraception and the ends of marriage. The bishops were not certain whether the Pope was ordering them to make these alterations or whether he was simply making suggestions for them to discuss. If his comments were for the bishops to discuss, then it had to be decided if his suggested alterations were substantial. Technically, the time for substantial alterations had lapsed.

On November 25, Cardinal Léger had an audience with the Pope to clarify the matter. The Pope issued a

---

100. Alberigo (ed), *History of Vatican II* (bibliog. III), vol. 2, 530–31.

101. *Acta Synodalia* (bibliog. III), vol. 4, part 6, 591.

102. Vorgrimler (ed), *Commentary on the Documents of Vatican II* (bibliog. III), vol. 5, 66–67.

response, via the Secretary of State, in which said he considered his suggested alterations to be of great importance. He said his wording was not fixed, however, and could be changed provided the meaning was not lost. Moreover, he was willing for his suggested alterations to be added to all the others submitted by bishops and thus dealt with in due course, but he alone was to decide whether the final wording was acceptable.[103]

With regard to contraception, Paul VI wanted the schema to include references to *Casti connubii* and Pius XII's allocution. The commission examining the bishops' suggestions decided to put these references in a footnote. This footnote also cites Paul VI's allocution to the cardinals in June 1964, when he announced the establishment of a papal commission to study certain problems which the Council had left for the Pope to decide.[104] The footnote concludes that the Council would not provide concrete solutions to the questions concerning population, the family, and births. Instead, it says that the Pope will make a judgment once the papal commission has completed and presented its findings.[105] In the final text of *Gaudium et spes*, this became footnote 14 attached to article 51.[106] In 1968, Paul VI issued the document *Humanae vitae* which gave

---

103. Mackin, *What is Marriage?* (bibliog. III), 263–64.

104. Paul VI (bibliog. I), Address to the Sacred College of Cardinals, 23 June 1964.

105. "Quaedam quaestiones quae aliis ac diligentioribus investigationibus indigent, iussu Summi Pontificis, Commissioni pro studio populationis, familiae et natalitatis traditae sunt, ut postquam illa munus suum expleverit, Summus Pontifex iudicium ferat. Sic stante doctrina Magisterii, S. Synodus solutiones concretas immediate proponere non intendit."

106. *Sacrosanctum* (bibliog. III), 763. English translation in Flannery (ed), *Vatican Council II* (bibliog. III), 955.

his judgment and upheld the prohibition on artificial contraception.[107]

Concerning the ends of marriage, Paul VI wished to remove the word *also* (*etiam*) from what became article 50 of the final version of *Gaudium et spes*. Although this is only one word, its removal made a significant change. The article explained that marriage and conjugal love are ordered toward the procreation and education of children. This is indeed the understanding of marriage put forward in the second appendix to Schema 13. The next sentence then began, "Hence the true practice of conjugal love and the whole meaning of family life which results from it also have this aim."[108]

This sentence is ambiguous. It could mean that the true practice of conjugal love and the whole meaning of family life is also ordered toward the procreation and education of children. This interpretation gives a narrow understanding of conjugal love and family life. But there is a second possible interpretation. That is, the true practice of conjugal love and the whole meaning of family life have various purposes —one of which is *also* the procreation and education of children. This interpretation acknowledges that although procreation and education is an essential part of conjugal love and family life, there are other dimensions too.

The removal of *also*, as requested by Paul VI, results in the article explaining that marriage and conjugal love are ordered toward the procreation and education of children and, "Hence the true practice of

107. Paul VI (bibliog. I), Encyclical, *Humanae vitae*, 25 July 1968. English translation in Flannery (ed), *Vatican Council II: More* (bibliog. III), 397–416.

108. "Unde verus amoris coniugalis cultus totaque vitae familiaris ratio

conjugal love and the whole meaning of family life which results from it have this aim." It can be seen that the loss of the word also removes any ambiguity. The article is now stating very clearly that the whole meaning of conjugal love and family life is procreation and education. It looked as if the 1917 Code's understanding of the primary ends of marriage was making a final stand. Indeed, it was not only the Pope who wanted *also* removed. Charles Scicluna, a senior canon lawyer who works in Rome, has noted that there were calls from 120 bishops for its removal.[109]

In order to comply with the Pope's wishes, the commission decided to remove the word also from the text. In order to preserve a balanced view of marriage, however, it inserted a clause of its own: "while not underestimating the other ends of marriage" (*non posthabitis ceteris matrimonii finibus*).[110] This revision and footnote 14 were presented to the Pope, he approved them, and the crisis was over. Finally, on December 7, the bishops met in public session and a solemn vote was taken. Out of 2,391 votes cast, 2,309 were in favor. Only 75 were against, with another 7 votes declared invalid.[111] *Gaudium et spes* had been approved.

---

inde oriens etiam eo tendunt." *Acta Synodalia* (bibliog. III), vol. 4, part 6, 477. Translation from Mackin, *What is Marriage?* (bibliog. III), 265. (The italics are mine.)

109. Scicluna, *The Essential Definition of Marriage* (bibliog. III), 172.

110. The text now reads, "Hence the true practice of conjugal love and the whole meaning of family life which results from it have this aim, while not underestimating the other ends of marriage." The Latin text is this: "Unde verus amoris coniugalis cultus totaque vitae familiaris ratio inde oriens, non posthabitis ceteris matrimonii finibus, eo tendunt." In *Sacrosanctum* (bibliog. III), 760. Also, Scicluna, *The Essential Definition of Marriage* (bibliog. III),172, and Mackin, *What is Marriage?* (bibliog. III), 265.

111. *Acta Synodalia* (bibliog. III), vol. 4, part 7, 860.

Marriage in *Gaudium et Spes*

Marriage is treated in the second part of *Gaudium et spes*. This part is titled "Some More Urgent Problems."[112] It is noteworthy that marriage is the first subject to be considered—in chapter one, in six articles numbered 47 to 52.[113] The priority given to marriage indicates that the Council was of the opinion that one must have a correct approach toward marriage before one is able to lessen many of the world's problems. The family is the basic unit that makes up society. It is the foundation of every country. Thus, national and international problems cannot be solved without a healthy understanding of marriage and family life.

Article 47 is concerned with marriage and the family in the modern world. It begins by stating the principle just outlined—that the well-being of each person and society depends upon the well-being of married life. It is for this reason that married couples need so much support. But marriage is undermined in the modern world by divorce, polygamy, and a casual attitude toward sex. The article outlines other problems facing married couples: selfishness, hedonism, and unlawful contraception.

The commission responsible for the final editing felt that the context makes it clear that the prohibition of contraception refers to artificial contraception, as opposed to natural methods such as periodic continence.[114] The article also says that poor social and economic

---

112. "De Quibusdam Problematibus Urgentioribus."

113. *Sacrosanctum* (bibliog. III), 753–66. English translation in Flannery (ed), *Vatican Council II* (bibliog. III), 949–57.

114. *Responsum 5 ad num.* 51 (*nunc 47*) in *Acta Synodalia* (bibliog. III), vol. 4, part 7, 473–74.

conditions threaten the family, as do problems with population growth. This article sets the scene for the rest of the chapter. Married couples do not live in an ideal world. On the contrary, they are faced with many problems which endanger their marriages. Indeed, the problems named do not even form an exhaustive list.[115] The article explains that the document must address this crisis.

This article also sets the scene for the rest of the chapter in another way; it speaks of marriage in terms of love. It describes marriage as a "community of love" (*communitas amoris*).[116] One Council Father suggested that this expression be replaced by "domestic community" (*communitas domestica*). The editing commission explained that they wished to retain the expression *communitas amoris* because it highlights two important aspects of the marital partnership, its life and love.[117]

Article 48 speaks of the sanctity of marriage and the family. It states that marriage is divinely instituted. An individual marriage is rooted in the covenant (*foedus*) of the couple.[118] It is brought into existence by their irrevocable consent. Through their consent, the man and woman surrender themselves to each other for their own good, as well as for the good of any future children and society. There were 190 bishops who were unhappy with the use of the word *covenant*. They

---

115. *Responsum 6b ad num. 51 (nunc 47)* in *Acta Synodalia* (bibliog. III), vol. 4, part 7, 474.

116. *Sacrosanctum* (bibliog. III), 753.

117. *Responsum 3a ad num. 51 (nunc 47)* in *Acta Synodalia* (bibliog. III), vol. 4, part 7, 473.

118. *Sacrosanctum* (bibliog. III), 754. Flannery often translates "*foedus*" as "contract." For example, Flannery (ed), *Vatican Council II* (bibliog. III), 950. It should be translated as "covenant", however.

preferred to use contract. They argued that this more juridical language enables the entry into marriage to be clearly described in terms of an exchange by the couple of rights and duties. In particular, the terminology would allow the article to use the 1917 Code's precise definition of marital consent as "an act of the will by which each party gives and accepts a perpetual and exclusive right over the body, ordered towards acts which are of themselves apt for the generation of children."[119]

Their fear was that the use of *covenant* could not give a precise understanding of marriage. The editing commission replied that the use of *contract* would give a view of marriage that was far too narrow. They reminded the bishops that the document under consideration was meant to encourage a dialogue with the world on pastoral matters. The use of such legal vocabulary would not assist in achieving this aim.[120] Moreover, marriage is so profound that it would be inadequate to speak of it simply in terms of rights and duties.[121]

I would say that the concept of marriage as a covenant is most helpful. In biblical terms, the covenant between God and humanity has both a divine element and a human element. The divine element is God's enduring and unconditional love for his people. The indissolubility of marriage can be seen as a share in this. The human element is humanity's response to God's love. Scripture

119. Canon 1081 §2: "Consensus matrimonialis est actus voluntatis quo utraque pars tradit et acceptat ius in corpus, perpetuum et exclusivum, in ordine ad actus per se aptos ad prolis generationem."

120. *Responsum 15 ad num. 52* (*nunc 48*) in *Acta Synodalia* (bibliog. III), vol. 4, part 7, 477.

121. *Responsa 25c & d ad num. 52* (*nunc 48*) in *Acta Synodalia* (bibliog. III), vol. 4, part 7, 481. Also, Vorgrimler (ed), *Commentary on the Documents of Vatican II* (bibliog. III), vol. 5, 234–35.

shows that this is not always constant. This element is reflected in the daily lives of married couples. That is, they may often fall short of the ideal and their mutual love may not be as strong and as constant as it should be, but they are not left to struggle by themselves. The divine element of marriage means that God is always with them to assist them in the daily realities of married life. It is by calling upon God's help that spouses are able to live up to the ideals of marriage.

Article 48 goes on to explain that God, the author of marriage, continues to pour out his blessings upon married couples. He has given marriage various benefits and ends. At this point, in a footnote, the document cites Saint Augustine's *De Bono Coniugali*. The editing commission refused, however, to order the ends of marriage hierarchically.[122] The article mentions some of the benefits of marriage—the continuation of mankind, as well as the personal and spiritual development of every member of the family and, indeed, of the whole human race. It explains that marriage is ordered to the procreation and education of children, which it describes as the crowning glory of married love.

Some bishops wanted the text to be changed to make it clear that a childless marriage is not deficient. The editing commission agreed with their sentiments, but thought that the text already made this sufficiently clear.[123] To uphold the value of childless marriages,

---

122. *Responsa 15 & 19b ad num. 52* (*nunc 48*) in Acta Synodalia (bibliog. III), vol. 4, part 7, 477–79. Also, Vorgrimler (ed), *Commentary on the Documents of Vatican II* (bibliog. III), vol. 5, 233.

123. *Responsum 23c ad num. 52* (*nunc 48*) in Acta Synodalia (bibliog. III), vol. 4, part 7, 479. Also, Vorgrimler (ed), *Commentary on the Documents of Vatican II* (bibliog. III), vol. 5, 234.

the commission refused to say that it is through fe-
cundity that marital love participates in God's love for
the Church—an idea that had been suggested by 151
bishops.[124]

Matthew 19:6 is quoted in regard to indissolubility:
"They are no longer two, therefore, but one flesh."[125] Thus,
the marriage bond is unbreakable. Here the article cites
Casti connubii. It explains that the bond of love which
exists between couples originates from God's love. Indeed, it is modeled on Christ's bond with the Church.

Again citing *Casti connubii*, article 48 states that the
marriage of Christians is a sacrament. Thus, Christ is
present to these couples, strengthening their marriage
and blessing them so that they can be good parents. It
is through family prayer that Christian parents are able
to inspire their children and lead them to salvation. In
return, children help to sanctify their parents and assist them in old age. When one spouse dies, the words
of Saint Paul are to be remembered: "Be considerate
to widows."[126] Widowhood is described as a continuation of marriage which should be given honor. This
is in reply to four bishops who asked if the text could
speak of widowhood and consecrated virginity. The
commission decided not to include any reference to
virginity, however, on the grounds that this chapter is
about marriage—virginity would be covered by other
Conciliar texts.[127]

---

124. *Responsum 28c ad num. 52 (nunc 48)* in *Acta Synodalia* (bibliog. III),
vol. 4, part 7, 483–84. Also, Vorgrimler (ed), *Commentary on the Documents of
Vatican II* (bibliog. III), vol. 5, 235.

125. *Sacrosanctum* (bibliog. III), 755.

126. 1 Timothy 5:3. *Sacrosanctum* (bibliog. III), 757.

127. *Responsum 41 ad num. 52 (nunc 48)* in *Acta Synodalia* (bibliog. III), vol.

The article concludes with a reminder that the love which is exchanged between family members is a share in Christ's love for the Church. When others see this love, they will be made aware of Christ's love. Hence, the Christian family witnesses to his love in the world. Some bishops were concerned that this emphasis on love could lead to the erroneous opinion that a marriage ceases to exist if the marriage partners stop loving each other. The commission disagreed. It felt that the article makes it clear that the indissolubility of the marriage bond is objective and does not depend upon the subjective disposition of the spouses. Moreover, the commission felt that the text spoke of marital love in such a way that it had to be understood in its most profound form and not only on the level of emotional love. [128]

Article 49 is concerned with marital love in particular. It explains that this love is eminently human in nature because it is rooted in the human will and embraces the good of the whole person. In fact, the Lord has elevated this love so that it is not only human but also participates in the divine love. Thus, marital love is greater than mere erotic attraction, which easily fades away. Moreover, the mutuality of the spouses' love corresponds to their equality. Once again, certain bishops were concerned about this emphasis on love. They feared that it would lead to the misunderstanding that a marriage entered into without love was automatically invalid. The

---

4, part 7, 487. Also, *Responsa 56a & 63 ad num. 53 (nunc 49)* in *Acta Synodalia* (bibliog. III), vol. 4, part 7, 490 & 492.

128. *Responsum 1 (modi generales) ad num.* 51–56 (nunc 47–52) in *Acta Synodalia* (bibliog. III), vol. 4, part 7, 471–72.

editing commission replied that the chapter on marriage
as a whole does not give this impression.[129]

The article goes on to speak of acts of sexual intercourse between husband and wife, which are described
as "honorable and worthy" (*honesti ac digni sunt*).[130]
These acts bring about an intimate and chaste union.
They give joy and gratitude, as well as express physically the mutual self-giving that is essential to marriage. It is noteworthy that the article talks of "the truly
human performance of these acts" (*modo vere humano
exerciti*).[131] The editing commission acknowledged that
not every act of intercourse necessarily tends toward
producing children—for example, during the infertile
period or when there is sterility.[132] In these cases, intercourse can still give joy and gratitude, as well as express the spouses' mutual self-giving. This leads one to
conclude that sexual intercourse can achieve purposes
other than producing children. Indeed, the commission
refused a request asking them to include in the next
article this clause: "Marital love is ordered toward the
primary end of marriage, which is children."[133]

Because marital love embraces the whole person,
it is present in both mind and body at all times—good
times and bad. Thus, it is always present and always
exclusive. It therefore excludes both divorce and adultery. The article acknowledges that married life is

---

129. *Responsum 51a ad num. 53 (nunc 49)* in *Acta Synodalia* (bibliog. III),
vol. 4, part 7, 489.
130. *Sacrosanctum* (bibliog. III), 758.
131. Ibid.
132. *Responsum 56d ad num. 53 (nunc 49)* in *Acta Synodalia* (bibliog. III),
vol. 4, part 7, 491. Also, Vorgrimler (ed), *Commentary on the Documents of
Vatican II* (bibliog. III), vol. 5, 241.
133. "Amor coniugalis ad finem primarium matrimonii, qui est proles,

difficult. It calls for courage on the part of spouses. They need to make sacrifices. To do this, they require help both on the supernatural and the natural level. With regard to the former, they need God's grace. Concerning the latter, they require proper instruction for marriage. They will also find invaluable the example of others who enjoy good Christian marriages.

Article 50 addresses the fruitfulness of marriage. It has been seen that Pope Paul VI intervened personally in the final drafting of this article. It acknowledges that marriage and conjugal love are, by nature, ordered to the procreation and education of children, who are described as the supreme gift of marriage. When spouses produce new life they are cooperating with God who is the Creator. It has already been noted that this description of procreation is not intended to underestimate the other ends of marriage.[134] Moreover, the commission refused to include a statement saying that marital love does not justify intercourse when it is independent of the intention to produce children. On the contrary, the commission opposed the suggested statement.[135] Thus, for example, sexual intercourse during the wife's infertile period is still legitimate.

Article 50 goes on to urge parents to seek the good of their children. They are to judge wisely in both material and spiritual matters. In doing so, they will not only benefit their children, but also their whole family,

---

ordinatur." *Responsum 72b ad num. 54 (nunc 50)* in *Acta Synodalia* (bibliog. III), vol. 4, part 7, 494–95.

134. *Responsum 71 ad num. 54 (nunc 50)* in *Acta Synodalia* (bibliog. III), vol. 4, part 7, 493–94.

135. *Responsum 67 (modi generales) ad num. 54 (nunc 50)* in *Acta Synodalia* (bibliog. III), vol. 4, part 7, 492. Also, Vorgrimler (ed), *Commentary on the Documents of Vatican II* (bibliog. III), vol. 5, 239.

society, and the Church. In order to make such judgments they are to inform their consciences by God's law, which is manifested through the Church. Once they have informed their consciences, they are to follow them.

The article gives special attention to those who, after prudent reflection and common decision, raise a large number of children.[136] It describes their task as courageous. This is a continuation of the article's call for parents to act wisely. That is, in order to have a large number of children, they should do so after careful consideration. This is because of the seriousness of their undertaking, both with regard to themselves and society. Moreover, the decision must be a joint one because the efforts of both parents will be required. Vorgrimler suggests that this reference to large families is intended to counter those who equate responsible parenting with having small families.[137]

There were 91 bishops who wanted the article to praise the adoption of orphans and other children without parental care. The commission was sympathetic but felt that this was already covered by the last article in the chapter on marriage (52 in the final version) which speaks more generally about the need to protect and help those who are deprived of the benefits of family life.[138]

136. "Inter coniuges qui tali modo muneri sibi a Deo commissio satisfaciunt, peculiariter memorandi sunt illi qui, prudenti communique consilio, magno animo prolem congruenter educandam etiam numerosiorem suscipiunt." *Sacrosanctum* (bibliog. III), 761.

137. Vorgrimler (ed), *Commentary on the Documents of Vatican II* (bibliog. III), vol. 5, 241.

138. *Responsum 73 ad num. 54 (nunc 50)* in *Acta Synodalia* (bibliog. III), vol. 4, part 7, 495.

The conclusion of article 50 is meant to provide a balance. It reminds one that marriage is not solely for procreation. It is, by nature, an indissoluble covenant between two people. Thus, mutual love must be manifested between the spouses. Moreover, this love must be allowed to grow and mature. This will not only benefit the spouses but also their children. Indeed, this love is so central to marriage that even if a couple is unable to have children, their marriage retains its character, value, and indissolubility.

With regard to marriage's character, the article describes it as "a whole manner and communion of life."[139] This description calls for two comments. First, it puts very succinctly the fact that marriage is essentially a unity created from two people. This unity is expressed by living in a way appropriate to marriage. That is, it is a manner of living, but it involves two individuals and so must also be a communion of life. Second, this manner of living and the communion of life must be all-embracing because marriage involves the whole person and the whole couple.

The next article, 51, looks at the relationship between married love and respect for human life. It begins with the acknowledgment that certain situations in the modern world hinder the exchange of marital love. These situations also make it difficult to have further children. When these problems arise, it is hard for spouses to preserve the intimate nature of their love. The article warns, however, that this can lead to greater

---

139. ". . . totius vitae consuetudo et communion." *Sacrosanctum* (bibliog. III), 761.

threats to marriage—infidelity, the insufficient education of existing children, and the refusal to have further
children.

The article goes on to teach that human life is to be
preserved from the moment of conception. Thus, abortion and infanticide are gravely wrong. Also, human
sexuality and human reproduction are above those of
the animals. Therefore, sexual intercourse is to be performed in a way that is fitting. In particular, marital
love must be harmonized with responsible procreation.
Sexual intercourse must respect both the total self-giving dimension of marital love, as well as the natural
laws associated with procreation. To achieve this, the
article states, good intentions are not enough; the objective norms must be followed. With regard to the regulation of births, these norms are taught by the Church
which interprets divine law. The article forbids those
methods of regulating births which are deemed by the
Church to be unlawful. This is the nature of chastity within marriage: to use one's sexual dimension in a
way that fosters love between spouses, promotes mutual self-giving, and conforms to the natural laws of
procreation.

It is at this point that one finds footnote 14, the contents of which were added at the request of Paul VI.
It has been seen that this footnote cites *Casti connubii*, Pius XII's allocution to Italian midwives, and the
allocution of Paul VI to the cardinals whereby he announces the establishment of a commission to study
matters relating to population, the family, and births.
This commission was requested to give its findings

to the Pope so that he could make the final judgment. The footnote ends with an explanation that it was not the Council's intention to propose definite solutions to these problems immediately.

Article 51 concludes by stating that the true meaning of human life and its creation cannot be understood simply from the perspective of this world. They have to be evaluated in the light of mankind's eternal destiny.

The final article in the chapter on marriage is number 52. It emphasizes that everyone has a duty to promote marriage and family life. It then goes on to outline the responsibilities of various groups—families, civil authorities, Christians, experts, priests, and organizations. It begins with the family, which it says is like "a school for human enrichment."[140] For this "school" to be successful, both parents must show affection and be involved in making decisions. Both the father and the mother have a role within the home. The article states the importance of the mother being present, especially when her children are young, but it acknowledges that the mother may have responsibilities outside the home. These do not have to be undermined provided her role within the home is safeguarded.

The education given to children should enable them to find their vocation in life—including religious ones. If they choose to marry, then they should be sufficiently prepared. Parents and teachers have an important part to play in this. The article cautions against forcing young people to marry or compelling them to choose a particular spouse.

---

140. "Familia schola quaedam uberioris humanitatis est." Ibid., 763.

The family is the basic unit of society. Thus, the prosperity of society is connected with that of the family. Also, it is within the family that the young have their first experience of society—for example, the mixing of different generations. Hence, the family environment enables the young to learn skills which will assist them later. It is for this reason that anyone with influence who works in society should promote family life. Ultimately, society will benefit.

The article states that civil authorities must recognize their "sacred duty"[141] to protect and foster marriage. They must also protect parents' rights with regard to procreation and education. There must also be adequate support for those without families. As just noted, the commission stated that this includes adoption.[142] With regard to Christians themselves, the article reminds them to promote family life by witnessing to the dignity of their own marriages. Also, they are to cooperate with all men and women of good will to promote marriage.

Experts in disciplines such as biology, medicine, social science, and psychology are considered next. They are encouraged to work together for the good of the family and to assist with the legitimate regulation of births. Next, the article says that priests must be properly trained to promote family life and to help married couples by their preaching, by their involvement in the liturgy, and by other means.

The article concludes by looking at the role of orga-

---

141. ". . . sacrum suum munus consideret." Ibid., 764.

142. *Responsum 119b ad num. 56 (nunc 52)* in *Acta Synodalia* (bibliog. III), vol. 4, part 7, 505. Also, *Responsum 73 ad num. 54 (nunc 50)* in *Acta Synodalia* (bibliog. III), vol. 4, part 7, 495.

nizations such as family associations. They should provide instruction and activities which assist the young, especially those who are married. They should also help these young people to carry out their Christian duties in the world. Finally, groups of married couples should give joint witness to the dignity of marriage.

A Summary of the Second Vatican Council and Marriage

The Second Vatican Council very nearly failed to issue any major statement on marriage. All attempts to produce a document on matrimony were unsuccessful and *Gaudium et spes* was threatened by last-minute concerns over its understanding of marriage. Despite these problems, there are eight Conciliar documents which consider marriage in a significant way. Of these, *Gaudium et spes* provides the fullest treatment.

It is noteworthy that *Gaudium et spes* puts love at the very center of marriage. Article 47 states that marriage is a "community of love" (*communitas amoris*).[143] Article 48 explains that the love between spouses is a share in Christ's love for his Church. Moreover, it speaks of the "intimate sharing of marital life and love" (*Intima communitas vitae et amoris coniugalis*).[144] I would say that this is in keeping with Saint Augustine's understanding of the fundamental nature of marital love.[145]

---

143. *Sacrosanctum* (bibliog. III), 753.
144. Ibid., 754.
145. Connery, "The Role of Love in Christian Marriage" (bibliog. III). Also, LaDue, "Conjugal Love and the Juridical Structure of Christian Marriage" (bibliog. III). Also, Montagna, *"Bonum Coniugum: Profili Storici"* (bibliog. III).

Indeed, article 48 names Augustine's *De Bono Coni-ugali* in a footnote. [146]

Article 49 develops the Conciliar document's teaching on love. It says that sexual intercourse allows such love to be expressed physically. As intercourse must be open to children, then it can be said that marital love is ordered toward children. The article also states that this love must embrace the whole person—body and mind. Furthermore, it must embrace the person at all times—both good and bad. Thus, it is always present in an exclusive way. Consequently, marital love excludes both divorce and adultery.[147] I wish to highlight the fact that article 49 of *Gaudium et spes* is actually teaching that marital love is more fundamental than the so-called three goods of Augustine. Indeed, each of these three goods depends upon marital love. That is, this love gives rise to sexual intercourse and so promotes the good of children. Also, it is exclusive and so upholds the good of unity and fidelity. Finally, it is perpetual and so preserves the good of indissolubility.

The fundamental nature of marital love is also taught by article 50. It states that this love is so central to marriage that even if a couple is unable to have children, their marriage retains its character, value, and indissolubility.[148] Once again, the Council is in accordance with Saint Augustine who says that a loving partnership is so central to marriage that it is not

---

146. Vatican II (bibliog. I), *Gaudium et spes,* 7 December 1965, art. 48 refers to Augustine's *De Bono Coniugali* (bibliog. III), in the context that God is the author and designer of marriage; *Sacrosanctum* (bibliog. III), 754.

147. *Sacrosanctum* (bibliog. III), 757–59.

148. Ibid., 759–61.

dependent upon the couple having children. He goes on to say that this bond of love remains even when they grow beyond the age for having children.[149]

---

149. Augustine, *De Bono Coniugali* (bibliog. III), 3.3; Migne (ed), *Patrologiae Latina* (bibliog. III), vol. 40, col. 375.

—3—

Description of the
1983 Code of Canon Law

The Drafting of the Code

IT IS NOT NECESSARY FOR ME to give a detailed history of
the drafting of the 1983 Code of Canon Law, but a summary would be useful. An excellent account has been
provided by the prominent American canon lawyer
John Alesandro, who was an official consultant during
the drafting stage.[1]

Although it was in January 1959 that Pope John
XXIII announced that he was going to convene a council and revise the 1917 Code of Canon Law, it was not
until March 1963 that he formed the first commission
to start the revision of the Code. In November of that
year the commission held its first plenary session. The
most important decision it made was to suspend its activity until the Second Vatican Council had concluded
its work. This decision proved to be fundamental with
regard to emphasizing the true role of canon law. The
cardinals on the commission realized that the Council would enrich the Church's theology, moral theology,

---

1. Alesandro, "The Revision of the *Code of Canon Law:* A Background
Study" (bibliog. III).

and ecclesiology. Thus, the revised Code would have to help implement these developments. That is, the new Code would be the Code of the Council.

In April 1967, under the chairmanship of Cardinal Pericle Felici, the Central Committee enunciated principles which would govern the drafting of the new Code. These principles were put before the Synod of Bishops which met later that year. After a few minor alterations, ten principles of revision were accepted.[2] In brief, the principles are as follows: (1) the new Code must be juridical in nature, explaining the rights and obligations of individuals, as well as protecting them; (2) it must distinguish between the external forum and the internal forum, while enabling them to complement each other; (3) it must foster pastoral care; (4) it should grant faculties to dispense from general laws;[3] (5) it should make use of the principle of subsidiarity; (6) it should protect the rights of every member of the Church; (7) it should determine the tribunals and procedures to be used in order to defend rights; (8) it should continue to determine ecclesiastical jurisdiction in terms of geography,[4] while allowing other criteria in those instances where they would be more appropriate;[5] (9) ecclesiastical penalties should be reduced to a minimum,

---

2. These are described in the Preface of the 1983 Code of Canon Law: *1983 Code* (bibliog. I), xvii–xxx, especially xxi–xxiii. Also, Alesandro, "The Revision of the Code of Canon Law" (bibliog. III), 106–10. Also, Cunningham, "Principles Guiding the Revision of the *Code of Canon Law*" (bibliog. III).

3. This incorporates the wishes of the diocesan bishops present at the Second Vatican Council, as expressed in *Vatican II* (bibliog. I), *Christus Dominus,* 28 October 1965, art. 8b.

4. Examples would include dioceses and parishes.

5. For example, the norms and customs of members of the Eastern Catholic Churches should be recognized and provided for, even if they are living within the territory of Latin-rite dioceses.

especially those which can be incurred automatically; and (10) the new Code should be organized systematically.

From April 1972 to November 1977, the schemas of the various sections of the revised Code were distributed throughout the world to conferences of bishops, religious superiors, departments of the Roman Curia, and pontifical universities. The commission invited comments and suggestions.[6] The Pope then closely examined the text with his own advisors. After further corrections, he promulgated the new Code of Canon Law on 25 January 1983. He did so in an apostolic constitution called *Sacrae disciplinae leges*.[7] A few days later, on the third day of February, the official text of the Code (*Codex Iuris Canonici*) was issued. Certain typographical errors were subsequently spotted and so a corrigenda was issued later that year on September 22. Finally, the new Code came into force on November 27, which was the first Sunday of Advent and so marked the start of a new year in the Church.[8] The ten month delay between the promulgation of the Code and it becoming law was to allow various members of the Church to become acquainted with it and to prepare for its implementation.

---

6. Alesandro, "The Revision of the *Code of Canon Law*" (bibliog. III), 111–21, 134–36.

7. John Paul II (bibliog. I), Apostolic Constitution, *Sacrae disciplinae leges,* 25 January 1983. This is given in the 1983 Code of Canon Law just before the Preface: *1983 Code* (bibliog. I), vii–xiv.

8. A special supplement to *Acta Apostolicae Sedis* (bibliog. III) 75 (1983) was issued. In it, the following can be found: *Sacrae disciplinae leges,* vii–xiv; *Praefatio,* xvii–xxx; *Codex Iuris Canonici,* 1–301; Index, 305–17; Corrigenda, 321–24.

Those Bound by the Code

The very first canon explains that the 1983 Code is meant only for the Latin tradition of the Catholic Church.[9] Thus, it does not apply to those Catholics of the Eastern or Oriental Churches. Their own Code (*Codex Canonum Ecclesiarum Orientalium*) was promulgated in October 1990 with the apostolic constitution *Sacri canones*.[10] This Code came into force on 1 October 1991.[11] Thus, with regard to members of the Eastern Catholic Churches, the practical consequence of canon 1 of the 1983 Code is very similar to that of canon 1 of the 1917 Code.[12] That is, they are generally not bound by the 1983 Code unless it is obvious from the context. Such exceptions would include matters of divine or natural law.

Although the first canon of the 1983 Code is similar to that of the 1917 Code, there is a fundamental difference between the two Codes. Canon 12 of the 1917 Code states that purely ecclesiastical laws contained within the Code generally apply to everyone who is baptized and has the use of reason and has completed his or her seventh year.[13] Thus, according to the 1917 Code, baptized Christians who were not members of the Catholic

---

9. Canon 1: "Canones huius Codicis unam Ecclesiam latinam respiciunt."

10. *Codex Canonum Ecclesiarum Orientalium* (bibliog. I), 18 October 1990.

11. Green, "Reflections on the Eastern Code Revision Process" (bibliog. III). Also, Metz, *"Le Nouveau Code"* (bibliog. III).

12. *1917 Code* (bibliog. I), canon 1: "Licet in Codice iuris canonici Ecclesiae quoque Orientalis disciplina saepe referatur, ipse tamen unam respicit Latinam Ecclesiam, neque Orientalem obligat, nisi de iis agatur, quae ex ipsa rei natura etiam Orientalem afficiunt."

13. *1917 Code* (bibliog. I), canon 12: "Legibus mere ecclesiasticis non tenentur qui baptismum non receperunt, nec baptizati qui sufficienti rationis usu non gaudent, nec qui, licet rationis usum assecuti, septimum aetatis annum nondum expleverunt, nisi aliud iure expresse caveatur."

Church were regarded as still bound by it—though it is very doubtful that this caused them much concern. The 1983 Code is more realistic. In canon 11 it states that Catholics are bound by it, provided they have the use of reason and have completed their seventh year.[14] Non-Catholics are only bound if the law is of divine or natural origin—or if they are bound indirectly.

An example of the latter would be when a non-Catholic marries a Catholic. As the Catholic is bound by the form of marriage, then so is the non-Catholic. This example is addressed by canon 1059 of the 1983 Code: "The marriage of Catholics, even if only one party is a Catholic, is governed not only by divine law but also by canon law, without prejudice to the competence of the civil authority in respect of the merely civil effects of the marriage."[15] The equivalent canon in the 1917 Code did not make any distinction between Catholics and Christians of other traditions: "The marriage of baptized persons is governed not only by divine law but also by canon law, without prejudice to the competence of the civil authority in respect of the merely civil effects of the marriage."[16] In summary, the 1917 Code generally applied to all Christians, except those

---

14. Canon 11: "Legibus mere ecclesiasticis tenentur baptizati in Ecclesia catholica vel in eandem recepti, quique sufficienti rationis usu gaudent et, nisi aliud iure expresse caveatur, septimum aetatis annum expleverunt."

15. My English translation is based on the one used in Caparros et al. (eds), *Code of Canon Law Annotated* (bibliog. III), 661. Canon 1059: "Matrimonium catholicorum, etsi una tantum pars sit catholica, regitur iure non solum divino, sed etiam canonico, salva competentia civilis potestatis circa mere civiles eiusdem matrimonii effectus."

16. *1917 Code* (bibliog. I), canon 1016: "Baptizatorum matrimonium regitur iure non solum divino, sed etiam canonico, salva competentia civilis potestatis circa mere civiles eiusdem matrimonii effectus."

of the Eastern or Oriental churches,[17] whereas the 1983
Code generally applies only to Catholics of the Latin
Church.

The Structure of the Code

The 1983 Code consists of 1,752 canons. This is fewer
than the 1917 Code, which has 2,414. One reason for
the decrease is that the 1983 Code has only 89 canons
concerning ecclesiastical penalties (canons 1311–99);
whereas the 1917 Code has 220 (canons 2195–2414).
This simplification is in accordance with the ninth principle of revision. Also, the 1917 Code contains canons
governing the processes of beatification and canoniza-
tion (canons 1999-2141). These processes are not dealt
with by the 1983 Code.

It has been seen that the 1917 Code uses the divi-
sions of law from the ancient Roman jurists. The jurists categorized the law into persons, things, and actions. The 1917 Code considers these three categories
after one on general norms. It then follows them with a
section on ecclesiastical penalties. Thus, the 1917 Code
consists of five books: (1) general norms (general principles); (2) persons (clergy, religious, laity); (3) things
(the sacraments, sacred places and times, divine worship, the Church's teaching authority, benefices, temporal goods); (4) actions (processes); and (5) penalties.

The 1983 Code was drafted with the intention of
implementing the teachings of the Second Vatican
Council, but this was an incredibly difficult task. There
were two main reasons for this. First, the teachings of

---

17. Bouscaren and Ellis, *Canon Law: A Text and Commentary* (bibliog. III),
18.

the various documents of the Council would have to be translated into legal language. This is indicated by the first principle of revision which says that the Code has to be juridical in nature. Second, the resulting Code would require an intelligible and systematic structure. This was highlighted by the tenth principle of revision. Despite some exceptions, some of which I shall give later, I would say that the final version of the 1983 Code is faithful to the teachings of the Council. Indeed, the official list of sources for the canons shows that very many of them are based on the Council—some verbatim.[18] The need to organize the Code systematically, however, results in its overall structure being similar to that of the 1917 Code.

The 1983 Code consists of seven books. The first book, like the 1917 Code, is on general norms. The second book is titled *The People of God* (*De Populo Dei*) and corresponds to the second book of the 1917 Code. This book has three parts. The first part considers the rights and obligations of the various members of the Church, in accordance with the first principle of revision. This part also gives norms governing associations of people in the Church. The second part deals with the hierarchical constitution of the Church and examines—in order—the Pope, the College of Bishops, cardinals, the Roman Curia, papal legates, dioceses and bishops, bishops' conferences, parish priests and parishes, assistant priests, and chaplains. The third part of the second book deals with institutes of consecrated life and societies of apostolic life (including both

18. *Pontificia Commissio Codici Iuris Canonici Authentice Interpretando* (bibliog. III).

religious and secular institutes). It can be seen that
the strict hierarchical ordering of the second and third
parts is very similar to that found in the pre-Conciliar
1917 Code.

The next three books of the 1983 Code consider matters which were contained in the third book of the 1917
Code. Thus, the third book of the 1983 Code deals with
the teaching office of the Church; the fourth book considers the sanctifying office of the Church (the sacraments, divine worship, sacred places and times); and the
fifth book examines temporal goods. In the 1917 Code,
the fourth and fifth books considered processes and penalties respectively. These are also examined by the last
two books of the 1983 Code, but in reverse order.

The canons on marriage are found primarily in the
fourth book of the Code, which is on the sanctifying
office of the Church. The first part of this book examines each of the seven sacraments in turn. Marriage
is the last of the sacraments to be considered. There
are 111 marriage canons, ranging from canon 1055 to
1165. This is comparable to the 1917 Code which has
132 such canons. One reason for the slight reduction
is that the 1983 Code has simpler rules concerning
impediments.

The layout of the marriage section of the 1983 Code
is exactly the same as that of the 1917 Code, except
that it omits two chapters found in the former Code.
It thus has ten chapters instead of twelve. The first
omitted chapter concerns impedient impediments.[19]
It will be seen that the simpler system of marriage

19. Chapter 3 of the marriage section in the *1917 Code* (bibliog. I).

impediments in the 1983 Code means that it no longer has this category. The other chapter from the 1917 Code to be omitted is chapter twelve on second marriages which consists of two canons (1142 and 1143). The ten chapters in the 1983 Code are preceded by eight introductory canons (1055 to 1062).

—4—

The Nature of Marriage

CANONS 1055 AND 1056 both consider the very nature of marriage. The official list of sources for canon
1055 §1 says that it is based upon canons 1012 §1 and
1013 §1 of the 1917 Code.[1] The first of these former canons states that Christ has raised the marriages of baptized spouses to the level of a sacrament.[2] The second
canon is the one which proved so controversial because
it speaks of the primary and secondary ends of marriage.[3] The list of sources for canon 1055 §1 also cites
three documents from Vatican II: *Lumen gentium*, articles 11 and 41; *Apostolicam actuositatem*, article 11;
and *Gaudium et spes*, article 48.[4]

Article 48 of *Gaudium et spes* opens by describing
marriage as the "intimate sharing of marital life and

---

1. *Pontificia Commissio Codici Iuris Canonici Authentice Interpretando*
(bibliog. III), 292.
2. *1917 Code* (bibliog. I), canon 1012 §1: "Christus Dominus ad sacramenti
dignitatem evexit ipsum contractum matrimonialem inter baptizatos."
3. *1917 Code* (bibliog. I), canon 1013 §1: "Matrimonii finis primarius est
procreatio atque educatio prolis; secundarius mutuum adiutorium et remedium
concupiscentiae."
4. *Sacrosanctum* (bibliog. III), 111–13, 167–70, 478–80, and 754–57. English
translation in Flannery (ed), *Vatican Council II* (bibliog. III), 361–63, 398–400,
778–80, and 950–52.

love."[5] This is used by the 1966 draft of what eventually became canon 1055 §1. This draft states, "Marriage is an intimate union of the whole of life between a man and a woman which, of its very nature, is ordered to the procreation and education of children."[6] However, unlike article 48, the draft omits any reference to marital love. One must acknowledge that those drafting the canon were faced with the problem that love is traditionally not a canonical term; it is internal to people and so is difficult to measure. But so is marital consent, to which, it will be seen, the marriage canons do refer. The first principle of revision is that the Code has to be juridical in nature. Love was not regarded as a juridical concept, so it was omitted. Hence the draft canon's description of marriage only speaks of the intimate sharing of life—and not life and love.

Although article 50 of *Gaudium et spes* is not cited as a source, the draft canon is very similar to it. The article describes marriage as "a whole manner and communion of life,"[7] while the canon calls it "an intimate union of the whole of life." There are two particular similarities. First, the communion (or union) of the man and the woman is said to be "of life" (*vitae*). It is a sharing of their daily lives. Second, this communion involves the "whole" (*totius*) of life—that is, it involves

---

5. "Intima communitas vitae et amoris coniugalis." *Sacrosanctum* (bibliog. III), 754.

6. "Matrimonium est intimam totius vitae coniunctionem inter virum et mulierem, quae, indole sua naturali, ad prolis procreationem et educationem ordinatur." *Pontificia Commissio Codici Iuris Canonici Recognoscendo* (bibliog. III), *Communicationes* 3 (1971), 70. This commission is currently called the *Pontificium Consilium de Legum Textibus.* These changes do not affect the title or the numbering of its journal. The *Pontificium Consilium de Legum Textibus* provides authentic interpretations of the 1983 Code when necessary.

7. ". . . totius vitae consuetudo et communio." *Sacrosanctum* (bibliog. III), 761.

every aspect of daily life at every level. The union is not limited either in scope or depth.

The 1966 draft's reference to the procreation and education of children shows that very early on in the process of revision these dimensions of marriage were regarded as so important that they had to be included in the description of marriage. Thus, in accordance with the Conciliar documents just mentioned, the canon needed to stress that marriage is the context in which children are born. Without these children, neither society nor the Church on earth would have a future. Moreover, the education of these children is vital if they are to be good members of society and the Church. In particular, unless they are educated in the faith, they will be ignorant of the means to salvation, as well as their role in the Church's mission.

Thus, the 1966 draft indicates that the procreation and education of children is important with regard to marriage. The draft does show, however, that there is no intention of repeating the controversial teaching of canon 1013 §1 of the 1917 Code, which stated that the procreation and education of children is the primary end of marriage. This is indeed faithful to article 50 of *Gaudium et spes*, which states that the emphasis on the procreation and education of children is made "while not underestimating the other ends of marriage."[8] Although the list of sources shows that the final version of canon 1055 §1 of the 1983 Code *uses* canon 1013 §1 of the 1917 Code, it is more accurate to say that it *replaces* it.[9]

---

8. ". . . non posthabitis ceteris matrimonii finibus." Ibid., 760.

9. *Pontificium Consilium de Legum Textibus* (bibliog. III), *Communicationes* 3 (1971), 69–80, and *Communicationes* 15 (1983), 221.

In 1977, the draft for canon 1055 §1 was revised. It states, "The marriage covenant, by which a man and a woman establish between themselves an intimate communion of their whole life, and which of its own very nature is ordered to the good of the spouses and to the procreation and education of children, has, between the baptized, been raised by Christ the Lord to the dignity of a sacrament."[10] This draft is closer to the Council's understanding of marriage than the one of 1966. It incorporates the term *covenant* (*foedus*) from article 48 of *Gaudium et spes*.[11] It also uses the word *communion* (*communio*) from article 50, as opposed to the term *union* (*coniunctio*).

The draft introduces the concept of the good of the spouses (*bonum coniugum*) as one of the ends of marriage. This expression could also be interpreted to mean "the well-being" of the spouses. Its insertion is connected with what canon 1013 §1 of the 1917 Code called the secondary end of marriage. This described the secondary purpose of marriage as mutual help and a remedy for concupiscence.[12] These elements are absorbed into the more general expression "the good of the spouses." This new term is also open to certain Conciliar teachings from documents just seen. For example, article 11 of *Lumen gentium* says that couples are to help each other attain holiness. Also, article 48 of *Gaudium et*

---

10. "Matrimoniale foedus, quo vir et mulier intimam inter se constituunt totius vitae communionem, indole sua naturali ad bonum coniugum atque ad prolis procreationem et educationem ordinatam, a Christo Domino ad sacramenti dignitatem inter baptizatos evectum est." *Pontificia Commissio Codici Iuris Canonici Recognoscendo, Communicationes* 9 (1977), 122–23.

11. *Pontificium Consilium de Legum Textibus* (bibliog. III), *Communicationes* 15 (1983), 222.

12. ". . . mutuum adiutorium et remedium concupiscentiae."

spes states that marriage is to help in the personal and spiritual development of the members of the family.

The expression *bonum coniugum* is sufficiently broad and even vague enough to include many aspects of marriage that have not found their way directly into the canons. For example, marital love could fall under this new heading. Certainly, the expression *bonum coniugum* seems to be the closest the compilers of the new Code come to speaking of love. They were aware that the breadth in meaning of this term would allow ecclesiastical judges to develop its interpretation.[13] I shall look at such developments later.

In the 1917 Code, canon 1012 §1 gave the traditional teaching that the marriage of baptized spouses is a sacrament. The 1977 draft concludes by repeating this. In doing so, the draft is also faithful to article 48 of *Gaudium et spes*, as well as *Casti connubii* and *Humanae vitae*, which are all cited as sources.[14]

The final version of canon 1055 §1, as promulgated,[15] reads, "The marriage covenant, by which a man and a woman establish between themselves a partnership of their whole life, and which of its own very nature is ordered to the good of the spouses and to the generation and education of children, has, between the baptized, been raised by Christ the Lord to the dignity of a sacrament."[16] The major difference between this final

---

13. *Pontificium Consilium de Legum Textibus* (bibliog. III), *Communicationes* 9 (1977), 79–80, 117–46, 345–78.

14. *Pontificia Commissio Codici Iuris Canonici Authentice Interpretando* (bibliog. III), 292.

15. *Pontificium Consilium de Legum Textibus* (bibliog. III), *Communicationes* 10 (1978), 86–127, and 15 (1983), 219–42.

16. Canon 1055 §1: "Matrimoniale foedus, quo vir et mulier inter se totius vitae consortium constituunt, indole sua naturali ad bonum coniugum atque ad

version and the 1977 draft is that marriage is no longer described as a "communion" (*communio*) of the whole of the life of the man and woman but as a "partnership" or "sharing" (*consortium*) of their whole life. The main reason why those editing the Code made this change is that the word *communion* is used elsewhere in the Code with other meanings. They decided to use another word in order to avoid ambiguity and confusion.[17]

For example, canon 912 speaks of "holy communion," meaning the Eucharistic species, and canon 333 §2 talks of "full communion" in the sense of ecclesial unity.[18] The eventual use of the word *consortium* shows the influence of Modestinus.[19] He was a student of the Roman jurist Ulpian. Ulpian died in 228, which illustrates when Modestinus was writing. Modestinus described marriage as a "partnership of the whole of life."[20] It is noteworthy that, despite the inclusion in canon 1055 §1 of many of the teachings of the Second Vatican Council, a central part of its understanding of

prolis generationem et educationem ordinatam, a Christo Domino ad sacramenti dignitatem inter baptizatos evectum est." My English translation is based on the one used in Caparros et al. (eds), *Code of Canon Law Annotated* (bibliog. III), 659.

17: *Pontificium Consilium de Legum Textibus* (bibliog. III), *Communicationes* 15 (1983), 222.

18: Canon 912: "Quilibet baptizatus, qui iure non prohibeatur, admitti potest et debet ad sacram communionem." Canon 333 §2: "Romanus Pontifex, in munere supremi Ecclesiae Pastoris explendo, communione cum ceteris Episcopis immo et universa Ecclesia semper est coniunctus; ipsi ius tamen est, iuxta Ecclesiae necessitates, determinare modum, sive personalem sive collegialem, huius muneris exercendi."

19: Scicluna, *The Essential Definition of Marriage* (bibliog. III), 21–46.

20: ". . . consortium omnis vitae . . ." *Digest* (bibliog. III), 23, 2, 1. Also, Gauthier, *Roman Law* (bibliog. III), 36. Canon 1055 §1 uses the word *totius* instead of *omnis*—as well as a different word order, which the Latin language allows.

marriage relies on a description given seventeen hundred years earlier.

The first paragraph of canon 1055, like canon 1012 §1 of the 1917 Code, says that the marriage of baptized spouses is a sacrament. Thus, the second paragraph follows this by stating, "Consequently, a valid marriage contract cannot exist between baptized persons without its being by that very fact a sacrament."[21] Three points need to be made. First, canon 1055 §2 is not only based upon canon 1012 §2 of the 1917 Code; it repeats it verbatim. Second, it is most surprising that this paragraph should speak of the marriage "contract"—rather than "covenant." The previous paragraph very carefully introduces the canons on marriage by employing the much richer term *covenant,* in accordance with *Gaudium et spes.* It could be argued that the editors of the new Code simply took the canon from the 1917 Code and overlooked the need to change *contract* to *covenant.* Unfortunately, even if this were the case, it does not explain why thirty-three of the marriage canons use contractual language—compared with only three that speak of marriage in terms of a covenant.[22]

It must be noted, however, that those drafting the new Code explained that the use of *covenant* was not

---

21: Canon 1055 §2: "Quare inter baptizatos nequit matrimonialis contractus validus consistere, quin sit eo ipso sacramentum."English translation in Caparros et al. (eds), *Code of Canon Law Annotated* (bibliog. III), 660.

22. Marriage canons using contractual language: Canons 1055 §2; 1058; 1073; 1085 §2; 1086 §3; 1089; 1094; 1095; 1096 §1; 1097 §2; 1098; 1101 §2; 1102 §1; 1104 §1; 1105 §1 1°, §4; 1106; 1108 §§1,2; 1114; 1115; 1116 §1; 1117; 1120; 1121 §§2,3; 1122 §§1,2; 1125 3°; 1127 §1; 1143 §1; 1144 §1; 1146; 1147; 1148 §2; 1149; and 1160. Marriage canons using covenantal language: Canons 1055 §1; 1057 §2; and 1063 4°.

intended to replace *contract*. On the contrary, it was meant to supplement it and enrich it because both terms apply to marriage.[23] Indeed, the term *contract* has legal connotations suitable for canon law. For example, it will be seen that canon 1101 §2 says that a party contracts marriage invalidly (*invalide contrahit*) if by a positive act of the will he or she excludes marriage itself or something essential to it when giving consent. This is an application of the legal principle that a contract is invalid if a party deliberately excludes something that is required. Despite the legal benefits of the term *contract*, however, it can be said that the lack of covenantal language means that the 1983 Code's marriage canons are by no means as rich as they could be.

The third point to be made about canon 1055 §2 is that it reaffirms the teaching that any marriage between baptized spouses is, by its very nature, a sacrament, irrespective of their own personal faith. Nevertheless, if the man and woman are the actual ministers of the marriage, bringing it about through their mutual consent, then to what extent is their level of faith important? This theological question is most pertinent in those cases where a man and a woman were baptized as babies but then had no Christian upbringing or education. Is it still reasonable to say that their marriage is a sacrament, even if they personally do not understand what a sacrament is? Indeed, the bishops present at the 1980 Synod on the role of the Christian family in the modern world called for the link between

---

23. *Pontificium Consilium de Legum Textibus* (bibliog. III), *Communicationes* 15 (1983), 222.

24. This was Proposition number 12 from the 1980 Synod of Bishops, in Grootaers and Selling, *The 1980 Synod of Bishops* (bibliog. III), 137, 350–51.

sacramental marriage and baptism to be re-examined.[24] Only a few years before, in 1977, the International Theological Commission said that there were problems in this area which still needed a satisfactory answer.[25]

The commission responsible for the revision of this canon said that the matter was a doctrinal one and not a canonical one. Thus, unless the official doctrine were to change, the canon would have to retain its traditional meaning.[26] The official document emanating from the 1980 Synod of Bishops was Pope John Paul II's *The Christian Family in the Modern World* (*Familiaris consortio*) of November 1981—an Apostolic Exhortation.[27] Despite the bishops' suggestion, article 68 of this papal document repeats the existing teaching that a marriage between baptized spouses is, by the very nature of things, a sacrament.[28] Hence, canon 1055 §2 reflects this official teaching.[29]

The next introductory canon also concerns the nature of marriage. This is canon 1056 which states,

---

25. Sharkey, (ed), *Texts and Documents 1969–1985* (bibliog. III), in particular, "Propositions on the Doctrine of Christian Marriage (1977)," 163–74. Of these, Proposition 2.3 is titled "Baptism, Real Faith, Intention, Sacramental Marriage," 167–68. Also, Cunningham, "Marriage and the Nescient Catholic" (bibliog. III). Also, Örsy, "Disputed Questions" (bibliog. III). Also, Lawler, "Faith, Contract, and Sacrament" (bibliog. III).

26. *Pontificium Consilium de Legum Textibus* (bibliog. III), *Communicationes* 9 (1977), 122–24, and *Communicationes* 15 (1983), 222. Also, Nowak, "Inseparability of Sacrament and Contract" (bibliog. III). Also, Burke, "The Sacramentality of Marriage: Canonical Reflections" (bibliog. III). Also, Himes, "The Intrinsic Sacramentality of Marriage" (bibliog. III). Also, Pompedda, "Faith and the Sacrament of Marriage" (bibliog. III), 33–65. Also, Faltin, "The Exclusion of the Sacramentality of Marriage" (bibliog. III), 66–104.

27. John Paul II (bibliog. I), Apostolic Exhortation, *Familiaris consortio*, 22 November 1981. English translation in Flannery (ed), *Vatican Council II: More* (bibliog. III), 815–98.

28. Flannery (ed), *Vatican Council II: More* (bibliog. III), 872–74.

29. Morrisey, *"L'Evolution du Texte des Canons 1055 et 1095"* (bibliog. III). This article has been particularly useful for my book.

"The essential properties of marriage are unity and indissolubility; in Christian marriage they acquire a distinctive firmness by reason of the sacraments."[30] The wording is virtually the same as canon 1013 §2 of the 1917 Code, which is cited as a source.[31] Other sources listed include article 48 of *Gaudium et spes* and article 25 of *Humanae vitae*. The latter article was originally written in the context of the Church's teaching concerning legitimate means of birth control.[32] It states that if married couples fail to live up to the Church's teaching, they are not to feel rejected by God. They are encouraged to turn to him in prayer and to trust in his infinite love and mercy. God will then strengthen couples with his grace and raise up those who have fallen into sin and put them on the path to holiness.

Canon 1013 §2 of the 1917 Code speaks of "*unitas ac indissolubilitas*." This is generally translated as "unity and indissolubility," but it is possible to translate it as "unity, as well as indissolubility". The revised canon 1056 uses "*unitas et indissolubilitas*." In the context of the rest of the canon, this expression can only be taken to mean unity and indissolubility. Hence, the revised canon makes it clear that indissolubility, as a property of marriage, is as important as unity.

The terms *unity* and *indissolubility* are to be inter-

---

30. Canon 1056: "Essentiales matrimonii proprietates sunt unitas et indissolubilitas, quae in matrimonio christiano ratione sacramenti peculiarem obtinent firmitatem." English translation in Caparros et al. (eds), *Code of Canon Law Annotated* (bibliog. III), 660.

31. *1917 Code* (bibliog. I), canon 1013 §2: "Essentiales matrimonii proprietates sunt unitas ac indissolubilitas, quae in matrimonio christiano peculiarem obtinent firmitatem ratione sacramenti." Also, *Pontificia Commissio Codici Iuris Canonici Authentice Interpretando* (bibliog. III), 292.

32. Flannery (ed), *Vatican Council II: More* (bibliog. III), 410–12.

preted as they are in the 1917 Code. Thus, *unity* means that the marriage involves an exclusive bond between the husband and wife which excludes any third person. *Indissolubility* means that the marriage is perpetual so that the bond cannot be broken, except by the death of one of the spouses. The fact that these properties are essential (*Essentiales matrimonii proprietates*) means that they are intrinsic to marriage—not optional extras.

The canon concludes by stating that these two properties are strengthened in the marriages of Christians because such marriages are sacraments. That is, Christian spouses will be helped by God to live up to the exclusive and perpetual nature of marriage.

It will shortly be seen that the property of indissolubility is not absolute. Although spouses cannot simply dissolve their marriages themselves, the 1983 Code does allow the dissolution of certain marriages—even sacramental ones. In this particular context, it will be noted that there is no significant difference between the 1917 Code and the 1983 Code.

—5—

Consent Brings a Marriage into Existence

IT HAS JUST BEEN SEEN that canons 1055 and 1056 describe the very nature of marriage. But what brings such a marriage into existence? This is explained by the next introductory canon—Canon 1057, which is in two parts. The first part reaffirms the important principle that it is the consent of the couple that brings a marriage into existence. Although the list of sources cites canon 1081 §1 of the 1917 Code as well as article 48 of *Gaudium et spes*, it can be seen that canon 1057 §1 focuses on the former—repeating it verbatim.[1]

It states, "A marriage is brought into being by the lawfully manifested consent of persons who are legally capable. This consent cannot be supplied by any human power."[2] It has been seen that the sources of the corresponding canon of the 1917 Code include the reply of Pope Nicholas I to the Bulgarians, the writings of Saint

---

1. *Pontificia Commissio Codici Iuris Canonici Authentice Interpretando* (bibliog. III), 292.
2. Canon 1057 §1: "Matrimonium facit partium consensus inter personas iure habiles legitime manifestatus, qui nulla humana potestate suppleri valet." English translation in Caparros et al. (eds), *Code of Canon Law Annotated* (bibliog. III), 660.

Ambrose, Saint Isidore of Seville, and the work attributed to Saint John Chrysostom. Thus, the teaching of canon 1057 §1 that consent makes marriage is part of a long tradition in the Church. This part of the canon emphasizes that the role of the couple's consent is so essential that no third party can supply it for them. Even if the man and woman are engaged, nobody can insist that they marry should one of them change his or her mind.[3]

Canon 1057 §1 states that those entering marriage must be "legally capable" (*iure habiles*) and that their consent must be "lawfully manifested" (*legitime manifestatus*). The former expression means that they must be free from any impediment to marriage. The latter means that the consent must be exchanged in accordance with the form prescribed by the Church.

The second paragraph of canon 1057 describes matrimonial consent. Although the first paragraph of canon 1057 repeats the corresponding canon of the 1917 Code verbatim, the second paragraph is very different from its predecessor. It has been seen that canon 1081 §2 of the 1917 Code states, "Matrimonial consent is an act of the will by which each party gives and accepts a perpetual and exclusive right over the body, ordered toward acts which are of themselves apt for the generation of children."[4]

---

3. This last point is encapsulated by canon 1062 §2: "No right of action to request the celebration of marriage arises from a promise of marriage, but there does arise an action for such reparation of harm as may be due." English translation in Caparros et al. (eds), *Code of Canon Law Annotated* (bibliog. III), 662. Canon 1062 §2: "Ex matrimonii promissione non datur actio ad petendam matrimonii celebrationem; datur tamen ad reparationem damnorum, si qua debeatur."

4. *1917 Code* (bibliog. I), canon 1081 §2: "Consensus matrimonialis est actus voluntatis quo utraque pars tradit et acceptat ius in corpus, perpetuum et exclusivum, in ordine ad actus per se aptos ad prolis generationem."

Although it must be acknowledged that matrimonial consent is an act of the will, it has been seen that the rest of the 1917 Code's definition cannot be sustained by the Church's tradition. Cardinal Gasparri gave very few references to support this definition of consent. Although he relied mainly on Gratian, none of his three references to Gratian actually uphold this definition with any strength. Thus, the 1917 Code gives an unfounded definition of marital consent which is biased toward the sexual and procreative aspects of marriage to the detriment of the other dimensions.

The official list of sources for canon 1057 §2 gives two references: canon 1081 §2 of the 1917 Code and article 8 of *Humanae vitae*. The first of these has just been seen. As for the second, it states that marital love is a gift from God—who himself is love. In marriage, spouses give themselves to each other in an exclusive manner. In doing so, they complement one another and collaborate with God in the generation and education of new life.[5] Canon 1057 §2 uses this concept of the spouses giving themselves to each other. It states, "Matrimonial consent is an act of the will by which a man and a woman by an irrevocable covenant mutually give and accept one another for the purpose of establishing a marriage."[6]

Like canon 1081 §2 of the 1917 Code, canon 1057 §2 describes matrimonial consent as an act of the will.

---

5. Flannery (ed), *Vatican Council II: More* (bibliog. III), 400.

6. Canon 1057 §2: "Consensus matrimonialis est actus voluntatis, quo vir et mulier foedere irrevocabili sese mutuo tradunt et accipiunt ad constituendum matrimonium." English translation based on Caparros et al. (eds), *Code of Canon Law Annotated* (bibliog. III), 660–61.

Unlike its predecessor, however, the revised canon does not give a narrow definition of this consent. Instead, it gives the broadest possible definition. That is, it simply states that marital consent involves the mutual giving and accepting of the spouses for the purpose of creating a marriage. Although this does include giving each other the right to intimate acts which can lead to the generation of children, the canon does not limit its definition to just the sexual side of marriage.[7]

I welcome this broader definition because it permits an appreciation of marriage that is wider and deeper than just a consideration of the sexual. Unlike the definition of the 1917 Code, this new definition of consent applies to those marriages where older couples, beyond child-bearing age, have married for the sake of companionship. The revised canon's broader definition is emphasized by its reference to an "irrevocable covenant." The fact that it is irrevocable means that the marriage is continuous. The use of the word *covenant* acts as a reminder that marriage involves the joining of two lives in their entirety. Hence, canon 1057 §2 explains that matrimonial consent brings a marriage into existence—a marriage which involves the ongoing sharing of every aspect of life. This is very different from Gasparri's narrow definition.

---

7. Burke, "The Object of the Marital Self-Gift as Presented in Canon 1057 §2" (bibliog. III).

—6—

Non-Consummated Marriages, Consummated Marriages, and the Act of Consummation

WHILE CANON 1057 introduces the role of consent in creating a marriage, canon 1061 introduces the concept of consummation. Its first paragraph provides a fundamental distinction between a non-consummated marriage and a consummated one. In doing so, it outlines essential qualities concerning the act of consummation.

Canon 1061 §1 concerns a valid marriage between two baptized persons. From canon 1055, especially paragraph 2, this marriage is considered to be a sacrament. Canon 1061 §1 describes the marriage as "ratified" (*ratum*) if it has not been consummated. If, on the other hand, it has been consummated, then it is "ratified and consummated" (*ratum et consummatum*). Canon 1061 §1 in full reads, "A valid marriage between baptized persons is said to be merely ratified, if it is not consummated; ratified and consummated, if the spouses have in a human manner engaged together in a conjugal act in itself apt for the generation of offspring: to

311

this act marriage is by its nature ordered and by it the spouses become one flesh.[1]

The list of sources for this paragraph cites the equivalent one of the 1917 Code (canon 1015 §1) and article 49 of *Gaudium et spes*.[2] There are two major differences between canon 1015 §1 of the 1917 Code and the revised canon. First, canon 1015 §1 of the former Code begins, "A valid marriage of baptized persons is said to be *ratified*, if it has not yet been completed by consummation."[3] It can be seen that this includes the words *not yet* (*nondum*) and *completed* (*completum est*). These words are not found in the new canon. They suggest that an unconsummated marriage is essentially deficient. That is, it will remain incomplete and wanting until it has been consummated.

I would say that it is most fortunate that these words have been omitted from the revised canon. It has been seen that Saint Augustine said that marriage is good primarily because of the fellowship between the spouses. It is within this fellowship that love and charity are exchanged. It has also been seen that the French scholars Ivo of Chartres, Hugh of Saint Victor, and Peter Lombard wrote of the centrality of love within marriage. Pius XI, in his encyclical *Casti connubii* also praised marital love. Thus, it would be true to say that a marriage with-

---

1. Canon 1061 §1: "Matrimonium inter baptizatos validum dicitur ratum tantum, si non est consummatum; ratum et consummatum, si coniuges inter se humano modo posuerunt coniugalem actum per se aptum ad prolis generationem, ad quem natura sua ordinatur matrimonium, et quo coniuges fiunt una caro." English translation based on Caparros et al. (eds), *Code of Canon Law Annotated* (bibliog. III), 662.

2. *Pontificia Commissio Codici Iuris Canonici Authentice Interpretando* (bibliog. III), 293.

3. "Matrimonium baptizatorum validum dicitur ratum, si nondum consummatione completum est."

out love is incomplete, but this cannot be said of a marriage that has not been consummated. There are many couples who have not consummated their marriages, perhaps because of age, but who are fulfilled because their lives are spent expressing their mutual love in other ways. Indeed, it has been noted already that *Gaudium et spes* speaks of marriage as the "intimate sharing of marital life and love" and as a "whole manner and communion of life."[4] Also, article 47 of this Conciliar document calls marriage a "community of love."[5] Thus, the sexual dimension of marriage is only one dimension among many in which love can be expressed.

Unfortunately, canon 1061 §1 still emphasizes the sexual dimension of marriage to the detriment of all the others. Its final part is virtually the same as that of its predecessor in the 1917 Code.[6] With regard to the act of sexual intercourse, canon 1061 §1 states that "to this act marriage is by its nature ordered and by it the spouses become one flesh." I do not doubt the truth of this statement, but it fails to take into account the broader context of marriage—that is, the mutual self-giving which must take place on a daily basis. The great similarity, in this respect, between canon 1015 §1 of the pre-Conciliar 1917 Code and the post-Conciliar canon 1061 §1 does not reflect that the Second Vatican Council ever happened.

---

4. "Intima communitas vitae et amoris coniugalis." From the opening words of art. 48. *Sacrosanctum* (bibliog. III), 754. ". . . totius vitae consuetudo et communio ." From art. 50. Ibid., 761.

5. ". . . communitate amoris." *Sacrosanctum* (bibliog. III), 753.

6. *1917 Code* (bibliog. I), canon 1015 §1: "Matrimonium baptizatorum validum dicitur ratum, si nondum consummatione completum est; ratum et consummatum, si inter coniuges locum habuerit coniugalis actus, ad quem natura sua ordinatur contractus matrimonialis et quo coniuges fiunt una caro."

WHAT BRINGS A MARRIAGE INTO EXISTENCE?

The second difference between canon 1061 §1 of the 1983 Code and its predecessor is that the revised canon gives conditions which have to be met in order for an act of sexual intercourse to be regarded as an act by which the marriage is consummated. There are two conditions. First, the act must be conducted in a "human manner" (*humano modo*). Second, it must be "apt for the generation of offspring" (*per se aptum ad prolis generationem*). Thus, according to this revised canon, a marriage cannot be said to be consummated in the canonical sense simply because the physical act of sexual intercourse has taken place.[7]

With regard to the expression *human manner*, this comes from article 49 of *Gaudium et spes*. This article speaks of "the truly human performance of these acts" (*modo vere humano exerciti*).[8] Canon 1061 §1 does not explain what are the characteristics of an act performed in a human manner, but it is possible to determine some of the more essential qualities.

If an act is human, then it pertains to the whole person—including the will. Hence, if an individual is forced to act against his will, then it can be said that his action is not performed in a truly human fashion. Indeed, canon 125 §1 in the book on general norms states, "An act performed as a result of force imposed from outside on a person who was quite unable to resist it, is regarded as not having taken place."[9] This general

7. Hudson, "Marital Consummation According to Ecclesiastical Legislation" (bibliog. III), in particular, 117–22.

8. *Sacrosanctum* (bibliog. III), 757–59.

9. Canon 125 §1: "Actus positus ex vi ab extrinseco personae illata, cui ipsa nequaquam resistere potuit, pro infecto habetur." English translation in Caparros et al. (eds), *Code of Canon Law Annotated* (bibliog. III), 142.

principle can be applied to marriage. An act of sexual intercourse in which the wife is forced to participate against her will by her husband cannot be said to be performed in a human manner. Thus, such an act cannot be considered to consummate their marriage. This conclusion was also reached by those responsible for editing canon 1061 §1.[10]

Similarly, a spouse who is heavily drugged cannot engage in sexual intercourse in a human manner because he or she does not have the use of reason. That is, he or she is unable to make a true decision about having intercourse. The editors of the canon agreed that aphrodisiacs are permissible to assist intercourse—provided that neither spouse loses the use of reason or becomes incapable of refusing intercourse.[11] It was not decided whether an act of intercourse in which the wife suffers grave pain can be regarded as conducted in a truly human manner. It is thus a matter of debate whether such a marriage can be said to be consummated in the canonical sense.[12]

I greatly welcome the inclusion of the expression *human manner*. If sexual intercourse is to be a truly physical expression of the loving self-giving that is so essential to marriage, then it must be acted out freely. This is indeed in accordance with the understanding of marriage as expressed by Pope John Paul II in his weekly audiences from July 1982 to July 1984.[13]

---

10. *Pontificium Consilium de Legum Textibus* (bibliog. III), *Communicationes* 6 (1974), 191–92.
11. Ibid., 192.
12. Ibid., 192–93. Also, Navarrete, *"De Notione et Effectibus"* (bibliog. III).
13. John Paul II, *The Theology of the Body* (bibliog. III), 304–85.

He explains that spouses' bodies have a sacramental aspect—making visible, and participating in, what is invisible.[14] That is, spouses manifest Christ's love for the Church and also their marital unity.

They express these through their bodies. It is as if their bodies speak for them, proclaiming Christ's love and their unity. Just as a prophet makes known the truth about God, then so their bodies reveal the truth about marriage. It is for this reason that Pope John Paul II speaks of the "prophetism of the body."[15] One consequence of this is that spouses must behave in conformity with the truths of marriage; otherwise their bodies act as false prophets. If one applies this to forced sexual intercourse, then one must conclude that the forced act of union cannot truly represent the genuine total self-giving that marriage involves. Pope John Paul also speaks of the "language of the body."[16] If this terminology is used, then forced sexual intercourse is a lie. That is, forced intercourse cannot truthfully express the voluntary self-giving that is at the center of marriage.

Those responsible for drafting canon 1061 §1 feared that the inclusion of the words *human manner* could result in an increase in the number of marriages that are not regarded as consummated. Consequently, they feared that there could be an uncontrollable number of petitions requesting the dissolution of non-consummated marriages.[17] I shall follow up on this point. It

---

14. Ibid., 304–06.
15. Ibid., 364.
16. Ibid., 398.
17. *Pontificium Consilium de Legum Textibus* (bibliog. III), *Communicationes* 9 (1977), 129.

will be seen very shortly that I am not in favor of continuing the practice of dissolving non-consummated marriages. But if the tradition is to continue, then the expression *human manner* must be taken seriously. I shall show that the fears of many of those responsible for the editing of canon 1061 §1 were justified because the expression *human manner* can be applied in a way that they had not considered.

The second condition for consummation given by canon 1061 §1 is that intercourse must be "apt for the generation of offspring" (*per se aptum ad prolis generationem*). Again this opens the way for an increase in petitions for dissolution. An example would clarify matters. Two people marry and during the course of their time together the man insists on using a prophylactic sheath (condom). Indeed, he never engages in intercourse without one. The relationship ends in separation and civil divorce. As no act of intercourse has been performed in a manner apt for the generation of children, then it could be argued that the marriage is not consummated canonically and so can be dissolved.

The remainder of canon 1061 can be examined briefly. Its second paragraph repeats almost verbatim its predecessor in the 1917 Code, canon 1015 §2. Canon 1061 §2 states, "If the spouses have lived together after the celebration of their marriage, consummation is presumed until the contrary is proven."[18] Thus, if the spouses lived together after the wedding and dissolution on

---

18. Canon 1061 §2: "Celebrato matrimonio, si coniuges cohabitaverint, praesumitur consummatio, donec contrarium probetur." English translation in Caparros et al. (eds), *Code of Canon Law Annotated* (bibliog. III), 662.

the grounds of non-consummation is being sought, then the onus is on proving the non-consummation.

Traditionally, three types of proof can be used. One involves a physical examination of the woman. This approach may not be possible if she refuses or if she is no longer intact as a result of other relationships. It is also possible that she lost her virginity to the man who became her husband, but before they married. In this case, the marriage would not be consummated in the canonical sense. The second type of proof involves the couple being interviewed. The truth of their evidence can then be supported by character witnesses. Also, there could be close friends or family members who are aware from intimate conversations that the marriage was never consummated.[19]

If the couple did not live together after the wedding, then a third approach could be used. This is described as *lack of opportunity*. For example, a soldier marries a woman. Immediately after the wedding he is driven back to his barracks and is sent overseas. While he is away, he is unfaithful and the marriage fails. The couple never lived together and so never had the opportunity to consummate their union.[20]

Canon 1061 §3 refers to invalid marriages. It repeats canon 1015 §4 of the former Code virtually verbatim. It states, "An invalid marriage is said to be putative if it has been celebrated in good faith by at least one party. It ceases to be such when both parties become certain

---

19. Woestman, *Special Marriage Cases* (bibliog. III), 18–19.
20. Ibid.

of its nullity."[21] The relevance of this canon can be understood by considering it in conjunction with canon 1137: "Children who are conceived or born of a valid or of a putative marriage are legitimate."[22] An example will illustrate the importance of these canons.

Two people marry and have children. The marriage fails and is later declared null by a marriage tribunal. The decision of the tribunal means that the marriage never truly existed. Thus, the children were not conceived or born within a marriage. It is a common concern among those seeking a declaration of nullity that their children will be regarded as illegitimate should the declaration be made. These two canons provide a pastoral solution to the problem. It can be said that at the time the children were conceived or born their parents *believed* that their marriage was valid. They thus had their children in good faith. It was only later that they became aware that they were not truly married. Canon 1061 §3 calls the marriage at the time the children were conceived or born *putative*. Then, canon 1137 states that the children of this putative marriage are to be considered legitimate.

---

21. Canon 1061 §3: "Matrimonium invalidum dicitur putativum, si bona fide ab una saltem parte celebratum fuerit, donec utraque pars de eiusdem nullitate certa evadat." English translation in Caparros et al. (eds), *Code of Canon Law Annotated* (bibliog. III), 662. Paragraph 3 of canon 1015 of the 1917 Code is not reproduced in the 1983 Code. This paragraph calls the valid marriage of two unbaptized persons "legitimate" (*legitimum*). It thus acknowledges that non-Christians are able to marry. Although this is not in the revised Code, its omission is certainly not meant to undermine the marriages of the unbaptized.

22. Canon 1137: "Legitimi sunt filii concepti aut nati ex matrimonio valido vel putativo." English translation ibid., 717.

—7—

The Dissolution of
Non-Consummated Marriages

WITH REGARD TO OBTAINING dissolution of a non-consummated marriage, the canons governing the correct procedure are found in the seventh book of the 1983 Code. This book deals with processes. The relevant canons are numbered 1697 to 1706. The first canon states that only the spouses themselves have the right to seek dissolution of a non-consummated marriage: "The spouses alone, or indeed one of them even if the other is unwilling, have the right to seek the favor of a dispensation from a ratified and non-consummated marriage."[1] Two observations are called for. First, a husband or wife can seek the dissolution against the other spouse's wishes.

This rule may seem most unusual but it is meant to protect an innocent party. For example, a woman marries but her marriage is never consummated. The reason for the non-consummation is that her husband

---

1. Canon 1697: "Soli coniuges, vel alteruter, quamvis altero invito, ius habent petendi gratiam dispensationis super matrimonio rato et non consummato." English translation in Caparros et al. (eds), *Code of Canon Law Annotated* (bibliog. III), 1046.

is having an adulterous affair with another woman. He engages in intercourse only with the other woman and loses physical interest in his own wife. The other woman is not married and so he does not want his marriage dissolved because he fears that would make him free to marry her. He thus opposes any dissolution of the non-consummated marriage because it provides him with an excuse for not making a true commitment to either woman. According to canon 1697, his wife can request dissolution despite his unwillingness.

The second observation is that the spouse, or spouses, have a right to seek the dissolution. That is, they have a right to ask for it, but the canon describes the dissolution as a "favor." Thus, although they have a right to request it, they do not have a right for their request to be granted.

Canon 1698 §1 states that only the Apostolic See can make the judgment as to whether the dissolution should be granted: "Only the Apostolic See gives judgment on the fact of the non-consummation of a marriage and on the existence of a just reason for granting the dispensation."[2] This canon shows that two elements are needed in order for the favor to be granted: proof of non-consummation and a just reason for the dissolution. The second element is as important as the first. This is because the dissolution is a "favor". That is, even the incontrovertible fact of non-consummation does not give the spouse, or spouses, the "right" to the dissolution. There must be an appropriate reason in order to convince the Apostolic

---

2. Canon 1698 §1: "Una Sedes Apostolica cognoscit de facto inconsummationis matrimonii et de exsistentia iustae causae ad dispensationem concedendam." English translation ibid., 1047.

See that the favor should be granted.[3] In the example just given, it would seem possible that the wife would be granted the dissolution. If the husband were to change his mind, however, and be the party seeking the dissolution so that he could marry his mistress, it would seem unlikely that it would be granted.

The apostolic constitution of Pope John Paul II, *Pastor Bonus*, outlines the work of the Roman Curia and explains the responsibilities of each of its departments. In article 67, it states that the Congregation for Divine Worship and the Discipline of the Sacraments is the appropriate department of the Apostolic See to make the judgment as to whether the dissolution should be given.[4] This Congregation does not actually give the dissolution, however. It merely decides whether it should be granted. Canon 1698 §2 states, "The dispensation, however, is given by the Roman Pontiff alone."[5] This point is reaffirmed by canon 1142 which summarizes matters: "A non-consummated marriage between baptized persons or between a baptized party and an unbaptized party can be dissolved by the Roman Pontiff for a just reason, at the request of both parties or of either party, even if the other is unwilling."[6]

---

3. Orlandi, *"De Casibus 'Difficilioribus'"* (bibliog. III). Also, Pompedda, *"La Nozione di Matrimonio 'Rato e Consumato'"* (bibliog. III).

4. John Paul II (bibliog. I), Apostolic Constitution, *Pastor Bonus*, 28 June 1988. Latin text with English translation in Caparros et al. (eds), *Code of Canon Law Annotated* (bibliog. III), 1166–1279.

5. Canon 1698 §2: "Dispensatio vero ab uno Romano Pontifice conceditur." English translation in Caparros et al. (eds), *Code of Canon Law Annotated* (bibliog. III), 1047.

6. Canon 1142: "Matrimonium non consummatum inter baptizatos vel inter partem baptizatam et partem non baptizatam a Romano Pontifice dissolvi potest iusta de causa, utraque parte rogante vel alterutra, etsi altera pars sit invita." English translation ibid., 719. Again, canon 1142 states that the dissolution can take place even if one of the parties objects.

Why is it that only the Pope can grant the dissolution? The Code of Canon Law uses two principles concerning indissolubility. The first is that in the marriages of the baptized, indissolubility is strengthened because these marriages are sacramental (as seen in canon 1056). The second is that when sacramental marriages are consummated they become absolutely indissoluble. The strengthening of indissolubility through sacramental marriage and consummation must be understood, though, as the strengthening of an indissolubility that exists naturally in all marriages. Thus, to dissolve an unconsummated marriage involves breaking a bond between the spouses. Although this bond does not possess absolute indissolubility, it does possess a certain indissolubility by the very nature of marriage itself. Therefore, no human power can dissolve what has been established by nature. It is for this reason that it is taught that only the Pope can dissolve unconsummated marriages. He does so not as head of the Church but as Vicar of Christ. That is, he does not use human power but allows God to act through him. He becomes an instrument of divine power. Consequently, it is God who dissolves unconsummated marriages.[7]

What about the dissolution of a consummated sacramental marriage? Canon 1141 states, "A marriage which is ratified and consummated cannot be dissolved by any human power or by any cause other than death."[8] Although the list of sources for this canon

---

7. Woestman, *Special Marriage Cases* (bibliog. III), 6–7.
8. Canon 1141: "Matrimonium ratum et consummatum nulla humana potestate nullaque causa, praeterquam morte, dissolvi potest." English translation in Caparros et al. (eds), *Code of Canon Law Annotated* (bibliog. III), 719.

includes *Casti connubii* and article 48 of *Gaudium et spes* (both of which refer to indissolubility), the main source is canon 1118 of the 1917 Code—which canon 1141 repeats nearly verbatim.[9] Canon 1141 acknowledges that the death of a spouse dissolves a ratified and consummated marriage. Can anything or anyone else? The canon states that no human power can do so. Thus, not even the Pope acting as *head of the Church* can dissolve such a marriage.

This canonical restriction notwithstanding, can the Pope dissolve this type of marriage using his ministerial power? That is, can God work through him to bring about the dissolution? From the canon itself the answer to this question is not clear. The canon does state that, apart from death, the dissolution of a consummated sacramental marriage cannot be brought about by any human power "or by any cause" (*nullaque causa*). This could be taken to mean that even divine power cannot be invoked to dissolve such a marriage.

At this point I give two cautions. First, one must be careful not to read too much into the expression *or by any cause*. Second, the canon must not be interpreted so as to restrict God; he is not bound by the 1983 Code of Canon Law. It is thus possible that God could act through the Pope to dissolve consummated sacramental marriages. As Woestman observes, however, "Although some writers maintain that the Pope has such power, it must be remarked that no Pope has exercised it, or has given evidence that he thought that he

---

9. *Pontificia Commissio Codici Iuris Canonici Authentice Interpretando* (bibliog. III), 311.

possessed the authority to do so as the Vicar of Christ."[10] Indeed, various Popes have indicated that they do not have this authority.[11] Pope John Paul II reaffirmed this position in his annual address to the Rota in January 2000.[12]

I am disappointed that the dissolution of non-consummated marriages has remained in the 1983 Code. I am disappointed for two reasons. First, the historical basis for the practice is weak. Second, the practice seems to ignore the teaching of the Second Vatican Council on marriage. I shall expand upon these two objections in turn.

It has been seen that canon 1142 summarizes the dissolution of non-consummated marriages. An examination of its origins shows that the only official source given is canon 1119 of the 1917 Code.[13] Canon 1119 states that an unconsummated marriage between baptized spouses or between a baptized spouse and an unbaptized one can be dissolved. It explains that the dissolution can take place by solemn religious profession or, for a just reason, by a dispensation from the Apostolic See.[14] Under the 1917 Code, whichever method of

---

10. Woestman, *Special Marriage Cases* (bibliog. III), 10. Also, Lawler, "Blessed Are the Spouses Who Love" (bibliog. III).

11. Huizing, "Canonical Implications of the Concept of Marriage in the Conciliar Constitution *Gaudium et spes*" (bibliog. III), in particular, 119–23. Also, Abate, *Il Matrimonio nell'Attuale Legislazione Canonica* (bibliog. III), 2nd edition, 230–42.

12. John Paul II (bibliog. I), Address to the Roman Rota, 21 January 2000. Also, Kowal, *"L'Indissolubilità del Matrimonio Rato e Consumato: Status Quaestionis"* (bibliog. III).

13. *Pontificia Commissio Codici Iuris Canonici Authentice Interpretando* (bibliog. III), 311.

14. *1917 Code* (bibliog. I), canon 1119: "Matrimonium non consummatum inter baptizatos vel inter partem baptizatam et partem non baptizatam, dissolvitur tum ipso iure per sollemnem professionem religiosam, tum per dispensationem

dissolution was used, the Apostolic See had to be involved because a dispensation was required for a married person to enter the novitiate of a religious order.[15]

Where did canon 1119 come from? It has been seen that Cardinal Gasparri cites certain ecclesiastical authorities. Of these, the most influential ones are the Council of Trent and Pope Alexander III.[16] The Council of Trent wanted to uphold the Church's practices against the criticisms of Protestant Reformers. In the sixth canon of its Doctrine Concerning the Sacrament of Marriage, the Council stated definitively that a non-consummated marriage can be dissolved by one of the spouses entering solemn religious life.[17] Gasparri quotes Alexander III to show that non-consummated marriages can also be dissolved for reasons other than religious profession. He cites Alexander's decretal *Ex publico* which argued that when Jesus condemned those who divorced and remarried, he was referring only to those who attempted to leave consummated marriages.[18] That is, unconsummated marriages do not fall under Jesus's prohibition and so can be dissolved. It might be considered surprising that Alexander III should interpret Scripture in this way, but I would say that it is even more shocking that Gasparri should use this very decretal to support a canon.

I have shown that Alexander III was heavily influenced by Gratian. Gratian wrote his *Decretum* some-

---

a Sede Apostolica ex iusta causa concessam, utraque parte rogante vel alterutra, etsi altera sit invita."

15. *1917 Code* (bibliog. I), canon 542 1°.
16. Gasparri (ed), *Codex Iuris Canonici Fontes* (bibliog. III), 319–20.
17. Denzinger, *Enchiridion Symbolorum* (bibliog. III), 416.
18. Alexander III (bibliog. I), decretals, 1159–81: *Ex publico*.

time between 1139 and 1155. Alexander was elected Pope shortly afterwards in 1159. By that time, Gratian's work had influenced many parts of the Church. I have explained how Gratian claimed to have taken two valid traditions within the Church and synthesized them. These are supposedly the Roman tradition which taught that a marriage is brought into existence by the couple's consent and the Germanic tradition which taught that consummation creates marriage. Undoubtedly, the Roman tradition did teach that consent makes marriage, but I have shown that it cannot be said that the so-called Germanic tradition simply focused on consummation. The effect of Gratian's *Decretum* was that a marriage was not regarded as complete until it had been consummated sexually. In practical terms, this meant that the marriage did not enjoy absolute indissolubility until consummated. This led to the general practice of dissolving non-consummated marriages.

By the time of Alexander III, it was difficult for him to go against this practice. He thus defended it by using means available to him—which, it has been seen, included interpreting Scripture in such a way that it showed Jesus of Nazareth defending twelfth-century Church practice. The custom of dissolving non-consummated marriages continued into the twentieth century. Cardinal Gasparri was asked to codify the laws and practices of the Church—not to question them. Thus, the dissolution of non-consummated marriages found its way into the 1917 Code with extremely weak sources to support it. It then found its way from there into the 1983 Code.

My second reason for opposing the inclusion of the dissolution of non-consummated marriages in the revised Code is much briefer. That is, it lessens the teaching of the Second Vatican Council. To repeat what I said earlier, the Council speaks of marriage as a "community of love," the "intimate sharing of marital life and love," and a "whole manner and communion of life."[19] If consent creates marriage, then from that very moment there exists a community of love that incorporates every dimension of life. I have no doubt that the final part of canon 1061 §1 is true. That is, marriage is by its nature ordered toward that act which is in itself apt for the generation of offspring and which unites the spouses in one flesh. But to dissolve a marriage on the grounds that it is not consummated is to emphasize its sexual dimension to the detriment of all its other dimensions. A couple may be very happily married for a long time but may never have consummated the marriage. Everyday they exchange love and charity, but what value is being placed on their marriage by saying that it does not enjoy absolute indissolubility? The couple may love each other dearly, but canon 1142 teaches that their marriage could, in theory, be dissolved by the stroke of a pen.

Are my views contrary to the Catholic Church's official teaching? What about the sixth canon from the Council of Trent's *Doctrine Concerning the Sacrament of Marriage*? With regard to Trent, it must be noted that it upheld the practice of dissolving

---

19. Vatican II (bibliog. I), *Gaudium et spes,* 7 December 1965, arts. 47, 48, and 50 respectively.

non-consummated marriages by religious profession—
as opposed to a general dissolution of non-consummated marriages. Moreover, I am not saying that the
Pope is unable to dissolve such marriages. I have explained that any dissolution is a favor which does not
have to be granted. I am merely asking if, in the light
of the Second Vatican Council, it still makes sense to
grant this favor? In this modern world, many people,
not just Catholics, look to the Church and the Pope to
uphold moral standards. In particular, they want marriage and its traditional values, such as indissolubility,
to be protected. I acknowledge that it is not for me to
question the actions of the Pope, but a re-examination
of the practice of dissolving non-consummated marriages may be beneficial.

—8—

Pastoral Care
and Marriage Preparation

THE INTRODUCTORY MARRIAGE canons are followed by the first chapter. This is titled "Pastoral Care and the Prerequisites for the Celebration of Marriage."[1] The chapter consists of canons 1063 to 1072. The first canon, number 1063, is important because it highlights the intention to base the 1983 Code on the teaching of the Second Vatican Council. Canon 1063 opens by reminding pastors that they have an obligation to ensure that their ecclesial communities provide assistance to married couples.[2] The official list of sources for this canon shows that it is based upon three documents from the Second Vatican Council: *Gaudium et spes*, *Lumen gentium*, and *Sacrosanctum Concilium*.[3]

This canon is divided into four parts, each of which suggests how married couples can be helped. The first

---

1. *"De cura pastorali et de iis quae matrimonii celebrationi praemitti debent."* English translation of title in Caparros et al. (eds), *Code of Canon Law Annotated* (bibliog. III), 663.

2. Canon 1063: "Pastores animarum obligatione tenentur curandi ut propria ecclesiastica communitas christifidelibus assistentiam praebeat, qua status matrimonialis in spiritu christiano servetur et in perfectione progrediatur."

3. *Pontificia Commissio Codici Iuris Canonici Authentice Interpretando* (bibliog. III), 294.

part says that everyone, children and adults, are to be instructed in Christian marriage and in the role of Christian spouses and parents. This ongoing instruction is
to be achieved through preaching, catechesis, and the
various means of communication at the Church's disposal.[4] The second part refers to the more immediate preparation of engaged couples for marriage.[5] The
third part states that a fruitful celebration of the wedding ceremony will itself help prepare couples for marriage.[6] Finally, the fourth part of canon 1063 refers to
ongoing support for those who have already married.[7]

It can be seen that canon 1063 is very much based on
the documents of the Second Vatican Council. The same
cannot be said of the rest of the canons in this first chapter of marriage canons. This is not meant as a criticism.
The remaining canons cover very practical and essential
aspects of the preparations for marriage. These canons
are just as necessary after the Council as they were before it and so they repeat a number of the equivalent canons from the 1917 Code. For example, canon 1065 refers
to spiritual preparations for marriage. Canons 1066 to
1070 refer to the publication of marriage banns and the
pre-marriage investigation to ensure that there is no reason why a marriage cannot be celebrated.

Canon 1071 §1 lists particular groups of people
who should not be allowed to marry until the minister

---

4. Vatican II (bibliog. I), *Gaudium et spes,* 7 December 1965, arts. 47 and
52.

5. Ibid., art. 52.

6. Vatican II (bibliog. I), *Sacrosanctum Concilium,* 4 December 1963, arts.
19, 59, and 77.

7. Vatican II (bibliog. I), *Gaudium et spes,* 7 December 1965, art. 52: and
Lumen gentium, 21 November 1964, art. 41.

has obtained permission. These include those with no fixed address[8] and those who have publicly rejected the Catholic faith.[9] Canon 1071 §1, 6° repeats the instruction of the former canon 1034 that permission must be obtained from the local ordinary before celebrating the marriages of minors who want to marry against their parents' reasonable wishes or without their knowledge.[10] It has been noted that Luther regarded such marriages to be invalid. The Council of Trent took the opposing view and said that these marriages are valid, but it said that they should be discouraged.[11] Canon 1067 §2 of the 1917 Code stated that those who marry below the civil legal age still marry validly provided they are above the minimum age set by the Church, but it asked priests to discourage such marriages and to respect civil law. This instruction is repeated in canon 1072 of the 1983 Code.[12]

---

8. Canon 1071 §1, 1°: "matrimonio vagorum." This repeats *1917 Code* (bibliog. I), canon 1032.

9. Canon 1071 §1, 4°: "matrimonio eius qui notorie catholicam fidem abiecerit." This repeats 1917 Code (bibliog. I), canon 1065. Those drafting 4° acknowledged that, in practice, it is not always clear when the rejection of the Catholic faith is public and when it is not. Thus, it is not always certain when permission for the marriage is required. *Pontificium Consilium de Legum Textibus* (bibliog. III), *Communicationes* 9 (1977), 144.

10. Canon 1071 §1, 6°: "matrimonio filii familias minoris, insciis aut rationabiliter invitis parentibus."

11. Denzinger, *Enchiridion Symbolorum* (bibliog. III), 417–18.

12. Canon 1072: "Curent animarum pastores a matrimonii celebratione avertere iuvenes ante aetatem, qua secundum regionis receptos mores matrimonium iniri solet."

—9—

The Impediment of Impotence

The Present Law on Impotence

THE SECOND CHAPTER OF the 1983 Code's marriage section runs from canon 1073 to canon 1082. It is titled "Diriment Impediments in General."[1] Earlier, I noted that the 1983 Code has a simpler system of impediments than the previous Code. When I examined the 1917 Code, I explained that it distinguishes between two types of impediment: the impedient impediment (*impedimentum impediens*) and the diriment impediment (*impedimentum dirimens*). The former prohibits a marriage, but should the marriage go ahead, then it is valid albeit unlawful. The latter actually invalidates a marriage.

The 1983 Code of Canon Law has simplified matters and only considers diriment impediments—that is, impediments which invalidate marriage.[2] For the sake of validity, the competent ecclesiastical authority has to dispense the impediment before the marriage is celebrated. Obviously, this is not possible if the impediment

---

1. "De impedimentis dirimentibus in genere." English translation of title in Caparros et al. (eds), *Code of Canon Law Annotated* (bibliog. III), 667.

2. *Pontificium Consilium de Legum Textibus* (bibliog. III), *Communicationes* 9 (1977), 132–37, and *Communicationes* 10 (1978), 126.

is of natural or divine law. The first canon in this chapter thus states, "A diriment impediment renders a person incapable of validly contracting a marriage."[3] With regard to the revised Code, I shall often use the word *impediment* without the qualifying term *diriment* because it is no longer necessary to distinguish between the two types of impediment.[4]

The third chapter of the marriage canons goes from canon 1083 to canon 1094. It is titled "Individual Diriment Impediments."[5] As the name suggests, the canons of this chapter give the various impediments to marriage. Canon 1084 §1 states, "By reason of its very nature, marriage is invalidated by antecedent and perpetual impotence to have sexual intercourse, whether on the part of the man or on that of the woman, whether absolute or relative."[6] There are two sources listed for this paragraph.[7] The first source is canon 1068 §1 of the 1917 Code. The second is a letter from the Sacred Congregation for the Doctrine of the Faith[8] issued in 1977. I shall examine each of these sources.

Canon 1068 §1 of the former Code states, "By reason of the law of nature itself, marriage is invalidated by antecedent and perpetual impotence, whether on the

---

3. Canon 1073: "Impedimentum dirimens personam inhabilem reddit ad matrimonium valide contrahendum." English translation in Caparros et al. (eds), *Code of Canon Law Annotated* (bibliog. III), 667.

4. *Pontificium Consilium de Legum Textibus* (bibliog. III), *Communicationes* 10 (1978), 359.

5. "De impedimentis dirimentibus in specie." English translation of title in Caparros et al. (eds), *Code of Canon Law Annotated* (bibliog. III), 674.

6. Canon 1084 §1: "Impotentia coeundi antecedens et perpetua, sive ex parte viri sive ex parte mulieris, sive absoluta sive relativa, matrimonium ex ipsa eius natura dirimit." English translation ibid., 675.

7. *Pontificia Commissio Codici Iuris Canonici Authentice Interpretando* (bibliog. III), 299.

8. As the Congregation for the Doctrine of the Faith was then called.

part of the man or on the part of the woman, whether known by the other or not, whether absolute or relative."[9] It can be seen that the canon in the 1983 Code is very similar to this one. In my section on the 1917 Code, I examined the canon on impotence. It would be helpful if I were to give a summary.

Canon 1068 §1 gives two criteria which both have to be met in order for the impotence to be an impediment. First, it has to be "antecedent" (*antecedens*)—that is, actually existing at the time the marriage is celebrated. Second, it must be "perpetual" (*perpetua*). It has been noted that one commentary states that if the impotence can be cured, but only by means that are illicit or dangerous, then it is still deemed to be perpetual.[10] The canon explains that if the impotence is antecedent and perpetual then the marriage cannot take place. I shall refer to this type of impotence as *canonical impotence* in order to distinguish it from impotence which does not meet these criteria. Thus, canon 1068 §1 states that canonical impotence invalidates marriage—irrespective of whether it is the man or the woman who suffers the impotence, irrespective of whether or not the other party knows about the condition, and irrespective of whether the condition would manifest itself with any sexual partner (absolute impotence) or with just a particular individual or class of individuals (relative impotence).[11]

---

9. *1917 Code* (bibliog. I), canon 1068 §1: "Impotentia antecedens et perpetua, sive ex parte viri, sive ex parte mulieris, sive alteri cognita sive non, sive asboluta sive relativa, matrimonium ipso naturae iure dirimit."

10. Bouscaren and Ellis, *Canon Law: A Text and Commentary* (bibliog. III), 525. Also, Boccafola, *The Requirement of Perpetuity for the Impediment of Impotence* (bibliog. III), 142–43.

11. Ritty, "Invalidity of Marriage by Sexual Anomalies" (bibliog. III).

It has been noted that Cardinal Gasparri cites Gratian as one of the main sources for canon 1068 §1.[12] Once again, the shadow of this twelfth-century scholar can be seen. In my section on Gratian, I showed that he taught that if a man enters marriage and proves to be impotent, then his wife can leave him and marry another.[13] It is not clear whether Gratian regarded the first marriage to be dissolved or simply not to exist in the first place. In favor of the former explanation, he says, "Behold, the inability to pay the debt dissolves the bond of marriage."[14] The reference to debt refers to marital debt, which according to Gratian was the mutual obligation to engage in sexual intercourse with, and at the behest of, the other spouse.[15]

With regard to the second explanation, Gratian also suggests that the woman can leave her impotent husband and marry another man because the first marriage never truly existed. In modern canonical terminology, this would be equivalent to saying that the former marriage was invalid because of the impotence. Gratian bases his argument for this on the Church's practice in his time of allowing remarriage in cases of impotence.

It has been seen that Gratian is strict in his understanding of divorce and remarriage. Indeed, when he

---

12. Gasparri (ed), *Codex Iuris Canonici Pii X* (bibliog. III), 304.

13. Gratian, *Concordia* (bibliog. III), Part 2, Case 27, Question 2, dictum after ch. 29.

14. "Ecce, inpossibilitas coeundi, si post carnalem copulam inventa fuerit in aliquo, non solvit coniugium." Gratian, *Concordia* (bibliog. III), Part 2, Case 27, Question 2, dictum after ch. 29.

15. Gratian, *Concordia* (bibliog. III), Part 2, Case 27, Question 2, dictum after ch. 18, ch. 19, dictum after ch. 26, and dictum after ch. 28. Also, Case 30, Question 1, ch. 2, and Case 32, Question 2, dictum after ch. 2, and Case 33, Question 5, ch. 5 and dictum after ch. 11. Also, Brundage, *Law, Sex, and Christian Society* (bibliog. III), 241.

considers the possible exceptive clause in Matthew's Gospel,[16] he concludes that it in fact provides no exception to the rule that spouses cannot separate and marry others.[17] With this strict interpretation of divorce and remarriage in mind, Gratian can only explain the Church's practice of allowing someone to remarry in a case of impotence by saying that there was never a marriage in the first place.[18] Gratian does not seem to consider the possibility, however, that the actual practice of allowing remarriage in cases of impotence is wrong. If this were so, then there would be no need to doubt the validity of the marriage involving impotence.

Earlier, I showed how Gratian takes the well-founded tradition that consent makes marriage and corrupts it by very dubiously adding the role of consummation. Consequently, he teaches that a marriage is created by the consent of the spouses but that it is not complete until it has been consummated by sexual intercourse. Whether Gratian regards a marriage involving impotence to be open to dissolution or simply invalid, it can be said that he believes it to be gravely deficient because of the inability to perform intercourse. Thus, impotence is a "natural inability" (*naturali impossibilitate*) to complete a marriage.[19] As seen earlier, although Gratian's *Decretum* was never an official legal text, it influenced many Popes and, eventually, Cardinal Gasparri.

The examination so far of canon 1068 §1 of the 1917 Code raises the question of what actually counts as im-

---

16. Matthew 19:9.

17. Gratian, *Concordia* (bibliog. III), Part 2, Case 32, Question 7, ch. 16, and dictum after ch. 16.

18. Ibid., Case 27, Question 2, dictum after ch. 29.

19. Ibid., Case 33, Question 1, dictum after ch. 3.

potence? In brief, it is the inability to perform the marital act. Traditionally, the Church has regarded the true performance of the marital act to require three things from the husband and two corresponding things from the wife. For the man, he must be able to have an erection, penetrate his wife's vagina, and ejaculate within the vagina. Consequently, the woman must be able to receive the man's penis in her vagina and permit ejaculation in it. If one of these elements is missing, then there is some form of impotence.[20] The notions of erection and penetration by the man and reception by the woman are fairly straightforward. But the concept of ejaculation has proved difficult canonically.

A source used by Gasparri for canon 1068 §1 is a letter from Pope Sixtus V to the Bishop of Navarre, who was the papal representative in Spain.[21] The letter was written in 1587 and is known by its opening words *Cum frequenter*.[22] In this letter, Sixtus V states that eunuchs and spadones cannot marry. The difference between eunuchs and spadones, as understood by Sixtus, is not clear. It could be that both terms refer to men who have been castrated but that eunuchs, unlike spadones, have been done so in order to hold a particular office. In his canon law doctoral thesis, however, Owen Oxenham suggests, "Etymologically, eunuchs are those who are born without testicles; spadones are those who are deprived of them by castration."[23] He goes on to warn, "The terminology in this matter was not, and still is

---

20. Although not necessarily formal "canonical impotence."
21. Gasparri (ed), *Codex Iuris Canonici Pii X* (bibliog. III), 304.
22. Sixtus V (bibliog. I), Letter, *Cum frequenter,* 27 June 1587.
23. Oxenham, *Canon 1068 and the Notion of* "Verum Semen" (bibliog. III), 122.

not, constant."[24] What is certain is that the letter of Sixtus V refers to men who, for whatever reason, are without testicles. Sixtus explains that such men are unable
to emit "true semen" (*verum semen*).[25]

The meaning of *true semen* and its connection with
the bar on marriage have never been absolutely clear.
Oxenham helps clarify matters. He first explains what
it could not mean in *Cum frequenter*. It could not be a
term meant to distinguish semen which originates in
the testicles from semen which does not. This is because "the complex origin of the various constituents
of the seminal fluid was not known in 1587."[26] Neither
could it refer to fertile semen, or semen which contained
spermatozoa, because these were not understood in the
sixteenth century, and it was already established that
sterility does not prohibit marriage.[27]

Oxenham then explains that, by the time of Sixtus V,
four things about men without testicles would have been
observed: they do not produce offspring, their ejaculate
is different to that of others, they experience difficulty
when copulating, and they are not satisfied sexually by
their efforts to copulate.[28] The first two of these observations would have led to the conclusion that men without testicles are sterile—that is, they lack "true semen."
Because sterility was not a bar to marriage, however,

---

24. Ibid.

25. "Cum frequenter in istis regionibus Eunuchi quidam, et Spadones, qui
utroque teste carent, et ideo certum ac manifestum est, eos verum semen emittere
non posse.." Gasparri (ed), *Codex Iuris Canonici Fontes* (bibliog. III), vol. 1,
col. 298.

26. Oxenham, *Canon 1068 and the Notion of* "Verum Semen" (bibliog. III),
122.

27. Ibid., 122–23.

28. Ibid., 123.

these first two observations would not have prevented eunuchs and spadones from marrying. It is the last two observations which would have cast doubts on whether men without testicles can engage in sexual intercourse properly. I agree with Oxenham that Sixtus V comes to the conclusion that eunuchs and spadones are unable to perform the marital act fully. Therefore, his letter's prohibition on them marrying is based on the fact that he regards them to be canonically impotent.[29]

Prior to *Cum frequenter*, some ecclesiastical authorities allowed eunuchs and spadones to marry while others did not. The letter settled the debate by stating that they cannot marry. The letter was based upon two established legal principles: sterility in itself does not prohibit marriage, and impotence does prohibit marriage. The letter did not change either of these principles.

Cum frequenter did cause confusion, however. This is because it refers to "true semen." If Oxenham's interpretation of *Cum frequenter* is correct, then the ability to emit "true semen" is not necessary for marriage. This is because any inability to emit it is a matter of sterility and not impotence, and thus, is not a bar to marriage. But if the letter is taken to mean that the ability to emit "true semen" is necessary for marriage, then a wider group of men would fall under the letter's bar to marriage.[30] This became particularly true in the twentieth century with the development of vasectomy operations. Can men with vasectomies marry? Their ejaculate does not originate in the testicles and so is not

29. Ibid., 123–24.
30. Zalba, *"Decretum circa Impotentiam"* (bibliog. III). Also, Gordon, *"Adnotationes Quaedam De Valore Matrimonii Vivorum"* (bibliog. III).

"true semen." If "true semen" is required, then they cannot marry.

In 1977, the Sacred Congregation for the Doctrine of the Faith issued a decree which asks and then answers two questions.[31] It states,

> The Sacred Congregation for the Doctrine of the Faith has always held that those who have had a vasectomy and other persons in similar conditions are not to be prohibited from marriage because their impotence is not verified with certainty.
>
> Now, having examined this type of practice and after repeated studies by this Sacred Congregation, as well as by the Commission for the Revision of the Code of Canon Law, the Most Eminent and Most Reverend Fathers of this Sacred Congregation, in the plenary session held on Wednesday the 11th May 1977, decided to reply to the following doubts proposed by them:
>
> 1. Whether impotence which invalidates marriage consists of an incapacity, which is antecedent and perpetual, either absolute or relative, to complete conjugal intercourse?
> 2. In so far as the reply is affirmative, whether for conjugal intercourse, the ejaculation of semen elaborated in the testicles is necessarily required?
>
> To the first: *In the Affirmative.* To the second: *In the Negative.*[32]

---

31. Sacred Congregation for the Doctrine of the Faith (bibliog. I), Decree, *Circa Impotentiam quae Matrimonium Dirimit,* 13 May 1977.

32. Sacra Congregatio pro Doctrina Fidei semper retinuit a matrimonio non esse impediendos eos qui vasectomiam passi sunt aliosque in similibus condicionibus versantes eo quod non certo constaret de eorum impotentia. Iam vero, inspecta tali praxi et post iterata studia ab hac Sacra Congregatione necnon a Commissione Codici Iuris Canonici recognoscendo peracta, Em.mi ac Rev.mi Patres huius S. Congregationis, in consessu plenario feriae IV, die 11 maii 1977 habito, propositis Sibi dubiis, quae sequuntur, respondendum decreverunt:

1.Utrum impotentia, quae matrimonium dirimit, consistat in incapacitate, antecedenti quidem et perpetua, sive absoluta sive relativa, perficiendi copulam coniugalem.

Two days after the plenary session, Pope Paul VI approved the decree and ordered that it be published, which it was that day. Although the decree consists of two questions, its introductory paragraph is also important. This paragraph states the principle that no man is to be prevented from marrying if his impotence is not certain. This principle would also apply to women. The decree then goes on to ask and answer the first question. This reaffirms the traditional teaching, as given in canon 1068 §1 of the 1917 Code, that impotence invalidates marriage if it is antecedent and perpetual. Moreover, it is irrelevant whether the impotence is absolute or relative. This first question and answer state that impotence is any incapacity to complete conjugal intercourse. The second question and answer then state that conjugal intercourse can be completed without the ejaculation of semen elaborated in the testicles.

The decree of 1977 thus allows men who have undergone vasectomy operations to marry. The rule behind this decision is that while impotence prevents marriage, sterility does not. If Oxenham's understanding of *Cum frequenter* is correct, then Sixtus V would have agreed fundamentally with the decree of 1977. That is, if eunuchs and spadones are to be barred from marriage, then it is because they suffer impotence, not because they are sterile.

I have indicated that others, however, interpreted *Cum frequenter* to mean that "true semen" is required in order to marry. Thus, certain ecclesiastical

---

2. Quatenus affirmative, utrum ad copulam coniugalem requiratur necessario eiaculatio seminis in testiculis elaborati. Ad primum: Affirmative. Ad ecundum: Negative.

authorities would have prevented men from marrying on the grounds that they could not ejaculate semen that had been elaborated in the testicles. Moreover, following this interpretation of *Cum frequenter*, some tribunals would have declared marriages involving such men to be invalid. These ecclesiastical authorities and tribunals would have had to change their policies in the light of the 1977 declaration.[33] Indeed, when Pope Paul VI gave his annual address to the judges of the Roman Rota in January 1978, he reminded them of the decree and the need to continue to adhere strictly to this and other official teachings of the Church.[34]

Canon 1068 §1 of the 1917 Code and the 1977 declaration are sources for canon 1084 §1 of the 1983 Code. In February 1970, those responsible for the drafting of the new canon decided that it would not be appropriate to give a definition of sexual intercourse. Any fixed definition might not cover unforeseen cases. Their discussions show that they too, like the 1977 decree which followed them, regarded the ability to have sexual intercourse to be necessary for marriage. Also, like the later decree, they did not see sterility as a bar. For example, a woman who cannot conceive because her vagina is closed at the entrance of the womb is regarded as capable of marriage provided her vagina is able to receive a penis. Similarly, a woman without a womb or ovaries can marry as long as she can engage in intercourse.[35]

---

33. Lefebvre, *"La Questione del 'Verum Semen'"* (bibliog. III). Also, McGrath, *A Controversy Concerning Male Impotence* (bibliog. III).

34. Paul VI (bibliog. I), Address to the Roman Rota, 28 January 1978. English translation in Woestman (ed), *Papal Allocutions* (bibliog. III), 144–49.

35. *Pontificium Consilium de Legum Textibus* (bibliog. III), *Communicationes* 6 (1974), 176–98.

The second paragraph of canon 1084 of the 1983 Code is based upon the second paragraph of canon 1068 of the former Code, which it repeats nearly verbatim.[36] It states, "If the impediment of impotence is doubtful, whether the doubt be one of law or one of fact, the marriage is not to be prevented nor, while the doubt persists, is it to be declared null."[37] This paragraph uses the principle found in the opening paragraph of the 1977 decree—namely, that individuals should not be prevented from marrying if there exists a doubt about their impotence. This is based upon an even more fundamental principle that marriage is a natural state and so individuals must not be prevented from marrying except for a well-founded reason. Their right to marry cannot be superseded by a doubtful opinion about their ability to have intercourse. Similarly, such doubtful opinions cannot challenge the validity of marriages. To do so would undermine the stability of marriage and family life. Those drafting the canon wished to emphasize this second point to prevent tribunals declaring marriages invalid on the grounds of impotence when there is insufficient proof.[38]

Paragraph 3 of canon 1084 is concerned with sterility. Sterility is different from impotence in that it does not prevent sexual intercourse from taking place,

---

36. *Pontificia Commissio Codici Iuris Canonici Authentice Interpretando* (bibliog. III), 299.

37. Canon 1084 §2: "Si impedimentum impotentiae dubium sit, sive dubio iuris sive dubio facti, matrimonium non est impediendum nec, stante dubio, nullum declarandum."English translation in Caparros et al. (eds), *Code of Canon Law Annotated* (bibliog. III), 675.

38. *Pontificium Consilium de Legum Textibus* (bibliog. III), *Communicationes* 9 (1977), 361.

although such intercourse will not produce offspring. It has already been noted that, traditionally within the Church, sterility is not regarded as an impediment to marriage. In the 1917 Code, canon 1068 §3 states, "Sterility neither invalidates nor prevents marriage."[39] This is the source for canon 1084 §3.[40] Those drafting this new paragraph decided to add an exceptive clause, however, so that it now reads, "Sterility neither forbids nor invalidates marriage, without prejudice to the provisions of canon 1098."[41] Canon 1098 states, "A person contracts invalidly who enters marriage inveigled by deceit, perpetrated in order to secure consent, concerning some quality of the other party, which of its very nature can seriously disrupt the partnership of conjugal life."[42]

Although canon 1098 is in the fourth chapter of the marriage canons, which deals with consent, it is worth examining it now. This is a new canon which had no counterpart in the 1917 Code.[43] It is based upon the principle that a marriage is brought into existence by the consent of the couple. It also acknowledges that it is possible for someone to be deceived into marrying. An example will clarify matters. A woman has a

---

39. *1917 Code* (bibliog. I), canon 1068 §3: "Sterilitas matrimonium nec dirimit nec impedit."

40. *Pontificia Commissio Codici Iuris Canonici Authentice Interpretando* (bibliog. III), 299.

41. Canon 1084 §3: "Sterilitas matrimonium nec prohibet nec dirimit, firmo praescripto can. 1098." English translation based on Caparros et al. (eds), *Code of Canon Law Annotated* (bibliog. III), 676.

42. Canon 1098: "Qui matrimonium init deceptus dolo, ad obtinendum consensum patrato, circa aliquam alterius partis qualitatem, quae suapte natura consortium vitae coniugalis graviter perturbare potest, invalide contrahit." English translation in Caparros et al. (eds), *Code of Canon Law Annotated* (bibliog. III), 690.

43. *Pontificia Commissio Codici Iuris Canonici Authentice Interpretando* (bibliog. III), 301–02.

casual relationship with a man in which they have sexual intercourse. She tells him that she is pregnant and that he must be the father. From this information the man decides to marry her. Thus, at the wedding ceremony, he gives consent. The woman is not pregnant, however, and only said she was in order to fool him into marrying her. He has given consent purely on the basis that he thought she was pregnant with his child. If he had known that she was not pregnant, he would never have consented to marrying her. Consequently, his consent is gravely deficient. As consent makes marriage, then the marriage is invalid.

The reference to canon 1098 in canon 1084 §3 is an indication to tribunals that, although sterility in itself does not invalidate a marriage, it might be possible for a marriage to be declared invalid when there has been deceit concerning the sterility.[44] For example, a man is aware that he is sterile and meets a woman he knows is very anxious to have children. He tells her that she can have children by him if they marry. Overcome with joy she marries him. The marriage is not invalid because of his sterility, but because her consent is gravely deficient as the result of a lie which she believed.

At this point it is worth noting that canon 1068 §1 of the 1917 Code stated that canonical impotence on the part of the man or the woman invalidates marriage irrespective of whether the other party is aware of it. As it does not matter whether the other party knows, this clause has been omitted from the revised canon 1084

---

44. *Pontificium Consilium de Legum Textibus* (bibliog. III), *Communicationes* 7 (1975), 59, and *Communicationes* 9 (1977), 361–62.

§1. Is it possible for a marriage to be declared invalid in accordance with canon 1098 if one party knows that he or she is impotent and deceives the other into marrying? The answer is in the affirmative, but most tribunals would probably declare the marriage invalid because of the impotence and not the deceit.

Possible Developments of the Law on Impotence

I am disappointed that canon 1084 §1 states that canonical impotence is an impediment to marriage. It repeats the teaching of the 1917 Code, which is based heavily on Gratian. I have shown that Gratian took the well-established tradition that consent makes marriage and introduced the notion that a marriage is not complete until it has been consummated. Thus, those suffering from impotence are unable to complete a marriage and so are not allowed to marry.

Another criticism I have of canon 1084 §1 is that it reduces marriage to just the sexual dimension. As with the canons concerning the dissolution of non-consummated marriages, which I examined earlier, I would say that it ignores the other aspects of marriage. In particular, it fails to acknowledge the teaching of the Second Vatican Council that marriage is a "community of love" which involves the "intimate sharing of marital life and love." It also ignores the Conciliar teaching that marriage is a "whole manner and communion of life."[45]

I have referred to the discussions of those who

---

45. Vatican II (bibliog. I), *Gaudium et spes,* 7 December 1965, arts. 47, 48, and 50.

drafted the canon. Without wishing to take their words out of context, it must be said that their debates do appear to reduce women to mere receptacles for penises. That is, a woman can marry as long as she has a vagina which can receive a penis and allow ejaculation. It is not even relevant whether the vagina leads to the womb or whether she is fertile. This is very far from the Conciliar understanding that marriage involves a deep sharing of every aspect of life.

It also ignores the fact that many people marry for companionship. For these people, the sexual side is not important. It is noteworthy that the "Order of the Celebration of Marriage" allows the minister to omit references to having children in those cases where the spouses are no longer young.[46] I must acknowledge that this is not intended for the marriages of those who are impotent—this would not be allowed by canon 1084 §1. Instead it refers to cases of sterility, in particular those caused by old age. Thus, although such marriages are not open to the possibility of children, they must be open to consummation. Despite being open to consummation, however, this may not happen in practice because the man and woman have married for friendship. For them, the omission of references to children in the wedding ceremony implies there will be no intercourse during the marriage—even if this was not the intention of those who drafted the rite of marriage.

I have said that I am disappointed that the 1983

---

46. Sacred Congregation of Rites (bibliog. I), *Ordo Celebrandi Matrimonium*. English text in The International Commission on English in the Liturgy, *The Rites of the Catholic Church* (bibliog. III), 715–, in particular, 726, 731, 735, 741, 744, 749–50, 753, and 755–58.

Code of Canon Law cites canonical impotence as an impediment to marriage. But in defense of the 1983 Code, it could be argued that canonical impotence is an impediment of natural law and so those editing the Code had no choice but to include it as an impediment. It is thus necessary to consider whether or not it is of natural law.[47] Those who drafted canon 1084 §1 were unanimous that impotence is incompatible with the very nature of marriage, so the impediment must be of natural law. They wanted the final wording to make this clear—which it does.[48] This teaching is in continuity with canon 1068 §1 of the 1917 Code which states that marriage, by the law of nature itself, is invalidated by canonical impotence. Indeed, this has been the position of various experts in canon law and moral theology for a long time.[49]

To say that impotence is an impediment of natural law, however, means that it applies to all marriages at all times. With regard to this, I think that it is impossible to say with certainty that the Church, before Gratian, banned those with impotence from marrying. Consequently, I would say that it is possible that the impediment is only of ecclesiastical law and so can be dispensed by ecclesiastical authorities. Such a development in thinking could be compared with the development arising from the 1977 decree of the Sacred Congregation for the Doctrine of the Faith. Before this

---

47. David, B, *L'Impuissance est-elle un Empêchement de Droit Naturel ou Positif?* (bibliog. III).

48. *Pontificia Commissio Codici Iuris Canonici Recognoscendo, Communicationes* 7 (1975), 41–62, and *Communicationes* 15 (1983), 228–29.

49. For example, Noldin and Schmitt, *Summa Theologiae Moralis* (bibliog. III), 577.

decree, many ecclesiastical authorities interpreted the letter *Cum frequenter* of Sixtus V in such a way that they disallowed men who were unable to produce "true semen" from marrying. But these same authorities had to change their understanding of impotence in the light of the 1977 decree. They had to start allowing such men to marry. It must be acknowledged that many of these authorities had previously said that such marriages were prohibited by natural law itself.

Another reason why the impediment of impotence might be regarded as being only of ecclesiastical law is that the Church's understanding of marriage has widened and deepened to incorporate every aspect of shared marital life. I have already illustrated this last point by referring to the documents of the Second Vatican Council. I would maintain that those who are impotent are able to marry. For example, the physically disabled are created in the image and likeness of God. Not only do they receive God's love, but they are able to share it with others. They are able to form a partnership of love and share their daily lives. They cannot simply be excluded from marriage. They cannot be deprived of the benefits of all the other dimensions of marriage solely because they are unable to engage in the one dimension of sexual intercourse. Moreover, the sexual side of marriage involves more than just the conjugal act. If they are not allowed to marry, then they cannot enjoy other legitimate sexual acts.

Pastorally, priests and others responsible for marriage preparation often try to be as flexible as possible with regard to allowing people with suspected impotence to marry. When asked for pastoral advice, many canon lawyers emphasize the fact that canon 1084 §1 states that the impotence must be perpetual. They then explain that the constant development of new medicines and surgical techniques makes it very difficult to say with certainty that an individual's impotence is perpetual. Therefore, paragraph 2 of the canon—which says that a marriage is not to be prevented if there is a doubt about the existence of canonical impotence—applies, and the individual suffering suspected impotence may marry. Although I agree with this reasoning, I do not think that it goes far enough.

If canonical impotence is an impediment purely of ecclesiastical law, then there are two possible consequences. First, it need not be in the Code of Canon Law at all. That is, the Church could remove it from the list of impediments. The second possibility is that it could remain as an impediment, but that it could be dispensed by the appropriate ecclesiastical authority, such as a diocesan bishop or a vicar general.

At present, however, the official teaching of the Catholic Church is that canonical impotence is an impediment of natural law. That is, no human authority can dispense from it. At this point, I would draw a comparison with the dissolution of non-consummated marriages. It has been seen that although absolute indissolubility applies only to sacramental marriages that have been consummated, every marriage possesses a certain degree of indissolubility by the very nature of marriage. Thus, no human power can dissolve a non-consummated marriage. In spite of this, the Pope is able to dissolve such a marriage using his ministerial power. That is, God works through the Pope and dissolves the marriage. In this age of increased divorce, surely if the Pope can be used as an instrument of God to dissolve marriages, then he can also be used as an instrument to help create them. That is, he can use his ministerial power to dispense from the impediment of impotence in individual cases.

With regard to the dissolution of non-consummated marriages, Woestman states that the Pope cannot just claim he is using ministerial power. On the contrary, he must have a just reason. Woestman observes, "Since the dispensation is an exercise of the Pope's vicarious [that is, ministerial] power, a just cause is necessary for him to act validly. The cause must be proportionate to the gravity of the dissolution of the ratified marriage. In general, all just causes are ultimately the salvation of souls (*salus animarum*)."[50] By analogy, this can be applied to the dispensation from the impediment of impotence.

Thus, dispensation could be given for a just and proportionate reason. For example, it could be said that such a reason exists if the couple suffering from impotence are fully aware of the type of marriage they would be entering. That marriage would still be a community of love in which they share their lives,[51] helping each other attain holiness through prayer,[52] and enabling each other to witness to Christ's love to the rest

---

50. Woestman, *Special Marriage Cases* (bibliog. III), 19.
51. Vatican II (bibliog. I), *Gaudium et spes,* 7 December 1965, arts. 47 and 50.
52. Vatican II, *Lumen gentium,* 21 November 1964, art. 11.

of the world.[53] This loving partnership, for them, would not involve sexual intercourse, but it would still involve other licit intimate acts which express marital love and affection.

To summarize my analysis of canon 1084 and its treatment of impotence, I would say that the development of this canon has been unduly influenced by such authors as Gratian. Once again, too much emphasis has been put on sexual intercourse at the expense of all the other dimensions of marriage. The canon undermines the rich understanding of marriage that the Second Vatican Council has provided. It is debatable whether the impediment is of ecclesiastical law or natural law. If it is the former, then the Church can either stop treating it as an impediment or allow it to be dispensed. On the other hand, if it is of natural law, then it could still be possible for the Pope to use his ministerial power to dispense from it in individual cases. Thus, whether it is of ecclesiastical or natural law, people suffering from impotence, such as the physically handicapped, would no longer be excluded from the married state. That is, they too could enter a marriage that is a community of love in which they profoundly share their lives.

---

53. Vatican II (bibliog. I), *Gaudium et spes,* 7 December 1965, art. 48.

—10—

Requirements for Matrimonial Consent: Mental Faculty, Knowledge, and Genuineness

IT HAS BEEN SEEN that the 1983 Code repeats the traditional teaching that consent brings a marriage into existence (canon 1057 §1). It also describes consent as an act of the will (canon 1057 §2). But this raises a question: How is matrimonial consent arrived at in the mind? The fourth chapter of the marriage canons (1095 to 1107) is called "Matrimonial Consent,"[1] and behind it is a particular view of how matrimonial consent is attained.

An individual (say, a man) considers whether he should marry a particular woman. To help him decide, he has certain knowledge at his disposal. This knowledge consists of information about marriage and what it involves. He also has information about the woman. Finally, he has self-knowledge. He processes this information and, accordingly, decides whether he should marry the woman. This process presumes that the in-

---

1. *"De consensu matrimoniali."* English translation of title in Caparros et al. (eds), *Code of Canon Law Annotated* (bibliog. III), 684.

dividual has three things in order for genuine matrimonial consent to be given: sufficient *knowledge* with
which to make a decision, a sufficient critical *faculty*
with which to process this knowledge, and a *genuine*
desire to marry in the light of the knowledge which
he has processed. This understanding of matrimonial
consent is somewhat mechanical. That is, it regards the
human person to be very similar to a computer. Data is
fed into the machine and an answer is duly given. Despite this mechanical approach, however, it does provide access to the very complex process of giving matrimonial consent.[2]

The three factors that are needed to give consent
enable the main canons of chapter four to be divided
into three parts: canon 1095, which governs the *faculty*
that is needed to decide whether to marry; canons 1096
to 1100, which consider the *knowledge* that is required;
and canons 1101 to 1103, which examine how *genuine*
is the consent that is finally given. The next three chapters of this book (11, 12, and 13) will consider each of
these in turn, although there will inevitably be some
overlap.

---

2. Ladislas Örsy observes that this understanding of how consent is given
is actually based upon traditional scholastic categories (intellect and will). He
suggests that the canons on consent might need to be revised in the light of
modern psychology. Örsy, *Marriage in Canon Law* (bibliog. III).

—11—

The Mental Faculty
Required for Valid Consent

The Present Law Concerning
the Required Mental Faculty

CANON 1095 HAS NO EQUIVALENT IN THE 1917 CODE—a
fact which is corroborated by its official list of sources.[1]
This canon consists of three parts. It states,

> The following are incapable of contracting marriage:
> 1° those who lack sufficient use of reason;
> 2° those who suffer from a grave lack of discretion
>   of judgment concerning the essential
>   matrimonial rights and obligations to be
>   mutually given and accepted;
> 3° those who, because of causes of a psychological
>   nature, are unable to assume the essential
>   obligations of marriage.[2]

---

1. *Pontificia Commissio Codici Iuris Canonici Authentice Interpretando* (bibliog. III), 301.

2. Canon 1095:

Sunt incapaces matrimonii contrahendi:

1° qui sufficienti rationis usu carent;

2° qui laborant gravi defectu discretionis iudicii circa iura et officia matrimonialia essentialia mutuo tradenda et acceptanda;

3° qui ob causas naturae psychicae obligationes matrimonii essentiales assumere non valent.

English translation in Caparros et al. (eds), *Code of Canon Law Annotated* (bibliog. III), 684–87.

The principles behind canon 1095 are that consent makes marriage and that the act of giving consent must be a "human act"— that is, one which sufficiently involves the use of the intellect and the will. These principles have been used continuously within the Church's jurisprudence.[3] The first part of canon 1095 refers to those who are unable to give matrimonial consent because they cannot do so rationally. Such persons do not possess sufficient reason in order to perform a human act, such as validly entering marriage.

The psychological problem which results in the lack of sufficient reason can be either permanent or temporary.[4] A permanent disorder is a severe mental illness where the individual always lacks the use of reason.[5] A temporary disorder is where the individual does have lucid periods. With regard to the latter, if such a case went before a tribunal, it would be for the judges to decide whether the individual had been in a long enough period of rationality to have given genuine matrimonial consent.[6] For example, if the person suffers from serious alcoholism, it would be a matter of determining to what degree he or she was under the influence of alcohol at the time of agreeing to marry and giving consent. Again, an individual might be suffering

---

3. Masala, Rotal decision of 17 December 1985 (bibliog. II). Also, Jarawan, Rotal decision of 19 June 1984 (bibliog. II). Also, Huot, Rotal decision of 29 January 1981 (bibliog. II). Also, Ferraro, Rotal decision of 6 February 1979 (bibliog. II). Also, Bruno, Rotal decision of 20 July 1973 (bibliog. II).

4. Palombi, R, "I Disturbi di Personalità e la Loro Valutazione Canonica" in Bonnet et al. (eds), L'Incapacità di Intendere (bibliog. III), 171–217. Also, Egan, "The Nullity of Marriage" (bibliog. III).

5. Pinto, Rotal decision of 2 May 1977 (bibliog. II).

6. Sabattani, Rotal decision of 24 February 1961 (bibliog. II).

from schizophrenia and on medication to keep it under control. Ecclesiastical judges would need to consider whether the individual had been taking the medication and, if so, whether it had provided him or her with sufficient mental stability.[7]

Canon 1095 2° is used frequently by tribunals to declare marriages invalid.[8] This ground refers to those individuals who are not able to evaluate critically the essential rights and obligations of marriage at the time of marrying. Although they are able to act rationally (and hence do not come under canon 1095 1°), their decision-making process is gravely restricted. For example, an individual may be suffering from a personality disorder so that the person has a problem with an impulsive personality.[9] The degree of the disorder is such that the individual does not just have a slight quirk of personality but a major problem. If it can be proved that this person entered marriage, not because of making an informed decision, but because he or she was driven into it by an irresistible and uncontrollable psychological force, then it can be said that the decision was not a truly human one. Consequently, the consent is invalid and so is the marriage.

A similar example involves psychological immaturity. Nobody can expect a very young child to marry because the child is totally unaware of the complexities of marriage and the associated obligations. Even if the child were to express a desire to marry, he or she

---

7. Stankiewicz, Rotal decision of 5 April 1979 (bibliog. II). Also, Lesage and Morrisey, *Documentation on Marriage Nullity Cases* (bibliog. III), 118–23, 246–52, 288–99.

8. Provost, "Canon 1095 2° Seen From Its Sources" (bibliog. III).

9. Pinto, Rotal decision of 9 December 1983 (bibliog. II).

would not be taken seriously. The child is unable to make an informed decision proportionate to the major step of entering marriage. An adult suffering from psychological immaturity may be found to be no more capable of making a proper decision about marrying than a child. Thus, any marriage he or she attempts would be invalid.[10]

When canon 1095 1° was examined, it was seen that an alcoholic can be so impaired by alcohol that he or she acts irrationally. It is also possible that an alcoholic, although able to perform rational acts, is unable to make a proper evaluation about marrying because the addiction has dulled that person's critical faculty.[11] The same can be said of those suffering from drug addiction.[12]

It is also possible that an individual's critical faculty is restricted by psychological factors that are not medical disorders. For example, a young woman might discover that she is pregnant as a result of premarital sexual intercourse.[13] She fears what her parents will think if she remains an unmarried mother. Thus, she experiences severe pressure to marry. It might be that this pressure is purely subjective, existing only in her mind. But if this internal pressure is such that she finds herself compelled to marry, without being able to evaluate critically whether she should, then the marriage is invalid. Again, her consent has not been given in a human manner.

10. Colagiovanni, Rotal decision of 11 December 1985 (bibliog. II).. Also, Guiry, "Immaturity, Maturity, and Christian Marriage" (bibliog. III). Also, Colagiovanni, *"Immaturità"* (bibliog. III)..
11. Ragni, Rotal decision of 26 November 1985 (bibliog. II).
12. Colagiovanni, Rotal decision of 8 May 1984 (bibliog. II).
13. Ragni, Rotal decision of 11 July 1986 (bibliog. II).

Canon 1095 3° concerns an individual who is suffering from a psychological disorder which means that the person is incapable of married life. At a wedding ceremony the individual might be quite capable of expressing marital consent and the associated vows and promises. The psychological disorder means, however, that this person is actually incapable of living out these promises.[14] Thus, the individual is consenting to something that he or she cannot do. Thus, the consent lacks true meaning; it is invalid, and so is the marriage.

It is necessary to distinguish *assuming* the essential obligations of marriage from *fulfilling* them. Canon 1095 3° clearly states that the incapacity must involve "assuming" (*assumere*) the essential marital obligations. Thus, the psychological incapacity must exist at the time marital consent is given (at the wedding). It is at this point that the spouses assume their obligations. This is very different from fulfilling their obligations. For example, a man enters marriage and is capable of assuming his marital duties. Later, during the course of the marriage, he has an accident and suffers a head injury. Because of consequent brain damage, he is unable to fulfill the promises he made at his wedding— for instance, he starts to act violently toward his wife and children.

The marriage cannot be declared invalid because of the accident. This is because, by the laws of cause and effect, it is not possible for a future event (the accident) to affect an earlier event (the validity of the

---

14. McGrath, "On the Gravity of Causes" (bibliog. III).

marriage on the wedding day). Otherwise, all spouses would live with the uncertainty that unforeseen future events could make their marriages invalid. In conclusion, canon 1095 3° refers only to the capacity to *assume* the essential obligations of marriage—and not to the capacity to *fulfill* them. Consequently, the psychological incapacity which renders the marriage invalid must exist at the time of the wedding. It might be that the problem exists in a latent form at the wedding and only manifests itself later in the course of the marriage. Whether the problem is latent or has already manifested itself, however, it must *exist* at the time of the wedding in order to prevent the essential obligations of marriage from being assumed. Canonists call a problem which exists at such a time *antecedent*.

Comparisons Made between Psychological Incapacity and Impotence

The fact that the psychological cause must be antecedent means that a comparison can be drawn between canon 1095 3° (concerning psychological incapacity) and canon 1084 §1 (concerning impotence). Both these canons require the problem to be antecedent. Some ecclesiastical judges have emphasized the comparison between these two canons. It has already been seen that canon 1084 §1 requires impotence to be perpetual in order for it to prevent and invalidate marriage.[15] Consequently, some Rotal judges, such as Pinto, have said that the psychological incapacity referred to in canon

---

15. Pinto, Rotal decision of 20 February 1987 (bibliog. II), especially 573.

1095 3° must also be perpetual if it is to invalidate marriage. This argument means that not only must the psychological problem exist at the time of consent, but it must also be incurable.[16] Other Rotal judges, such as Pompedda and Bruno, disagree and say that an analogy cannot be made between the conditions for psychological incapacity and those for canonical impotence.[17] They argue that if the psychological incapacity has to be permanent, then canon 1095 3° would say so explicitly, in the same way that canon 1084 §1 does.

I am personally very cautious about using the analogy with canon 1084 §1 for two reasons. The first is that I certainly do not regard canon 1084 §1 to be a model canon with which to compare others. I have already expressed doubts about its development and its contents. My second reason against using canon 1084 §1 as an analogy is that it does not refer to a similar situation at all.

The premise behind canon 1084 §1 is that marriage is initiated by the mutual consent of the couple and is completed by sexual intercourse. I have already expressed my concerns about this view of marriage. Nevertheless, putting my objections to one side, the 1983 Code's understanding of marriage is such that if there can be no intercourse because of impotence, then the marriage cannot be completed. Consequently, when a man and a woman exchange their consent on their wedding day, if it can be ascertained that at no point in the future will they be able to engage in sexual intercourse

16. Doran, Rotal decision of 1 July 1988 (bibliog. II).

17. Pompedda, Rotal decision of 19 October 1990 (bibliog. II), especially 159. Also, Bruno, Rotal decision of 19 July 1991 (bibliog. II), especially 171.

with each other, then the marriage is invalid in accordance with canon 1084 §1. But if there is a possibility that they will be able to perform just *one* act of intercourse, then the marriage cannot be declared invalid. This is because just *one* act of intercourse is sufficient to consummate the marriage. Therefore, the canon on impotence is about the impossibility of *one* act. The same cannot be said about the psychological incapacity referred to in canon 1095 3°, however. This incapacity refers to the living-out of the essential obligations of marriage. That is, it refers to an *ongoing* situation—not a single event.

An example will make this clear. Two men enter marriage on the same day in different ceremonies. The first man suffers from an impotence-related problem; the second man has a grave psychological disorder which manifests itself in violence and cruelty. According to canon 1084 §1, if the first man's impotence is permanent, then his marriage is invalid because he is unable to consummate it. But if there is a chance that at some point in the future he will be able to engage in *one* act of intercourse with his wife, then the marriage cannot be said to be invalid.

Now, if the analogy between psychological incapacity and impotence is used so that the psychological incapacity must be permanent for there to be invalidity, then the following conclusion about the second man's marriage is reached. That is, if his condition is permanent and he can never live out the essential obligations of marriage, then his marriage is invalid. If there is a possibility that his condition is not permanent, however, and that at some future time he will be able to live out the essential obligations of marriage, even for *one* day, then the marriage cannot be declared invalid. This is tantamount to saying that his marriage cannot be declared invalid because one day he might stop beating his wife and treating her cruelly. I would say that this example of *reductio ad absurdum* illustrates that the analogy regarding the perpetuity of impotence cannot be applied directly to the duration of psychological incapacity.

Indeed, the Canadian professor of canon law, Lynda Robitaille, has observed that Rotal jurisprudence is now tending away from the requirement that the psychological incapacity be perpetual. But the question of perpetuity is still of some relevance. Canon 1095 3° refers to the *inability* to assume the essential obligations of marriage. Thus, the psychological problem must make it *impossible* for the individual to assume these obligations—as opposed to just making it *difficult*. Robitaille notes that although the psychological problem does not have to be permanent, its incurability can sometimes indicate that the problem is of such gravity that it does give rise to a genuine inability.[18]

Some ecclesiastical judges have made another comparison between impotence and psychological incapacity. Canon 1084 §1 says that the impotence can be either absolute or relative. I have already explained that absolute impotence means that the sufferer is unable to perform intercourse with any partner; relative impotence means that the sufferer is unable to engage in intercourse with particular persons. Rotal judges such

---

18. Robitaille, "Another Look at Perpetuity" (bibliog. III).

as Pinto and Serrano have argued that psychological incapacities to marriage can also be relative. That is, an individual might be unable to assume the essential obligations of marriage with a particular person but be able to do so with another. Pinto and Serrano have said that a relative incapacity is sufficient to declare a marriage invalid in accordance with canon 1095 3°. [19]

However, other Rotal judges argue that canon 1095 3° only refers to psychological incapacities which are absolute.[20] Burke says that, according to canon 1095 3°, a marriage is invalid only if the individual has a psychological incapacity with respect to the essential obligations of marriage—not with respect to the other party. That is, the incapacity is not relative to the other person; it is absolute. Pompedda agrees with Burke. He says that canon 1084 §1 includes cases of relative impotence because it explicitly says so, but canon 1095 3° makes no such reference to relative incapacity. Pompedda acknowledges that impotence can be used as an analogy, but he says that most judges would now only consider absolute psychological incapacities to invalidate marriage.[21]

Stankiewicz raises two further objections to the notion of relative incapacity.[22] First, relative impotence is an objective fact based on physical evidence. For

19. Pinto, Rotal decision of 12 February 1982 (bibliog. II). Also, Serrano, Rotal decision of 15 November 1977 (bibliog. II).

20. Burke, "Some Reflections on Canon 1095" (bibliog. III), especially 138–42.

Also, Burke, Rotal decision of 27 October 1994 (bibliog. II),.

21. Pompedda, Rotal decision of 19 October 1990 (bibliog. II), especially 160.

22. Stankiewicz, Rotal decision of 25 October 2001 (bibliog. II).

example, a serious discrepancy in the size of the man's sexual organs and the woman's can be verified medically so that the inability to have sexual intercourse can be ascertained with certainty—but relative incapacity is subjective. A husband might claim that he is unable to be married to his wife but that he could be married to somebody else. It is not possible to verify such a claim. The man might not be putting sufficient effort into the marriage. He might not be calling upon God for assistance. His claim is purely subjective.

The second objection of Stankiewicz is that relative incapacity places the inability within the relationship of the couple. That is, to say that a marriage is invalid because of some relative incapacity means that the man is capable of being married to somebody else and that the woman is also able to be married to someone else. Therefore, the inability cannot exist in either of them. Thus, it must exist in their relationship. This is not in accordance with canon 1095 3°, which clearly places the inability within one of the parties. Indeed, only an individual can suffer from a psychological problem—a relationship cannot.

The question of relative incapacity, like that of permanency, is worthy of its own book. Although I cannot enter the full complexities of the debate, I can say that canon 1084 §1 on impotence has its own problems and so its application to canon 1095 3° cannot produce a healthy understanding of that canon.

Despite the differences in interpretation of canon 1095 3° by the various judges at the Rota, they have accepted a number of incapacitating psychological factors

in accordance with this canon.[23] Among these factors
are paranoid schizophrenia,[24] nymphomania,[25] antisocial personality,[26] homosexuality,[27] and post-traumatic
stress disorder.[28] The fact that an individual has one of
these does not, in itself, make a marriage invalid. But
if the psychological factor is such that the conditions of
canon 1095 3° are met, then there is invalidity.

Applying the Present Law Concerning the Mental Faculty to Consummation

It has been noted that some judges have applied canon 1084 §1, concerning impotence, to canon 1095 3°. I
wish to suggest that paragraphs 1 and 2 of canon 1095
can be applied to consummation. I have already stated that I think the well-established view that consent
makes marriage has been undermined by the introduction of the notion that consummation strengthens the
indissolubility of marriage. Earlier, I explained how the
Catholic Church teaches that even a sacramental marriage can be dissolved if it has not been consummated,
but once consummated, the marriage is absolutely indissoluble. Thus, although the exchange of consent is
essential to marriage, consummation plays a vital role
as far as indissolubility is concerned. I have also stated
that I have doubts about the continuation of the practice of dissolving non-consummated marriages, especially in the light of the teachings of the Second Vati-

---

23. Mendonça, "Recent Rotal Jurisprudence" (bibliog. III).
24. Fiore, Rotal decision of 5 March 1985 (bibliog. II).
25. Stankiewicz, Rotal decision of 14 November 1985 (bibliog. II).
26. Stankiewicz, Rotal decision of 19 November 1985 (bibliog. II). Also, Mendonça, "Antisocial Personality" (bibliog. III).
27. Funghini, Rotal decision of 19 December 1994 (bibliog. II).
28. Faltin, Rotal decision of 29 November 1995 (bibliog. II).

can Council. If this practice is to continue, however, I suggest that criteria be applied to consummation the same as they are to consent.

It has been seen that if an individual lacks sufficient reason (canon 1095 1°), then his or her giving of consent cannot be performed in a human way. Similarly, if the individual's capacity to evaluate the essential rights and obligations of marriage is gravely limited, then he or she cannot decide, in a human manner, whether to marry (canon 1095 2°). Ecclesiastical tribunals spend an extremely high proportion of time examining the process of consenting to marriage, especially with regard to whether it has been conducted in a truly human manner. But what about consummation?

Earlier, when canon 1061 §1 was considered, it was noted that if a marriage is to be regarded as consummated, then sexual intercourse must take place in a "human manner" (*humano modo*). Despite this criterion, which comes from article 49 of the Conciliar document *Gaudium et spes*,[29] very little is done to see whether marriages have been consummated in a human fashion.

Canon 1095 1° uses the principle that an act must be performed rationally in order for it to be truly human. If this is applied to sexual intercourse, then there immediately exists a whole area of possible future jurisprudence. It has been seen that canon 1095 1° acknowledges that any psychological problem affecting rational behavior may be either permanent or temporary—provided it exists at the time of the wedding.

---

29. *Sacrosanctum* (bibliog. III), 758.

With regard to intercourse, permanent psychological problems could gravely affect an individual's reason so that he or she does not consummate rationally. It is also highly possible that a spouse could engage in sexual intercourse with a temporary, but grave, impairment to his or her faculty to reason. For example, he or she could be drunk or under the influence of drugs (or a combination of the two).

Another example of a temporary impairment could be described as "the heat of passion." That is, a spouse becomes so sexually excited that he or she engages in intercourse with an uncontrollable desire. The individual feels unable to refrain from intercourse. There might even be a part of him or her that does not want to have intercourse. Indeed, he or she might even be aware that it is not a "good idea," but the individual feels compelled to do so by desire and, perhaps, may even regret performing the act immediately it is completed and the "heat of passion" subsides.

Canon 1095 2° is based on the principle that the decision to enter marriage must be a human one. In order for this to be the case, an individual requires three things: a sufficiently developed mental faculty, sufficient knowledge, and adequate psychological freedom in which to make a genuine decision. These three factors were enunciated by Pinto shortly after the 1983 Code came into force.[30] These criteria can also be applied to an individual's decision to consummate marriage.

With regard to a sufficiently developed mental faculty, canon 1095 2° requires parties to be mature

---

30. Pinto, Rotal decision of 14 December 1984 (bibliog. II).

enough to make a decision about whether to marry. Now, if the act of consummation is to be truly human, then this criterion must also apply to it. Couples must be sufficiently mature to appreciate the true meaning of the act, as well as its canonical implications. The act must not be seen just on the physical level. It has been noted that Pope John Paul II speaks of the "prophetism of the body" and the "language of the body."[31] Thus, the physical union that takes place in intercourse must reflect the ongoing intimate union of the lives of the spouses, as well as Christ's love for his Church. Sexual intercourse between married couples, especially for the first time, is a most profound event from the interpersonal perspective, as well as theologically and legally. Consequently, it calls for sufficient maturity and due consideration.

Once again, this opens up a whole new area of possible future jurisprudence where a couple consummates the marriage with a grave lack of discretion of judgment. It is noteworthy that the Council of Trent saw the need for spiritual preparation for consummation. Toward the end of the first chapter of Trent's *Decree Concerning the Reform of Matrimony* (commonly known as *Tametsi*) it encouraged couples to go to Confession and to attend Mass before marrying. If they were unable to do so, then they were exhorted to receive these sacraments at least three days before consummating their marriage.[32]

With regard to sufficient knowledge, how many bap-

---

31. John Paul II, *The Theology of the Body* (bibliog. III), 364, 398.
32. English translation in Schroeder (tr), *The Canons and Decrees of the Council of Trent* (bibliog. III), 185.

tized spouses, when they engage in sexual intercourse for the first time, have sufficient knowledge to comprehend the significance of what they are doing? That is, how many know that, not only are they consummating their marriage, but that they are making it absolutely indissoluble? The answer is, quite simply, very few. As for an awareness that they are participating in the indissoluble bond that exists between Christ and his Church, hardly any would possess such knowledge.

The following example might help to explain my point. Two practicing Catholics marry. For various reasons, they do not immediately consummate the marriage, perhaps because of ill health or because one of them is called away from home on work. Their relationship becomes unsteady and begins to deteriorate. They decide to do their best to keep the relationship going. Consequently, they have sexual intercourse in the hope that it will heal the differences between them. Unfortunately, it does not and the marriage fails. Now, if they had known that the act of intercourse was going to make their marriage absolutely indissoluble, they might have thought twice about it. That is, if they had been aware of the canonical implications of the act, they might have left the marriage unconsummated and, consequently, open to dissolution.

With regard to psychological freedom, canon 1095 2° requires individuals to have sufficient internal freedom in which to make a genuine decision about entering marriage. Similarly, it could be argued that spouses should have such freedom in which to decide whether to consummate their marriage. Any grave restriction on this freedom (for example, psychological pressure to have intercourse) may result in the act being less than human.[33] Various psychological factors could give rise to this situation so that, although the individual has the use of reason, he or she feels compelled to have intercourse—even if the other party is not responsible for the pressure experienced. For example, a wife suffers from grave psychological immaturity and is still under the control of her parents. Her sisters have all married and provided their mother with grandchildren. The wife in question is made to feel a total failure by her mother for not producing children. Consequently, she feels inescapable pressure to participate in sexual intercourse.

In conclusion, I have suggested that the principles behind the first two paragraphs of canon 1095 be applied to the act of consummation. Canon 1061 §1 says that consummation must be performed in a human manner. Consequently, there must be sufficient rationality and judgment on the part of each spouse. I have thus suggested possible new areas of future jurisprudence—although a married couple might have had sexual intercourse with each other, they might not have done so in a human manner, in which case their marriage is not consummated canonically and so is open to dissolution.

I acknowledge that my suggested areas of jurisprudence could be dismissed as absurd, but they are logical conclusions of the present law which states that,

---

33. Heredia, *"Importancia Canónica de la Primera Cópula Conyugal"* (bibliog. III).

although a marriage is created by the consent of the couple, it is not absolutely indissoluble until it has been consummated. I am merely applying the same scrutiny to consummation as tribunals do every day to the exchange of consent. Thus, any apparent absurdity is because of the emphasis placed on consummation. I therefore argue that if my suggested developments to jurisprudence are not acceptable, then there should be serious consideration as to whether the connection between consummation and indissolubility should be dropped. In this case, indissolubility would be linked solely with the exchange of consent at the very beginning of marriage. This indeed would have been the case if it had not been for the influence of such people as Hincmar of Rheims and, especially, Gratian.

—12—

The Knowledge Required
for Valid Consent

CANONS 1096 TO 1100 refer to the knowledge an individual must have in order to give marital consent. Of these, canons 1097 and 1098 are concerned with the knowledge that is required of the intended spouse, while canons 1096 and 1099 are connected with the nature of marriage.

With regard to the knowledge an individual must have of the person he or she is marrying, canon 1097 §1 quite simply states that if he or she marries the wrong person, then the marriage is invalid.[1] This is because the person is really consenting to marry somebody else.[2] The second paragraph of canon 1097 states, "Error about a quality of the person, even though it be the reason for the contract, does not render a marriage invalid unless this quality is directly and principally intended."[3] An example will help. A woman has sexu-

---

1. Canon 1097 §1: "Error in persona invalidum reddit matrimonium."
2. Navarrete, *"Error in Persona (c. 1097 §1)"* (bibliog. III). Also, Villeggiante, *"L'Error in Persona"* (bibliog. III).
3. English translation in Caparros et al. (eds), *Code of Canon Law Annotated* (bibliog. III), 689. Canon 1097 §2: "Error in qualitate personae, etsi det causam contractui, matrimonium irritum non reddit, nisi haec qualitas directe et principaliter intendatur." Also, Hilbert, *"Error in Qualitate Personae (c. 1097 §2)"* (bibliog. III).

al relationships with more than one man and becomes pregnant. She decides to marry the father of the child, but the man she marries turns out not to be the father. In this case, the man she marries does not have the quality that she directly and principally intends. Her mistake is tantamount to marrying the wrong person. Consequently, the marriage is invalid.

Canon 1097 is based upon canon 1083 of the 1917 Code.[4] This former canon concluded with a particular case of error. It said that a marriage is invalid "if a free person contracts marriage with a person whom he or she believes to be free, but who is on the contrary a slave, in the proper sense of slavery."[5] This part of the canon has not been reproduced in the 1983 Code. Although slavery is rare, it is possible for people to find themselves in other forms of slavery—for example, alcohol addiction. In this instance, canon 1097 §2 could still cover the case where an individual marries another person believing him or her to be free from an addiction to alcohol.[6]

Canon 1098 is similar to canon 1097, but the erroneous opinion held by one party is the result of deceit.[7] This

4. *Pontificia Commissio Codici Iuris Canonici Authentice Interpretando* (bibliog. III), 301. Also, Carmignani Caridi, "The *'Error Personae vel Qualitatis Personae'* in Rotal Jurisprudence" (bibliog. III).

5. *1917 Code* (bibliog. I), canon 1083 §2, 2°: "Si persona libera matrimonium contrahat cum persona quam liberam putat, cum contra sit serva, servitute proprie dicta." It has been seen that Ivo of Chartres also taught that a free person who marries a slave, believing him or her to be free, does so invalidly. *Epistula ccxlii* (bibliog. III); Migne (ed), *Patrologiae Latina* (bibliog. III), vol. 162, cols. 249–50. It has also been seen that, prior to Ivo of Chartres, Pope Leo I taught that any marriage between a free person and a slave is invalid *irrespective* of whether the free person knows of the servile condition of the other. This is because marriage must be between two equals. Leo I (bibliog. I), *Epistula clxvii, circa* 458–59.

6. Palestro, Rotal decision of 24 June 1987 (bibliog. II).

7. Bonnet et al. (eds), *Errore e Dolo* (bibliog. III). Also, Boccafola, "Deceit and Induced Error about a Personal Quality" (bibliog. III), 692–710.

canon was examined in conjunction with canon 1084 §3 on sterility and so no further analysis is needed.[8]

With regard to the knowledge that is required of marriage itself, canon 1096 §1 states, "For matrimonial consent to exist, it is necessary that the contracting parties be at least not ignorant of the fact that marriage is a permanent partnership between a man and a woman, ordered to the procreation of children through some form of sexual cooperation."[9] The second paragraph says that it is presumed that anyone who has reached puberty has such knowledge,[10] but this presumption can be overturned by contrary evidence.

It can be seen that the first paragraph of canon 1096 refers to four items of knowledge. The first is that marriage is a permanent partnership. The second is that it is between a man and a woman. The third is that it is ordered toward the procreation of children. The fourth item concerns sexual activity.

It must be explained that the knowledge required by canon 1096 is so basic that an individual might possess it and still lack sufficient knowledge to marry. This is because other knowledge is called for by canon 1095 2°, which requires an individual to have sufficient knowledge in connection with the "essential matrimonial rights and obligations." Two examples will clari-

---

8. See Chapter 9 of this second part.

9. Canon 1096 §1: "Ut consensus matrimonialis haberi possit, necesse est ut contrahentes saltem non ignorent matrimonium esse consortium permanens inter virum et mulierem ordinatum ad prolem, cooperatione aliqua sexuali, procreandam." English translation in Caparros et al. (eds), *Code of Canon Law Annotated* (bibliog. III), 687–88.

10. Canon 1096 §2: "Haec ignorantia post pubertatem non praesumitur."

fy what I mean. First, a young man attempts to marry but has absolutely no awareness that marriage is a permanent partnership. His upbringing has been such that he regards marriage as just another transient relationship. This ignorance of marriage is so fundamental that, according to canon 1096, his consent is invalid and so is the marriage.

The second example is of a man who knows that marriage is a permanent partnership between a man and a woman, ordered to the procreation of children through some form of sexual cooperation. He thus satisfies canon 1096. Nevertheless, he has a personality disorder which makes him very immature, dependent upon his mother and unable to think for himself. He gravely lacks self-awareness—that is, knowledge of himself. His ignorance of himself means that he cannot make a proper evaluation as to whether he should enter marriage.[11] Thus, although his knowledge satisfies canon 1096, it does not satisfy canon 1095 2°.

It is noteworthy that canon 1096 links the third item of knowledge with the fourth. That is, children are produced through some form of sexual cooperation. What the canon does not do is link the first item of knowledge with the fourth. That is, there is no connection made, even superficially, between permanency and sexual intercourse. It must be acknowledged that canon 1096 is concerned with the minimum amount of knowledge parties must have in order to exchange matrimonial consent. Considering the Church's emphasis on the role of intercourse with regard to indissolubility, however, it

---

11. Serrano, Rotal decision of 12 November 1982 (bibliog. II).

does seem somewhat surprising that neither this canon, nor any other, expects parties to have at least some
knowledge of the effect of intercourse on indissolubility.

Canon 1099 also considers the nature of marriage.
It states, "Provided it does not determine the will, error
concerning the unity or the indissolubility or the sacramental dignity of marriage does not vitiate matrimonial consent."[12] This canon is based primarily on canon 1084 of the 1917 Code,[13] "Simple error concerning
the unity or the indissolubility or the sacramental dignity of marriage, even though it be the reason for the
contract, does not vitiate matrimonial consent."[14] Both
these canons make a distinction between the intellect
and the will. Error concerning the given properties of
marriage pertains to the intellect, but the giving and receiving of matrimonial consent is an act of the will, not
of the intellect. Consequently, if the error contained in
the intellect does not affect the will, then it cannot undermine matrimonial consent. This can be described as
"simple error"—as in canon 1084 of the 1917 Code.

The revised canon clarifies matters. Its opening words
acknowledge that error can affect the will, "Provided it
does not determine the will." If such a case came before
an ecclesiastical tribunal, it would be for the judges to
decide whether the error had affected the will to such a

---

12. Canon 1099: "Error circa matrimonii unitatem vel indissolubilitatem aut
sacramentalem dignitatem, dummodo non determinet voluntatem, non vitiat
consensum matrimonialem." English translation in Caparros et al. (eds), *Code of
Canon Law Annotated* (bibliog. III), 691.

13. *Pontificia Commissio Codici Iuris Canonici Authentice Interpretando*
(bibliog. III), 302.

14. *1917 Code* (bibliog. I), canon 1084: "Simplex error circa matrimonii
unitatem vel indissolubilitatem aut sacramentalem dignitatem, etsi det causam
contractui, non vitiat consensum matrimonialem."

degree that the matrimonial consent was in fact invalid.[15] An example will help explain canon 1099.

A man was brought up in a family where nobody was married. His parents continuously moved from one relationship to another. Consequently, when he married, he had no understanding of the indissolubility of marriage. On the contrary, he thought marriage was just another type of temporary relationship. It can be said that he suffered from error concerning the indissolubility of marriage. Nevertheless, his marriage would only be invalid if the error had influenced his will and had undermined his act of consent. It might be that he went through the wedding ceremony with no intention of establishing a permanent relationship with the woman. This is because he was not even aware of such a concept. In this case the marriage would be invalid. On the other hand, it might be that although he was not aware of the indissolubility of marriage, he still intended to remain with his wife until death because of his love for her. In this case, his error concerning indissolubility did not affect his will and so did not invalidate the marriage.[16]

The qualities of marriage referred to by canon 1099

---

15. Vann, *"Dolus:* Canon 1098 of the Revised Code of Canon Law" (bibliog. III). Also, Sumner, *"Dolus* as a Ground for Nullity of Marriage" (bibliog. III).

16. Ladislas Örsy states that although canon law may make a clear distinction between the intellect and the will, modern psychology does not. He suggests that knowledge contained in the intellect nearly always influences the will. If it does not, comments Örsy, then it might be an indication that the individual is suffering from a serious personality disorder. I have already stated that a human act must involve sufficient use of both the intellect and the will. To ignore the effect of the intellect on the will is to undermine the fact that the decision to marry must be a human act involving both intellect and will. Also, one must be careful not to separate out too much the working of the intellect from that of the will. To do so would be to split the unity of the human mind. Örsy, *Marriage in Canon Law*

are unity, indissolubility, and sacramental dignity. It can be seen that this list has remained unchanged since the 1917 Code. But the Second Vatican Council has emphasized that marriage is a covenant, a partnership of the whole of life and a community of love. What about error concerning love? In the example I have just given, what if the man had been brought up in an environment where women were treated badly? He could easily have entered marriage without any awareness that he was to love his wife. In such a case, it might be that the marriage could be declared invalid under another canon, for example, canon 1095 2°—for he lacked awareness of the essential rights and obligations of marriage. As for canon 1099, at present it does not allow for such a marriage to be declared invalid. I shall return to the question of the exclusion of love in the next section when I consider canon 1101.

Finally, canon 1100 states, "Knowledge of, or opinion about, the nullity of a marriage does not necessarily exclude matrimonial consent."[17] This canon is based upon canon 1085 of the 1917 Code and repeats it virtually verbatim.[18] Canon 1100 can be applied to a wedding ceremony. It might be that one or both parties

---

(bibliog. III), 140–42. In order for an ecclesiastical judge to declare a marriage invalid in accordance with canon 1099, he would need to have moral certainty that the error in the intellect has affected the will. Örsy says that, in practice, the error will always have affected the will. I would suggest that canon 1099 can be harmonized with Örsy's position by saying that although the error has most probably influenced the will and thus the decision to marry, the judge would need to be certain that the will has been *gravely* affected.

17. Canon 1100: "Scientia aut opinio nullitatis matrimonii consensum matrimonialem non necessario excludit." English translation based on Caparros et al. (eds), *Code of Canon Law Annotated* (bibliog. III), 692.

18. *Pontificia Commissio Codici Iuris Canonici Authentice Interpretando* (bibliog. III), 302.

goes through a wedding aware that the marriage is invalid—perhaps because of an impediment or because
they are not following due canonical form. This does
not necessarily mean that their consent is lacking. They
might genuinely intend to give themselves to each other in marriage but a marriage cannot exist because of
the impediment or the lack of form. The fact that their
consent exists means that it might be possible for the
marriage to be made valid at some later date.

—13—

The Required Genuineness of Consent

The Exclusion of Marriage
or an Essential Element or Essential Property

THE AGE-OLD PROBLEM with consent is that it is an internal act of the will and so cannot be seen. Consequently, for legal purposes, the consent must be manifested externally. This is traditionally done at a wedding ceremony. The first paragraph of canon 1101 makes an important presumption: "The internal consent of the mind is presumed to conform to the words or the signs used in the celebration of a marriage."[1] This presumption is basically about truth. That is, it is to be presumed that the bride and groom mean what they say at a wedding when they express their matrimonial consent. Thus, they are presumed to give genuine consent and so create a valid marriage. Without this presumption, the validity of any marriage would always be open to question and so would lack legal stability.

---

1. Canon 1101 §1: "Internus animi consensus praesumitur conformis verbis vel signis in celebrando matrimonio adhibitis." This repeats canon 1086 §1 of the 1917 Code almost verbatim. See also *Pontificia Commissio Codici Iuris Canonici Authentice Interpretando* (bibliog. III), 302. English translation in Caparros et al. (eds), *Code of Canon Law Annotated* (bibliog. III), 692.

It can be seen that canon 1101 §1 refers not only to words used at a wedding but also signs. This would include weddings where one party, or both, cannot speak —perhaps because of an impairment or because of problems in language (although canon 1106 allows the use of a trustworthy interpreter). With regard to signs, the principle remains the same—they are presumed to be truthful and to express genuine consent.[2]

But what if an individual's words or actions at a wedding ceremony do not correspond to his or her internal consent? In this case, it is possible for the presumption of canon 1101 §1 to be overturned. The second paragraph of the canon states, "If, however, either or both of the parties should by a positive act of the will exclude marriage itself or any essential element of marriage or any essential property, such a party contracts invalidly."[3] This paragraph is frequently used by tribunals when they examine the validity of marriages.

Canon 1101 §2 is based on canon 1086 §2 of the 1917 Code.[4] This earlier canon stated, "If, however, either or both of the parties should by a positive act of the will exclude marriage itself or every right to the conjugal act, or some essential property of marriage, such

---

2. Canon 1101 §1 is an application of the general norm given in canon 124 §2, "A juridical act which, as far as its external elements are concerned, is properly performed is presumed to be valid." English translation of canon 124 §2 based on Caparros et al. (eds), *Code of Canon Law Annotated* (bibliog. III), 141. Canon 124 §2: "Actus iuridicus quoad sua elementa externa rite positus praesumitur validus."

3. Canon 1101 §2: "At si alterutra vel utraque pars positivo voluntatis actu excludat matrimonium ipsum vel matrimonii essentiale aliquod elementum, vel essentialem aliquam proprietatem, invalide contrahit." English translation based on Caparros et al. (eds), *Code of Canon Law Annotated* (bibliog. III), 693.

4. *Pontificia Commissio Codici Iuris Canonici Authentice Interpretando* (bibliog. III), 302.

a party contracts invalidly."[5] Traditionally, this canon of the 1917 Code was known as the "simulation" canon.[6] It refers to a wedding ceremony where either or both parties express matrimonial consent externally, but this expression is not genuine—it merely simulates true consent. The canon gives two types of simulation, *total* and *partial*. Total simulation is when the simulating party (or parties) goes through a wedding ceremony without intending to marry. As the canon states, marriage itself is excluded by a positive act of the will. Therefore, at the wedding, two things occur simultaneously. The first is that the party concerned does not intend to marry. The second is that this party falsely manifests a desire to marry.[7]

Rotal jurisprudence provides many examples of total simulation.[8] For example, an unmarried mother wishes her son to be regarded as legitimate. Consequently, she goes through a wedding ceremony, but she does not actually want to be married. For her, the ceremony is not about entering marriage but about making her son appear legitimate.[9] In another case, a woman celebrates a wedding with a man from another country. She has no intention of marrying him, however. She simply uses the ceremony to obtain citizenship of his country.[10] An-

---

5. *1917 Code* (bibliog. I), canon 1086 §2: "At si alterutra vel utraque pars positivo voluntatis actu excludat matrimonium ipsum, aut omne ius ad coniugalem actum, vel essentialem aliquam matrimonii proprietatem, invalide contrahit."

6. Bouscaren and Ellis, *Canon Law: A Text and Commentary* (bibliog. III), 561–63.

7. Moneta, P, "*La Simulazione Totale*," in Bonnet et al. (eds), *La Simulazione del Consenso Matrimoniale Canonico* (bibliog. III), 45–56.

8. Mendonça, (ed), *Rotal Anthology* (bibliog. III).

9. Bruno, Rotal decision of 8 July 1975 (bibliog. II).

10. Bruno, Rotal decision of 21 March 1980 (bibliog. II).

other example is of an individual who uses the ceremony as an excuse to move out of the home of her uncle and aunt, of whom she is frightened.[11]

The concept of total simulation is also found in canon 1101 §2 of the 1983 Code, which speaks of the exclusion of marriage itself. Consequently, Rotal judges still use this ground to declare marriages null.[12] For example, there is the case of a woman who was engaged but, as the wedding approached, realized that she did not want to marry her fiancé. She felt unable to withdraw from the wedding because everything had been arranged and a lot of money spent. Consequently, she went through the wedding ceremony but without any intention of marrying. Thus, although she followed the prescribed words of the ceremony, she did not mean them.[13]

The second type of simulation referred to by canon 1086 §2 of the 1917 Code is called partial simulation. This is not the exclusion of marriage itself but the exclusion of every right to the conjugal act (*omne ius ad coniugalem actum*) or some essential property of marriage (*essentialem aliquam matrimonii proprietatem*). The exclusion of the right to sexual intercourse naturally means that procreation is also excluded. The exclusion of some essential property of marriage, according to canon 1013 §2 of the former Code, involves the exclusion of unity or indissolubility.[14] Therefore, in the

11. Fiore, Rotal decision of 17 June 1981 (bibliog. II).
12. Johnson, "Total Simulation in Recent Rotal Jurisprudence" (bibliog. III).
13. Serrano, Rotal decision of 20 January 1994, (bibliog. II).
14 *1917 Code* (bibliog. I), canon 1013 §2: "Essentiales matrimonii proprietates sunt unitas et indissolubilitas, quae in matrimonio christiano peculiarem obtinent firmitatem ratione sacramenti."

1917 Code, partial simulation means that one party, or both, follows the prescribed words and actions at a wedding but does not consent to every essential dimension of marriage. That is, he or she excludes one or more of the following: the conjugal act and children; the unity of marriage which entails fidelity to one's spouse; indissolubility, which acknowledges the on-going sanctity of marriage.[15] It has been seen that these three dimensions coincide with what has become known as the "three goods" of marriage from Saint Augustine. In his *On the Good of Marriage* (*De Bono Coniugali*), Augustine says that each of these three aspects of marriage is good in itself—consequently, marriage as a whole is good.[16]

Therefore, jurisprudence has treated partial simulation, according to the 1917 Code, as the exclusion of one or more of Saint Augustine's three goods of marriage. Such an exclusion means that true matrimonial consent is not given, and the marriage is invalid as a consequence. For example, a marriage which went before the Rota was declared null because one party went through the wedding ceremony without any intention of having children—that is, the good of children was excluded. The individual concerned was aware that her husband and other members of his family suffered from diabetes. Consequently, she did not want any children in case they too were afflicted with this complaint.[17]

---

15. Picard, *"Exclusion de la Procréation"* (bibliog. III). Also, Doyle, "A New Look at the *Bonum Fidei*" (bibliog. III). Also, Fellhauer, "The Exclusion of Indissolubility" (bibliog. III).

16. Augustine, *De Bono Coniugali* (bibliog. III), 24.32; Migne (ed), *Patrologiae Latina* (bibliog. III), vol. 40, cols. 394–95.

17. Parisella, Rotal decision of 25 March 1971 (bibliog. II).

In another case, a man participated in a wedding while in a sexual relationship with another woman. Thus, although he promised to remain faithful, he actually had a contrary intention. Indeed, he maintained his relationship with the other woman even after the wedding. The marriage was declared null because he had excluded the good of fidelity.[18] Finally, it can be noted that marriages have also been declared null because the good of indissolubility has been excluded—that is, either or both parties have celebrated a wedding without intending the marriage to be permanent. Very often, such an exclusion of indissolubility is caused by a divorce mentality. That is, an individual regards divorce to be so commonplace that he or she has entered marriage with an intention to divorce should the relationship prove difficult.[19]

The 1983 Code uses a different wording for partial simulation. Canon 1101 §2 speaks of the exclusion of any essential element of marriage (*matrimonii essentiale aliquod elementum*) or any essential property (*essentialem aliquam proprietatem*). With regard to the essential *elements* of marriage, it has been seen that canon 1055 §1 says that marriage is, by its very own nature, ordered to the procreation and education of children. As for the essential *properties* of marriage, it has been noted that canon 1056 says that these are unity and indissolubility (hence, repeating the teaching of the 1917 Code). Consequently, it can be said that partial simulation, according to the 1983 Code, still involves

18. Bejam, Rotal decision of 19 October 1974 (bibliog. II).
19. Egan, Rotal decision of 13 November 1978 (bibliog. II)..

the exclusion of one or more of the three goods of marriage enumerated by Augustine.[20] Therefore, marriages are still declared null on the grounds that one or both spouses have excluded the good of children,[21] the good of unity (or fidelity)[22] and the good of indissolubility.[23]

An increasing number of ecclesiastical judges regard partial simulation to relate to a fourth aspect of marriage. Canon 1101 §2 refers to the exclusion of the essential elements or properties of marriage. It has just been noted that canon 1055 §1 is used to provide the teaching that the procreation and education of children is an essential element of marriage, while canon 1056 lists the essential properties as unity and indissolubility. Canon 1055 §1 not only says that marriage, by its very nature, is ordered to the procreation and education of children, but that it is also ordered to the good of the spouses (*bonum coniugum*). I have already considered this canon and have made the comment that I think this is the closest the 1983 Code comes to referring to marital love.

Traditional jurisprudence shows that if the good of children is excluded, then the marriage is null. Canon 1055 §1 seems to suggest that the exclusion of the good of the spouses also gives rise to nullity. Indeed, the commission responsible for the drafting of the 1983 Code stated that the *bonum coniugum* is an essential

20. Woestman (ed), Simulation of Marriage (bibliog. III), 277–359.

21. For example, De Lanversin, Rotal decision of 5 April 1995 (bibliog. II). Also, Candelier, *"Le 'Bonum Prolis': Doctrine et Évolution de la Jurisprudence"* (bibliog. III).

22. For example, Faltin, Rotal decision of 31 May 1995 (bibliog. II). Also, Franceschi, *"L'Oggetto dell'Esclusione"* (bibliog. III).

23. For example, Bottone, Rotal decision of 8 June 2000 (bibliog. II). Also, Stankiewicz, *"La Simulazione del Consenso"* (bibliog. III).

element of marriage.[24] If it is an essential element, then canon 1101 §2 does say that the exclusion of *any* essential element (*matrimonii essentiale aliquod elementum*) results in invalidity.

Although more and more judges regard the exclusion of the good of the spouses as a cause for nullity, they give different canonical reasons why this should be so.[25] In his cases, the Rotal judge Cormac Burke argues that the *bonum coniugum* is not a fourth good of marriage. He prefers to keep to the traditional triple *bona* attributed to Saint Augustine. Burke acknowledges that the exclusion of the *bonum coniugum* does result in invalidity, but he claims that the *bonum coniugum* involves nothing that is not already covered by the other three goods. Thus, for Burke, the exclusion of the good of the spouses really means the exclusion of one or more of the traditional goods of children, unity, or indissolubility. Consequently, he does not believe that canon 1101 §2 allows tribunals to declare marriages null under the separate heading of the exclusion of the good of the spouses. Although this good might have been excluded, tribunals must consider cases under the exclusion of one or more of the three traditional goods.[26]

Other Rotal judges go further than Burke concern-

24. *Pontificium Consilium de Legum Textibus* (bibliog. III), *Communicationes* 15 (1983), 221.

25. DeLuca, L, *"L'Esclusione del 'Bonum Coniugum'"* in Bonnet et al. (eds), *La Simulazione del Consenso Matrimoniale Canonico* (bibliog. III), 125–37. Also, Pereira, "The Debate Relating to the *Bonum Coniugum*" (bibliog. III). Also, Pfnausch, "The Good of the Spouses" (bibliog. III). Also, Dewhirst, "*Consortium Vitae, Bonum Coniugum* and their Relation to Simulation: A Continuing Challenge to Modern Jurisprudence" (bibliog. III).

26. Burke, "The *Bonum Coniugum* and the *Bonum Prolis*—Ends or Properties of Marriage" (bibliog. III). Also, Burke, "Progressive Jurisprudential Thinking" (bibliog. III). Also, Burke, "Simulated Consent" (bibliog. III).

ing the exclusion of the *bonum coniugum*. For example, Di Felice agrees with Burke that to go through a wedding ceremony excluding the good of the spouses does result in invalidity. Unlike Burke, though, he suggests that such an exclusion is a distinct ground for tribunals to use. Thus, Di Felice believes that there are four possible grounds for partial simulation—the three traditional ones plus the exclusion of the good of spouses.[27] Although he does not give a description of the *bonum coniugum*, by the rules of logic, it can be said that it must contain aspects of marriage that are not contained in the other three goods—otherwise it would not be a distinct ground.

I welcome the introduction of the concept of the good of the spouses (*bonum coniugum*) into the Church's law. This addresses the problem raised by the Italian jurist Arturo Jemolo in 1941, which I referred to earlier. He gave a hypothetical case in which a man marries a woman intending to have children, to be faithful, and not to divorce. He thus intends all three of the traditional goods of marriage, but he also intends not to love his wife—he intends to be cruel to her. It has been seen that, according to the simulation canon of the 1917 Code, this exclusion of love did not give rise to an invalid marriage. The 1983 Code is different. Canon 1101 §2, in conjunction with canon 1055 §1, allows tribunals to declare Jemolo's hypothetical marriage null because the man excluded the good of the spouses at the time of the wedding.

Although it is possible to interpret the 1983 Code in

---

27. Di Felice, Rotal decision of 19 June 1984 (bibliog. II), especially 350.

such a way that the marriage described by Jemolo can be declared null through partial simulation, I personally would go one step further. Earlier, I examined Augustine's work *On the Good of Marriage* (*De Bono Coniugali*). In it, Augustine wishes to show that marriage is good. He does refer to the so-called triple *bona*. He explains that each is good in itself and so marriage as a whole is good, but his examination of the three goods is far from central to his work. Before he gives his relatively brief consideration of the three goods, he writes much more on the fact that marriage is good because of the love and friendship that exists between the husband and wife. Indeed, for Augustine, this is the principal reason why marriage is good.[28]

The traditional three goods of marriage, which are often used in Augustine's name, are only peripheral to his consideration of marriage. With this in mind, I would say that to exclude love, to exclude the intention of protecting and fostering the good of one's spouse, is to exclude something so fundamental to marriage that it is much more than the exclusion of just an essential element or property of marriage. If one wants to use Augustine's framework and wishes to be faithful to it, then I say that the exclusion of the good of the spouses is the very exclusion of marriage itself. Thus, unlike Burke or Di Felice, I do *not* think such an exclusion should be treated as partial simulation. On the contrary, I regard it as total simulation.

I believe that my understanding of the matter is the most faithful to Augustine. Furthermore, it makes the

28. Augustine, *De Bono Coniugali* (bibliog. III), 1.1 and 3.3; Migne (ed), *Patrologiae Latina* (bibliog. III), vol. 40, cols. 373–75.

most sense with regard to the Jemolo case. The reason why this hypothetical case is so shocking is indeed because the man is intending to exclude something that will undermine the marriage so greatly that the inclusion of the three traditional goods becomes irrelevant. That is, openness to children, fidelity, and the intention of maintaining the permanence of marriage all become meaningless in the absence of love and the desire to protect and foster the good of one's spouse.

To support my view, I also appeal to the teaching of the Second Vatican Council. The *Pastoral Constitution on the Church in the Modern World* (*Gaudium et spes*), which cites Augustine's *De Bono Coniugali* in a footnote,[29] describes marriage as a "community of love" (*communitas amoris*) in article 47.[30] Article 48 then explains that the love between spouses is a share in Christ's love for his Church. Moreover, it speaks of the "intimate sharing of marital life and love" (*intima communitas vitae et amoris coniugalis*).[31] These two articles put marital love at the very center of the relationship between the spouses. This is indeed in keeping with Augustine's understanding of the fundamental nature of marital love.[32]

Article 49 develops the document's teaching on love. It says that sexual intercourse allows this love to be expressed physically. As intercourse must be open

---

29. Vatican II (bibliog. I), *Gaudium et spes*, 7 December 1965, art. 48 refers to Augustine's *De Bono Coniugali* (bibliog. III), in the context that God is the author and designer of marriage. *Sacrosanctum* (bibliog. III), 754.

30. *Sacrosanctum* (bibliog. III), 753.

31. Ibid., 754.

32. Connery, "The Role of Love in Christian Marriage" (bibliog. III). Also, LaDue, "Conjugal Love" (bibliog. III). Also, Montagna, "*Bonum Coniugum: Profili Storici*" (bibliog. III).

to children, then it can be said that marital love is ordered toward children. The article also states that this
love must embrace the whole person—body and mind.
Furthermore, it must embrace the person at all times—
both good and bad. Thus, it is always present in an exclusive way. Consequently, marital love excludes both
divorce and adultery.[33] I wish to highlight the fact that
article 49 of *Gaudium et spes* is actually teaching that
marital love is more fundamental than the so-called
three goods of Augustine. Indeed, each of these three
goods depends upon marital love. That is, this love
gives rise to sexual intercourse and so promotes the
good of children. Also, it is exclusive and so upholds
the good of unity and fidelity. Finally, it is perpetual
and so preserves the good of indissolubility.

The fundamental nature of marital love is also taught
by article 50. It states that this love is so central to marriage that even if a couple is unable to have children,
their marriage retains its character, value, and indissolubility.[34] Once again, the Council is in accordance
with Saint Augustine who says that a loving friendship
is so central to marriage that it is not dependent upon
the couple having children. He goes on to say that this
bond of love remains even when they grow beyond the
age for having children.[35]

In summary, the 1983 Code does speak of the good
of the spouses—to which marital love belongs. But I
think that the good of the spouses is more than just an

---

33. *Sacrosanctum* (bibliog. III), 757–59.
34. Ibid., 759–61.
35. Augustine, *De Bono Coniugali* (bibliog. III), 3.3; Migne (ed), *Patrologiae Latina* (bibliog. III), vol. 40, col. 375.

element of marriage—albeit an essential one. This is because both Saint Augustine and the Second Vatican Council regard marital love to be fundamental to marriage, even more so than the three traditional goods of children, unity, and indissolubility. Indeed, these three goods depend upon marital love for their continuation. I would say that when love itself is excluded, when there is no desire to uphold and promote the good of one's spouse, then the very meaning of marriage is excluded so that nothing remains. It is for this reason that I argue that such an exclusion is actually total simulation.

I acknowledge that love is not a canonical concept. Indeed, it does not appear in the 1983 Code. Marital love cannot be seen or measured, but the same can be said of the actions of the mind by which marital consent is given. Despite this, matrimonial consent is referred to many times in the 1983 Code. Also, ecclesiastical tribunals are able to use external evidence to judge whether true consent has been given. Therefore, the same tribunals can use visible evidence to ascertain whether love has been excluded. Although the 1983 Code does not speak of marital love, it does refer to the good of the spouses. Hopefully, jurisprudence will continue to develop so that ecclesiastical judges will increasingly regard love to be at the very center of what is meant by the good of the spouses. By the time the Code is revised in the future, it would be most fitting if love's essential role within marriage had been established by jurisprudence. Then love would have become a canonical term and could be included in a future Code.

Marriage Celebrated Subject to a Condition

Canon 1102 is concerned with conditional consent (sometimes called conditioned consent). Unfortunately, this canon is based primarily upon canon 1092 of the 1917 Code rather than upon the documents of the Second Vatican Council.[36] When canon 1092 of the former Code was examined, it was seen that it allowed spouses to attach conditions to their matrimonial consent. The 1917 Code allowed conditions concerning the past, the present, and the future to be added. Of these three temporal possibilities, conditions concerning the future proved to be the most complicated.

The following example of a condition concerning the future has already been seen: "I marry you here and now on the condition that my parents agree tomorrow."[37] In such a case, the validity of the marriage is suspended until the condition is fulfilled. Thus, if the parents give their approval, then the marriage is valid; otherwise it is invalid.[38] I have already commented that the period between the couple consenting to marry with the attached condition and the condition being fulfilled (and thus the marriage becoming valid) is one of matrimonial limbo. It is thus not surprising that the 1983 Code no longer allows conditions concerning the future. Canon 1102 §1 of the revised Code simply states, "Marriage cannot be validly contracted subject to a condition concerning the future."[39]

---

36. *Pontificia Commissio Codici Iuris Canonici Authentice Interpretando* (bibliog. III), 302.

37. Bouscaren and Ellis, *Canon Law: A Text and Commentary* (bibliog. III), 569.

38. Ibid., 569–70.

39. Canon 1102 §1: "Matrimonium sub condicione de futuro valide contrahi

Paragraph 2 of canon 1102 does allow conditions to be attached to matrimonial consent if they are about the past or the present: "Marriage entered into subject to a condition concerning the past or the present is valid or not, depending upon whether the basis of the condition exists or not."[40] This effectively repeats the fourth and final part of canon 1092 of the 1917 Code.[41] Consequently, a marriage involving a condition about the past or the present is valid depending on whether or not the condition is met.[42] For example, "I marry you if you have not been to prison" (past), or "I marry you if you are a virgin" (present). Thus, in the first example, if the individual has not been to prison then the marriage is valid; if he or she has, then it is invalid. Similarly, in the second example, if the intended partner is a virgin, then the marriage is valid; if not, then it is invalid.[43]

One particular type of condition that is important is the so-called *conditio potestativa*. This is best described as a condition concerning a promise about the future.[44] An example will help to explain. A woman suffers from severe asthma and her boyfriend is a heavy

---

nequit." English translation in Caparros et al. (eds), *Code of Canon Law Annotated* (bibliog. III), 694. Also, *Pontificium Consilium de Legum Textibus* (bibliog. III), *Communicationes* 15 (1983), 234.

40. Canon 1102 §2: "Matrimonium sub condicione de praeterito vel de praesenti initum est validum vel non, prout id quod condicioni subest, exsistit vel non." English translation based on Caparros et al. (eds), *Code of Canon Law Annotated* (bibliog. III), 695.

41. *1917 Code* (bibliog. I), canon 1092 4°: "Si de praeterito vel de praesenti, matrimonium erit validum vel non, prout id quod conditioni subest, exsistit vel non."

42. Robitaille, "Conditioned Consent" (bibliog. III).

43. Bouscaren and Ellis, *Canon Law: A Text and Commentary* (bibliog. III), 570.

44. Caparros et al. (eds), *Code of Canon Law Annotated* (bibliog. III), 695. Also, Parisella, Rotal decision of 10 January 1980 (bibliog. II). Also, Pompedda, Rotal decision of 26 May 1981 (bibliog. II).

smoker. For medical reasons, she does not wish to be married to somebody who smokes and so she agrees to marry him on the condition that he will not smoke ever again. This is clearly a condition concerning the future and so, according to canon 1102 §1, the marriage is regarded as invalid.

What if, however, she agrees to marry him on the condition that he *promises* not to smoke again? In this case, the condition is concerned with the present and so falls under canon 1102 §2. That is, the condition is not connected with whether he will smoke again but with whether he *promises now* not to smoke. Thus, if he makes a genuine promise, then the marriage is valid; if he does not, then the marriage is invalid. It is irrelevant whether he actually manages to keep his promise. That is, the validity of the marriage does not depend upon whether he smokes again in the future.

Canon 1102 concludes with paragraph 3, which simply states that a condition concerning the past or present may only be attached with the written permission of the appropriate local ecclesiastical authority. Such permission, however, is only required for *lawfulness*.[45] Thus, in the example just given, the woman with the asthma should obtain written permission in order to add the condition that her boyfriend promises not to smoke again, but even without this permission the condition is recognized by the Church—even though it is technically unlawful. Indeed, many of the parties whose cases go before tribunals because of conditional consent have not obtained such written permission.

---

45. Canon 1102 §3: "Condicio autem, de qua in §2, licite apponi nequit, nisi cum licentia Ordinarii loci scripto data."

I certainly welcome the fact that canon 1102 now excludes conditions concerning the future from being added to matrimonial consent, but I think that the canon should go further. The example of the woman with asthma and whether the condition about her boyfriend's smoking is of the future or the present would be perfectly acceptable if marriage were merely a contract. The whole legal basis behind this canon, as well as its counterpart in the 1917 Code, is that parties are free to add conditions to a contract. Marriage is much more than a contract, however. It has been seen that article 48 of *Gaudium et spes* speaks of marriage as a covenant (*foedus*).[46] Moreover, the covenant that exists between spouses reflects and participates in the covenant that God has made with his people. The very nature of God's covenant is that it is unconditional.[47] Throughout the Old Testament, there are many instances when his people desert him, yet he maintains his covenant with them. Therefore, conditions attached to matrimonial consent undermine the unconditional love that marriage is supposed to involve.

Marriage involves the "intimate sharing of marital life and love."[48] This sharing touches every aspect of daily life. Thus, article 50 of *Gaudium et spes* calls marriage "a whole manner and communion of life." Earlier, it was seen that canon 1055 §1 reflects this article and describes marriage as "an intimate union of the whole of life."[49] I have already explained that this

46. *Sacrosanctum* (bibliog. III), 754.
47. Kirchschläger, "Marriage as Covenant: A Biblical Approach to a Familiar Notion" (bibliog. III).
48. "Intima communitas vitae et amoris coniugalis." Vatican II (bibliog. I), *Gaudium et spes*, 7 December 1965, art. 48, in *Sacrosanctum* (bibliog. III), 754.
49. ". . . totius vitae consuetudo et communio." Ibid., 761.

means that the marital union is not limited either in depth or in scope. That is, the union involves a total self-giving that is created by the mutual consent of the couple. Consequently, their consent must also be total. If spouses add conditions to their consent, then the consent is not total. A condition added to consent is equivalent to saying, "I give myself to you totally in marriage and I accept you totally, however there is the following exception . . . ." This is also contrary to the description of marital love given in article 9 of *Humanae vitae*. This article describes it as "fully human" and "total." It thus involves the whole person in an unconditional and unlimited manner.[50]

Consequently, I would say that conditional consent can no longer be tolerated. It treats marriage as a mere contract, not as an unconditional covenant. Furthermore, it cannot express the total self-giving that marriage involves. For this reason, I welcome canon 826 of the 1990 Eastern Code. It simply states, "Marriage based on a condition cannot be validly celebrated."[51] This canon succinctly promotes the Conciliar understanding of marriage. Hopefully, the Latin tradition of the Catholic Church will soon do the same.

Marriage Entered Because of Force or Grave Fear

If matrimonial consent is to be genuine, then the parties must give it freely. That is, they must not be made to give consent because of force or grave fear, other-

---

50. *Acta Apostolicae Sedis* (bibliog. III) 60 (1968), 486. Also, Mackin, "Conjugal Love and the Magisterium" (bibliog. III), in particular, 290–96.

51. 1990 Eastern Code, canon 826: "Matrimonium sub condicione valide celebrari non potest."

wise they are not truly consenting to marriage in a human manner. Canon 1103 encapsulates this teaching: "A marriage is invalid which was entered into by reason of force or of grave fear imposed from without, even if not purposely, from which the person has no escape other than by choosing marriage."[52] This canon applies the principle given in canon 1057 §1, seen earlier—no human power can supply the consent for the parties.

Canon 1103 is based on canon 1087 of the 1917 Code.[53] The major difference between the two canons is that the revised canon has the phrase "even if not purposely" added. This allows the canon to cover those instances where an individual feels compelled to marry even if those responsible are unaware. For example, the person could live in a household where there is domestic violence between his or her parents. The parents do not realize that their actions are gravely harming the individual. He or she might feel that the only way out of the frightening situation is to marry. Although the parents are responsible for the individual's decision to marry, they have not brought about the marriage purposely.

---

52. Canon 1103: "Invalidum est matrimonium initum ob vim vel metum gravem ab extrinseco, etiam haud consulto incussum, a quo ut quis se liberet, eligere cogatur matrimonium." English translation based on Caparros et al. (eds), *Code of Canon Law Annotated* (bibliog. III), 695.

53. *1917 Code* (bibliog. I), canon 1087 §1: "Invalidum quoque est matrimonium initum ob vim vel metum gravem ab extrinseco et iniuste incussum, a quo ut quis se liberet, eligere cogatur matrimonium."

§2: "Nullus alius metus, etiamsi det causam contractui matrimonii nullitatem secumfert." Also, *Pontificia Commissio Codici Iuris Canonici Authentice Interpretando* (bibliog. III), 302. Also, Pellegrino, *"La 'Vis et Metus'"* (bibliog. III).

Indeed, it is possible to imagine instances where those responsible for the marriage are actually opposed to it. For example, a young woman might be suffering from sexual abuse by her stepfather. She sees marriage as the only way to escape. Although he might be against the marriage (because it deprives him of his victim), he is responsible for the woman's decision to marry. This decision is not made freely, so her matrimonial consent is not genuine.

—14—

The Prescribed Ceremony
by Which Consent is Given

The Form of Marriage

IT HAS BEEN SEEN HOW a man and a woman attain matrimonial consent mentally. That is, they use their critical faculties to analyze knowledge about marriage and about themselves. Provided they do not have ulterior motives or are acting under pressure, they each arrive at a genuine decision to marry. Nevertheless, this consent to marry is within the mind and so cannot be seen, heard, or verified. It thus has to be expressed externally. The fifth chapter of the marriage canons (1108 to 1123) is titled, "The Form of the Celebration of Marriage" and prescribes how matrimonial consent is to be exchanged.[1]

It has already been seen that the Council of Trent wished to prevent abuses and so called for marriages to be celebrated publicly. It did this through its decree *Tametsi*. Later, the Sacred Congregation of the Council issued the decree *Ne temere* which simplified the rules

---

1. *"De forma celebrationis matrimonii."* English translation of title in Caparros et al. (eds), *Code of Canon Law Annotated* (bibliog. III), 701.

laid down by Trent and made them more effective. The norms of *Ne temere* were incorporated into the 1917 Code. For the purposes of this book, it is sufficient to say that the 1983 Code basically repeats the previous Code's canons on the form of marriage.[2] But there are four major differences which I wish to highlight. I shall consider the first three in this section because they are based upon canons from the fifth chapter of the marriage canons. The fourth difference will be considered in the next section when mixed marriages are examined.

The first difference concerns the fact that the Second Vatican Council, in article 29 of *Lumen gentium*, said that the permanent diaconate should be restored in the Latin Church.[3] This article also explains the various functions of deacons—among which is the celebration of marriages. Consequently, the canons of the 1917 Code had to be altered to include references to deacons. Thus, canons 1108 §1, 1111 §1, and 1116 §2 of the 1983 Code now list deacons among those who can celebrate marriages. Indeed, these canons have among their sources article 29 of *Lumen gentium*.[4]

The second major difference is that canon 1112 §1 of the 1983 Code allows a diocesan bishop to delegate lay people to celebrate marriages if he has no priests or deacons—provided his conference of bishops has approved it and the Holy See has given permission.[5]

2. *Pontificia Commissio Codici Iuris Canonici Authentice Interpretando* (bibliog. III), 304–07.

3. *Sacrosanctum* (bibliog. III), 149–50. English translation in Flannery (ed), *Vatican Council II* (bibliog. III), 387.

4. *Pontificia Commissio Codici Iuris Canonici Authentice Interpretando* (bibliog. III), 304–05.

5. Canon 1112 §1: "Ubi desunt sacerdotes et diaconi, potest Episcopus dioecesanus, praevio voto favorabili Episcoporum conferentiae et obtenta licentia Sanctae Sedis, delegare laicos, qui matrimoniis assistant."

Paragraph 2 of this canon says that suitable lay people should be chosen who are capable of giving appropriate marriage instructions to couples and who can celebrate marriages in a fitting manner.[6] No such canon existed in the 1917 Code. Although the list of sources for this canon does not cite the Second Vatican Council,[7] it can be said that the use of lay people in celebrating marriages is certainly a response to the major Conciliar concept that lay people have an essential role to play within the Church.[8] In fact, prior to the 1983 Code, the Holy See had been allowing lay people to be delegated to celebrate marriages in those areas of the world where there were shortages of clergy.[9] These permissions were based on the principle that, in the Latin tradition of the Catholic Church, a marriage is brought into existence by the consent of the couple, not by the action of the person leading the celebration of the marriage. Thus, the insertion of this new canon was a recognition and a codification of an existing practice; it was not as revolutionary as some of the editors of the Code had initially thought.[10]

The third difference is that canon 1117 of the revised Code releases a particular group of people from the requirement to follow the canonical form of mar-

---

6. Canon 1112 §2: "Laicus seligatur idoneus, ad institutionem nupturientibus tradendam capax et qui liturgiae matrimoniali rite peragendae aptus sit."

7. *Pontificia Commissio Codici Iuris Canonici Authentice Interpretando* (bibliog. III), 305.

8. For example, *Vatican II* (bibliog. I), *Lumen gentium,* 218 November 1964; *Gaudium et spes,* 7 December 1965; and *Apostolicam actuositatem*, 18 November 1965.

9. A useful commentary is in Caparros et al. (eds), *Code of Canon Law Annotated* (bibliog. III), 705.

10. *Pontificium Consilium de Legum Textibus (bibliog. III), Communicationes* 8 (1976), 221, and *Communicationes* 10 (1978), 92–94.

riage. This group comprises those Catholics who have defected from the Catholic Church by a formal act. This is stipulated in canon 1117: "The form prescribed above is to be observed if at least one of the parties contracting marriage was baptized in the Catholic Church or received into it and has not by a formal act defected from it, without prejudice to the provisions of canon 1127 §2."[11] Someone who has formally defected from the Catholic Church can also validly marry an unbaptized person without a dispensation (canon 1086 §1).[12]

It can be seen that the Code's reference to formal defection has important canonical consequences. Thus, the defection must be externally verifiable. That is, it has to be a definite act.[13] Mere non-attendance of Mass is not sufficient; the person must decide to leave the Catholic Church. In 2006 the Pontifical Council for Legislative Texts explained that the individual formally defecting from the Catholic Faith must communicate his or her decision to the local Ordinary (for example, diocesan bishop or vicar general) or the parish priest. The individual's baptismal entry must then be amended to include the fact that formal defection has

---

11. Canon 1117: "Statuta superius forma servanda est, si saltem alterutra pars matrimonium contrahentium in Ecclesia catholica baptizata vel in eandem recepta sit neque actu formali ab ea defecerit, salvis praescriptis can. 1127 §2." Canon 1127 §2 allows a Catholic to be dispensed from the canonical form of marriage when marrying a baptized non-Catholic. This canon will be examined very shortly. English translation in Caparros et al. (eds), *Code of Canon Law Annotated* (bibliog. III), 707.

12. Canon 1086 §1: "Matrimonium inter duas personas, quarum altera sit baptizata in Ecclesia catholica vel in eandem recepta nec actu formali ab ea defecerit, et altera non baptizata, invalidum est."

13. *Pontificium Consilium de Legum Textibus* (bibliog. III), Communicationes 8 (1976), 54–56, and 10 (1978), 96–98. Also, the commentary on canon 1117 in Caparros et al. (eds), *Code of Canon Law Annotated* (bibliog. III), 707–08.

14. *Pontificium Consilium de Legum Textibus* (bibliog. III), Letter, *Actus*

occurred.[14] It is because of these complexities that, at the time of this book being published, Pope Benedict XVI announced that formal defection would be removed from the Church's matrimonial law. Thus, the exceptions to the law granted by the Code to those who have formally defected will cease.[15]

Mixed Marriages and Marriages Celebrated Secretly

The sixth chapter of the marriage canons considers mixed marriages[16]—that is, marriages between Catholics and baptized non-Catholics. This chapter goes from canon 1124 to canon 1129. The list of sources for these canons shows that they are based primarily on a document from Pope Paul VI, issued in 1970, called *Matrimonia mixta.*[17] For the purposes of my book, I only need to consider canon 1127, which gives rise to the fourth major difference between the 1983 Code and the former Code with regard to the canonical form of marriage.

The difference is that canon 1127 §2 of the 1983 Code introduces a certain flexibility in order to respond to ecumenical needs. That is, when a Catholic marries a baptized non-Catholic, if they can only follow the canonical form of marriage with grave

---

Formalis Defectionis ab Ecclesia Catholica (Prot. N. 10279/2006), 13 March 2006. Also, Stenson, " Concept and Implications" (bibliog. III). Also, Lopez Gallo, "Formal Defection from the Catholic Church" (bibliog. III). Also, Read, "Formal Defection: The End of the Road?" (bibliog. III). Also, Read, "Not Quite the End of the Road!" (bibliog. III).

15. Benedict XVI, *Motu Proprio, Omnium* in *mentem*, 26 October 2009

16. *"De matrimoniis mixtis."*

17. *Pontificia Commissio Codici Iuris Canonici Authentice Interpretando* (bibliog. III), 307–09. Also, Paul VI (bibliog. I), Motu Proprio, *Matrimonia* mixta, 31 March 1970. Also, Filipiak, *"Matrimonia Mixta: Commentarium"* (bibliog. III). Also, Tomko, *"Adnotationes"* (bibliog. III).

difficulty, then they can be dispensed from it by the local ordinary.[18] An example will help to explain. A Catholic woman is engaged to a man who is a practicing member of the Church of England. Moreover, his father is the local vicar. When they discuss the arrangements for their wedding, it becomes very clear that his father and the rest of his family would be extremely upset if the father could not conduct the ceremony. In this case, the Catholic woman could obtain a dispensation from the canonical form of marriage so that she could validly marry in a ceremony in the Church of England conducted by her fiancé's father.[19]

If the Catholic party does not obtain a dispensation from canonical form and attempts to marry a baptized non-Catholic in a ceremony outside the Catholic Church, then the marriage is considered to be invalid. But paragraph 1 of the same canon provides an exception to this.[20] This is when the Catholic party marries an Orthodox Christian.

It has been seen that article 18 of the Second Vatican Council's *Decree on the Eastern Catholic Churches* (*Orientalium Ecclesiarum*) responded to the calls

---

18. Canon 1127 §2: "Si graves difficultates formae canonicae servandae obstent, Ordinario loci partis catholicae ius est ab eadem in singulis casibus dispensandi, consulto tamen Ordinario loci in quo matrimonium celebratur, et salva ad validitatem aliqua publica forma celebrationis; Episcoporum conferentiae est normas statuere, quibus praedicta dispensatio concordi ratione concedatur."

19. Canon 1129 also allows such a dispensation from canonical form to be granted when a Catholic marries an unbaptized person. Canon 1129: "Praescripta can. 1127 et 1128 applicanda sunt quoque matrimoniis, quibus obstat impedimentum disparitatis cultus, de quo in can. 1086 §1."

20. Canon 1127 §1: "Ad formam quod attinet in matrimonio mixto adhibendam, serventur praescripta can. 1108; si tamen pars catholica matrimonium contrahit cum parte non catholica ritus orientalis, forma canonica celebrationis servanda est ad liceitatem tantum; ad validitatem autem requiritur interventus ministri sacri, servatis aliis de iure servandis."

from the Eastern Catholic Bishops and made the canonical form of marriage only for lawfulness and not for validity when an Eastern Catholic married an Orthodox Christian—provided a sacred minister was present. Because of the validity of Orthodox orders, this meant that a Catholic could validly marry an Orthodox Christian in an Orthodox wedding ceremony without the need for a dispensation from canonical form.[21]

This norm is codified by canon 1127 §1.[22] It is noteworthy that the canon applies the norm to Latin-rite Catholics (for whom the 1983 Code is intended, according to canon 1). Thus, when a Latin-rite Catholic marries an Orthodox Christian in an Orthodox ceremony, he or she should obtain a dispensation from canonical form. But even without such a dispensation, the marriage is still valid. With regard to marriages between Eastern Catholics and Orthodox Christians (to which *Orientalium Ecclesiarum* was actually referring), these are dealt with by canon 834 §2 of the Eastern Code.[23] Again, canonical form is only for lawfulness. Because the Eastern theology of marriage is different, however, the sacred minister who is to be present has to be a priest, not a deacon. This priest must bless the couple.[24]

21. *Sacrosanctum* (bibliog. III), 233–34. English translation in Flannery (ed), *Vatican Council II* (bibliog. III), 447–48.

22. *Pontificia Commissio Codici Iuris Canonici Authentice Interpretando* (bibliog. III), 308.

23. *1990 Eastern Code* (bibliog. I), canon 834 §2: "Si vero pars catholica alicui Ecclesiae orientali sui iuris ascripta matrimonium celebrat cum parte, quae ad Ecclesiam orientalem acatholicam pertinet, forma celebrationis matrimonii iure praescripta servanda est tantum ad liceitatem; ad validitatem autem requiritur benedictio sacerdotis servatis aliis de iure servandis."

24. Connolly, "Contrasts in the Western and Eastern Approaches to Marriage" (bibliog. III). Also, Prader, *Il Matrimonio in Oriente e Occidente* (bibliog. III), 194–99. Also, Pospishil, *Eastern Catholic Marriage Law* (bibliog. III), 371–73. Also, Pospishil, *Interritual Marriage Law Problems* (bibliog. III), 134.

The seventh chapter of marriage canons consists of canons 1130 to 1133 and is titled "The Secret Celebration of Marriage."[25] In the 1917 Code, this type of marriage was called a "marriage of conscience" (*matrimonium conscientiae*) and was covered by canons 1104 to 1107. With the exception of a few very minor changes, the present Code repeats the canons of the 1917 Code.[26]

25. "*De matrimonio secreto celebrando.*" English translation of title in Caparros et al. (eds), *Code of Canon Law Annotated* (bibliog. III), 715.

26. *Pontificia Commissio Codici Iuris Canonici Authentice Interpretando* (bibliog. III), 309.

—15—

The Effects of Marriage

ONCE MATRIMONIAL CONSENT has been formulated in the mind and exchanged externally using the prescribed form, there is a marriage. What are the consequences of this marriage? The eighth chapter of marriage canons is called "The Effects of Marriage" and runs from canon 1134 to canon 1140.[1] The equivalent chapter in the 1917 Code was the ninth chapter of marriage canons with the same title. This chapter consisted of canons 1110 to 1117. A simple comparison of the two Codes shows that, apart from canon 1135, the canons of the new Code effectively repeat those of the 1917 Code.

Canon 1135 states, "Each spouse has an equal obligation and right to whatever pertains to the partnership of conjugal life."[2] This canon replaces canon 1111[3] of the 1917 Code which states, "Both spouses, from the very beginning of the marriage, have an equal right and

---

1. *"De matrimonii effectibus."* English translation of title in Caparros et al. (eds), *Code of Canon Law Annotated* (bibliog. III), 716.

2. Canon 1135: "Utrique coniugi aequum officium et ius est ad ea quae pertinent ad consortium vitae coniugalis." English translation in Ibid., 717.

3. *Pontificia Commissio Codici Iuris Canonici Authentice Interpretando* (bibliog. III), 310. *1917 Code* (bibliog. I), canon 1111: "Utrique coniugi ab ipso matrimonii initio aequum ius et officium est quod attinet ad actus proprios coniugalis vitae."

obligation with regard to those acts proper to the conjugal life." It has been seen that Gratian is a source for
canon 1111.[4] Although this canon agrees with Gratian
on one important point, it disagrees with him on another. Gratian said that a husband and wife have equal
rights with regard to sexual intercourse. This is indeed
the teaching of canon 1111 of the 1917 Code. But Gratian said that the right to sexual intercourse originates
with the first act of intercourse. That is, it comes about
via consummation and not via the exchange of consent.
Thus, spouses are not bound to have intercourse, but
once they do, either spouse can demand it on any subsequent occasion.[5] It has been noted that this gave rise
to the practice whereby, in the first two months of their
marriage, spouses could either consummate their marriage or one of them could enter religious life, leaving
the other free to remarry.[6] This is different from canon 1111, which states that the right to intercourse exists "from the very beginning of the marriage." Thus,
under the 1917 Code, a spouse could no longer simply
leave a marriage and enter religious life—a dispensation from the Holy See was needed.

Canon 1135 of the 1983 Code develops canon 1111
of the former Code in two ways. First, it speaks of an
"equal obligation and right" (*aequum officium et ius*),
as opposed to an "equal right and obligation" (*aequum*

---

4. Gasparri (ed), *Codex Iuris Canonici Pii X* (bibliog. III), 318. Also, Gasparri
(ed), *Codex Iuris Canonici Fontes* (bibliog. III), vol. 9, cols. 44–47. References
to Gratian: Gratian, *Concordia* (bibliog. III), Part 2, Case 27, Question 2, ch. 24;
Case 32, Question 2, ch. 3; and Case 33, Question 5, chapters 1–3, 5, 6, and 11.

5. Gratian, *Concordia* (bibliog. III), Part 2, Case 32, Question 2, ch. 3; and
Case 33, Question 5, chapters 5 and 11.

6. Ibid, Case 27, Question 2, dictum after ch. 26, and dictum after ch. 28. Also,
Case 33, Question 5, dictum after ch. 11, and dictum after ch. 20.

ius et officium). This simple transposition of words emphasizes the duties spouses have—especially toward each other. The second and more fundamental development is that canon 1135 extends these obligations and rights to every aspect of marital life—"the partnership of conjugal life" (*consortium vitae coniugalis*). The former canon had restricted these obligations and rights to the sexual acts of marriage (*actus proprios coniugalis vitae*). I welcome this development because it is in keeping with the Conciliar understanding that marriage is a partnership of the whole of life.

I have noted that this present chapter of canons is based upon canons 1110 to 1117 of the 1917 Code, but one of these is not reproduced in the 1983 Code. This canon is number 1112 which states, "Unless the contrary is provided by special law, the wife shares in the status of her husband with regard to canonical effects."[7] I shall give two examples from the 1917 Code. First, canon 93 §1 says that the wife shares in her husband's domicile.[8] Second, concerning where people are to be buried, canons 1223 §2 and 1229 §2 speak of wives being buried with their husbands.[9] The fact that canon 1112 is not reproduced shows that the new Code is trying to promote equality between husbands and wives. This is very much in keeping with canon 1135,

---

7. *1917 Code* (bibliog. I), canon 1112: "Nisi iure speciali aliud cautum sit, uxor, circa canonicos effectus, particeps efficitur status mariti."

8. *1917 Code* (bibliog. I), canon 93 §1: "Uxor, a viro legitime non separata, necessario retinet domicilium viri sui; amens, domicilium curatoris; minor, domicilium illius cuius potestati subiicitur."

9. *1917 Code* (bibliog. I), canon 1223 § 2: "Uxor et filii puberes in hac electione prorsus immunes sunt a maritali vel patria potestate." *1917 Code* (bibliog. I), canon 1229 §2: "Pro uxore attenditur sepulcrum viri, et, si plures habuerit, sepulcrum ultimi."

just considered, which speaks of the *equal* obligations and rights of both spouses.[10]

With regard to the two examples I have just given from the 1917 Code, the new Code has revised the appropriate canons in order to give greater equality between spouses. Thus, canon 104 of the 1983 Code does speak of the "common domicile or quasi-domicile" of spouses, but recognizes the fact that they can have separate domiciles or quasi-domiciles.[11] Also, canon 1180 §2 states that everyone may choose his or her place of burial, unless prohibited by law[12]—thus, wives do not have to be buried with their husbands. These two revised canons are examples of the greater emancipation of wives in the 1983 Code and hence their equality with their husbands.

---

10. *Pontificium Consilium de Legum Textibus (bibliog. III), Communicationes* 5 (1973), 75–76, and *Communicationes* 10 (1978), 105.

11. Canon 104: "Coniuges commune habeant domicilium vel quasi domicilium; legitima separationis ratione vel alia iusta de causa, uterque habere potest proprium domicilium vel quasi-domicilium."

12. Canon 1180 §2: "Omnibus autem licet, nisi iure prohibeantur, eligere coemeterium sepulturae."

—16—

The Dissolution
of Non-Sacramental Marriages

Introduction

THE NINTH CHAPTER of marriage canons is called "The Separation of the Spouses."[1] This chapter is divided into two articles. Article 1 is called "The Dissolution of the Bond"[2] and consists of canons 1141 to 1150. Article 2 is called "Separation While the Bond Remains"[3] and runs from canon 1151 to canon 1155. Thus, this chapter considers two types of occasion when spouses separate: article 1 examines those cases where the spouses separate and the marriage is actually dissolved; article 2 considers those instances where the spouses no longer cohabit but are still married. For the purposes of this book, only article 1—that is, cases where the bond of marriage is dissolved—needs to be examined.

Canon 1141 states, "A marriage which is ratified and consummated cannot be dissolved by any human

---

1. *"De separatione coniugum."* English translation of title in Caparros et al. (eds), *Code of Canon Law Annotated* (bibliog. III), 719.
2. *"De dissolutione vinculi."* English translation of title ibid.
3. *"De separatione manente vinculo."* English translation of title ibid., 724.

power or by any cause other than death."[4] I have already examined this canon. It has been seen that it gives two conditions, both of which must be met in order for a marriage to be absolutely indissoluble. The first is that the marriage must be a ratified marriage. That is, it must be a valid marriage between baptized spouses.[5] It has been seen that the Catholic Church teaches that such a marriage is automatically a sacrament. Thus, the first condition for absolute indissolubility is equivalent to saying that the marriage must be a sacrament.[6] The second condition given by canon 1141 is that the marriage must then be consummated.

If a particular marriage does not satisfy both of these condition, then it is not absolutely indissoluble and so is open to dissolution. Therefore, canon 1141 implicitly gives two types of marriage which can be dissolved. The first type comprises those marriages which are not ratified. That is, those marriages which are not a sacrament. These are usually called "non-sacramental marriages." The second type of marriage which can be dissolved comprises those which have not been consummated. These two types of marriage dissolution are covered by article 1.

I have already examined the Church's practice of dissolving non-consummated marriages. This leaves the other type of dissolution to be analyzed—the dissolution of non-sacramental marriages. This form of dissolution can be subdivided into the Pauline

---

4. Canon 1141: "Matrimonium ratum et consummatum nulla humana potestate nullaque causa, praeterquam morte, dissolvi potest." English translation ibid., 719.
5. Canon 1061 §1.
6. Canon 1055 §2.

Privilege (canons 1143 to 1147) and more particular cases (canons 1148 to 1149). I shall examine these two subdivisions in turn. Finally, I shall consider dissolutions "in Favor of the Faith" which are not covered by the 1983 Code but are granted by the Pope.

The Pauline Privilege

Canon 1143 §1 gives a basic outline of the circumstances under which the Pauline Privilege applies.[7] That is, two unbaptized people marry and one of them subsequently receives baptism. The baptism does not necessarily have to be in the Catholic Church. The other party leaves the baptized spouse. The Pauline Privilege allows the baptized party to enter a new marriage. When the baptized person enters a new marriage, the former marriage is dissolved. The second paragraph of canon 1143 says that the unbaptized party is to be considered to have left the baptized spouse if he or she refuses to live peacefully with the baptized party "without offense to the Creator" (*sine contumelia Creatoris*). It further stipulates that the baptized party must not have given the other party a just reason to depart.[8]

The expression, *sine contumelia Creatoris*, covers a wide range of possibilities where the unbaptized party does not actually leave the matrimonial home but refuses to live with the baptized party in a way that is conducive to the sanctity or harmony of marriage. Woestman

---

7. Canon 1143 §1: "Matrimonium initum a duobus non baptizatis solvitur ex privilegio paulino in favorem fidei partis quae baptismum recepit, ipso facto quo novum matrimonium ab eadem parte contrahitur, dummodo pars non baptizata discedat."

8. Canon 1143 §2: "Discedere censetur pars non baptizata, si nolit cum parte baptizata cohabitare vel cohabitare sine contumelia Creatoris, nisi haec post baptismum receptum iustam illi dederit discedendi causam."

gives examples: The unbaptized spouse "refuses to permit the Catholic education of the children, tries to destroy the faith of the Catholic spouse, tries to lead the Catholic party into serious sin, [or] by quarrels and provocation makes conjugal peace impossible."[9] (If the baptized spouse had received baptism in a non-Catholic tradition, then the same description could be used but with the word *Christian* inserted in the place of *Catholic*.)

The canons in the 1983 Code governing the Pauline Privilege effectively repeat those of the 1917 Code (canons 1120–24, and 1126). Indeed, the former canons are cited as sources for the new ones.[10] With regard to the 1917 Code, it has been seen that Gasparri uses Gratian as a source for canon 1120 §1, which introduces the canons on the Pauline Privilege.[11] Once again, Gratian proves to be influential with regard to the 1917 Code and, consequently, the 1983 Code.

I have already examined Gratian's contribution to the Pauline Privilege.[12] He bases it on two arguments. His first focuses yet again on the role of sexual intercourse within marriage. That is, intercourse between unbaptized spouses cannot make present the indestructible bond that exists between Christ and the Church. Consequently, such a marriage is not absolutely indissoluble. Indeed, the couple can dissolve the marriage by divorcing.[13]

It can be seen that Gratian is applying the same emphasis on sexual intercourse as he does when he consid-

9. Woestman, *Special Marriage Cases* (bibliog. III), 40.

10. *Pontificia Commissio Codici Iuris Canonici Authentice Interpretando* (bibliog. III), 311–12.

11. Gasparri (ed), *Codex Iuris Canonici Pii X* (bibliog. III), 320. Also, Gasparri (ed), *Codex Iuris Canonici Fontes* (bibliog. III), vol. 9, col. 45.

12. Gratian, *Concordia* (bibliog. III), Part 2, Case 28, Question 2.

13. Ibid., Question 1, dictum after ch. 17.

ers the initiation and completion of marriage, as well as impotence. I have already argued that this emphasis on consummation is in fact a corruption of a genuine tradition within the Church which teaches that consent alone brings an indissoluble marriage into existence. Moreover, Gratian's emphasis is based on nothing more than sources which are either false or taken out of context.

Gratian's second argument uses Saint Paul's First Letter to the Corinthians. "But if the unbeliever chooses to leave, then let the separation take place: in these circumstances, the brother or sister [that is, the Christian spouse] is no longer tied. But God has called you to live in peace."[14] It has been seen that Gratian interprets the expression "no longer tied" to mean that the marriage no longer exists—thus allowing a second marriage.[15] However, it has been noted that there is no support for this particular interpretation. It is indeed surprising that someone like Gratian should allow the Pauline Privilege since he is extremely strict with regard to divorce. For example, it has been seen that he does not accept that Matthew's Gospel allows divorce and remarriage even in the case of adultery.[16] His interpretation of the text from Saint Paul is not consistent with this.

Although it would be false to claim that the use of the Pauline Privilege began with Gratian, it is true to say that his treatment of it in the *Decretum* did influence many Popes. Benedict XIV promoted the use of the Privilege and was of the opinion that the dissolution

---

14. 1 Corinthians 7:15.

15. Gratian, *Concordia* (bibliog. III), Part 2, Case 28, Question 2, especially dictum after ch. 2.

16. Ibid., Case 32, Question 7, ch. 16, and dictum after ch. 16. The reference in Matthew is 19:9.

of the first marriage takes place when the baptized party actually enters the second marriage.[17] It has been seen that Benedict is the main source for canon 1126 of the 1917 Code, which repeated his understanding of when it is that the first marriage is dissolved.[18] Canon 1126 has been absorbed into canon 1143 §1 of the 1983 Code.[19]

I acknowledge that my analysis of the Pauline Privilege is somewhat limited and that the subject is deserving of a book of its own. I have shown, however, that it is doubtful scripturally and that its historical development owes a great deal to Gratian's bias toward the importance of sexual intercourse within marriage. Finally, irrespective of whether the Privilege is well-founded or not, it certainly can be said that its use could be seen to undermine the Church's teaching on the permanence of marriage. That is, it is a counter-sign in this modern world, with its very prevalent divorce mentality. This mentality caused grave concerns at the 1980 Synod of Bishops[20] and was regarded as an urgent problem by Pope John Paul II, who addressed the matter in *Familiaris consortio*.[21]

---

17. Benedict XIV (bibliog. I), Epistle, *Postremo mense,* 28 February 1747. Also, Benedict XIV (bibliog. I), Apostolic Constitution, *Apostolici ministerit,* 16 September 1747.

18. *1917 Code* (bibliog. I), canon 1126: "Vinculum prioris coniugii, in infidelitate contracti, tunc tantum solvitur, cum pars fidelis reapse novas nuptias valide iniverit." Also, Gasparri (ed), *Codex Iuris Canonici Pii X* (bibliog. III), 322. Also, Gasparri (ed), *Codex Iuris Canonici Fontes* (bibliog. III), vol. 9, col. 154.

19. *Pontificia Commissio Codici Iuris Canonici Authentice Interpretando* (bibliog. III), 311.

20. The bishops spoke of their concerns about the increase in divorce in Propositions 13 and 14. Grootaers and Selling, *The 1980 Synod of Bishops* (bibliog. III), 139–40, 351–53.

21. Articles 6–7, 83–84. English text in Flannery (ed), *Vatican Council II: More (bibliog. III), 818–20, 887–89.*

Extensions to the Pauline Privilege

The second subdivision of dissolution cases consists of canons 1148 and 1149. There is a direct line between these two canons and the three constitutions of the sixteenth century seen earlier: *Altitudo, Romani Pontificis,* and *Populis.*[22] It has been noted how these constitutions were issued to deal with particular pastoral problems in certain parts of the world.

Altitudo and *Romani Pontificis* were concerned with those unbaptized men, with more than one unbaptized wife, who requested baptism in the Church. *Populis* considered those unbaptized men who were separated from their unbaptized wives by reason of slavery and who sought baptism.[23] Canon 1125 of the 1917 Code then extended the application of these constitutions to other parts of the world with similar problems.[24] It is this canon from the former Code which is the basis for canons 1148 and 1149 of the 1983 Code.[25] To be more precise, canon 1148 is based upon the constitutions *Altitudo* and *Romani Pontificis,* while canon 1149 is based upon *Populis.*

---

22. Paul III (bibliog. I), Apostolic Constitution, *Altitudo,* 1 June 1537, in *1917 Code* (bibliog. I), 750–51. Also, Pius V (bibliog. I), Apostolic Constitution, *Romani Pontificis,* 2 August 1571, in *1917 Code* (bibliog. I), 751–52. Also, Gregory XIII (bibliog. I), Apostolic Constitution, *Populis,* 25 January 1585, in *1917 Code* (bibliog. I), 752–54.

23. *Populis* applied to both monogamous and polygamous marriages.

24. *1917 Code* (bibliog. I), canon 1125: "Ea quae matrimonium respiciunt in constitutionibus Pauli III *Altitudo,* 1 Iun. 1537; S. Pii V *Romani Pontificis,* 2 Aug. 1571; Gregorii XIII *Populis,* 25 Ian. 1585, quaeque pro peculiaribus locis scripta sunt, ad alias quoque regiones in eisdem adiunctis extenduntur."

25. *Pontificia Commissio Codici Iuris Canonici Authentice Interpretando* (bibliog. III), 312–13.

Canon 1148 considers the baptism into the Catholic Church of those who have more than one wife or husband. Paragraph 1 states, "When an unbaptized man who simultaneously has a number of unbaptized wives, has received baptism in the Catholic Church, if it would be a hardship for him to remain with the first of the wives, he may retain one of them, having dismissed the others. The same applies to an unbaptized woman who simultaneously has a number of unbaptized husbands."[26] The second paragraph states that when it is decided which spouse is to remain, the marriage is to be celebrated according to canonical form and with any required permissions or dispensations.[27] The third paragraph then says that adequate provision must be made for the needs of those who have been dismissed.[28]

It can be seen that canon 1148 develops the norms of *Romani Pontificis* in two main ways. First, if the man is not to remain with his first wife, then priority is no longer given to any wife who wishes to be baptized with him. Consequently, the man is virtually free to choose any wife he likes. The only condition the canon gives is that he should remain with his first wife unless

---

26. Canon 1148 §1: "Non baptizatus, qui plures uxores non baptizatas simul habeat, recepto in Ecclesia catholica baptismo, si durum ei sit cum earum prima permanere, unam ex illis, ceteris dimissis, retinere potest. Idem valet de muliere non baptizata, quae plures maritos non baptizatos simul habeat." English translation in Caparros et al. (eds), *Code of Canon Law Annotated* (bibliog. III), 722.
27. Canon 1148 §2: "In casibus de quibus in §1, matrimonium, recepto baptismo, forma legitima contrahendum est, servatis etiam, si opus sit, praescriptis de matrimoniis mixtis et aliis de iure servandis."
28. Canon 1148 §3: "Ordinarius loci, prae oculis habita condicione morali, sociali, oeconomica locorum et personarum, curet ut primae uxoris ceterarumque dimissarum necessitatibus satis provisum sit, iuxta normas iustitiae, christianae caritatis et naturalis aequitatis." Also, *Pontificium Consilium de Legum Textibus* (bibliog. III), *Communicationes* 10 (1978), 115.

this would be a hardship (*durum*) for him. In practice, the term *hardship* is sufficiently vague to be easily established. The canon is not stating that it must be impossible for him to remain with his first wife or even seriously difficult. The second development is that the canon also applies to women with more than one husband. The combined effect of these developments is that canon 1148 makes the dissolution of non-Christian marriages more available.

Canon 1149 virtually repeats the norms given in *Populis*. It states, "An unbaptized person who, having received baptism in the Catholic Church, cannot re-establish cohabitation with his or her unbaptized spouse because of captivity or persecution can contract another marriage, even if the other party has in the meantime received baptism, without prejudice to the provisions of canon 1141."[29] The reference to canon 1141 means that the convert may enter another marriage even if his or her first spouse has also been baptized, provided they have not consummated their marriage while both being baptized. This is because such consummation would make the marriage ratified and consummated—hence, absolutely indissoluble.[30] In practice, the convert will not know whether his or her first spouse has been baptized because they have been separated by circumstances outside their control—captivity or persecution.

---

29. Canon 1149: "Non baptizatus qui, recepto in Ecclesia catholica baptismo, cum coniuge non baptizato ratione captivitatis vel persecutionis cohabitationem restaurare nequeat, aliud matrimonium contrahere potest, etiamsi altera pars baptismum interea receperit, firmo praescripto can. 1141." English translation based on Caparros et al. (eds), *Code of Canon Law Annotated* (bibliog. III), 723.

30. *Pontificium Consilium de Legum Textibus* (bibliog. III), *Communicationes* 10 (1978), 112–16.

This separation will also mean that, in practice, there would be no opportunity to engage in sexual intercourse should the first spouse have been baptized too.

Canons 1148 and 1149 both rely upon the Pauline Privilege, insofar as they involve the dissolution of a marriage between two unbaptized spouses, one of whom subsequently receives baptism. These two canons also develop the Pauline Privilege, however, because they do not require the spouse of the baptized party to refuse to live with him or her peacefully without offense to the Creator. Historically, with regard to canon 1148, this development came about because men with more than one wife sometimes could not remember which wife had been their first. Consequently, it was not possible to determine whether the unbaptized wife would live peacefully with her newly baptized husband. With regard to canon 1149, the impossibility of determining the unbaptized spouse's intentions came about because the couple was forcibly separated by slavery. I have already shown that the scriptural and historical bases for the Pauline Privilege are weak. Therefore, the same can be said about canon 1148 and canon 1149, which are founded on the Pauline Privilege.

Dissolution in Favor of the Faith

It has been seen that the principle behind the Pauline Privilege is that a marriage between two unbaptized spouses is not a sacrament, so when they engage in sexual intercourse they cannot participate in the indissoluble bond that exists between Christ and his Church. The present position of the Catholic Church is that *both* spouses must be baptized in order for their marriage to be a sacrament. This has been noted when canon 1055 was examined. Therefore, according to the Church's official teaching, a marriage between a baptized person and an unbaptized person is not a sacrament. Consequently, the same reasoning can be applied to it as in the case of the Pauline Privilege. That is, a marriage where only one spouse is baptized cannot participate in the indissoluble bond between Christ and the Church. In canonical language, such a marriage is not ratified (canon 1061 §1) and so is not absolutely indissoluble (canon 1141).

This wider application of the principle behind the Pauline Privilege opens up a whole new group of marriages that can be dissolved. Woestman gives an excellent account of the historical development of this new type of dissolution—called "in Favor of the Faith" (*in Favorem Fidei*).[31] This new type of dissolution developed during the twentieth century. Woestman says that the first publicized case was in 1920. Another dissolution was granted in April 1924 to a woman in the diocese of Breslau in Germany. This particular case illustrates how the dissolution works.

The woman was a baptized non-Catholic who had married a Jew. The marriage ended in divorce and she wished to marry a Catholic. Her first marriage was not a sacrament because her Jewish husband was not baptized. Consequently, the marriage was dissolved so that she could marry the Catholic party. Another case was in November 1924 and came from the Diocese of

---

31. Woestman, *Special Marriage Cases* (bibliog. III), 53–60.

428 WHAT BRINGS A MARRIAGE INTO EXISTENCE?

Helena in Montana.[32] An unbaptized man was married to a baptized woman of the Anglican Communion. After a divorce, his wife entered a second union and he wished to be baptized in the Catholic Church and marry a Catholic. Again, the first marriage was not a sacrament, so Pope Pius XI dissolved it.[33]

In October 1941, Pope Pius XII gave the annual papal address to the Rota.[34] In it he reaffirms that a sacramental marriage which has been consummated is absolutely indissoluble. He goes on to say that other marriages do not have this degree of indissolubility. Consequently, they can be dissolved "not only in virtue of the Pauline Privilege, but also by the Roman Pontiff in virtue of his ministerial power."[35] Pius XII then explains that this exercise of ministerial power is based upon the fact that the Pope is Christ's minister. That is, the power used is Christ's power—the Pope uses it vicariously. Consequently, non-sacramental marriages can be dissolved not only by the Pauline Privilege but also by divine power.[36] It is noteworthy that Pius XII also bases this latter type of dissolution on the ambiguous passage of Saint Paul. But, for Pius, there is no ambiguity: "'The brother or sister is not bound. It is to peace that God has called you" (1 Cor 7:15), that is, there remains no bond, no servitude, when God dissolves it and thus allows a party to pass licitly to a new marriage." [37]

---

32. Donnelly, "The Helena Decision of 1924" " (bibliog. III).
33. Woestman, *Special Marriage Cases* (bibliog. III), 53–54.
34. Pius XII (bibliog. I), Address to the Sacred Roman Rota, 3 October 1941. English translation in Woestman (ed), *Papal Allocutions* (bibliog. III), 11–16.
35. Woestman (ed), *Papal Allocutions* (bibliog. III), 14.
36. Tomko, *"De Dissolutione Matrimonii"* (bibliog. III).
37. Woestman (ed), *Papal Allocutions* (bibliog. III), 15.

In December 1973, the Sacred Congregation for the Doctrine of the Faith, as it was then called, issued a document which not only upholds the practice of dissolving marriages where only one party is baptized but also gives norms governing the preparation of such cases.[38] Although the later 1983 Code does not deal explicitly with these cases, it is still the practice of the Church to allow such marriages to be dissolved. Indeed, new norms were issued by the Congregation for the Doctrine of the Faith in April 2001.[39] This new document begins by considering the Pauline Privilege. It bases it explicitly on verse 15 of chapter 7 of Saint Paul's First letter to the Corinthians. It continues, "Consequently, the Pauline Privilege was already established as a fully defined theological-canonical institute by the beginning of the thirteenth century."[40] It is significant that the document refers to this period, which is shortly after Gratian's *Decretum*, published around the middle of the twelfth century. The document then gives a brief history of how the Pauline Privilege was extended and eventually gave rise to dissolutions in Favor of the Faith.[41]

My doubts about the Pauline Privilege mean that I also have grave concerns about dissolutions in Favor of the Faith. My concerns are heightened by the fact that people, including non-Catholics, look toward the

38. Sacred Congregation for the Doctrine of the Faith (bibliog. I), Instruction, *Ut Notum Est,* 6 December 1973. English translation in Woestman, *Special Marriage Cases* (bibliog. III), 129–34. The Latin original was never published in the *Acta Apostolicae Sedis.* Also, Labelle, *"Les Incidences Pastorales"* (bibliog. III).

39. Congregation for the Doctrine of the Faith (bibliog. I), Instruction, *Normae de Conficiendo Processu pro Solutione Vinculi Matrimonialis in Favorem Fidei,* 30 April 2001.

40. Ibid. (English text), 5.

41. Ibid. (English text), 5–11.

Catholic Church and the Pope for the protection of moral values—including the sanctity of marriage. The Church's practice of dissolving marriages can be a counter-sign to the permanence of marriage. Dissolutions in Favor of the Faith are favors granted by the Pope. I have no doubt that he can grant such favors. Without daring to suggest what the Pope should or should not do, however, I think the time has come to reassess whether such favors should be granted so that the Church's teaching on the sanctity of marriage may be strengthened.

—17—

The Validation of Marriage

IT HAS BEEN SEEN that canon 1057 §1 states, "A marriage is brought into being by the lawfully manifested consent of persons who are legally capable. This consent cannot be supplied by any human power."[1] Implicit in this canon are three reasons why a marriage could be invalid: there has been a lack of genuine matrimonial consent in one or both of the parties; this consent has not been "lawfully manifested"—that is, canonical form has not been followed; or the parties are not "legally capable" because of the existence of an impediment.

Sometimes an invalid marriage can be made valid. This is explained in the tenth and final chapter of the marriage canons in the 1983 Code, which is called "The Validation of Marriage"[2] and consists of canons 1156 to 1165. For example, a marriage which is invalid because canonical form has not been followed can be made valid by celebrating again—this time following canonical

---

1. Canon 1057 §1: "Matrimonium facit partium consensus inter personas iure habiles legitime manifestatus, qui nulla humana potestate suppleri valet." English translation in Caparros et al. (eds), *Code of Canon Law Annotated* (bibliog. III), 660.

form. Also, a marriage which is invalid because of an impediment can be made valid once the impediment either ceases or, if it is possible, is dispensed.

What about a marriage which is invalid because of a lack of consent by one or both of the parties? The canons in this chapter are based firmly on the age-old principle given in canon 1057 §1 that a marriage is brought about by the consent of the couple. Moreover, as this canon explains, if a marriage is invalid because of a lack of such consent, nobody else can supply this consent.[3] Thus, such a marriage will remain invalid until genuine matrimonial consent is given by both of the parties themselves.

---

2. *"De matrimonii convalidatione."* English translation of title ibid., 727.

3. O'Rourke, "Considerations on the Convalidation of Marriage" (bibliog. III). Also, Bogdan, L, "Simple Convalidation of Marriage in the 1983 Code of

GENERAL CONCLUSION

THE QUESTION—What brings a marriage into existence?—has given me a focus with which to examine the Catholic Church's law concerning marriage. In the General Introduction to this book, I state that I hope to contribute three things to the field of canon law: a re-examination of those primary sources which are often quoted in regard to matrimonial law, as well as a re-examination of the historical development of that law; an objective evaluation of the present law of marriage, in particular that found in the 1983 Code of Canon Law; and suggestions for possible development of the present law of marriage. In this general conclusion, I shall draw together the findings of my book under these three headings.

The Primary Sources and Historical Development

In order to show my contribution to understanding the primary sources and historical development of matrimonial law, it would be helpful if I were to paraphrase three statements that are often made. These illustrate the currently held views on the subject. I shall then comment on each.

Statement 1: Saint Augustine gives three "goods" of marriage—namely, children, fidelity, and indissolubility. Each one of these is good in itself and so makes marriage, as a whole, good. The emphasis on these three goods is thus based on Augustine and is an essential part of the Church's teaching.

Comments: I have shown that Augustine did indeed say that these three aspects of marriage are good and so marriage as a whole is good. But I have also shown that this was merely an addendum to his main argument as to why marriage is good. Augustine teaches that the primary reason why marriage is good is because of the companionship that exists between the spouses. It is within this companionship that love and charity are exchanged. Moreover, this exists from the very start of the marriage and does not depend upon the spouses having sexual intercourse or producing children.

The emphasis on Augustine's three goods of marriage is to the detriment of his main argument about companionship and love. Thus, it is easy to overlook the tradition within the Church which has highlighted the importance of love. For example, in twelfth-century France, there were Peter Lombard, Ivo of Chartres, and Hugh of Saint Victor. Marital love is also described most eloquently in Pius XI's encyclical *Casti connubii* and Paul VI's encyclical *Humanae vitae*. Augustine's three goods of marriage found their way into the 1917 Code and then into the 1983 Code; whereas the rather non-canonical concept of love did not. This must not detract, however, from the fact that there has always been a firm tradition within the Church which teaches the importance of marital love.

Statement 2: Originally, the Roman tradition emphasized the role of the spouses' consent in creating a marriage, whereas the Germanic tradition emphasized the role of cohabitation and sexual intercourse. The Church synthesized these to say that marriage begins with consent but that it is not complete until it has been consummated sexually.

Comments: I have shown that it is true that the Roman tradition did emphasize the role of consent. This tradition existed in the pre-Christian empire and also within the Christian period. The teaching that consent brings a marriage into existence is found in the works of Pope Nicholas I, Saint Ambrose, Saint Isidore of Seville, Saint Augustine, and in a work attributed to Saint John Chrysostom.

What about the Germanic tradition? I have shown that one cannot simply talk of a Germanic tradition. *Germanic* is a generic term for the non-Graeco-Roman tribes such as the Goths, Vandals, Alans, Suevi, and Visigoths. Also, within these various Germanic tribes, one finds various ways in which people married. Thus, the expression, *Germanic tradition*, is too simplistic. Having said that, I have shown that within these tribes there were three main ways in which marriages came into existence: marriage by purchase, marriage by abduction, and marriage by mutual consent. Of these, the first two ways eventually died out leaving marriage by mutual consent as the main way in which people married. I have shown how cohabitation and sexual intercourse were important legally, but only as proof that consent had been given. Thus, it is wrong to say that consent was not primary within the Germanic tribes.

Therefore, there was no fundamental difference between the Roman tradition and the "Germanic tradition." Both regarded consent as an essential part in the creation of a marriage. This means that it was not necessary for the two traditions to be synthesized because they were already in agreement. Despite this, a so-called synthesis was provided in the twelfth century by the influential writer Gratian. I have shown how he took genuine sources which teach that consent makes marriage. I have also shown how he took other sources which seem to teach that it is sexual intercourse which brings a marriage into existence. Unfortunately, these latter sources were either false or taken out of context. The consequence of this is that Gratian does not provide us with a synthesis of two genuine traditions. On the contrary, he took the genuine tradition that consent creates marriage and he polluted and diluted it with a false tradition that sexual intercourse creates marriage. The result is the teaching that a marriage begins with consent but that it is not complete until there has been intercourse.

Gratian's "synthesis" places a new emphasis on sexual intercourse. This has two major consequences. The first is that an unconsummated marriage is not regarded as complete and so can be dissolved. The second consequence is that canonical impotence prevents a true marriage. Gratian's *Decretum* influenced Pope

Alexander III and Pope Innocent III. Through them, it influenced the entire Church.

Statement 3: The Catholic Church upholds the indissolubility of marriage. It permits a few exceptions and has a firm basis for doing so.

Comments: I have explained how every marriage has a degree of indissolubility so that spouses on their own authority cannot just decide to separate and remarry. But the Catholic Church teaches that only certain marriages are *absolutely* indissoluble. These are sacramental marriages (that is, where both spouses are baptized) which have been consummated sexually. If the marriage has not been consummated, it can be dissolved. Similarly, if either spouse, or both, is not baptized, then the marriage can be dissolved.

With regard to the dissolution of non-consummated marriages, I have shown that Gratian has been particularly influential. For him, a non-consummated marriage is not complete and so can be dissolved. He argues that sexual intercourse between baptized spouses makes present the symbolism of Christ and his Church. That is, it participates in the indissoluble bond that exists between Christ and the Church. Thus, sexual intercourse makes a Christian marriage absolutely indissoluble. But an analysis of Gratian's *Decretum* reveals a flaw in his argument. He bases his position on a text from Pope Leo I. In it, he shows how Leo taught that sexual intercourse between baptized spouses makes present the symbolism of Christ and his Church. Unfortunately, Gratian uses Leo's words out of context. In fact, the original text has nothing to do with sexual intercourse. Thus, as far as indissolubility is concerned, there is no firm foundation for Gratian's distinction between a consummated marriage and an unconsummated one.

With regard to the dissolution of non-sacramental marriages, the earliest type was the Pauline Privilege—where neither spouse was baptized at the time of entering the marriage. This is based upon a passage from Saint Paul's First Letter to the Corinthians.[1] It has been seen how this text can be interpreted in two ways. In one interpretation, the baptized party is not bound *to live* with his or her non-baptized spouse. In the other interpretation, the baptized party is not bound *by the marriage* and so is free to remarry.

Once again, Gratian has been extremely influential in this area. Despite the strength of the first interpretation of Saint Paul's text, Gratian chooses the second. Again, Gratian supports his position by explaining that sexual intercourse between baptized spouses makes present the symbolism of Christ and his Church. He argues that if the spouses are not baptized, then such symbolism cannot be made present and so the marriage cannot become absolutely indissoluble. Thus, the marriage is open to dissolution. It can be seen that, once more, Gratian supports his argument by misusing Pope Leo I's reference to the symbolism of Christ and the Church.

If one accepts the principle that non-sacramental marriages can be dissolved, then those marriages where one spouse is baptized and the other is not are

Canon Law" (bibliog. III), 511–31.

also open to dissolution. It has been seen that the first part of the twentieth century saw the start of the practice of dissolving such marriages by what has become known as dissolutions in Favor of the Faith. As with the other types of dissolution, I have absolutely no doubt that they can be done. But, considering the basis for them and the need for the Church to be seen to uphold the permanence of marriage, I wonder if it is time to reconsider whether these favors should be granted.

An Evaluation of the Present Law of Marriage

Before I provide an evaluation of the present law, it is necessary to establish objective criteria. The first would be its primary sources. Thus, my re-examination of these sources is pertinent. If the law is meant to be based upon these sources, then they must be correctly understood. Other criteria would be the genuine traditions within the Church. For example, I have examined the Roman tradition and the tradition within twelfth-century France. I have also clarified what could be understood by the expression *Germanic tradition*. Finally, the most important criteria are the documents of the Second Vatican Council.

The majority of the Church's law of marriage is found in the 1983 Code of Canon Law. It has been seen that Pope John XXIII announced that there was going to be this revised code at the same time as he explained that he was going to convene a council. The eventual decision to delay work on revising the Code until after the conclusion of the Council emphasizes that the new

Code was meant to implement the teaching of Vatican II. Thus, the 1983 Code is very much the Code of the Council. Therefore, the Conciliar documents are an excellent gauge for evaluating the 1983 Code's treatment of marriage.

Vatican II and Marriage Law—Not a Revolution

The first thing I wish to say about the present law of marriage is that it has not been revolutionized by the Second Vatican Council. I say this because there can be a tendency to think that the Council radically altered the Church's understanding of marriage in such a way that nearly two thousand years of teaching was reversed. This most certainly was not the case. Indeed, it has been seen that the Council nearly ended without any major statement on marriage. All attempts to produce a document focused solely on marriage failed to do so.

It is true to say that marriage is no longer understood in terms of primary and secondary ends. It has been seen how this caused major tensions both before and during the Council. Although the removal of the teaching about the primary and secondary ends is most welcome, however, it is not the reversal of centuries of Church teaching. The legal concept of the primary and secondary ends began with the 1917 Code. Cardinal Gasparri, who drew up that Code, issued an official list of sources on which each law is based. It has been noted that the 1917 Code's canon 1013 §1 on the primary and secondary ends of marriage lacks historical support. Thus, the removal of the primary and secondary ends should be seen simply as the reversal of about fifty years of Church teaching.

Again, it is true to say that marriage is now spoken of as a covenant and not a contract, but I would suggest that this is not revolutionary. Marriage has never been seen as just a contract—but always as a sacred contract. Also, it is difficult to see what practical difference the use of the term *covenant* has made. The Church's law has not been radically altered. Indeed, while the first paragraph of canon 1055 of the 1983 Code introduces the canons on marriage by describing it as a covenant, the very next paragraph calls marriage a contract. Indeed, the rest of the marriage canons tend to use contractual language.

Finally, concerning the "revolutionary" effect of the Council—canon 1055 §1 of the 1983 Code gives the beautiful description of marriage as the partnership of the whole of life, but this is far from innovative. The Roman jurist Modestinus used this description. To obtain some idea of when he was writing, he was a student of Ulpian who was murdered in 228.

The Present Law's Faithfulness to Vatican II

My analysis of the present law of marriage has shown that it is generally faithful to the teaching of the Second Vatican Council. I shall draw out four main areas where the 1983 Code implements the vision of the Council concerning marriage.

1. Marriage and the Mission of the Church: Vatican II's *Dogmatic Constitution on the Church* (*Lumen gentium*) and its *Decree on the Apostolate of the Laity* (*Apos-*

tolicam actuositatem) both emphasize that all people are called to holiness—not just celibates. Moreover, all members of the Church have a vital role to play in the Church's mission. In particular, articles 11 and 41 of *Lumen gentium* state that married couples are to help each other attain holiness and that they are the first teachers of the faith to their children. These important points are picked up by the first paragraph of the opening canon of the marriage section in the 1983 Code.[2] The paragraph states that marriage is by its own very nature ordered to "the good of the spouses" (*bonum coniugum*) and to the generation and education of children. I have shown how the inclusion of the concept of "the good of the spouses" is a major advancement and is the closest the present law comes to speaking about marital love.

2. A Broader Understanding of Marriage: The answer to the question—What brings a marriage into existence?—is answered by canon 1057 §1. Quite simply, it is the consent of the couple. The second paragraph then goes on to describe the nature of this consent. It states that matrimonial consent is an act of the will by which the man and woman give themselves to each other for the purpose of establishing a marriage. This canon's predecessor in the 1917 Code restricted its consideration of matrimonial consent to just the sexual dimension of marriage. That is, it stated that through their consent, the parties exchange rights to sexual acts apt for the generation of children.[3] The new canon speaks in general terms, however, which is in keeping with

1. 1 Corinthians 7:15.
2. Canon 1055 §1.

the traditional teaching that marriage *in its entirety* is created by consent. This is certainly in accord with the teaching of Vatican II, especially article 48 of the Council's *Pastoral Constitution on the Church in the Modern World* (*Gaudium et spes*) which describes marriage as the intimate sharing of marital life and love.

The Council also emphasized the all-embracing nature of marriage by dropping the notion of the primary and secondary ends. It has been seen that even at the very end of the Council, this was an issue which threatened the publication of *Gaudium et spes*. The last-minute changes by Pope Paul VI suggested that marriage is directed toward the procreation and education of children. But it was agreed to add the phrase "while not underestimating the other ends of marriage."[4] This is adopted by canon 1055 §1, which states that marriage is ordered to the good of the spouses and to the generation and education of children.

Marriage's comprehensive nature is also highlighted by the Council's description of marriage as a covenant.[5] The opening words of the first marriage canon (1055 §1) remain faithful to the Council and use this description. I have already suggested that it does not seem to make any difference legally whether *covenant* or *contract* is the term used. I acknowledge, however, that *covenant* is a more biblical and much richer term than *contract*. Therefore, it is unfortunate that most of the canons which follow canon 1055 §1 still speak of marriage in contractual terms.

---

3. *1917 Code* (bibliog. I), canon 1081.

4. "non posthabitis ceteris matrimonii finibus." Vatican II (bibliog. I), *Gaudium et spes*, 7 December 1965, art. 50, in *Sacrosanctum* (bibliog. III), 760.

It has been seen that the canons on the effects of marriage basically repeat the corresponding ones in the 1917 Code, but one genuine development is the 1983 Code's canon 1135. In accordance with the Conciliar understanding of marriage, this extends the obligations and rights of marriage to every area of marital life. Thus, unlike canon 1111 of the former Code which spoke of rights and obligations only in connection to the sexual acts of marriage,[6] canon 1135 speaks of them in relation to whatever pertains to "the partnership of conjugal life."[7] This partnership is also fostered by the new Code's emphasis on the equality of husband and wife. Thus, canon 1135 states that they have equal obligations and rights. This is very different from the 1917 Code which spoke of the wife sharing in the rights of her husband. The wife now enjoys her own rights.

With regard to the rights of a wife, the new description of consummation is most welcome.[8] That is, sexual intercourse must be performed in a "human manner."[9] This expression has its basis in article 49 of *Gaudium et spes*. It acknowledges that the wife must consent to sexual intercourse. Again, this fosters the broader understanding of marriage. Sexual intercourse must be understood in terms of the whole marriage. It is an act which should manifest the love and mutual respect which exist between the spouses. At the same time, the act should enable this love and respect to increase even more.

3. Continuous Pastoral Care: The canons concern-

---

5. Vatican II (bibliog. I), *Gaudium et spes*, 7 December 1965, art. 48.
6. "actus proprios coniugalis vitae."
7. "consortium vitae coniugalis."
8. Canon 1061 §1.

ing pastoral care and preparations for the celebration of marriage also foster the Second Vatican Council's teaching on marriage. For example, canon 1063 draws on *Gaudium et spes*, the *Constitution on the Sacred Liturgy (Sacrosanctum Concilium)*, and *Lumen gentium* when it speaks of ongoing catechesis concerning marriage for everyone from childhood to maturity, immediate preparations for engaged couples, a fruitful celebration of the wedding liturgy, and continuous support for those who are married.

4. Flexibility Concerning the Marriage Ceremony: The canons on the form of marriage (that is, how weddings are to be celebrated) are also faithful to the Council. The canons from the 1917 Code have been adapted so as to speak of deacons celebrating weddings (in keeping with article 29 of *Lumen gentium*). The revised canons also provide a pastoral solution for those areas of the world where there is a shortage of clergy. Canon 1112 allows lay people to be delegated to celebrate weddings in such areas. Although the list of sources for this canon does not cite the Second Vatican Council,[10] the canon is an application of the general Conciliar concept that lay people have a vital role to play within the Church.[11]

At the Council, the bishops from the Eastern Catholic Churches called for the canonical form of marriage to be only for lawfulness, not for validity, when Eastern Catholics marry baptized Orthodox Christians. That

9. "humano modo."

10. *Pontificia Commissio Codici Iuris Canonici Authentice Interpretando* (bibliog. III), 305.

11. For example, the Conciliar documents *Lumen gentium*, 21 November 1964; *Gaudium et spes*, 7 December 1965; and *Apostolicam actuositatem*, 18

is, when an Eastern Catholic marries a member of the Orthodox Church, the marriage should be recognized even if the wedding takes place within the Orthodox Church without any permission being granted from the Catholic Church.[12] When the Eastern Code of Canon Law was promulgated in 1990, canon 834 §2 allowed this. Moreover, canon 1127 §1 of the 1983 Code grants this concession to those marriages involving Latin-rite Catholics and Orthodox Christians.

Differences between the Present Law and Vatican II

This examination of the present law of marriage has also shown areas where it does not seem to be in accord with the teachings of the Second Vatican Council. I suggest that the canons concerned have generally found their way into the 1983 Code because of what could be called *canonical inertia*. That is, they were in the 1917 Code and so it was easier to transfer them to the new Code, rather than reconsider whether they should be in it at all. I shall highlight two main areas.

1. Remnants of a Contractual Understanding: Although the Second Vatican Council spoke of marriage in terms of a covenant, the 1983 Code still uses contractual language. I have already suggested that it possibly does not matter legally which term is used, but there is definitely one area of the present law where a contractual understanding puts it contrary to the Conciliar understanding of marriage. The area of law concerned is conditional consent (sometimes called conditioned

November 1965.

12. The Decree on the Eastern Catholic Churches: *Vatican II* (bibliog. I),

consent).[13] The notion of adding conditions to marital
consent is treating marriage as a contract where conditions can be added to the transaction by the parties.
But if marriage is to be compared to a covenant, as
the Council taught, then it must be unconditional as is
God's love for his people. Indeed, article 9 of Pope Paul
VI's encyclical *Humanae vitae* describes marital love
as "total"—it is unconditional and unlimited.

2. Emphasis on the Sexual Dimension and not on Love:
While the Council speaks of marriage as a community
of love and also as the intimate sharing of marital life
and love,[14] there are elements of the present law which
still emphasize the sexual dimension of marriage to the
detriment of the other dimensions—such as love. That
is, the Council's treatment of marital love is not transferred into the revised Code. It could be argued that
love is not a canonical concept because it is invisible
and is difficult to describe in legal language. But marital consent is also invisible and is a most complicated
concept. Despite these problems, ecclesiastical tribunals spend a lot of their time discussing marital consent. Thus, love could also be included in the canons of
the Code. I have explained that the nearest the present
Code comes to talking about love is when it uses the
expression "the good of the spouses."[15] I certainly welcome the inclusion of this expression, but the Conciliar
emphasis on marital love is not found in the Code.

Orientalium Ecclesiarum, 21 November 1964, art. 18.
    13. Canon 1102.
    14. "communitas amoris" and "intima communitas vitae et amoris coniugalis."
Vatican II (bibliog. I), *Gaudium et spes,* 7 December 1965, arts. 47 and 48,
respectively.

The absence of love in the Code is most obvious
when one considers canon 1101 §2 on simulation and
how ecclesiastical tribunals apply their understanding of Saint Augustine to it. For Augustine, the principal reason why marriage is good is because of the
love and friendship that exists between the spouses. He
then adds a very brief supplement to his argument. He
explains that there are three aspects of marriage (children, fidelity, and permanence) which are themselves
good and so make marriage as a whole good. When tribunals apply canon 1101 §2, they can declare marriages
invalid if one of these three aspects is deliberately excluded by a party at the time he or she enters the marriage. This is called *partial simulation*.

But what about the exclusion of love (as in the hypothetical case put forward by Arturo Jemolo)? I welcome the fact that more tribunals are declaring marriages invalid because the good of the spouses has been
excluded. But there is still great hesitation about using
the actual term *love*—as if it has no place in law. I acknowledge that the term can be understood purely sub-
jectively. It is also possible, however, to describe objective criteria for marital love—for example, recognizing
the needs of one's spouse and the call for self-sacri-
fice.

It has been seen that during the drafting of the 1983
Code it was felt that any attempt to define love would
result in giving it a fixed legal description which would
lack the necessary flexibility and would fail to do justice to what love actually is. Nevertheless, although the
Code could mention marital love, it need not attempt a

definition of it. Descriptions of marital love could be provided by judges when they give their decisions about marriage cases. That is, jurisprudence would gradually provide objective descriptions of love.

Another example of where the Code might be expected to mention love is in connection with canon 1099 concerning error. It has been seen that in certain circumstances this canon allows a marriage to be declared invalid if one of the parties was in error about the unity, indissolubility, or sacramental dignity of marriage. As love is so central to marriage, then error concerning it can also have most damaging consequences.

Although Gratian's *Decretum* was never the official law of the Church, it proved to be highly influential. According to Gratian, a marriage begins with the consent of the couple but is not absolutely indissoluble until it has been consummated sexually. This gave credibility to the practice of dissolving non-consummated marriages. I have stated that I believe this practice does not fit comfortably with the Conciliar understanding of marriage. While Vatican II speaks of the intimate sharing of the whole of life, the dissolution of an unconsummated marriage focuses on purely one dimension—the sexual. I also think that such a practice could easily be a counter-sign with regard to the permanence and sanctity of marriage.

Gratian's *Decretum* has also promoted the Pauline Privilege within the Church. That is, only sexual intercourse between two baptized spouses can make present the indissoluble bond that exists between Christ and his Church. Thus, if the spouses are not baptized, then the marriage can be dissolved. I have shown that this principle is also applied to those marriages where only one spouse is baptized (dissolutions in Favor of the Faith). The present law of the Church continues to allow the Pauline Privilege and dissolutions in Favor of the Faith. I still have concerns that these dissolutions could be seen to undermine the Church's teaching on the permanence of marriage. Moreover, Gratian's original reasoning for such dissolutions focuses on the role of sexual intercourse—which, in the light of the Council, is only one aspect of marriage.

I have explained that another effect of Gratian's emphasis on sexual intercourse is that impotence is regarded as an impediment to marriage. Again, I believe that this ignores the totality of marriage as taught by the Second Vatican Council. Instead, it focuses on just the sexual dimension of marriage. Those suffering from impotence can still establish communities of love where marital life and love are intimately shared. Thus, the fact that they are not permitted to marry could be regarded as discriminatory. I do acknowledge that the official position of the Catholic Church is that this is an impediment of natural law and so it cannot simply be removed from the law. I shall soon return to this when I conclude by giving some possible areas for development of the law.

Possible Developments of the Present Law of Marriage

I shall conclude my analysis of the present law of marriage by daring to suggest some possible areas for development. These suggestions come from my re-examination of the law's primary sources, its historical development, and how it compares with the Second Vatican Council's vision of marriage. I wish to mention six areas.

1. It should no longer be permitted to add conditions to marital consent. I have already indicated that this promotes a contractual understanding of marriage. The Second Vatican Council described marriage as a covenant whereby each spouse gives himself or herself totally and unreservedly to the other, and the 1990 Code of Canon Law for the Eastern Catholic Churches says that any conditions attached to a marriage make it invalid.[16] Hopefully, the Latin tradition of the Church will follow suit.

2. Love must be central to the canon law of marriage. Although the Code could not be expected to provide a definition of marital love, it could refer to it. This would provide a basis for judges to build up a new area of jurisprudence giving a description of love using objective Christian criteria. Obviously, care must be taken to avoid any errors based on subjectivism—for example, one common error would be the false claim that a marriage only remains in existence as long as the spouses love each other.

---

15. "bonum coniugum."

452 WHAT BRINGS A MARRIAGE INTO EXISTENCE?

3. To go through a wedding ceremony with the intention of excluding love is not just to exclude a *part* of marriage; it is to exclude marriage *itself.* Canon lawyers would call this "total simulation." This answers the concerns of Arturo Jemolo. To go through a wedding ceremony and deliberately exclude fidelity, permanence, or children is to exclude an essential part of marriage, but to exclude love is something more fundamental. It is to exclude marriage itself.

4. I humbly suggest that those in authority in the Church reconsider whether the practice of dissolving unconsummated marriages should continue. The same can be said for the Pauline Privilege and dissolutions in Favor of the Faith. I have absolutely no doubt that these favors can be granted, but I have already raised two concerns regarding them. The first is about the primary sources which are often used to promote these practices. My second concern is that there is a possibility that such dissolutions could be interpreted so as to undermine the Church's teaching on the permanence and sanctity of marriage.

5. I have already explained that I think the present marriage law overemphasizes consummation. One consequence of this is the practice of dissolving unconsummated marriages. If this practice is to continue, then I would suggest that the same criteria be applied to consummation that are applied to consent. The 1983 Code has introduced a new criterion for consummation—it has to be performed "in a human manner." The insertion of this clause was to prevent marriages being regarded as consummated if sexual intercourse has only been achieved through force. Moreover, the term also means that the man and woman must have sufficient awareness of what they are doing. But how many couples consummate their marriages in the knowledge that they are making them absolutely indissoluble and that they are participating in the indissoluble bond that exists between Christ and his Church? Accordingly, I would suggest that there are many marriages, even with offspring, which could be dissolved because they have never been truly consummated "in a human manner." If the practice of dissolving unconsummated marriages is to continue, this could possibly open up a new area of jurisprudence.

6. Permanent impotence is officially regarded as a bar to marriage based on natural law. I wish to suggest two things. The first suggestion is that those in authority reconsider whether impotence is an impediment of natural law. My examination of Saint Augustine and the Second Vatican Council shows that love is central to marriage. Moreover, sexual intercourse is only one aspect of the whole of married life. Those suffering from impotence, such as the disabled and the elderly, can still enter a partnership of love. If, however, impotence is an impediment of natural law, then it cannot simply be removed from the Code. In this case, my second suggestion is that it be considered whether the Pope could use his ministerial power to dispense from the impediment in individual cases. That is, the same power used to dissolve non-consummated marriages could be used to help the creation of marriages. I acknowledge, however, that it is not for me to say what the Pope can and cannot do!

Finally

The question—What brings a marriage into existence?—might appear to have no practical consequences. But I have shown that the answer given by such people as Gratian has resulted in the role of sexual intercourse being overemphasized. I have explained how the 1917 Code introduced the concept of the primary and secondary ends into the Church's understanding of marriage. Eventually, this concept was removed by the Second Vatican Council and the resulting 1983 Code. I suggest that the next development within the canon law of marriage should involve restoring the balance away from the sexual back toward marital love seen as a whole. The Second Vatican Council began the process of restoring this balance. Through prayer and reflection, this process will continue. I hope that this book, in its own little way, may be of some use.

BIBLIOGRAPHY

This Bibliography is divided into three sections:

I.) Official ecclesiastical documents (arranged by date);

II.) Rotal decisions (arranged alphabetically by author, by date); and

III.) Other primary and all secondary sources (arranged alphabetically by author, by date).

All biblical excerpts are from this source (unless stated to be otherwise):

Wansbrough, H (general editor), *The New Jerusalem Bible*, Standard Edition, Darton, Longman and Todd, London, 1985.

Other biblical texts consulted include the following:

Berry, G, *Interlinear Greek-English New Testament*, Broadman, Nashville, TN, USA, 1985.

Souter, A (ed), *Novum Testamentum Graece*, Clarendon, Oxford, 1910.

Section I

OFFICIAL
ECCLESIASTICAL DOCUMENTS
(arranged by date)

The following abbreviations are used to point to works in this section:

1917 Code: *Codex Iuris Canonici Pii X*, 1917. (See below for details.)

1983 Code: *Codex Iuris Canonici Auctoritate Ioannis Pauli*, 1983. (See below for details.)

1990 Eastern Code: *Codex Canonum Ecclesiarum Orientalium*, 1990. (See below for details.)

Innocent I, *Ad Exsuperium*, 20 February 405, in Migne (ed), *Patrologiae Latina* (bibliog. III), vol. 20, cols. 495–501.

Eleventh Council of Carthage, canon 8, *circa* 407, in Migne (ed), *Patrologiae Latina* (bibliog. III), vol. 67, cols. 215–16.

Leo I, *Epistula clix (Ad Nicetam)*, 21 March 458, in Migne (ed), *Patrologiae Latina* (bibliog. III), vol. 54, cols. 1135–40.

————, *Epistula clxvii (Ad Rusticum)*, *circa* 458–59, in Migne (ed), *Patrologiae Latina* (bibliog. III), vol. 54, cols. 1198–1209.

Council of Friuli, *circa* 796–97, in Migne (ed), *Patrologiae Latina* (bibliog. III), vol. 99, cols. 283–302.

Nicholas I, *Responsa ad Consulta Bulgarorum*, 13 November

866, in Migne (ed), *Patrologiae Latina* (bibliog. III), vol. 119, cols. 978–1016.

Alexander III, decretals, 1159–81:

> *Solet frequenter*, in Friedberg (ed), *Quinque Compilationes Antiquae* (bibliog. III), *Compilatio Prima, Book 4, title 4, ch. 4.*
>
> *Consuluit*, in Friedberg (ed), *Quinque Compilationes Antiquae* (bibliog. III), *Compilatio Prima*, Book 4, title 16, ch. 2.
>
> *Ex transmissa*, in Gregory IX, *Decretales* (bibliog. III), 2, 13, 8.
>
> *Verum post consensum*, in Gregory IX, *Decretales* (bibliog. III), 3, 32, 2.
>
> *Ex publico*, in Gregory IX, *Decretales* (bibliog. III), 3, 32, 7.
>
> *De illis autem*, in Gregory IX, *Decretales* (bibliog. III), 4, 1, 5.
>
> *Ex parte C.*, in Gregory IX, *Decretales* (bibliog. III), 4, 1, 9.
>
> *Veniens ad apostolicam*, in Gregory IX, *Decretales* (bibliog. III), 4, 1, 13.
>
> *Quum locum*, in Gregory IX, *Decretales* (bibliog. III), 4, 1, 14.
>
> *Veniens ad nos*, in Gregory IX, *Decretales* (bibliog. III), 4, 1, 15.
>
> *Commissum*, in Gregory IX, *Decretales* (bibliog. III), 4, 1, 16.
>
> *De illis*, in Gregory IX, *Decretales* (bibliog. III), 4, 2, 9.
>
> *Quod nobis*, in Gregory IX, *Decretales* (bibliog. III), 4, 3, 2.
>
> *Licet praeter*, in Gregory IX, *Decretales* (bibliog. III), 4, 4, 3.
>
> *Tua fraternitas*, in Gregory IX, *Decretales* (bibliog. III), 4, 4, 4.
>
> *De illis*, in Gregory IX, *Decretales* (bibliog. III), 4, 5, 3.
>
> *Significavit nobis*, in Gregory IX, *Decretales* (bibliog. III), 4, 7, 2.
>
> *Pervenit ad nos*, in Gregory IX, *Decretales* (bibliog. III), 4, 8, 1.
>
> *Quoniam ex multis*, in Gregory IX, *Decretales* (bibliog. III), 4, 8, 2.
>
> *Proposuit nobis M.*, in Gregory IX, *Decretales* (bibliog. III), 4, 9, 2.

Ex literis, in Gregory IX, *Decretales* (bibliog. III),
4, 14, 1.
Ex literis, in Gregory IX, *Decretales* (bibliog. III),
4, 15, 3.
Literae quas tua, in Gregory IX, *Decretales*
(bibliog. III), 4, 16, 1.

Innocent III, decretals, 1198–1216:
    Ex parte tua, in Gregory IX, *Decretales* (bibliog.
    III), 3, 32, 14.
    Constitutus in praesentia, in Gregory IX,
    Decretales (bibliog. III), 3, 32, 15.
    Quum apud sedem, in Gregory IX, *Decretales*
    (bibliog. III), 4, 1, 23.
    Tua nos duxit, in Gregory IX, *Decretales*
    (bibliog. III), 4, 1, 26.
    Tuas dudum, in Gregory IX, *Decretales*
    (bibliog. III), 4, 4, 5.
    Per tuas, in Gregory IX, *Decretales* (bibliog. III),
    4, 5, 6.
    De infidelibus, in Gregory IX, *Decretales*
    (bibliog. III), 4, 14, 4.
    Fraternitatis tuae, in Gregory IX, *Decretales*
    (bibliog. III), 4, 15, 6.
    Quanto te, in Gregory IX, *Decretales* (bibliog.
    III), 4, 19, 7.
    Gaudemus in Domino, in Gregory IX, *Decretales*
    (bibliog. III), 4, 19, 8.

Honorius III, decretal, 1216–27: *Literae vestrae*, in Gregory IX,
Decretales (bibliog. III), 4, 15, 7.

Paul III, Apostolic Constitution, *Altitudo*, 1 June 1537, in *1917
Code* (bibliog. I), 750–51 (Document VI).

Council of Trent, Session 7, *Decretum de Sacramentis*, 3 March
1547, in Denzinger, *Enchiridion Symbolorum* (bibliog.
III), 381–84.

———, Session 21, *Doctrina de Communione sub utraque Specie
et Parvulorum*, 16 July 1562, in Denzinger, *Enchiridion
Symbolorum* (bibliog. III), 404–07.

———, Session 24, *Doctrina de Sacramento Matrimonii*, 11 November 1563, in Denzinger, *Enchiridion Symbolorum*
(bibliog. III), 415–17.

————, Session 24, *Canones super Reformatione circa Matrimonium: Decretum Tametsi*, 11 November 1563, in Denzinger, *Enchiridion Symbolorum* (bibliog. III), 417–18.

Pius V, Apostolic Constitution, *Romani Pontificis*, 2 August 1571, in *1917 Code* (bibliog. I), 751–52 (Document VII).

Gregory XIII, Apostolic Constitution, *Populis*, 25 January 1585, in *1917 Code* (bibliog. I), 752–54 (Document VIII).

Sixtus V, Letter, *Cum frequenter*, 27 June 1587, in Gasparri (ed), *Codex Iuris Canonici Fontes* (bibliog. III), vol. 1, cols. 298–99.

Benedict XIV, Declaration, *Matrimonia quae in locis*, 4 November 1741, in Denzinger, *Enchiridion Symbolorum* (bibliog. III), 500–501.

————, Epistle, *Postremo mense*, 28 February 1747, in Gasparri (ed), *Codex Iuris Canonici Fontes* (bibliog. III), vol. 2, col. 62–91.

————, Apostolic Constitution, *Apostolici ministerit*, 16 September 1747, in Gasparri (ed), *Codex Iuris Canonici Fontes* (bibliog. III), vol. 2, cols. 119–22.

————, Brief, *Singulari nobis*, 9 February 1749, in Denzinger, *Enchiridion Symbolorum* (bibliog. III), 511–12.

Leo XIII, Encyclical, *Arcanum*, 10 February 1880, in *Acta Sanctae Sedis* (bibliog. III) 12 (1879), 385–402.

Sacred Congregation of the Council, Response, *Ventimilien*, 19 May 1888, in *Acta Sanctae Sedis* (bibliog. III) 21 (1888), 162–81.

————, Decree, *Ne temere*, 2 August 1907, in *Acta Sanctae Sedis* (bibliog. III) 40 (1907), 525–30.

Codex Iuris Canonici Pii X Pontificis Maximi Iussu Digestus, Benedicti Papae XV Auctoritate Promulgatus, Praefatione Emi. Petri Card. Gasparri et Indice Analytico-Alphabetico Auctus, Typis Polyglottis Vaticanis, Vatican City, 1917.

Pius XI, Encyclical, *Casti connubii*, 31 December 1930, in *Acta Apostolicae Sedis* (bibliog. III) 22 (1930), 539–92.

Holy Office, Decree, *Circa Can. 1127 Codicis Iuris Canonici*, 10 June 1937, in *Acta Apostolicae Sedis* (bibliog. III) 29 (1937), 305–06.

Pius XII, Address to the Sacred Roman Rota, 3 October 1941, in *Acta Apostolicae Sedis* (bibliog. III) 33 (1941), 421–26.

Holy Office, Decree, *De finibus matrimonii*, 1 April 1944, in *Acta Apostolicae Sedis* (bibliog. III) 36 (1944), 103.

Pius XII, Encyclical, *Mediator Dei*, 20 November 1947, in *Acta Apostolicae Sedis* (bibliog. III) 39 (1947), 521–600.

————, Motu Proprio, *Decretum ne temere*, 1 August 1948, in *Acta Apostolicae Sedis* (bibliog. III) 40 (1948), 305–06.

————, Motu Proprio, *Crebrae allatae*, 22 February 1949, in *Acta Apostolicae Sedis* (bibliog. III) 41 (1949), 89–117.

————, *Allocutio Conventui Unionis Italicae inter Obstetrices*, 29 October 1951, in *Acta Apostolicae Sedis* (bibliog. III) 43 (1951), 835–54.

————, Motu Proprio, *Cleri sanctitati*, 2 June 1957, in *Acta Apostolicae Sedis* (bibliog. III) 49 (1957), 433–603.

John XXIII, Encyclical, *Pacem in Terris*, 11 April 1963, in *Acta Apostolicae Sedis* (bibliog. III) 55 (1963), 257–304.

Vatican II, *Sacrosanctum Concilium*, 4 December 1963, in *Acta Apostolicae Sedis* (bibliog. III) 56 (1964), 97–138.

Paul VI, Address to the Sacred College of Cardinals, 23 June 1964, in *Acta Apostolicae Sedis* (bibliog. III) 56 (1964), 581–89.

Vatican II, *Lumen gentium*, 21 November 1964, in *Acta Apostolicae Sedis* (bibliog. III) 57 (1965), 5–71.

————, *Orientalium Ecclesiarum*, 21 November 1964, in *Acta Apostolicae Sedis* (bibliog. III) 57 (1965), 76–89.

Paul VI, Address to the Commission for the Study of Problems of Population, Family and Birth, 27 March 1965, in *Acta Apostolicae Sedis* (bibliog. III) 57 (1965), 388–90.

Vatican II, *Christus Dominus*, 28 October 1965, in *Acta Apostolicae Sedis* (bibliog. III) 58 (1966), 673–701.

——, *Apostolicam actuositatem*, 18 November 1965, in *Acta Apostolicae Sedis* (bibliog. III) 58 (1966), 837–64.

——, *Gaudium et spes*, 7 December 1965, in *Acta Apostolicae Sedis* (bibliog. III) 58 (1966), 1025–1120.

Paul VI, Address to the National Congress of the Italian Society of Obstetrics and Gynaecology, 29 October 1966, in *Acta Apostolicae Sedis* (bibliog. III) 58 (1966), 1166–70,

——, Encyclical, *Humanae vitae*, 25 July 1968, in *Acta Apostolicae Sedis* (bibliog. III) 60 (1968), 481–503.

Sacred Congregation of Rites, Decree, *Ordo Celebrandi Matrimonium*, Typis Polyglottis, Vatican City, 1969.

Paul VI, Motu Proprio, *Matrimonia mixta*, 31 March 1970, in *Acta Apostolicae Sedis* (bibliog. III) 62 (1970), 257–63.

Sacred Congregation for the Doctrine of the Faith, Instruction, *Ut Notum Est*, 6 December 1973. (Not in *Acta Apostolicae Sedis*.) English translation in Woestman, *Special Marriage Cases* (bibliog. III), 129–34.

——, Decree, *Circa Impotentiam quae Matrimonium Dirimit*, 13 May 1977, in *Acta Apostolicae Sedis* (bibliog. III) 69 (1977), 426.

Paul VI, Address to the Roman Rota, 28 January 1978, in *Acta Apostolicae Sedis* (bibliog. III) 70 (1978), 181–86.

John Paul II, Apostolic Exhortation, *Familiaris consortio*, 22 November 1981, in *Acta Apostolicae Sedis* (bibliog. III) 74 (1982), 81–191.

——, Apostolic Constitution, *Sacrae disciplinae leges*, 25 January 1983, in *Acta Apostolicae Sedis* (bibliog. III) 75-Supplement (1983), vii–xiv.

Codex Iuris Canonici Auctoritate Ioannis Pauli PP. II Promulgatus, Libreria Editrice Vaticana, Vatican City, 1983. Also in *Acta Apostolicae Sedis* (bibliog. III) 75-Supplement (1983), 1–301.

John Paul II, Motu Proprio, *Recognito Iuris Canonici*, 2 January 1984, in *Acta Apostolicae Sedis* (bibliog. III) 76 (1984), 433–34.

————, Apostolic Constitution, *Pastor Bonus*, 28 June 1988, in *Acta Apostolicae Sedis* (bibliog. III) 80 (1988), 841–924, 1867.

————, Apostolic Constitution, *Sacri canones*, 18 October 1990, in *Acta Apostolicae Sedis* (bibliog. III) 82 (1990), 1033–44.

Codex Canonum Ecclesiarum Orientalium, Auctoritate Ioannis Pauli PP. II Promulgatus, Typis Polyglottis Vaticanis, Vatican City, 1990. Also in *Acta Apostolicae Sedis* (bibliog. III) 82 (1990), 1032–1363, 1702.

John Paul II, Address to the Roman Rota, 21 January 2000, in *Acta Apostolicae Sedis* (bibliog. III) 92 (2000), 350–55.

Congregation for the Doctrine of the Faith, Instruction, *Normae de Conficiendo Processu pro Solutione Vinculi Matrimonialis in Favorem Fidei*, 30 April 2001, Typis Vaticanis, Vatican City, 2001.
English text in Congregation for the Doctrine of the Faith, Instruction, *Norms on the Preparation of the Process for the Dissolution of the Marriage Bond in Favour of the Faith: Official Latin Text and English Translation*, Typis Vaticanis, Vatican City, 2003.

Pontificium Consilium de Legum Textibus, Letter, *Actus Formalis Defectionis ab Ecclesia Catholica* (Prot. N. 10279/2006), 13 March 2006.
English text in *Canon Law Society of Great Britain and Ireland Newsletter* 147 (September 2006), 9–11.

————, Benedict XVI, Motu Proprio, *Omnium* in *mentem*, 26 October 2009

Section II

ROTAL DECISIONS
(arranged alphabetically by author, by date)

Anné, Rotal decision of 25 February 1969, *Tribunalis Apostolici Sacrae Romanae Rotae Decisiones* 61 (1969), 174–92.

Bejam, Rotal decision of 19 October 1974, *Tribunalis Apostolici Sacrae Romanae Rotae Decisiones* 66 (1974), 648–53.

Bottone, Rotal decision of 8 June 2000, *Ius Ecclesiae* 13 (2001), 734–46.

Bruno, Rotal decision of 20 July 1973, *Tribunalis Apostolici Sacrae Romanae Rotae Decisiones* 65 (1973), 600–611.

———, Rotal decision of 8 July 1975, *Tribunalis Apostolici Rotae Romanae Decisiones* 67 (1975), 473–84.

———, Rotal decision of 21 March 1980, *Tribunalis Apostolici Rotae Romanae Decisiones* 72 (1980), 199–208.

———, Rotal decision of 19 July 1991, *Monitor Ecclesiasticus* 117 (1992), 167–85.

Burke, Rotal decision of 27 October 1994, *Studia Canonica* 30 (1996), 533–52.

Colagiovanni, Rotal decision of 8 May 1984, *Monitor Ecclesiasticus* 109 (1984), 327–34.

———, Rotal decision of 11 December 1985, *Monitor Ecclesiasticus* 111 (1986), 173–81.

De Lanversin, Rotal decision of 5 April 1995, *Ius Ecclesiae* 11 (1999), 125–36.

Di Felice, Rotal decision of 19 June 1984, *Apostolici Rotae Romanae Tribunalis Decisiones* 76 (1984), 346–56.

Doran, Rotal decision of 1 July 1988, *Monitor Ecclesiasticus* 114 (1989), 329–46.

Egan, Rotal decision of 13 November 1978, *Tribunalis Apostolici Rotae Romanae Decisiones* 70 (1978), 474–82.

Fagiolo, Rotal decision of 30 October 1970, *Tribunalis Apostolici Sacrae Romanae Rotae Decisiones* 62 (1970), 978–90.

Faltin, Rotal decision of 31 May 1995, *Ius Ecclesiae* 8 (1996), 121–44.

———, Rotal decision of 29 November 1995, *Monitor Ecclesiasticus* 121 (1996), 72–83.

Ferraro, Rotal decision of 6 February 1979, *Ephemerides Iuris Canonici* 35 (1979), 297–306.

Fiore, Rotal decision of 17 June 1981, *Apostolici Rotae Romanae Tribunalis Decisiones* 73 (1981), 326–33.

———, Rotal decision of 5 March 1985, *Ius Canonicum* 27 (1987), 225–31.

Funghini, Rotal decision of 19 December 1994, *Monitor Ecclesiasticus* 121 (1996), 33–57.

Huot, Rotal decision of 29 January 1981, *Il Diritto Ecclesiastico* 92-2 (1981), 480–86.

Jarawan, Rotal decision of 19 June 1984, *Apostolici Rotae Romanae Tribunalis Decisiones* 76 (1989), 367–79.

Masala, Rotal decision of 17 December 1985, *Monitor Ecclesiasticus* 112 (1987), 188–209.

Palestro, Rotal decision of 24 June 1987, *Monitor Ecclesiasticus* 112 (1987), 472–83.

Parisella, Rotal decision of 25 March 1971, *Tribunalis Apostolici Sacrae Romanae Rotae Decisiones* 63 (1971), 207–12.

————, Rotal decision of 10 January 1980, *Tribunalis Apostolici Rotae Romanae Decisiones* 72 (1980), 1–8.

Pinto, Rotal decision of 2 May 1977, *Ephemerides Iuris Canonici* 35 (1979), 244–48.

————, Rotal decision of 12 February 1982, *Monitor Ecclesiasticus* 107 (1982), 448–57.

————, Rotal decision of 9 December 1983, *Apostolici Rotae Romanae Tribunalis Decisiones* 75 (1983), 695–701.

————, Rotal decision of 14 December 1984, *Monitor Ecclesiasticus* 113 (1988), 445–54.

————, Rotal decision of 20 February 1987, *Ius Ecclesiae* 1 (1989), 569–81.

Pompedda, Rotal decision of 26 May 1981, *Apostolici Rotae Romanae Tribunalis Decisiones* 73 (1981), 307–11.

————, Rotal decision of 19 October 1990, *Ius Ecclesiae* 4 (1992), 153–61.

Ragni, Rotal decision of 26 November 1985, *Il Diritto Ecclesiastico* 97-2 (1986), 29–40.

————, Rotal decision of 11 July 1986, *Il Diritto Ecclesiastico* 97-2 (1986), 475–87.

Sabattani, Rotal decision of 24 February 1961, *Tribunalis Apostolici Sacrae Romanae Rotae Decisiones* 53 (1961), 116–32.

Serrano, Rotal decision of 15 November 1977, *Tribunalis Apostolici Rotae Romanae Decisiones* 69 (1977), 457–67.

————, Rotal decision of 12 November 1982, *Il Diritto Ecclesiastico* 94-2 (1983), 3–9.

————, Rotal decision of 20 January 1994, *Monitor Ecclesiasticus* 122 (1997), 361–66.

Stankiewicz, Rotal decision of 5 April 1979, *Monitor Ecclesiasticus* 104 (1979), 425–42.

————, Rotal decision of 14 November 1985, *Il Diritto Ecclesiastico* 97-2 (1986), 324–33.

————, Rotal decision of 19 November 1985, *Il Diritto Ecclesiastico* 97-2 (1986), 311–24.

————, Rotal decision of 25 October 2001, *Anuario Argentino de Derecho Canónico* 10 (2003), 333–60.

Wynen, Rotal decision of 22 January 1944, *Acta Apostolicae Sedis* (bibliog. III) 36 (1944), 179–200.

Section III

OTHER PRIMARY
AND ALL SECONDARY SOURCES
(arranged alphabetically by author, by date)

The following abbreviation is used to point to works in this section:

> **Digest**: **Krueger et al. (eds)**, *Corpus Iuris Civilis*. (See **Krueger** for details.) English translation: **Watson (ed)**, *The Digest of Justinian*. (See **Watson** for details.) References to *The Digest of Justinian / Corpus Iuris Civilis* will take this form: *Digest* (bibliog. III), book number, title number, fragment number, paragraph number.

In this section, primary sources are in **boldface type**.

1980 Synod of Bishops, "A Message to Christian Families in the Modern World," ***Origins*** **10 (1980), 321–25.**

Abate, A, *Il Matrimonio nell'Attuale Legislazione Canonica*, 2nd edition, Urbaniana University Press, Rome, 1982.

———, *Il Matrimonio nella Nuova Legislazione Canonica*, Urbaniana University Press, Rome, 1982.

***Acta Apostolicae Sedis*, Typis Polyglottis Vaticanis, Rome, 1909–.**

Acta et Documenta Concilio Oecumenico Vaticano II Apparando: Series I (Antepraeparatoria) **and** ***Series II (Praeparatoria)*, Typis Polyglottis Vaticanis, Rome, 1960–.**

469

Acta Sanctae Sedis, Typis Polyglottis Vaticanis, Rome, 1865–1908. This publication was succeeded by *Acta Apostolicae Sedis*—the official gazette of the Holy See.

Acta Synodalia Sacrosancti Concilii Oecumenici Vaticani II, Typis Polyglottis Vaticanis, Rome, 1970–80.

Alberigo, G (ed), *History of Vatican II*, Komonchak, J (editor of English version), 5 volumes, Orbis, Maryknoll, NY, USA, 1995–2006.

Alesandro, J, *Gratian's Notion of Marital Consummation*, Officium Libri Catholici, Rome, 1971.

————, "The Revision of the *Code of Canon Law*: A Background Study," Studia *Canonica* 24 (1990), 91–146.

Ambrose, St., *Liber de Institutione Virginis*, in Migne (ed), *Patrologiae Latina* (bibliog. III), vol. 16: cols. 319–48.

Aquinas, St. Thomas, *Summa Theologica (Editio Altera Romana)*, 6 volumes, vol. 5, *Tertiae Partis Supplementum*, Forzani and Co., Rome, 1894.

Augustine, St., *De Genesi contra Manichaeos*, in Migne (ed), *Patrologiae Latina* (bibliog. III), vol. 34: cols. 173–220.

————, *De Bono Coniugali*, in Migne (ed), *Patrologiae Latina* (bibliog. III), vol. 40: cols. 373–96. English translation in Augustine, "On the Good of Marriage" in Wilcox (trans), *The Fathers* (bibliog. III), vol. 27, 9–51.

————, *De Sancta Virginitate*, in Migne (ed), *Patrologiae Latina* (bibliog. III), vol. 40: cols. 397–428.

————, *Contra Julianum*, in Migne (ed), *Patrologiae Latina* (bibliog. III), vol. 44: cols. 641–874. English translation in Augustine, "Against Julian," in Schumacher (trans), *The Fathers* (bibliog. III), vol. 35.

Barrett, R, "Reflections on the *Bonum Coniugum*," *Monitor Ecclesiasticus* 124 (1999), 514–35.

Barry, J, "The Tridentine Form of Marriage: Is the Law Unreasonable?" *The Jurist* 20 (1960), 159–78.

Bassett, W (ed), *The Bond of Marriage: An Ecumenical and Inter-disciplinary Study*, The University of Notre Dame Press, London, 1968.

Béraudy, R, "*Le Mariage des Chrétiens*," *Nouvelle Revue Théologique* 104 (1982), 50–69.

Bernard, J, "*Sens de la Forme de Mariage*," *Revue de Droit Canonique* 30 (1980), 187–205.

Bersini, F, "*Il Decreto circa L'Impotenza che Dirime il Matrimonio e la Problematica da esso Suscitata*," *Il Diritto Ecclesiastico* 90-2 (1979), 228–41.

Bertolino, R, "*Gli Elementi Constitutivi del 'Bonum Coniugum'*: *Stato della Questione*," *Monitor Ecclesiasticus* 120 (1995), 557–86.

Boccafola, K, *The Requirement of Perpetuity for the Impediment of Impotence*, Gregorian University, Rome, 1975.

———, "Deceit and Induced Error about a Personal Quality," *Monitor Ecclesiasticus* 124 (1999), 692–710.

Bogdan, L, "Simple Convalidation of Marriage in the 1983 Code of Canon Law," *The Jurist* 46 (1986), 511–31.

Bonnet, P, et al. (eds), *La Simulazione del Consenso Matrimoniale Canonico*, (*Studi Giuridici* XXII), Libreria Editrice Vaticana, Vatican City, 1990.

———, et al. (eds), *Errore e Dolò nel Consenso Matrimoniale Canonico*, (*Studi Giuridici* XXXIX), Libreria Editrice Vaticana, Vatican City, 1995.

———, et al. (eds), *L'Incapacità di Intendere e di Volere nel Diritto Matrimoniale Canonico (can. 1095 nn. 1–2)*, (*Studi Giuridici* LII), Libreria Editrice Vaticana, Vatican City, 2000.

Bouscaren, T, and Ellis, A, *Canon Law: A Text and Commentary*, 2nd edition, The Bruce Publishing Company, Milwaukee, WI, USA, 1951.

Brown, P, *The Rise of Western Christendom: Triumph and Diversity AD 200–1000*, Blackwell, Oxford, 1996.

Brundage, J, *Law, Sex, and Christian Society in Medieval Europe*, The University of Chicago Press, Chicago, 1987.
——, *Sex, Law and Marriage in the Middle Ages*, (Collected Studies Series CS397), Variorum Publishers, Aldershot, England, 1993.

Buckley, T, *What Binds Marriage? Roman Catholic Theology in Practice*, Geoffrey Chapman Publishers, London, 1997.

Bullough, V, and Brundage, J (eds), *Sexual Practices and the Medieval Church*, Prometheus Press, Buffalo, 1982.

Burchard of Worms, *Decretorum Libri Viginti*, in Migne (ed), *Patrologiae Latina* (bibliog. III), vol. 140: cols. 537–1058.

Burke, C, "The *Bonum Coniugum* and the *Bonum Prolis*—Ends or Properties of Marriage?" *The Jurist* 49 (1989), 704–13.

——, "Some Reflections on Canon 1095," *Monitor Ecclesiasticus* 117 (1992), 133–50.

——, "The Sacramentality of Marriage: Canonical Reflections," *Monitor Ecclesiasticus* 119 (1994), 545–66.

——, "The Object of the Marital Self-Gift as Presented in Canon 1057 §2," *Studia Canonica* 31 (1997), 403–21.

——, "Progressive Jurisprudential Thinking," *The Jurist* 58 (1998), 437–78.

——, "Simulated Consent," *Forum* 9 (1998), 65–82.

Candelier, G, "*L'Impuissance, Empêchement et Sign d'une Incapacité*," *Revue de Droit Canonique* 44 (1994), 93–145.

——, "Le 'Bonum Prolis': Doctrine et Évolution de la Jurisprudence," *Studia Canonica* 34 (2000), 197–246.

Caparros, E, and Thériault, M, and Thorn, J (eds), *Code of Canon Law Annotated*, Wilson & Lafleur Limited, Montreal, 1993.

Carcopino, J, *Daily Life in Ancient Rome*, Penguin Books, Harmondsworth, 1956.

Carlen, C (ed), *The Papal Encyclicals 1873–1903*, McGrath Publishing Company, Raleigh, NC, USA, 1981.
Carmignani Caridi, S, "The '*Error Personae vel Qualitatis Personae*' in Rotal Jurisprudence," *Forum* 3 (1992), 67–96.

Cavallera, F, *Thesaurus Doctrinae Catholicae ex Documentis Magisterii Ecclesiastici*, Gabriel Beauchesne and Sons, Paris, 1936.

Celeghin, A, "*Sacra Potestas: Quaestio Post-Conciliaris*," *Periodica* 84 (1985), 165–225.

Chadwick, H, *The Early Church* (*The Pelican History of the Church*, vol. 1), Penguin Books, Harmondsworth, Middlesex, 1983.

Chrysostom, St. John (attributed to), *Opus Imperfectum in Matthaeum, Homilia xxxii*, in Migne (ed), *Patrologiae Graeca* (bibliog. III), vol. 56: cols. 798–805.

Cicognani, A, *Canon Law: I, Introduction to the Study of Canon Law; II, History of the Sources of Canon Law; III, A Commentary on Book I of the Code*, O'Hara, J, and Brennan, F (trans), 2nd edition, Dolphin Press, Philadelphia, 1935.

Ciprotti, P, "*Nullité et Dissolution du Mariage: Aspects Anciens et Récents*," *L'Année Canonique* 32 (1989), 179–95.

Clark, E (editor), *St. Augustine on Marriage and Sexuality*, The Catholic University of America Press, Washington, D.C., 1996.

Colagiovanni, E, "*Immaturità: Per un Approccio Interdisciplinare alla Comprehensione ed Applicazione del Can. 1095, no. 2 et 3*," *Monitor Ecclesiasticus* 113 (1988), 337–59.

Colish, M, *Peter Lombard*, 2 volumes, E.J.Brill, New York, 1994.

Collins, R, *Divorce in the New Testament*, (Good News Studies 38), Michael Glazier, Wilmington, DE, USA, 1992.

Connery, J, "The Role of Love in Christian Marriage: A Historical Overview," *Communio* 11 (1984), 244–57.

Connolly, P, "Contrasts in the Western and Eastern Approaches to Marriage," *Studia Canonica* 35 (2001), 357–402.

Coriden, J, *The Indissolubility Added to Christian Marriage by Consummation: An Historical Study of the Period from the End of the Patristic Age to the Death of Pope Innocent III (Excerpts),* Catholic Book Agency, Rome, 1961.

Cornes, A, *Divorce and Remarriage: Biblical Principles and Pastoral Practice*, William B. Eerdmans Publishing Company, Grand Rapids, MI, USA, 1993.

Cosgrove, A, "Consent, Consummation and Indissolubility: Some Evidence from Medieval Ecclesiastical Courts," *The Downside Review* 109 (1991), 94–104.

Cunningham, R, "Principles Guiding the Revision of the Code of Canon Law," *The Jurist* 30 (1970), 447–55.

———, "Marriage and the Nescient Catholic: Questions of Faith and Sacrament," *Studia Canonica* 15 (1981), 263–83.

———, "When Gratian Worked for the Tribunal," *The Jurist* 56 (1997), 632–56.

Dacanay, A, *"Matrimonium Ratum: Significatio Termini,"* *Periodica* 89 (1990), 69–89.

Damizia, G, *"Vasectomia e Matrimonio,"* *Apollinaris* 51 (1978), 146–93.

D'Avack, P, *"Il Problema dell'Impotenza nel Matrimonio Canonico,"* *Revue de Droit Canonique* 28 (1978), 123–29.

David, B, *L'Impuissance est-elle un Empêchement de Droit Naturel ou Positif?* Gregorian University, Rome, 1981.

Decker, R, "Institutional Authority versus Personal Responsibility in the Marriage Sections of Gratian's *A Concordance of Discordant Canons*," *The Jurist* 32 (1972), 51–65.

Denzinger, H, *Enchiridion Symbolorum, Definitionum et Declarationum de Rebus Fidei et Morum; quod Primum Editit Henricus Denzinger; et quod Funditus Retractavit Auxit Notulis Ornavit Adolfus Schönmetzer S.I.*, 33rd edition, Herder, Rome, 1965.

Dewhirst, J, "*Consortium Vitae, Bonum Coniugum* and their Relation to Simulation: A Continuing Challenge to Modern Jurisprudence," *The Jurist* 55 (1995), 794–812.

Digest: Krueger et al. (eds), *Corpus Iuris Civilis*. (See Krueger for details.) English translation: Watson (ed), *The Digest of Justinian*. (See Watson for details.) References to *The Digest of Justinian / Corpus Iuris Civilis* will take this form: *Digest* (bibliog. III), book number, title number, fragment number, paragraph number.

Di Mattia, G, "*La Dottrina sulla Forma Canonica del Matrimonio e la Proposta per un suo Reisame*," *Apollinaris* 44 (1971), 471–522.

Doms, H, *The Meaning of Marriage*, (translated by Sayer, G), Sheed and Ward, London, 1939.

Donnelly, F, "The Helena Decision of 1924," *The Jurist* 34 (1976), 442–49.

Doyle, T, "A New Look at the *Bonum Fidei*," *Studia Canonica* 12 (1978), 5–40.

———, et al. (editors), *Marriage Studies*, 5 volumes at present, Canon Law Society of America/Catholic University of America, Washington, D.C., 1980–.

Dunderdale, E, "The Canonical Form of Marriage: Anachronism or Pastoral Necessity?" *Studia Canonica* 12 (1978), 41–55.

Egan, E, "The Nullity of Marriage for Reason of Insanity or Lack of Due Discretion of Judgment," *Ephemerides Iuris Canonici* 39 (1983), 9–53.

Faltin, D, "The Exclusion of the Sacramentality of Marriage with

476   WHAT BRINGS A MARRIAGE INTO EXISTENCE?

Particular Reference to the Marriage of Baptized Non-Be-
lievers" in Doyle, T, et al. (eds), *Marriage Studies* (bibliog. III).

Fee, G, *The First Epistle to the Corinthians*, (The New International Commentary on the New Testament), William B.
Eerdmans Publishing Company, Grand Rapids, MI, USA,
1987.

Fellhauer, D, "The Exclusion of Indissolubility: Old Principles and
New Jurisprudence," *Studia Canonica* 9 (1975), 105–33.

Filipiak, M, *"Matrimonia Mixta: Commentarium,"* *Ephemerides
Iuris Canonici* 26 (1970), 346–51.

**Flannery, A (general editor), *Vatican Council II: The Conciliar
and Post Conciliar Documents*, Costello Publishing
Company, New York, 1981 (revised edition).**

**―――― (general editor), *Vatican Council II: More Post Con-
ciliar Documents*, (Vatican Collection, vol. 2), Costello
Publishing Company, New York, 1982.**

Flint, V, *"Hinkmar von Reims. De Divortio Lotharii Regis et
Theutbergae Reginae* (Short Notice)," *Journal of Ecclesiastical History* 46 (1995), 168.

Franceschi, H, *"L'Oggetto dell'Esclusione del 'Bonum Fidei' nella Giurisprudenza della Rota Romana,"* *Ius Ecclesiae* 12
(2000), 757–83.

Frend, W, *The Rise of Christianity*, Darton, Longman and Todd,
London, 1984.

**Friedberg, A (ed), *Quinque Compilationes Antiquae nec non
Collectio Canonum Lipsiensis*, Bernhard Tauchnitz
Publisher, Leipzig, 1882.**

Gallagher, C, "Marriage in the Revised Canon Law for the Eastern
Churches," *Studia Canonica* 24 (1990), 69–90.

**Gasparri, P (ed), *Codex Iuris Canonici Pii X Pontificis Maximi
Iussu Digestus, Benedicti Papae XV Auctoritate Promulgatus, Praefatione, Fontium Annotatione et Indice***

Analytico-Alphabetico, Typis Polyglottis Vaticanis, Rome, 1917.

——— (ed), *Codex Iuris Canonici Fontes*, 9 volumes, Typis Polyglottis Vaticanis, Rome, 1923–39.

Gauthier, A, *Roman Law and Its Contribution to the Development of Canon Law*, 2nd edition, Saint Paul University, Ottawa, 1996.

Germovnik, F, and Thériault, M, *Indices ad Corpus Iuris Canonici*, 2nd edition, Saint Paul University, Ottawa, 2000.

Gietl, A (ed), *Sentenzen Rolands nachmals Papstes Alexander III*, Herder, Freidburg im Breisgau, 1891.

Gordon, I, *"Adnotationes Quaedam De Valore Matrimonii Vivorum Qui Ex Toto Secti Sunt a Tempore Gratiani Usque ad Breve 'Cum Frequenter,'" Periodica* 66 (1977), 171–247.

Grant, R, *Augustus to Constantine: The Thrust of the Christian Movement in the Roman World*, Collins, London, 1971.

Gratian, *Concordia Discordantium Canonum*, in Richter, A, and Friedberg, A (eds), *Corpus Iuris Canonici*, 2nd edition, 2 volumes, vol. 1, *Pars Prior: Decretum Magistri Gratiani*, Bernhard Tauchnitz Publisher, Leipzig, 1922.

Green, T, "The Revised Schema *De Matrimonio*: Text, Reflections," *The Jurist* 40 (1980), 57–127.

———, "Reflections on the Eastern Code Revision Process," *The Jurist* 51 (1991), 18–37.

Gregory IX, *Decretales Gregorii Papae IX*, in Richter, A, and Friedberg, A (eds), *Corpus Iuris Canonici*, 2nd edition, 2 volumes, vol. 2, *Pars Secunda: Decretalium Collectiones*, Bernhard Tauchnitz Publisher, Leipzig, 1922, columns 1–928. References take this form: Gregory IX, *Decretales* (bibliog. III), book number, title number, chapter number.

Grootaers, J, and Selling, J, *The 1980 Synod of Bishops "On the Role of the Family": An Exposition of the Event and an Analysis of Its Texts*, (Bibliotheca Ephemeridum Theologicarum Lovaniensium, vol. 64), Leuven University Press, Louvain, Belgium, 1983.

Guindon, A, "Case for a 'Consummated' Sexual Bond before a 'Ratified' Marriage," *Église et Théologie* 8 (1977), 137–81.

Guiry, R, "Immaturity, Maturity and Christian Marriage," *Studia Canonica* 25 (1991), 93–114.

Heany, S, *The Development of the Sacramentality of Marriage from Anselm of Laon to Thomas Aquinas*, Catholic University of America Press, Washington, D.C., 1963.

Heredia, C, "*Importancia Canónica de la Primera Cópula Conyugal*," *Anuario Argentino de Derecho Canónico* 8 (2001), 57–74.

Hilbert, M, "*Error in Qualitate Personae (c. 1097 §2)*," *Periodica* 87 (1998), 403–42.

Hillman, E, "Polygamy and the Council of Trent," *The Jurist* 33 (1973), 358–76.

Himes, M, "The Intrinsic Sacramentality of Marriage: The Theological Ground for the Inseparability of Validity and Sacramentality in Marriage," *The Jurist* 50 (1990), 198–220.

Hincmar of Rheims, *De Nuptiis Stephani, et Filiae Regimundi Comitis*, in Migne (ed), *Patrologiae Latina* (bibliog. III), vol. 126: cols. 132–54.

———, *De Divortio Lotharii et Tetbergae*, in Migne (ed), *Patrologiae Latina* (bibliog. III), vol. 125: cols. 619–772.

Huber, J, "*Indissolubilitas Matrimonii, estne Norma Iuridica an Praeceptum Morale?*" *Periodica* 89 (1990), 91–118.

Hudson, J, "Marital Consummation According to Ecclesiastical Legislation," *Studia Canonica* 12 (1978), 93–123.

Hugh of St. Victor, *De Beatae Mariae Virginitate*, in Migne (ed), *Patrologiae Latina* (bibliog. III), vol. 176: cols. 857–76.

————, *De Sacramentis Fidei Christianae*, in Migne (ed), *Patrologiae Latina* (bibliog. III), vol. 176: cols. 173–618.

————, *De Sacramento Coniugii*, in Migne (ed), *Patrologiae Latina* (bibliog. III), vol. 176: cols. 479–520.

Husslein, J (ed), *Social Wellsprings*, 2 volumes, vol. 2,

Eighteen Encyclicals of Social Reconstruction by Pius XI, Bruce Publishing Company, Milwaukee, WI, USA, 1943.

The International Commission on English in the Liturgy, *The Rites of the Catholic Church as Revised by Decree of the Second Vatican Ecumenical Council and Published by Authority of Pope Paul VI*, Study Edition, 2 volumes, vol. 1, Pueblo Publishing Company, New York, 1976.

Isidore of Seville, St., *Libri Etymologiarum*, in Migne (ed), *Patrologiae Latina* (bibliog. III), vol. 82: cols. 73–728.

Ivo of Chartres, *Decretum*, in Migne (ed), *Patrologiae Latina* (bibliog. III), vol. 161: cols. 47–1036.

————, *Panormia*, in Migne (ed), *Patrologiae Latina* (bibliog. III), vol. 161: cols. 1045–1344.

————, *Epistula xcix*, in Migne (ed), *Patrologiae Latina* (bibliog. III), vol. 162: cols. 118–19.

————, *Epistula cxxxiv*, in Migne (ed), *Patrologiae Latina* (bibliog. III), vol. 162: cols. 143–44.

————, *Epistula cxlviii*, in Migne (ed), *Patrologiae Latina* (bibliog. III), vol. 162: cols. 153–54.

————, *Epistula ccxlii*, in Migne (ed), *Patrologiae Latina* (bibliog. III), vol. 162: cols. 249–50.

Jedin, H, *A History of the Council of Trent*, Graf, E (trans), 2 volumes, vol. 2, *The First Sessions at Trent 1545–1547*, Thomas Nelson and Sons Ltd., Edinburgh, 1961.

Jemolo, A, *Il Matrimonio nel Diritto Canonico*, Vallardi, Milan, 1941.

John Paul II, *The Theology of the Body: Human Love in the Divine Plan*, Pauline Books and Media, Boston, 1997.

Johnson, J, "Total Simulation in Recent Rotal Jurisprudence," *Studia Canonica* 24 (1990), 383–425.

Joyce, G, *Christian Marriage: An Historical and Doctrinal Study*, 2nd edition, Sheed and Ward, London, 1948.

Kasper, W, *Theology of Christian Marriage*, Crossroad Publishers, New York, 1981.

Kelleher, S, "Relative and Absolute Incapacity to Marry," *The Jurist* 29 (1969), 326–31.

Kirchschläger, W, "Marriage as Covenant: A Biblical Approach to a Familiar Notion," *Intams* 8 (2002), 153–62.

Kitchen, P, "Matrimonial Intention and Simulation," *Studia Canonica* 28 (1994), 347–406.

Kowal, J, "*L'Indissolubilità del Matrimonio Rato e Consumato: Status Quaestionis*," *Periodica* 90 (2001), 273–304.

Krueger, P, et al. (eds), *Corpus Iuris Civilis*, 3 volumes, vol. 1, *Institutiones, Digesta*, Weidmann, Berlin, 1928.

Labelle, J.-P, "*Les Incidences Pastorales de la Dissolution du Mariage Non Sacramentel en Faveur de la Foi*," *Studia Canonica* 33 (1999), 27–70.

LaDue, W, "Conjugal Love and the Juridical Structure of Christian Marriage," *The Jurist* 34 (1974), 36–67.

Larrainzar, C, "*El Decreto de Graciano del Códice Fd*," *Ius Ecclesiae* 10 (1998), 421–89.

Latourelle, R (ed), *Vatican II—Assessment and Perspectives: Twenty-Five Years After (1962–1987)*, 3 volumes, Paulist Press, Mahwah, NJ, USA, 1988–89.

Lawler, M, "Faith, Contract, and Sacrament in Christian Marriage: A Theological Approach," *Theological Studies* 52 (1991), 712–31.

————, *Marriage and Sacrament: A Theology of Christian Marriage*, The Liturgical Press, Collegeville, MN, USA, 1993.

————, "Blessed Are the Spouses Who Love, for Their Marriages Will Be Permanent: A Theology of the Bonds in Marriage," *The Jurist* 55 (1995), 218–42.

Lefebvre, C, "*La Questione del 'Verum Semen': Evoluzione della Dottrina e della Prassi*," *Monitor Ecclesiasticus* 102 (1977), 356–62.

Lehman, H (general editor), *The Christian in Society*, (Luther's Works, volumes 44–47), Fortress Press, Philadelphia, 1962–71.

Lesage, G, "The *Consortium Vitae Coniugalis*: Nature and Applications," *Studia Canonica* 6 (1972), 99–113.

————, and Morrisey, F, *Documentation on Marriage Nullity Cases*, Saint Paul University, Ottawa, 1973.

Liddell, H, and Scott, R, *An Intermediate Greek-English Lexicon: Founded upon the Seventh Edition of Liddell and Scott's Greek-English Lexicon*, Clarendon Press, Oxford, 1972.

Lopez Gallo, P, "Formal Defection from the Catholic Church," *Monitor Ecclesiasticus* 123 (1998), 620–46.

Mackin, T, "Conjugal Love and the Magisterium," *The Jurist* 36 (1976), 263–301.

————, *Marriage in the Catholic Church: What is Marriage?* Paulist Press, New York, 1982.

————, *Marriage in the Catholic Church: Divorce and Remarriage*, Paulist Press, New York, 1984.

Malone, R, and Connery, J (eds), *Contemporary Perspectives in Christian Marriage*, Loyola University Press, Chicago, 1984.

McAreavey, J, *The Canon Law of Marriage and the Family*, Four Courts Press, Dublin, 1997.

McGrath, A, *A Controversy Concerning Male Impotence*, Gregorian University, Rome, 1988.

———, "On the Gravity of Causes of a Psychological Nature in the Proof of Incapacity to Assume the Essential Obligations of Marriage," *Studia Canonica* 22 (1988), 67–75.

Meier, J, *Matthew*, (New Testament Message 3), Michael Glazier, Wilmington, DE, USA, 1980.

Mendonça, A, "Antisocial Personality and Nullity of Marriage," *Studia Canonica* 16 (1982), 5–213.

———, "The Effect of Paranoid Personality Disorder on Matrimonial Consent," *Studia Canonica* 18 (1984), 253–89.

———, "Recent Rotal Jurisprudence on the Effects of Sexual Disorders on Matrimonial Consent," *Studia Canonica* 26 (1992), 209–33.

——— (ed), *Rotal Anthology: An Annotated Index of Rotal Decisions from 1971 to 1988*, Canon Law Society of America, Washington, D.C., 1992.

———, "Narcissistic Personality Disorder: Its Effects on Matrimonial Consent," *Studia Canonica* 27 (1993), 97–143.

Metz, R, "*Le Nouveau Code des Canons des Eglises Orientales*," *Revue de Droit Canonique* 42 (1992), 99–117.

Migne, J.-P (ed), *Patrologiae Cursus Completus: Series Latina*, Garnier Fratres, Paris, 1844–. References take this form: Migne (ed), *Patrologiae Latina* (bibliog. III), volume number: column number(s).

——— (ed), *Patrologiae Cursus Completus: Series Graeca*, Petit Montrouge, Paris, 1857–. References take this form: Migne (ed), *Patrologiae Graeca* (bibliog. III), volume number: column number(s).

Montagna, E, "*Bonum Coniugum: Profili Storici*," *Monitor Ecclesiasticus* 120 (1995), 399–431.

Morrisey, F, "*L'Evolution du Texte des Canons 1055 et 1095*," *Studia Canonica* 19 (1985), 17–29.

Moulton, H (ed), *The Analytical Greek Lexicon Revised*, Zonder-van Publishing House, Grand Rapids, MI, USA, 1978.

Muller, W, *Huguccio: The Life, Works, and Thought of a Twelfth-Century Jurist*, (*Studies in Medieval and Early Modern Canon Law*, vol. 3), The Catholic University of America Press, Washington, D.C., 1994.

Murtagh, C, "The Judicial Importance of *Amor Coniugalis*," *The Jurist* 33 (1973), 377–83.

——, "The *Consortium Vitae* and Some Implications of the Juris-prudence on *Verum Semen*," *Studia Canonica* 8 (1974), 123–31.

Navarrete, U, "*De Notione et Effectibus Consummationis Matri-monii*," *Periodica*, 59 (1970), 618–60.

——, "*Potestas Vicaria Ecclesiae. Evolutio Historica Concep-tus atque Observationes Attenta Doctrina Concilii Vati-cani II*," *Periodica* 60 (1971), 415–86.

——, "*De Natura et de Applicatione Decreti S. Cong. pro Doc-trina Fidei diei 13 Maii 1977 circa Impotentiam Viri*," *Periodica* 68 (1979), 305–26.

——, "*Error in Persona (c. 1097 §1)*," *Periodica* 87 (1998), 351–401.

——, *Errore e Simulazione nel Matrimonio Canonico*, Editrice Pontificia Università Gregoriana, Rome, 1999.

Noldin, H, and Schmitt, A, *Summa Theologiae Moralis: Iuxta Co-dicem Iuris Canonici*, 23rd edition, 3 volumes, vol. 3, *De Sacramentis*, F. Rauch, Innsbruck, 1935.

Noonan, J, "Novel 22" in Bassett, W (ed), *The Bond of Marriage* (bibliog. III), 41–96.

——, *Power to Dissolve: Lawyers and Marriage in the Courts of the Roman Curia*, Belknap Press of Harvard University Press, Cambridge, MA, USA, 1972.

——, "Gratian Slept Here: The Changing Identity of the Fa-ther of the Systematic Study of Canon Law," *Traditio* 35 (1979), 145–72.

Nowak, J, "Inseparability of Sacrament and Contract in the Marriages of the Baptized," *Studia Canonica* 12 (1978), 315–63.

O'Callaghan, D, "Studies in Moral Questions: How Far is Christian Marriage Indissoluble?" *Irish Theological Quarterly* 40 (1973), 162–73.

Orlandi, G, "*De Casibus 'Difficilioribus' in Processibus Super Matrimonio Rato et Non Consummato,*" *Monitor Ecclesiasticus* 110 (1985), 246–52.

O'Rourke, J, "The Faith Required for the Privilege of the Faith Dispensation," *The Jurist* 36 (1976), 450–55.

———, "Considerations on the Convalidation of Marriage," *The Jurist* 43 (1983), 387–91.

Örsy, L, "Faith, Sacrament, Contract and Christian Marriage: Disputed Questions," *Theological Studies* 43 (1982), 379–98.

———, *Marriage in Canon Law: Texts and Comments, Reflections and Questions,* 2nd edition, Dominican Publications, Dublin, 1988.

Otten, W, "Augustine on Marriage, Monasticism, and the Community of the Church," *Theological Studies* 59 (1998), 385–405.

Oxenham, O, *Canon 1068 and the Notion of* Verum Semen, Gregorian University, Rome, 1961.

Pagé, R, "Marriage: Sacrament of Love or Sacrament of Bond?" *Studia Canonica* 34 (2000), 5–21.

Palmer, P, "Christian Marriage: Contract or Covenant," *Theological Studies* 33 (1972), 617–65.

Patres Collegii S. Bonaventurae (eds), *Petri Lombardi, Libri IV Sententiarum,* 2 volumes, College of Saint Bonaventure, Quaracchi near Florence, 1946.

Pellegrino, P, "*La 'Vis et Metus' (can. 1103) nel Codex Iuris Canonici,*" *Ius Canonicum* 37 (1997), 529–58.

Pennington, K, *Popes, Canonists and Texts 1150–1550*, (Collected Studies Series CS412), Variorum Publishers, Aldershot, England, 1993.

Pereira, V, "The Debate Relating to the *Bonum Coniugum*," *Monitor Ecclesiasticus* 126 (2001), 364–96.

Peter Lombard, *Sententiarum Libri Quatuor, Liber IV*, in Migne (ed), *Patrologiae Latina* (bibliog. III), vol. 192: cols. 839–962. References take this form: Peter Lombard, *Sententiarum* (bibliog. III), distinction number: chapter number(s).

Pfnausch, E, "The Good of the Spouses in Rotal Jurisprudence: New Horizons," *The Jurist* 56 (1996), 527–56.

Picard, N, "*Exclusion de la Procréation selon le Droit Matrimonial Ecclésial*," *Studia Canonica* 10 (1976), 37–74.

Pivonka, L, "Ecumenical or Mixed Marriages in the New Code of Canon Law," *The Jurist* 43 (1983), 103–24.

Poirel, D, "Love of God, Human Love: Hugh of St. Victor and the Sacrament of Marriage," *Communio* 24 (Spring 1997), 99–109.

Pompedda, M, "*La Nozione di Matrimonio 'Rato e Consumato' Secondo il Can. 1061 §1 del C.I.C. e Alcune Questioni Processuali di Prova in Merito*," *Monitor Ecclesiasticus* 110 (1985), 339–64.

————, "Faith and the Sacrament of Marriage—Lack of Faith and Matrimonial Consent: Juridical Aspects," in Doyle, T, et al. (eds), *Marriage Studies* (bibliog. III), vol. 4, 33–65.

***Pontificia Commissio Codici Iuris Canonici Authentice Interpretando, Codex Iuris Canonici Auctoritate Ioannis Pauli PP. II Promulgatus: Fontium Annotatione et Indice Analytico-Alphabetico Auctus*, Libreria Editrice Vaticana, Vatican City, 1989.**

***Pontificia Commissio Codici Iuris Canonici Recognoscendo* (now *Pontificium Consilium de Legum Textibus*; see next item).**

Pontificium Consilium de Legum Textibus (originally *Pontificia Commissio Codici Iuris Canonici Recognoscendo*), Rome, *Communicationes*, 1969 – .

Pospishil, V, *The Law on Marriage: Interritual Marriage Law Problems*, Universe Editions, Chicago, 1962.

————, *Eastern Catholic Marriage Law According to the Code of Canons of the Eastern Churches*, Saint Maron Publications, Brooklyn, NY, USA, 1991.

Prader, J, *Il Matrimonio in Oriente e Occidente*, (*Kanonika* 1), Pontifical Institute for Oriental Studies, Rome, 1992.

Provost, J, "Canon 1095 2° Seen From Its Sources," *The Jurist* 56 (1996), 824–74.

Raad, I, "*Prima e Dopo Il Decreto del 13 Maggio 1977 della S. Cong. per la Dottrina della Fede circa L'Impotenza*," *Ephemerides Iuris Canonici* 36 (1980), 70–96.

Read, G, "Formal Defection: The End of the Road?" *Canon Law Society of Great Britain and Ireland Newsletter* 128 (December 2001), 71–75.

————, "Formal Defection: Not Quite the End of the Road!" *Canon Law Society of Great Britain and Ireland Newsletter* 147 (September 2006), 12–15.

Reynolds, P, "Marriage, Sacramental and Indissoluble: Sources of the Catholic Doctrine," *The Downside Review* 109 (1991), 105–50.

Ritty, C, "Invalidity of Marriage by Sexual Anomalies," *The Jurist* 23 (1963), 394–422.

Roberts, W (ed), *Commitment to Partnership: Explorations of the Theology of Marriage*, Paulist Press, New York, 1987.

Robinson, G, "Unresolved Questions in the Theology of Marriage," *The Jurist* 43 (1983), 69–102.

Robitaille, L, "Conditioned Consent: Natural Law and Human Positive Law," *Studia Canonica* 26 (1992), 75–110.

————, "Another Look at Perpetuity: Revisiting the Jurisprudential Criteria for Canon 1095 3°," *Studies in Church Law* 1 (2005), 315–58.

Roman, J (ed), *"Summa d'Huguccio sur le Decret de Gratien d'apres le Manuscrit 3891 de la Bibliotheque Nationale, Causa XXVII, Questio II," Nouvelle Revue Historique de Droit Français et Etranger* **27** (1903), 745–805.

Sacrosanctum Oecumenicum Concilium Vaticanum II, Constitutiones, Decreta, Declarationes, **Typis Polyglottis Vaticanis, Rome, 1966.**

Schillebeeckx, E, *Marriage: Human Reality and Saving Mystery*, Sheed and Ward, London, 1976.

Schoovaerts, M, *"L'Amour et le Mariage selon les Lettres d'Yves de Chartres," Studia Canonica* 22 (1988), 305–25. (Professor Schoovaerts tends to write using his middle name Gustaaf.)

Scicluna, C, *The Essential Definition of Marriage According to the 1917 and 1983 Codes of Canon Law: An Exegetical and Comparative Study*, University Press of America, Lanham, MD, USA, 1995.

Schroeder, H (trans), *The Canons and Decrees of the Council of Trent*, **Tan Books and Publishers Inc., Rockford, IL, USA, 1978.**

Schumacher, M (trans), *The Fathers of the Church*, vol. 35, *Against Julian / Saint Augustine*, **The Catholic University of America Press, Washington, D.C., 1957.**

Sharkey, M (ed), *International Theological Commission: Texts and Documents 1969–1985*, **Ignatius Press, San Francisco, 1989.**

Smith, W, *A Classical Dictionary of Biography, Mythology, and Geography*, 20th edition, John Murray, London, 1889.

Societas Goerresiana (editing group), *Concilium Tridentinum: Diariorum, Actorum, Epistularum, Tractatuum Nova Collectio*, **13 volumes, Herder, Freiburg, 1901–85.**

Stankiewicz, A, *"La Simulazione del Consenso per l'Esclusione dell'Indissolubilità,"* Ius Ecclesiae 13 (2001), 653–71.

Stenson, A, "The Concept and Implications of the 'Formal Act of Defection,'" *Studia Canonica* 21 (1987), 175–94.

Sumner, P, *"Dolus* as a Ground for Nullity of Marriage," *Studia Canonica* 14 (1980), 171–94.

Thaner, F (ed), *Summa Magistri Rolandi nachmals Papstes Alexander III*, Wagner'schen, Innsbruck, 1874.

Tomko, J, *"Adnotationes in Motu Proprio 'Matrimonia Mixta,'"* Monitor Ecclesiasticus 95 (1970), 171–87.

————, *"De Dissolutione Matrimonii in Favorem Fidei eiusque Fundamento Theologico,"* Periodica 64 (1975), 99–140.

Treggiari, S, "Divorce Roman Style: How Easy and How Frequent was it?" in Rawson, B (ed), *Marriage, Divorce and Children in Ancient Rome*, Clarendon Press, Oxford, 1996, 32–33.

Vadakumcherry, J, "Marriage Laws in the *Code of Canon Law* and the *Code of Canons of the Eastern Churches,"* Studia Canonica 26 (1992), 437–60.

Van de Wiel, C, *History of Canon Law*, (Louvain Theological & Pastoral Monographs 5), Peeters Press, Louvain, 1991.

Van Hoecke, W, and Welkenhuysen, A (eds), *Love and Marriage in the Twelfth Century*, Leuven University Press, Louvain, 1981.

Vann, K, *"Dolus*: Canon 1098 of the Revised Code of Canon Law," *The Jurist* 47 (1987), 371–93.

Vennes, G, *"De la Capacité et de l'Incapacité 'Relative' dans les Causes de Mariage,"* Studia Canonica 11 (1977), 145–52.

Vernay, J, *"Les Dissolutions du Lien Matrimonial en Droit Canonique,"* L'Année Canonique 32 (1989), 139–52.

Viejo-Ximénez, J, "'*Concordia' y 'Decretum' del Maestro Graciano*," *Ius Canonicum* 39 (1999), 333–57.

Villeggiante, S, "*L'Error in Persona*," *Monitor Ecclesiasticus* 125 (2000), 524–49.

Vogel, C, "The Role of the Liturgical Celebrant in the Formation of the Marriage Bond" in Doyle, T, et al. (eds), *Marriage Studies* (bibliog. III), vol. 2, 67–87.

Vorgrimler, H (general editor), *Commentary on the Documents of Vatican II*, 5 volumes, Burns & Oats Ltd., London, 1967–69.

Walsh, M, *Roots of Christianity*, Grafton Books (Collins), London, 1986.

Watson, A (ed), *The Digest of Justinian*, 4 volumes, University of Pennsylvania Press, Philadelphia, 1985.

Weigand, R, "*Magister Rolandus und Papst Alexander III*," *Archiv für Katholisches Kirchenrecht* 149 (1980), 3–44.

Wernz, F, *Ius Decretalium ad Usum Praelectionum in Scholis Textus Canonici sive Iuris Decretalium*, 6 volumes, vol. 1, Ex Officina Libraria Giachetti, Prato, 1913.

Wilcox, C (trans), *The Fathers of the Church: A New Translation*, vol. 27, *Treatises on Marriage and other Subjects / Saint Augustine*, The Catholic University of America Press, Washington, D.C., 1985.

Winroth, A, *The Making of Gratian's Decretum*, Cambridge University Press, Cambridge, 2000.

Woestman, W, "Dissolution of a Ratified but Non-Consummated Marriage: A Procedure Sinking into Oblivion?" *Studia Canonica* 21 (1987), 195–97.

——— (ed), *Papal Allocutions to the Roman Rota 1939–1994*, Saint Paul University, Ottawa, 1994.

———, *Special Marriage Cases: Non-Consummation, Pauline Privilege, Favour of Faith, Separation of Spouses, Vali-*

dation-Sanation, Presumed Death, 3rd edition, Saint Paul University, Ottawa, 1994.

———— (ed), *Simulation of Marriage Consent: Doctrine, Jurisprudence, Questionnaires*, Saint Paul University, Ottawa, 2000.

Wojnar, M, "Interritual Law in the Revised Code of Canon Law," *The Jurist* 42 (1983), 191–98.

Wrenn, L (ed), *Divorce and Remarriage in the Catholic Church*, Newman Press, New York, 1973.

————, "Refining the Essence of Marriage," *The Jurist* 45 (1986), 532–51.

————, *Annulments*, 6th edition, Canon Law Society of America, Washington, D.C., 1996.

Zalba, M, "*Decretum circa Impotentiam quae Dirimit Matrimonium et Breve 'Cum Frequenter' Sixti V*," *Periodica* 68 (1979), 5–58.

————, "*Fides et Matrimonium*," *Periodica* 90 (1991), 93–105.

Index

491